"This extraordinary book is the most comprehensive summary I know of analyses and data covering the United States today. Jones describes a nihilistic postmodernism, a rapacious capitalism, the plutocratic destruction of democracy, the illusory construction of our sensibilities and appetites, and more! These dynamics are basic to the diminishment of our churches and an ongoing assault on the common good. Into this morass Jones offers a significant remnant strategy for dying churches."

—**Tex Sample**, Pastor, Trinity United Methodist Church, Kansas City, Missouri

"Rarely in the pages of one book do we find both a penetrating and solidly informed analysis of our present cultural situation and a visionary prescription for the church's future. Spurning efforts to reverse declining interest in the church by quick fixes, Paul Jones draws upon his long experience as a theologian and spiritual director to outline how a remnant church of the future, based on 'pure faith,' can bear witness in a post-Christian world."

—**Neal F. Fisher**, President emeritus and Senior Scholar in Theology, Garrett-Evangelical Theological Seminary

"All of us who are paying attention are sensing the coming of a spiritual winter that calls into question all that we believe. In this book, which is both challenging and comforting, W. Paul Jones analyzes the forms of idolatry that contemporary society presents to the church and the reasons why people of faith must prepare to live as a remnant people in a new reality. No one is better equipped with the gifts of mind and spirit than W. Paul Jones to help us understand what is happening to the church and why, and what it will mean for all of us to live faithfully in a post-Christian world."

—**William Boyd Grove**, Bishop, retired, the United Methodist Church

"I have participated in the church-growth models that Jones criticizes, spending much of my career working to increase numbers of people in church. But I also admit that those models have done little to ease the decline and the lack of authentic discipleship that he accurately describes in the twenty-first-century church. Given the hurt and division of our time, we need voices advocating for deeper spirituality and authentic discipleship. Paul Jones' vision for remnant community is not only biblical but compelling as well."

—**Bishop Bob Farr**, Missouri Conference of the United Methodist Church

"After a frank and brutally honest assessment of the impact postmodernism has had on Christianity, the church, and our culture, Jones offers a deeply compelling and hopeful path forward for Christian faith. This is one of the most spiritually honest and meaningful books I've read in a long time."

—**Adam Hamilton**, author of *The Lord's Prayer: The Meaning and Power of the Prayer Jesus Taught*

Remnant Christianity in
a Post-Christian World

Remnant Christianity in a Post-Christian World

Plight of the Modern Church

W. Paul Jones

WIPF & STOCK · Eugene, Oregon

REMNANT CHRISTIANITY IN A POST-CHRISTIAN WORLD
Plight of the Modern Church

Wipf & Stock
An Imprint of Wipf and Stock Publishers
199 W. 8th Ave., Suite 3
Eugene, OR 97401

www.wipfandstock.com

PAPERBACK ISBN: 978-1-7252-9484-4
HARDCOVER ISBN: 978-1-7252-9485-1
EBOOK ISBN: 978-1-7252-9486-8

10/27/21

For Cathleen Burnett,
sociologist and social justice advocate,
in appreciation of her encouragement and
patient research help.

And for the rest of my beloved extended family,
who continue to support me, whatever.

CONTENTS

PREFACE

I appreciate it when authors put the thesis of their books right up front. That way I can decide if the pilgrimage is likely to justify the reading. And if it seems so, then the thesis can help keep the path in mind, so that I do not become lost in the thicket of detail. Therefore, here is the thesis of this volume.

1. The decisive membership decline within the contemporary Christian churches is integrally tied to the consuming dynamic of our socioeconomic-secular society—in which there is no longer any force external to it with sufficient power or authority to halt or even significantly deter its self-destructive course. At this point in history, our global future is not hopeful.

2. Life within this formative ethos is such that Christian imagery is not only losing its conceivability and credibility, but the past motivations for belief have drastically lost their appeal—as answers to questions no longer being asked and healing of dilemmas no longer acknowledged. With these former bedrock points of contact no longer connecting with much width or depth, the demise in church membership will be relentless, one that is inevitable no matter how intense and creative any efforts to halt this erosion.

3. Consequently, the hope to which the church must now respond is trusting the divine promise that has appeared at other crisis points in history—that there will be raised up a faithful remnant with the determination to outlast whatever the concrete nature of our societal demise may turn out to be. While forging the anatomy of this faithfulness, the church must not dissipate her limited resources nor deflate

her spirits with false hopes of reversal. Instead, we need now to forge a plan for a remnant church and begin setting it in place.

4. This exile status necessitates distilling a minimal heart of preservable tradition sufficient to claim both personal and communal commitment, stripping excess baggage for the long haul.

5. Perseverance of the Christian faith will require not only this theological distillation but the emergence of a postmodern Christian spirituality purged by the very postmodernity that it opposes. Throughout much of its history, the appeal of Christianity has been instrumental. That is, its drawing power has been as a means to desirable and sought-after ends—whether in acquiring otherworldly rewards or this-worldly consequences, either way entailing advantage and/or success. But such promises are not only losing their likelihood but even more their appeal. Quaint is the beginning of John Wesley's ministry when several persons in desperation knocked on his door, pleading for help from the "wrath to come." Within a culture drained of need for any such negative protection, we Christians find ourselves at a place in history where we have never been before. Losing its lure as an instrumental means for preventable, desirable, or realizable ends, the only possible value left for faith must be found intrinsically. Without believable protection, advantage, or gain, lived faith must now find its meaning inherently—in being lived for its own sake. This means a Christian spirituality of pure faith, wagering subjunctively on its vision "as if" true, against modern odds to the contrary—yet strangely surmising that, even if it would turn out to be false, we would not wish to live otherwise.

6. Within a post-Christian world that has lost any defining narrative, the Christian gambles on one, all the while bereft of promise regarding not only recompense but consolation. The test of this radical faith is one's willingness to wager one's life upon it—gambling that the primal needs for being human intersect with the heart of the Christ event in disclosing unconditional love to be the inmost character of God. Faith as trusting such a God entails believing God's belief about us.

7. And yet, ironically, the grounding of this radical faith turns out to be not a matter of choosing, as if a reasoned conclusion. Thomas Merton ended *The Seven Story Mountain* by identifying his call as that of being one of the "burned ones." Being a serious Christian within our post-Christian modernity is rooted in being burned by the God question—branded, marked, and claimed in such a way that one is unable

to walk away, hang it up, or deny the insatiable void. However fragile the faith wager may feel, the proof of God is the struggle by those of us who find ourselves incapable of forfeiture—until, strangely, the question itself becomes the gift.

8. Our postmodern world is characterized by its denial of objective truth, insisting that what one sees depends on where one stands for the seeing. So we Christians must identify and reclaim our eucharistic standpoint from which to wager the meaning of life and history. There, through serious disciplining in spiritual practice, we can forge a unique disposition as our second nature—a habitual way of beholding and of being.

9. Perhaps the harshest threat to life's having a meaning is whether or not the works of our hands will have been in vain. The Christian vision wagers on the promise that our history and all of history is being redemptively woven into the tapestry of the kingdom of God. Therefore, the lifestyle to which Christians are called is to birth and cherish beauty; be generous stewards of the earth; ponder mystery; revel gratefully; care passionately; and intercede extravagantly amidst the world's enigmas, lifting the concrete example of suffering doggedly before the face of a God who has promised a new heaven and earth. The Christian shares freely of time, space, and possessions, assuming portions of the world's hurts, angers, and tragedies in order to help them die of malnutrition.

10. Recalling T. S. Eliot, the church must "set her own land in order . . . as London Bridge is falling down falling down falling down." A remnant structure must be of such a nature that it can function faithfully as both leaven and as ulcer in the stomach of the monster, strategizing by adapting clues from the past. Yet the remnant must not forget Origen's discernment that it is the blood of the martyrs that nourishes the roots of the church. Therefore, while preparing for the long haul, it needs to be with a humility born of knowing that Christians are the first to forfeit their lifeboat seats.

11. Finally, a story. There was once a priest who regularly took his exiled faithful secretly into the forest, and there lit a candle, told a story, said some prayers, and shared bread and wine. In time, some of the prayers became forgotten. And as he further aged, elements of the story became lost. Concerned lest the candle totally go out, the faithful remnant gathered anxiously around their ailing priest. "It is sufficient," he whispered, "simply to break the bread and share the cup, for that will tell the story."

CHAPTER ONE

POSTMODERN SECULARIZATION

Christianity's Silently Relentless Erosion

A CRISIS IN RECOGNITION

One need do no more than skim a recent issue of the *Christian Century*[1] to sense the widespread and ongoing dilemma of the modern church. Here it is hard to miss, confronted with such phrases as "irreversible decline," "desperation strategies," "loss of legitimacy," and "relentless membership loss." The descriptions are diverse, but the shadow is heavy—articles on denominational splits, pastoral approaches when a church closes, internal scandals, a snake-handling preacher bitten to death, and how to dispose of holy things when churches are sold. Also included is an interview with a clergy person's son whose novels are said to have touches of spirituality but are barren of religious themes or of church presence. There is a book review lamenting modernity as having lost all viable past. The cinema coverage is about two filmmakers who "leave you gasping with their vision of the meaninglessness of life," portraying a New York City drained of color, perpetually wintry, where most dreams go to seed. Then, for overseasoning, there is a poem entitled "Fear." Closing the magazine, one can taste with grittiness the pervasive grayness infecting the world in, around, and within which today's church is struggling, and within the churches themselves.

In 2014, a multimillion-dollar General Social Survey[2] funded by the National Science Foundation gives one of the most accurate reports on the American scene. Since 2012, 7.5 million persons have "left religion," with one in four persons indicating "none" as their "religious preference." This makes them 21 percent of the total population. Furthermore, church attendance

---

1. *Christian Century*, Mar. 19, 2014.
2. Grant, "Analysis: Seven Point Five Million," paras. 1, 4, 6–7.

is far from what it used to be, with a third of Americans (34 percent) never even having attended a worship service. This is a 3 percent increase in just two years. In the past ten years, the number of persons who "never pray" has risen from 10 percent to 15 percent. It is not simply the statistics that are overwhelming but, even more, the rapidity of decline.

This demise is particularly significant in that it is happening especially in areas that have traditionally been centers of Christian populations and influence, notably in the Western world. One in four Canadians no longer has any religious affiliation, which stands in startling contrast to 1991, when the figure was 12 percent.[3] In both England and Wales, there has been a 10 percent rise within the last ten years of those who no longer identify themselves as Christian, resulting in "no religion" being the single largest group.[4] This group is twice the size of identified Anglicans and four times the size of the Catholic population. At the same time, Anglican and Catholic churches lose at least ten members for every convert made. During the last decade, membership in the British Methodist Church has fallen by one-third, with attendance diminishing proportionally. Linda Woodhead, a sociologist at Lancaster University, concludes that Methodism in England "is totally dying out," and, based on current trends, "will disappear, very soon."[5] A 2016 study by St. Mary's University (London) indicates that only 48 percent of the population identified themselves as Christian, meaning that, for the first time, Christians are outnumbered by those claiming no religious affiliation.[6] Philip Jenkins, an expert on global Christianity, after analyzing church growth efforts in England, concludes that hope for a wide-ranging religious revival seems futile.[7] It is not farfetched, he ventures, to see Christian faith as confined to recent immigrants. A statistical projection done by the Spectator indicates that if the number of Christians in Britain continues to decline at the current rate, that country will have no more Christians by 2067.[8] Between 2001 and 2011, British churches as a whole have lost 5.3 million members—about 10,000 each week. In the 2016 British Social Attitudes Survey, for the first time in history, a majority of Britons reported having no religion.[9] This 53 percent reflects a 5 percent increase of "nones" since 2015 and 12 percent increase since 2002. The result is that many of the

3. "Canada's Changing Religious Landscape," graph 1.

4. Sherwood, "People of No Religion," para. 2.

5. Grundy, "Methodists in England," para. 4.

6. Bullivant, "Contemporary Catholicism in England," 3.

7. Jenkins, "Decline and Revival," para. 11.

8. Thompson, "Crisis of Faith," para. 1.

9. Dearie, "Survey: Majority of Britons," paras. 1–2.

347 Church of England churches presently vacant are centuries-old masterpieces, citadels of architecture, paintings, and stained glass, forced into rental for varied nonreligious activities without restrictions.

After centuries in which Ireland and Catholicism were near-synonymous, the rapidity of secularization there is setting historic records. From 2005 to 2011, the atheist/nonreligious population there has almost doubled, from 28 percent to 54 percent.[10] Philip Jenkins predicts in the *Christian Century* that Ireland will soon become "one of Europe's least religious countries,"[11] citing a Gallup survey showing that 44 percent of the Irish population declared themselves to be "not religious," with a further 10 percent claiming for themselves the atheist label.

Yet despite these alarming Irish statistics, those of almost every European country are still lower. Aside from Poland, where 42 percent of respondents attend church weekly, every other European country[12] has rates of attendance at or below 25 percent. Several countries in Scandinavia and Western Europe are in the single digits. France, for example, once deeply Christian, adorned with Gothic cathedrals and abundant monasteries, is now one of the most vehemently secular countries in Europe. Sunday attendance is the lowest ever, with tourists exceeding worshippers. In Sweden, only 6 percent of the population are churchgoers. Here and throughout Europe, this diminishment of active members has rendered tragic the income necessary for maintenance, resulting in a plethora of empty churches for sale. Many of these abandoned churches are ending up as secular commercial endeavors, indicative of which is a beautiful church in Arnhem, Netherlands, now impressive as a skating rink.[13] Roman Catholic leaders in that country estimate that, within a decade, two-thirds of their 1,600 churches will be closed. Protestant leaders there project that 700 churches will close by 2020.

Although Africa as a whole has been showing Pentecostal gains through a message of healing and prosperity, a recent WIN-Gallup poll indicates that even there—for example, in South Africa from 2005 to 2012— persons regarding themselves as religious have dropped from 83 percent to 64 percent,[14] a statistic that if extrapolated would parallel the vanishing point characterizing that of Europe as a whole. An international Pew

10. WIN-Gallup International, "Global Index of Religiosity," 3.

11. Jenkins, "Irish Nones," paras. 1, 13.

12. "How Religious Commitment Varies by Country among People of All Ages," in "Age Gap in Religion," para. 14.

13. Bendavid, "Europe's Empty Churches," paras. 2, 15.

14. Jenkins, "Secular South Africa," para. 11.

Research Center survey of one hundred countries[15] reported in 2018 that younger adults are those far less likely to identify with a religion, to believe in God, or to engage in any religious practices. The drop in the US was 17 percent, in Canada 28 percent, and in Germany 18 percent.

While in the past, the United States has appeared to be the most resistant major Western country to this religious diminishment, this is no longer so. Mainline church leadership is unable to remain in denial, being forced into realism by the failure of their previously ambitious reversal strategies, acknowledging with growing alarm this pattern of rapid membership erosion. No longer able to be disregarded are such facts as that between 2009 and 2019, the number of Americans who claim no religious affiliation has doubled, from thirty-nine million to sixty-eight million.[16] This makes the "nones" the fasting growing "religious" group in this country. The "nones" increased to 26 percent of the population, up from 17 percent, while Catholics declined from 23 percent to 20 percent, Protestants declined from 51 percent to 43 percent, and Evangelicals and Mormons remained somewhat stable at 25 percent and 2 percent of the population respectively. Persons identifying themselves as Christian have declined 12 percent in the past decade. Almost all reliable projections agree that this exponential diminishment will continue, if for no other reason than that present young adults are three times more likely to be religiously unaffiliated than are aging Americans. The Pew Research Center predicts that the number of "nones" will reach 1.2 billion by 2060.[17] Currently in the US, there are 26 percent who indicate no religious affiliation.[18] The shifting religious landscape in this country is like a pyramid. At the top are the Silent Generation (born 1928–1945), with 10 percent being unaffiliated. From there down, every age group shrinks, until the base occupied by millennials (born 1981–1996) shows 40 percent unaffiliated. Even ethnicity is no longer a stable factor, with Hispanic Americans who adhere to no religion having risen to 23 percent.

For a while, evangelical and conservative denominations appeared to be resisting this abandonment, seeming to indicate that the culprit in mainline Protestantism decline was its liberalism, that critics identified as having watered down the power and appeal of the gospel. In response, these Protestant churches began to emulate features characterizing evangelical worship—from screen projections to praise bands. Yet more recent

---

15. "Age Gap in Religion," para. 12.

16. "In U.S., Decline of Christianity," paras. 1–2, 16, 29.

17. "Changing Global Religious Landscape," para. 19.

18. Pew Research Center, "In U.S., Decline of Christianity," paras. 1, 10, 21.

studies are showing that, beginning in 2010, conservative churches have been accompanying liberal churches in overall decline, with these evangelical accommodations actually having alienated the traditional membership more than they have attracted unchurched youth. A massive study by the Public Religion Research Institute in 2017 discovered that the number of White evangelical Protestants fell from 23 percent of the US population in 2006 to 17 percent in 2016.[19] Today, only 11 percent of their membership is younger than thirty. Americans who say they have no religion now outnumber evangelical White Protestants. Those without religion have nearly doubled since 2003 (21 percent), while the number of White mainline Protestants has fallen from 18 percent to 13 percent. Membership in the conservative Southern Baptist Church, second to Catholics in size in this country, has dropped for thirteen straight years to its lowest numbers in sixty-four years, with a severe 5.5 percent decrease occurring within only the past three years. This denomination has one million fewer members now than a decade ago. "The loss of 288,000 church members last year brings total SBC membership to 14.5 million, down from its peak of 16.3 million in 2006. Average worship attendance remained relatively stable at 5.2 million. Total baptisms, a landmark metric for the denomination, fell by 4 percent to 235,748—the lowest number since World War II."[20]

The American Lutheran Church decline has been from nine million members in 1965 to seven million in 2013,[21] a percentage loss similar to that of the Evangelical Lutheran Church in America (ELCA) and the Lutheran Church Missouri Synod (LCMS). As with all other Protestant denominations, this diminishment is forcing a dramatic drop in national programs and offices.

The *Yearbook of American and Canadian Churches*[22] continues to provide a depressive overall picture, with heavy decline yearly in every mainline denomination. Among the three largest denominations, membership loss among Catholics was 1.1 percent in one year, Southern Baptists 0.15 percent, and United Methodists 1.22 percent. The decline in the Presbyterian USA churches is 3.45 percent, Episcopalians 2.71 percent, United Church of Christ 2.02 percent, and Missouri Synod Lutheran 1.45 percent. Consulting these yearbooks through the years discloses that decline has actually been happening since the turn of the century. What is new is that the current rate of membership loss is greater than ever before, with clear

19. D. Cox and Jones, "America's Changing Religious Identity," paras. 2, 4.

20. Shellnutt, "Southern Baptists See Biggest Drop," paras. 4–5.

21. Granquist, "Ways to Be Lutheran," para. 1.

22. Lindner, ed., *Yearbook of American and Canadian Churches 2010*.

projections that this decline will escalate as each younger generation finds religion increasingly less credible. One survey estimates that approximately 3,700 churches in the United States are closing each year.[23] The director of the usually optimistic Billy Graham Center at Wheaton College wrote in the *Washington Post* that America's mainline Protestants have "just twenty-three Easters left if current decline rates continue. It is not that the sky is falling down, but the floor is dropping out."[24]

It was the 2015 data provided by the Pew Foundation that finally succeeded in propelling this relentless diminution of US churches into the public domain. Alan Cooperman, director of their religion research, says of the downward trend that "it's big, it's broad, and it's everywhere."[25] During the seven years of doing these reports, atheists and agnostics have doubled in number. Mainline adults dropped by five million. Americans were found to be far less likely to identify themselves as religious "nones" than as Christians. There are 22.8 percent "nones," surpassing the number of Catholics, and are more than Evangelicals, Lutherans, United Methodists, and Episcopalians combined.[26] When the US Methodists merged with the Evangelical United Brethren in 1968, they had a combined membership of eleven million members, with the US population at 180 million. Presently the US membership of the United Methodist Church has declined to 6.7 million, while the US population has doubled.[27] In the 1960s, the Presbyterians had 4.3 million members and have since been reduced to 1.3 million.[28] During the same time, the Episcopal Church had 3.6 million members, with 1.8 million today.[29] The Disciples of Christ membership fell from 1.9 million to 382,000.[30]

Each successive age group is less connected to a church than their parents. Of those identified as growing up as Christians, one in five no longer call themselves Christian, and there are more than four former Christians for every convert.[31] Perhaps most telling is that the majority of "nones" do not identify themselves either as atheists or agnostics, but simply as "nothing in particular," which apparently characterizes as well their attitude

23. Dart, "Church-Closing Rate," para. 13.

24. Stetzer, "If It Doesn't Stem," para. 1.

25. Grossman, "Christians Lose Ground," para. 3.

26. Grossman, "Christians in Decline," para. 19.

27. Hahn, "US Dips below Majority," para. 12.

28. Rick Jones, "PC(USA) Statistics," para. 1.

29. Millard, "Two Thousand Nineteen Parochial Reports," para. 4.

30. Gryboski, "Disciples of Christ," para. 2.

31. "America's Changing Religious Landscape," para. 22.

toward social and political matters.[32] While a generation ago being a "none" would have risked public scorn, the new situation is such that Americans are much more comfortable in identifying themselves as religiously unaffiliated than with having religious convictions, which is what is suspect. Rod Dreher in the *American Conservative* concludes that "we are staring in the face of a European-style collapse" in religious observance that will be upon us "within a couple of generations."[33]

Further, discouragement is to be found in studies such as one by Christian Smith with Patricia Snell in which the Christianity of millennials who still identify themselves with Christianity is found to be surprisingly thin, both ethically and theologically. Smith calls their faith "moralistic therapeutic deism,"[34] which, when compared with the doctrines of historic biblical Christianity, is a pseudo religion. It is primarily a "feel-good spirituality," promising happiness and good feelings about oneself, functioning as a supportive correlate of a self-centered consumerist culture. Thus, while between 1990 and 2013 the proportion of Americans who identify themselves as Christians has declined from 78.4 percent to 71 percent, one might well begin regarding the term *identify* as quite ambiguous.[35] For example, what is one to make of the statistic in Google Trends for 2011–2013 indicating that the three states regarded as most highly religious (Alabama, Georgia, Mississippi) recorded the greatest number of internet searches for sexual content, gay and straight; while the states regarded as least religious (Vermont and New Hampshire) show the lowest number of such searches.[36] Although difficult to measure, a poll by Faith Communities Today also explored trends in "spiritual vitality" within churches over the last five years, drawing alarming conclusions. They found a 10 percent decline in "spirituality" within mainline Protestants, 18 percent within Evangelicals, and 15 percent among Catholics.[37] Catholics and evangelical traditions both showed a similar declining rate of "practicing commitment." In a 2019 Gallup poll employing phone conversations in all states, it was discovered that not only those claiming a religious identity declined in recent decades from 90 percent to 77 percent, but, even more telling, only 50 percent of Americans actually indicate membership in a church or other religious

---

32. "America's Changing Religious Landscape," para. 26.

33. Dreher, "Christianity in Collapse," para. 4.

34. C. Smith with Snell, *Souls in Transition*, 154.

35. "America's Changing Religious Landscape," para. 2.

36. MacInnis and Hodson, "Do American States," 138.

37. Roozen, "Negative Numbers," fig. 2.

body.[38] This is down from 73 percent at the turn of the century. What this means is that many who regard themselves as religious persons no longer see church membership as essential or important. While twenty years ago 62 percent of Generation X persons belonged to a church, only 42 percent of millennials at a comparable age are members.[39] With churches closing daily, persons will become less able to find convenient places of worship, accelerating membership decline.

Inevitably, this diminishment in church membership and participation in church life is bringing a drought in finances, forcing frugality of assets by closing local churches and consolidating others into trans-parishes or metaparish ministries and agencies. This financial erosion within mainline churches in the United States amounts to a one-year loss of $1.2 billion.[40] As a whole, current church giving is at its lowest level since the Great Depression, resulting in an increasing number of churches unable to afford full-time theologically trained clergy persons. Adjusted for inflation, giving to religion is essentially flat, increasing 0.5 percent in 2019 (a year in which total charitable giving rose 2.5 percent),[41] with contributions shifting to alternative nonprofit agencies. As a result, 30 percent of mainline churches have gone to lesser-trained bi-vocational paid ministers, with some of these churches increasingly resorting to part-time unpaid clergy whose income is gained from other employment. The number of Protestant seminary students fell from 31,532 in 2006 to 29,249 in 2012,[42] and many of those who do graduate are so squeezed by debt that they are prohibited from taking full-time positions at diminished salaries, let alone considering the part-time pastorates that are available. In Missouri, for example, over 40 percent of the United Methodist churches are now being served by "local pastors,"[43] which means persons who have at least been trained for ministry by attending a one-week licensing school. With no further requirements, these persons are granted the authority to perform all aspects of ministry, even the sacraments. Many of these bring with them backgrounds that are at odds with the theology and polity characterizing Methodism. The impact of this dynamic is alarming when compared with what a one-week training preparation would do to professions such as medicine, law, dentistry, and engineering.

38. J. Jones, "U.S. Church Membership Down," paras. 1–2, 9.

39. J. Jones, "U.S. Church Membership Down," paras. 13–14.

40. Musarra, "Churches Lost $1.2 Billion," para. 1.

41. Giving USA, *Giving USA 2020*, paras. 2, 12.

42. Grossman, "After Long Slump."

43. Missouri Conference of the UMC, *Conference Journal 2020*.

Likewise languishing financially are ecumenical ventures, so that once stable institutions such as the National Council of Churches (founded in 1950) are continuing to prune positions. Even though the Washington National Cathedral has undergone several rounds of program cuts and staff contractions, they have been forced to charge admission in order to survive.

A parallel diminishment is occurring with church publications. In 2013, the *Methodist Reporter*, one of the largest religious communication complexes, closed operations due to the demise of readership and thus income. Other closed publications include the *Progressive Christian, Episcopal Life, United Church News*, and the *Church Herald*. The *Christian Century*, a mainstay of mainline Protestantism, confessed in 2013 to its readership that "there is a chance that the *Century* and other Christian periodicals will not survive."[44] *Books & Culture*, started in 1995 under the umbrella of *Christianity Today*, has barely survived collapse for the moment with a philanthropic grant. But it was forced to close four of its own publications, laying off a quarter of its staff. *First Things* editor R. R. Reno reluctantly concludes that the diminishment of income within religious publishing is making it "very difficult to sustain a publication devoted to serious ideas."[45] In 2012, in spite of the apparent rise of interest in spirituality, two of the best publications in that field have been forced to close, *Weavings* with its intellectual focus and *Alive Now* with its informed piety. In an effort to survive, church publications are moving away from a news format, as well as editorial independence, and are becoming public relations vehicles. Characteristic of this change is the conversion of denominational newspapers into glitzy, glossy promotional magazines featuring random success stories with pictures of happy youth.

Diminishment is also happening through violence on the world scene. According to the International Society for Human Rights, 80 percent of worldwide religious discrimination is being perpetrated upon Christians.[46] Just this past year, as many as 310 million Christians globally suffered high to severe persecution in 73 nations. "Every day, eight Christians worldwide are killed because of their faith. Every week, 182 churches or Christian buildings are attacked. And every month, 309 Christians are imprisoned unjustly."[47]

Churches are being bombed and looted, and, in some cases, Christians are being forced to live in labor camps. Militant Islamists are increasingly violent in an increasing number of countries, threatening Christians

44. Buchanan, "Sustaining a Resource," para. 3.

45. Bailey, "Books & Culture Survives," para. 15.

46. World Watch Monitor, "Eighty Percent of Religious Discrimination," para. 1.

47. Casper, "Top Fifty Countries," paras. 1–5.

with the option of conversion or death. As violence escalates in Syria, evidence is indicating that the rich cultural involvement of Christianity there for the past two millennia will likely end. In Africa, persecution is particularly evident in such countries as Sudan, Nigeria, Libya, Central African Republic, Somalia, Kenya, and Yemen. The most tragic countries in this persecution are North Korea, Iraq, Syria, Iran, and Pakistan. The perceived identification of Christianity with US-European aggression in the Middle East is fermenting radical Islamic groups who celebrate in the name of Allah the enslaving and killing of Christians, particularly in such places as Iraq, Nigeria, and the Philippines.

This phenomenon of religious decline, however, is not only a Christian phenomenon. In Judaism, for example, while 90 percent of American Jews born before World War II identify themselves as Jewish by religion, one-third of Jews born after 1980 claim no religion at all.[48] Interfaith marriages are becoming increasingly common, and one-third of these couples have no intent of raising their children Jewish. A Pew Research Center poll among Jews reveals that 62 percent identified their Jewishness as either cultural or ancestral, with only 15 percent claiming that it has anything to do with religious belief.[49] While most Israeli Jews identify themselves as Jewish, 49 percent consider themselves secular, with one in five professing no belief in God.[50] Jonathan Tobin in *Commentary Magazine* concludes that, in three or four generations, there will be very few Jews left in the US.[51] Thus, it is not surprising to hear several Jewish leaders recognize in this increase of cultural Judaism an accomplishment that not even Hitler was able to perform. Likewise, a study in 2018 by the Pew Research Center indicates that 23 percent of Americans raised Muslim no longer identify with the faith, most of whom are second-generation immigrants who are rejecting the faith of their parents.[52]

There are also pessimistic statistics indicating diminishment within non-Christian religions around the world. At first glance, they do not appear as grim, with a poll by the Pew Research Center on Religion and Public Life indicating that 84 percent of the world's population of seven billion adheres to some form of religion.[53] This means that over eight persons in ten have some religious identification. Christianity is the largest

48. Goodstein, "Poll Shows Major Shift," para. 8.

49. "Portrait of Jewish Americans," para. 5.

50. "Israel's Religiously Divided Society," fig. 1, para. 7.

51. Tobin, "Loving Us to Death," para. 15.

52. Mohamed and Sciupac, "Share of Americans," para. 2

53. "Changing Global Religious Landscape," para. 12.

group with 2.3 billion adherents (31 percent). Muslims are second with 1.8 million members (24 percent), followed by approximately 1 billion Hindus (15 percent), Buddhists at 500 million (7 percent), Jews at 14 million (.2 percent), and 400 million persons (5.7 percent) practicing some form of folk tradition. Yet the third largest group, the one exhibiting the most significant growth, is composed of 1.1 billion persons (16 percent) who adhere to no religion. This is an alarming increase of 16.1 percent in eight years, disclosing a worldwide state of affairs never known before—that one out of six persons have no professed religion.

This decline can be geographically centered with 76 percent of these unaffiliated living in the Asia-Pacific—700 million in China.[54] There are six countries in which the religiously unaffiliated make up the majority of the population: the Czech Republic, Estonia, Hong Kong, Japan, and North Korea. In Japan, alarming trends in Buddhist and Shinto participation are prescient of other countries that are on the front lines of secularization, bringing deep financial trouble, the abandoning of temples and shrines, and Buddhist-related colleges being forced to relinquish their religious affiliation. Philip Jenkins predicts that around 49 percent of Japan's awe-inspiring temples and monasteries will cease to function by 2040, becoming at best commercially-based tourist attractions.[55] "In religious terms," he surmises, "Japan looks like Europe, only more so."

Another way to identify this overall demise in religion is in terms of the popular trend away from religion toward spirituality. Some church leaders take solace in this phenomenon, as when a LifeWay survey of Protestant millennials indicated that while one in five identify themselves as "nones," refusing the label of being religious, 72 percent of them were willing to accept the term spiritual.[56] Yet two out of three of these persons acknowledge rarely if ever praying, attend no worship of any kind, have never read the Bible, and do not read any spiritual books. The term they most often use to characterize their attitude toward the church is "indifference." Diana Butler Bass has found that many of those still willing to nod toward some identification with a faith tradition do so in name only.[57] She predicts that as our secular society becomes increasingly accepting, even affirming, of persons professing no religious ties, many of these persons will discontinue claiming any religious identification.

54. "Religiously Unaffiliated," in "Global Religious Landscape," paras. 4–5.

55. Jenkins, "Empty Buddhist Temples," paras. 5, 10.

56. Grossman, "Tracking the 'Nominals,'" paras. 15, 17.

57. Grossman, "Tracking the 'Nominals,'" paras. 22–23.

There are practical factors at work in this demise. Within Catholicism, the largest single Christian group in the United States, the tradition of creating parishes so that no person will be without a church bell to hear, this goal is no longer even close to viable. Not only are economic factors increasingly forcing the merging and closing of churches, but a major crisis is the alarming shortage of priests. Priestly attrition is due to a growing number of retirements, the allure of marriage, and the insufficiency of new vocations. Even with the slight increase recently in the number of seminarians, statistics show that even if all those in training would persevere to ordination, they would in no way even neutralize the number of present dropouts, retirements, and deaths. According to Dean R. Hoge, a sociologist at the Catholic University of America, for every hundred priests who retire, there are only thirty priests available to replace them.[58] Research by the Center for Applied Research in the Apostolate discloses that the total number of priests in the US has dropped from 58,632 in 1965 to 35,513 in 2020—a drop of 39 percent.[59] The number of priests who are in active ministry has dropped during this time from 94 percent to 65 percent. In 2019, 21 percent of US parishes no longer had a resident priest. Typical of the situation in large US cities is that, after a three-year study, the Pittsburgh diocese decided to reduce 188 parishes to 57, giving the repetitive reasons of diminishment of clergy and declining participation.[60] The number of available priests there will decline from the present 200 to 112 by 2025. A 2015 report by Future Church indicates that by 2019 half of the present full-time active priests will be eligible for retirement.[61] Father Bob Bonnot of the Association of US Catholic Priests indicates that many of this half "are counting the days to when they can retire from the relentless grind which is wearing them down, draining them not only of energy and often health but also of joy."[62] What will need to happen almost everywhere is the increased clustering of parishes with a lay administrator and a traveling priest, resulting in the decreasing availability of the Mass. The consequential increase in Protestant-like prayer services led by laity will be more like an expedient symptom than a creative solution. The significant waning of the altar bread business reflects graphically how this clergy diminishment is undermining the sacramental heart of Catholicism.

58. "Facts about the Priest Shortage," para. 1.

59. "U.S. Data over Time," in Center for Applied Research in the Apostolate, "Frequently Requested Church Statistics."

60. De Witt, "Pittsburgh Diocese Plans," para. 1.

61. "Priest Shortage at a Glance," para. 3.

62. Bonnot, "Merging, Megasizing and Marriage."

Increasing this difficulty, Katarina Schuth describes in her book *Seminary Formation* that while a significant number of parishioners are Vatican II Catholics, recently ordained seminarians have never experienced the pre-Vatican II church. As the result, they are enamored at finding possible solutions by returning to a romantic past, with authoritative cassocks, birettas, capes, and the clericalism of a Tridentine Latin Mass. Under Popes John Paul II and Benedict XVI, this post-Vatican II conservative reaction was encouraged, focusing on restoring doctrinal orthodoxy and tighter discipline in an attempt to reform the Vatican II reform. A result has been internal tension, with a diminishment of lay participation. A 2014 article by two Catholic priests in the *Catholic Missourian* acknowledges that "anyone involved with parish life knows the future looks bleak."[63] They document their appraisal by sharing that as a result of this conflictive confusion, 75 percent of confirmation candidates are leaving the faith within five years of confirmation, and 70 percent of those received into the Church through the demanding RCIA immersion program will still leave the Church within five years. Their further lament was that 85 percent of Generation X Catholics no longer attend Mass, and 90 percent of millennials never enter a church. And even among churchgoing Catholics, 40 percent no longer believe in a personal God.

The four primary ingredients being identified as grounding this Catholic crisis are, in order, the decreasing number of clergy, declining attendance, financial difficulties, and demographic shifts. A temporary respite in this country has been the importation of priests from third-world countries, yet this phenomenon is resulting in language, culture, and religious practice problems all their own. With an apparent papal determination to preserve celibacy and gender requirements for priesthood, coupled with an unwillingness to reinstate married Catholic clergy, priests are being stretched by multiple church assignments toward the breaking point. Morale is an escalating problem, with weariness and loneliness taking their physical toll, resulting in vulnerability regarding stress temptations and moral fatigue.

Such morale factors, however, are far from restricted to clergy. Deeply telling is a 2008 survey by Georgetown University's Center for Applied Research in the Apostolate revealing that while 77 percent of Catholics still express pride in being Catholic, 45 percent admit to being nonpracticing.[64] While Catholics once regarded Sunday Mass attendance as mandatory under threat of serious sin, this motivation is increasingly ineffective, with 68 percent of Catholics now regarding weekly mass as nonessential to their

---

63. Peckman and Berhorst, "Author Acknowledges Dismal Trends," 15.
64. Center for Applied Research in the Apostolate, "Catholic Beliefs and Attitudes," 1.

faith. Half of former Catholics have left institutional religion completely. In contrast to the unquestioned authority formerly awarded the Catholic hierarchy, now only 43 percent of Catholics look any longer to the pope and bishops for guidance in making moral decisions. Despite several decades of papal efforts to restore rigid obedience to Catholic teachings such as prohibitions against artificial birth control, nine out of ten Catholics no longer see any moral problem with that practice, with over two-thirds of Catholics being in noncompliance.[65] A 2012 Pew survey[66] indicates that in spite of rigorous hierarchical threats, only 15 percent of Catholics believe any longer that having an abortion is morally wrong. As for the permanence of marriage, only 19 percent believe that a divorce is immoral.[67]

As resident director of the Hermitage Spiritual Retreat Center, I find an increasing number of retreatants identifying themselves as "being raised Catholic" or being "nonpracticing Catholics." This supports the statistic that about one in ten adults in the US regard themselves as being "ex-Catholic."[68] Before the clergy sexual abuse was exposed and before the pandemic, a survey found that only 36 percent of members "attended Mass the previous week."[69]

Pope Benedict XVI, drawing upon the conservative leadings of John Paul II, loudly blames this demise on the collapse of what he calls Christian Europe. Such responses, largely oblivious of the larger dynamics at work, warranted church historian John R. Sommerfeldt to conclude in his *Christianity in Culture* that the possibility of a culture like that of the High or Middle Ages, permeated, directed, and held together by Christianity, seems so remote as to be absurd. Pope Benedict's analysis of this diminishment found blame in the "liberal misuse" of Vatican II (1960–1965). Pope John XXIIII had created Vatican II in order to "unfasten the windows of Catholicism to the fresh air of the modern world."[70] In so doing, the effort was to adapt the product so as to appeal better to modern conditions and sensitivities. This effort entailed the shift of emphasis from individual piety to communal formation, birthing such changes as vernacular liturgy, smaller group experimentation, participative music, regular homilies, and theological openness. The most significant shift, however, came in the motivation for becoming a person of faith. The former negative emphasis was on producing fear and

65. Kuruvilla, "Fifty Years Later," para. 18.

66. "Few Catholics See Contraceptive Use," para. 1.

67. Lipka, "Vatican Synod on Family," para. 4.

68. Masci and Smith, "Seven Facts about American Catholics," para. 3.

69. Catholic News Agency, "Survey Finds Correlation," para. 4

70. *Philadelphia Inquirer*, "John XXIII Opened Windows," para. 9.

threat of punishment, and the positive offering was on compensatory after-life rewards. But with Vatican II, the appeal became invitational, proffering in this life a sacramentally grounded communal living as an alternative to modern society's culture of loneliness and competitive individualism. This dissimilarity between pre- and post-Vatican II motivational appeal is at the heart of the internal strife endemic to present-day Catholicism.

Ralph Martin's recent book *Will Many Be Saved* is a revealing exacer-bation of this interior strain. In an effort at authoritative impact, the book is prefaced with enthusiastic endorsements by sixteen prominent arch-bishops, bishops, and Catholic professors.[71] The thesis is that the "massive apostasy" in the Catholic Church is rooted in the deep misunderstanding of Vatican II by progressives. Vatican II, they insist, was meant simply to correct what they admit might have been a previous overemphasis, but in no way was it intended to make any change in the primary meaning of and thus the reason for becoming Catholic. Thus, with all the authority that they could muster there came this unabashed declaration: the need to have "unashamedly stated" by Holy Mother Church that "the preaching of the gospel can make a life-or-death, heaven-or-hell difference"—for upon one's momentous Catholic decision, "the eternal destinies of human be-ings are really at stake."[72]

In heavy contrast, the intriguing figure of Pope Francis has appeared on the scene. As James Martin, editor-at-large of *America*, expresses it, this pope is insisting that the church be a "joyful community of believers completely un-afraid of the modern world," while accepting clear responsibility for a church fighting for its cultural life.[73] With conservative Catholics rallying around the theme of Vatican II having been misunderstood and misapplied, we now have a pope insisting upon a full implementation of Vatican II, in which the Church's concern must be with poverty, inequality, the role of women, di-vorcees, gay and lesbian persons, and ecumenical outreach. His insistence is upon following the totality of the Catholic social creed. The Church must become "poor for the poor," willing to become bruised, hurt, and dirty from being out in the streets, rather than being "a Church that is unhealthy from being confined and from clinging to its own security."[74]

This makes it a hard place for conservatives to find themselves, because the infallibility of papal authority has been one of their central tenets. There-fore, conservative legates are scurrying to reinterpret the pope's meanings,

71. R. Martin, *Will Many Be Saved,* i–iv.

72. R. Martin, *Will Many Be Saved,* 204.

73. J. Martin, "New Vision for the Church," para. 5.

74. Pope Francis, *Joy of the Gospel,* 25.

with traditionalist publications using diminutive modifiers and wealthy conservative Catholics simply threatening financial reprisals. The Catholic conservative wing is experiencing the fear of being displaced, a fate that the progressive wing had experienced under the reactionary tenures of two previous popes. Progressives, in turn, are no longer feeling marginalized and alienated but empowered to implement more fully Vatican II's reformative rediscovery of what they regard as being the heart of the gospel. Instead of attempting a return to a prior era where Catholic power operated within the halls of power, Pope Francis in his *Joy of the Gospel* has taken a radically contrasting stance. His call is not simply for a mercy ministry as supplemental aid for the poor and oppressed, but for a justice ministry that vigorously identifies the structural causes of poverty as residing in an unfettered capitalism. He declares that this "socioeconomic system is unjust at its roots" and judges it as "an economy of exclusion and inequality." Since "such an economy kills," it must be condemned, using the powerful words of St. John Chrysostom: "Not to share one's wealth with the poor is to steal from them and to take away their livelihood."[75] The analysis by this pope is a far cry from a Catholicism that threatens individuals with fear of hell and focuses upon otherworldly rewards. The demon he is confronting is not so much a personified Satan as a demonic system, for "we can no longer trust in the unseen forces and the invisible hand of the market."[76]

Pope Francis was quite aware of the dissension that his witnessing could cause and has caused—yet he sees no option but faithfulness to the gospel, as he sees it. To maintain a both/and compromise between the Church and present society is faithless, as is a diversion to otherworldliness rather than engaging modern society's exploitation. His is a global either/or vision in which the Church has responsible stakes in history's destiny. The choice is between two contrasting ways of having faith: "We can fear to lose the saved and we can want to save the lost." This is the internal plight of the Church, for "we stand at the crossroads of these two ways of thinking." Pope Francis seems determined that the previous censorious motivation that permitted accommodation with present-day societal powers will no longer be part of the Church's strategy.

Yet, sadly, any significant change that his propheticism might cause is likely to be internal to the Catholic Church, where some papal power remains. A majority of US Catholics regard the Church under his leadership as moving in the right direction—especially approving of his approach to clergy misconduct, the resistance to hierarchical obsession with power and

75. Pope Francis, *Joy of the Gospel*, 25, 27, 30.

76. Pope Francis, *Joy of the Gospel*, 103.

the accoutrements of wealth, reinterpreting teachings that obsessively focused on certain teaching taken out of context, and minimizing a particular
Catholic style from the past. But his proclamations can only make verbal
appeal to the world leaders of a global eco-political system rooted in blatant self-interest—urging them against their own self-interest to nevertheless become interested in the common good. His earlier pronouncements
were not threatening to these powers, as if intent on avoiding intimidation.
They were positive, gently inviting co-participation in helping to "set free
from sin, sorrow, inner emptiness and loneliness"[77] so that there could
be opened a new way of life, promising the joy of being "constantly born
anew." He attained the appeal and status of a rock star, with multiple polls
showing widespread admiration by 77 percent of Catholics and 59 percent of Americans.[78] Yet the cover of *The Joy of the Gospel* rightly identifies
that book as an apostolic exhortation, which probably accounts for why it
was thin in concrete strategies for confronting the present socioeconomic
dilemmas. Therefore, regardless of this extraordinary popularity and rare
courage being exerted from the most prestigious religious office in the
world, what is becoming clear is how greatly reduced religious authority
has become. His appeals were dutifully reported but disregarded by those
in power, for they were bereft of clout.

His early temperament was prophetic, but his manner was pastoral
and his plea nonthreatening—assuming that he shared with world leaders
a compassion capable of providing a negotiable point of contact. "Christian compassion is everything, and extends to everybody." His appeals have
increasingly expanded in scope, intensity, and explicitness—extending
compassion to gay persons, the divorced, and for those having abortions.
In fact, his declarations have become frantic. His posture has taken on a
globally systemic scope, as in his widely acclaimed encyclical *Laudato sì* (*On
Care for our Common Home*). Here, he identifies the very roots of climate
change as being the "self-destructive vices" of the rich countries. So grave
is his analysis that he is brought to declare that nothing can avert global
disaster short of a "bold cultural revolution" that transfigures the very way
in which humankind presently thinks. No less than the emergence of a "new
and universal solidarity" will halt the oncoming disaster, rooted as it is in a
disproportionate use of natural resources, living a culture of self-destructive
waste, and operating within the doomed inevitability of consumptive competition. No longer is he pleading for cooperation with the power barons

---

77. Pope Francis, *Joy of the Gospel*, 1.

78. Nortey and Gecewicz, "Three-Quarters of U.S. Catholics," paras. 2, 4.

of our global socioeconomic system but is now naming their system as the enemy itself, in need of direct confrontation.

While in Bolivia in July 2015, Pope Francis met with an international gathering of grassroots activists, intent on adding fuel to their fire by insisting on their "standing up to an idolatrous (economic) system which excludes, debases, and kills."[79] He insisted instead on creating an alternative economic social-political system that must emerge from a "logic of love." Both the public and ecclesiastical reaction to his daringly honest realism was diverse and intense, sufficient to grasp widespread attention—for a while. With honesty and realism, he had exposed that our international dilemma is so deep that nothing short of a global conversion can provide healing sufficient to birth even a modicum of sanity for survival. But in blatantly exposing our global crisis, what was likewise exposed was that the necessary solution is impossible to enact.

How ironic that this powerful insistence on transformation is being made by the spiritual leader of a Church ridden with scandal—as proof that such transformation is impossible, even within its own household. What is being exposed is a Church as the mighty Oz, the curtain having been pulled aside, exposing a tragic betrayal—not only by clergy called to lead but by bishops authorized to lead them. Before the face of a shocked world is emerging heavy evidence that Reinhold Niebuhr was right: the only Christian doctrine for which there is empirical evidence is the doctrine of original sin. Recently released was a blistering exposé from a state grand jury investigation regarding even the small Pennsylvania Altoona-Johnstown diocese of my birth.[80] Disclosed was the concealed sexual abuse perpetrated on hundreds of children by more than fifty priests over six decades, involving two bishops. The arenas of exploitation ranged the gamut from confessionals and orphanages to campsites, even within the cathedral itself. This was the third major probe into clergy sexual abuse in Pennsylvania, with prior grand jury investigations held in 2005 and 2011 in the Philadelphia area. Such are the exposures that are happening globally, now involving even religious orders. While one defense has been that the number of priests involved is commensurate with the general public as a whole, this does nothing to slake the loss of stature in the eyes of a public who rightly expects a far higher model of conversion. A clerical collar, once a sign of integrity, is now regarded by many of us who wear one as a badge of mistrust. The *State of Pastors* report commissioned by Pepperdine University found that only one-quarter of respondents had a "very positive" opinion of

79. Wooden, "In Bolivia, Francis Demands," para. 1.
80. "Attorney General Shapiro Details Findings."

pastors, with the same percentage having a "very negative" view.[81] The same percent marked the influence of pastors in their communities, with only 8 percent indicating any interest in hearing any pastor teach about controversial issues. What we see happening is that the church has not only lost her capacity for addressing power with power but is now forfeiting even its integrity for modeling empirical hope for a viable alternative.

Nor does the demise halt there. While Pope Benedict intensely laments the church's loss of influence and power in Europe, yearning for its restoration, such influence has recently been disclosed as involving highly questionable entanglements of Catholic leaders there with the seats of power and economic influence. Recently exposed, for example, was the complicity of Pope Pius XI in the rise of Mussolini's dictatorial power in Fascist Italy during the World War I era.[82] Likewise being widely documented is the church's involvement in centuries of exploitive third-world colonialism—marginalizing, exploiting, and excluding the very masses that Pope Francis now insists are "precious." The new atheists are burnishing the violent image of the Crusades as a mini-portrait that exposes the whole of the church's history as indelibly stained, making the case that a world without religion would be a far more peaceful one. Catherine Nixey's angry polemic *The Darkening Age: The Christian Destruction of the Classical World* identifies the dark ages as being when Christianity poisoned society and culture with "theocratic oppression" and "atrocities" of "ruthless destruction" that lasted for over a thousand years.

In her *Fields of Blood: Religion and the History of Violence*, Karen Armstrong attempts to defend the church against such charges, arguing that religion has been a scapegoat in contemporary explanations of violence. Yet even in making the case that Christianity has not been a motive in warfare through the ages, she is forced to acknowledge that when wars do happen, the countries involved readily use religion and its scriptures to bless as moral and righteous the violence being perpetrated. Thus, while religion is not a sole culprit in violence, Armstrong cannot exonerate it. Therefore, Pope Francis's appeal for radical transformation cannot pit the purity of faith against a system of exploitation, for a common sinful human propensity sullies both. As John B. Noss concludes his study of Christianity in *Man's Religions*, "no religion has expressed such high ideals, or been further from achieving them."[83] Again, being raised here is the question of

81. E. Miller and Christian Century Staff, "Survey Reveals Public's Skepticism," paras. 2, 4.

82. Kertzer, *Pope and Mussolini*.

83. Noss, *Man's Religions*, 571.

why anyone would ever again choose to be Christian, let alone participate in the life of any church.

This question of why has been emerging graphically in the plight of Catholic religious orders. These have traditionally been the spearhead of Catholic faithfulness, with poverty, chastity, and obedience being the evangelical vows that model for all other Christians the fullness of faith. Yet, ironically, with Vatican II, there began the great exit. By minimizing the traditional negative motivations of fear and punishment that focused on an afterlife, the reasons for remaining in a religious order were cut at the roots. No longer was monastic asceticism regarded as having greater merit than that accrued by a faithfully married Christian garage mechanic who was living out his vocation honestly for the good of his neighbors. "Whatever you do, do all to the glory of God" (1 Cor 10:31). This exiting is continuing even after fifty years, so that during the 2013–2018 time frame, 8 percent of religious men and 7.5 percent of religious women have left their orders.[84] While there were 181,000 nuns in 1966, presently there are fewer than 50,000.[85] The numbers for 2020 are stunning: 14,109 religious men and 41,357 religious women in the US.[86] In my own Trappist order, two-thirds of our monasteries globally have been officially determined to be "precarious," with these communities so fragile in numbers and age that formation of candidates is not permitted in them, even if there were any candidates to form.

When the abbot general of our order was asked to identify the most serious problem in our monasteries, his answer was quick and clear: "Numbers." The monastery of Thomas Merton, once numbering over 300 monks, now has numbers in the 70s. In most religious orders, the number of incoming novices does not come near to equaling the number of deaths. Highly revealing is the phenomenon that after each of our major wars, there has been a significant influx of postulants sufficient to rejuvenate our monasteries; but beginning with the Vietnam War, veterans disillusioned by our society have had no interest in exploring monasticism.

One of my favorite groups, the Sisters of Loretto, presently has a median age of eighty-four, being drained financially by the growing need to care for their aging sisters. Some of the older members recently recalled entering the order when there were over 1,200 members, sadly acknowledging their present situation in which their aging care needs to be done by a paid staff,

84. Esteves, "Vatican Statistics Show Decline."

85. McKenna, "Vatican Seeks to Bury the Hatchet," para. 16.

86. Center for Applied Research in the Apostolate, "Frequently Requested Church Statistics," table 1.

for only 120 nuns remain. Thus, after much evasion, they have begun selling off their properties around the country, consolidating in their motherhouse, which is now largely a geriatric center.

In one sense, detailing such depressing statistics is not necessary. Simply looking out upon most Sunday morning congregations of grey-haired worshippers is sufficient to ask how many of these will be alive in ten or at least twenty years. Recently, in having coffee with some of my United Methodist pastor friends, the mood was subdued, as they shared stories from their churches of demise in worshipers and finances. The modifier they kept using was "inevitable." Their hope was personal: early retirement. One of them received nods from the rest in expressing sadness over how few "growing congregations" had been assigned him during his career.

To understand this diminishment of Christianity, I personally need not go beyond my own family as a case study. My five daughters provide for me the faces of today's empty pews. As an ordained United Methodist, my wife and I raised them in a traditional mainline church environment. They willingly participated in weekly worship, Sunday school, daily vacation Bible school, youth groups, and church camp, being leaders in most church activities. They are now professional older adults living in various locations across the country. At Christmas, we continue to gather fondly as an extended family of seventeen, during which time they delight in exploring questions of meaning with me. Although no longer using Christian terminology or explicit reference, we continue to break bread and drink wine together— an act of renewed bonding and promised mutual support. Yet none of my daughters relates in any way to any church. They have no hostility toward Christianity but simply no longer feel any need for organized religion. Irrelevance is what has erased the church from their radar screens. Each feels contentedly full—with vocation, family, friends, causes, sports, music, reading, and yoga. For my benefit, they might occasionally use the word spiritual, especially in describing nature and the mountains that they abundantly climb. We have had friendly conversations about the spirituality that they can still affirm as a consensus. They sense that there may be something larger than themselves in the cosmos, something, if pushed, they might be willing to call God—but only if the name were divested of the literalistic baggage that they see especially conservative Christians as bringing to it. They are aware of some sort of presence in the awesome beauty of nature and in the love they experience within our extended family. They have a deep gratefulness for life itself and feel thankfully blessed by the diverse vibrancy of their living. They might think prayerfully of others who are in need yet are unsure about what that might mean or accomplish. They credit their Christian upbringing with instilling in them a passion for social justice, of desiring that the world be a bit better for their having participated in it. Occasionally, as needed, they might ask God for strength to do this. While recalling happily the hymns they sang as children, they acknowledge that much of their words and imagery are irreconcilable with what they now believe. They can make no sense of such doctrines as original sin, resurrection, ascension, and Trinity, and find repellent any God demanding the death of his Son in order to pay the price for human shortcomings. As they see it, human beings need to be responsible for the consequences of their own sins. As for an afterlife, maybe, as they reflect fondly on the death of their beloved mother at whose bedside they held vigil. Staring upward on a starry night, they will sometimes find themselves addressing her. Hope. But hell?—"Hell, no!" As for Jesus, they accept him as a rare teacher, who, along with other wise teachers such as Gandhi, model a moral lifestyle worth emulating. They find particularly distasteful the pettiness of church politics, seeing local congregations as reflecting characteristics not much different from those of most other organizations. They are particularly put off by the church's reactionary defense of the past rather than being a pioneer of a better future. Also bothersome are far-right churches with their crass literalism and social conservatism. All of my daughters were supportive of my ordination as a Catholic priest and my monastic participation—because "they seem to feed you." But they are a bit incredulous that I can feel at home in a church that will not ordain women and whose societal mission obsesses with abolishing abortion. On the other hand, they have visited appreciatively my monastery with its contemplative aura, which they can accept for its mindfulness. They might be willing to have their own vocations recognized as being their worship, and their church as being the groups with which they work on a common cause. If pushed, under some circumstances, they could use the word Christian in describing their values but are certain that the church would not regard these as sufficient for being called Christian. My daughters are fine persons of honed conscience, all of them with a passion for social justice. I am proud of them. Yet the Christian faith and especially the church that center my life are not for them, nor for those with whom they relate and have their being. I suspect that with my death, their theologizing may well end. These are the faces of the wide group identifying themselves as "nones."

Understandable, then, I can personally understand why prognosticators no longer cast much hope for the church's future. Their forecast is for a tsunami to sweep the church within a decade. This dynamic does not go unnoticed, with a 2014 Pew Research Center study indicating that 72 percent of Americans regard religion as having largely lost its influence on society.[87] Prescient are the increasingly number of articles in denominational publications caringly suggesting how congregations might prepare to die gracefully. But perhaps most staggering is the 2021 Gallup poll finding that over the past twenty-two years, Americans who identify themselves as belonging to a church, synagogue, or mosque have fallen from 70 percent in 1999 to 47 percent.[88]

OPERATIVE ECCLESIASTICAL STRATEGIES

It was not long ago that church leaders were inclined to dismiss the seriousness of this diminishment within the churches, at least publicly. Now the pendulum is swinging toward a near-frantic preoccupation with growth strategies, sounding the alarm that local congregations and even denominations might soon find themselves on the edge, unless something is done. Faced with this situation, these church leaders can hardly be faulted for being drawn toward strategy textbooks on successful corporate leadership. Relentless membership losses and financial drain bring dismal forecasts that force both denominational executives and local church pastors to function primarily as institutional CEOs. As a result, the emerging denominational strategies largely resemble the fourfold ones characterizing the CEOs of any floundering corporation:

1. Strategic placement of new facilities in growth areas, catering especially to the more affluent consumer; remodeling well-located facilities to appeal to current trends; and selling off or closing unprofitable sales centers.

2. Adapting the product(s) so as to appeal to changing cultural tastes.

3. Attracting new customers/clients through diverse sales gimmicks, creative advertising, and the use of technologically focused marketing.

4. Attempting to restore taste for a product that is losing its appeal.

New Facilities and Placement

Since 2007, the United Church of Christ denomination has begun 220 new churches.[89] The United Methodist Church reports establishing 684 new

---

87. Lipka, "Is Religion's Declining Influence," para. 2.
88. *Week* Staff, "Religion: Waning Influence," para. 1.
89. Dart, "UCC Has Been Progressive Pacesetter," paras. 17–18.

congregations from 2008 to 2012. The Presbyterian Church (USA) claims 115 new "worshipping communities." The apparent theory operating here, as with secular institutions, is that it is easier to start new churches than revive old ones. Yet David Roozen, director of the Hartford Institute for Religion Research, indicates that the track record in effectively starting and maintaining new congregations has been dismal, with only half of new church plants showing any success at all.[90] Adapting to what appeals often means resorting to cutesy worship that is loud and titillating, but devoid of much Christian substance.[91] New church starts may not result in much church growth by reaching the unchurched as they might in competitively drawing persons, congregations, and even judicatories out of existing churches and denominations.

The ecclesiastical equivalent of the commercial big-box multiplex appeal is the megachurch, with its own franchise of satellite campuses. These are strategically located in areas of affluent population growth, appealing to a researched diversity of amenities presumably sought by the upwardly mobile, efficiently and hospitably offered by trained professionals, atmosphered in a busy vibrancy associated with success, and packaged with a technologically targeted messaging, often as variations on themes of prosperity. The megachurch closest to me boasts "the largest stained-glass window in the world."

The current rage in secular corporate strategy, even where outlets are profitable, is remodeling, establishing the image of something new, part of the very latest, with glitzy advertising of constantly varied products and repackaging. While denominational leaders recognize the appeal of this approach, finances for more than tepid experimentation are largely limited to the affluent megachurches. McDonald's recent remodeling of nearly every franchise is a case in point, with rival corporations hustling to follow suit. Emblematic is the work of Lux Dei Design, a Christian church design company that has developed a McMass Project that builds McDonald restaurants inside churches to "draw a wider audience to the church."[92] How far such physical accommodation can go when finances are available is a glass church built in southern Taiwan, reaching a height of fifty-five feet in the shape of a massive high-heeled blue shoe. Hung Chao-chang, the spokesman for the enterprise, indicates that it is a bid at attracting more female worshippers.[93] His hope is that it will appeal especially to brides-to-be who

90. Dart, "UCC Has Been Progressive Pacesetter," para. 19.

91. J. Howell, "In Defense of Church," para. 9.

92. Pham, "Christian Group Hopes," paras. 2–3.

93. Agence France-Presse, "Taiwan Hopes to Entice Brides," para. 8.

want a unique and glamorous wedding venue. "I believe that this building will match their imagination."

A more modest approach has been the fad of a decade or so ago of adding a metal structure to existing churches, called a Family Life Center, to offer physical activities to middle-sized congregations. It is becoming clear now that for these centers to be an effective draw rather than simply an optional convenience, what is needed are expenditures for additional staff, increased utility costs, and competitive equipment. Even so, they are proving to be no match for the fast-growing secular health centers that can offer a professionally trained staff, diverse programs, and highly specialized paraphernalia, all at low cost. Thus, these church additions are becoming a liability, much as the fad fifty years ago of creating gymnasium space in downtown churches that featured bowling alleys.

Most megachurches are dependent upon the magnetic attraction of a rare pastor-celebrity, so that 73 to 80 percent of current megapastors have not only been the founders but have been the ongoing charismatic energy perpetuating their growth periods.[94] But diminishment sets in with the passing of their originating pastor. Furthermore, studies show that the power in megachurches tends to become consolidated in a few lay persons, as in Willow Creek Community Church.[95] This tendency makes them prone to a destructive abuse of power. In 1970, there were fewer than 100 megachurches;[96] in 2020, there are approximately 1,750 megachurches, making for at least one megachurch in nearly every Protestant denomination.[97] While these account for approximately 10 percent of Protestant churchgoers, they represent only half of 1 percent of the nearly 320,000 congregations struggling in the US.[98] This megachurch phenomenon will likely continue for a while, riding the momentum of current sales strategies. But as cultural tastes shift, it is likely that they will become as dated in appeal as commercial malls are becoming. As demography inevitably shifts the centers of growth, desirability, and affluence, megachurches, unlike commercial ventures, will be financially unable to liquidate their crystal cathedrals and move along with the dynamics, dotting landscapes with boarded-up religious versions of Toys R Us.

94. Bird and Thumma, "Megachurch 2020," 13.

95. In 2018, the church's entire senior leadership and elder board resigned, admitting to having mishandled abuse allegations.

96. Eagle, "More People, Looser Ties," para.1.

97. Bird and Thumma, "Megachurch 2020," 2.

98. Bird, "How Many Megachurches," para. 3.

Experts like David Eagle are less than impressed. Eagle makes a persuasive case that with modern families pulled in multiple directions, the appeal of the megachurch is really its anonymity in not making demands.[99] Therefore, he sees megachurches as actually representing a loosening of religious bonds, promoting lower levels of involvement than was the case with smaller churches. An indication of this is that large-church members are significantly less likely to attend weekly services regularly.

While megachurches may temporarily give some overall numerical respite, their successes are having a depressive effect on the majority of churches left behind, trapped within locations of economic and/or population decline. Even making minor cosmetic renovations is unlikely for such congregations, given the financial burden that most of them already bear. Facing pastors is the situation of deferred maintenance on aging and inefficient facilities, rising utility bills for unneeded space, ongoing mortgage payments, and salary costs especially encumbered by clergy health care costs. Understandably, then, such economics necessitate an attitude of coping and accommodation. It is a bit absurd to expect much prophetic preaching or significant social justice outreach from these congregations for whom financial survival depends on not upsetting a shrinking nucleus of aging providers. Controversy is the hobgoblin of survival. While fragile situations necessitate risk-taking, this is unlikely—for the shadow hovering over most of these churches is that of being one step away from no longer being able to afford a full-time pastor.

Such marginality often bubbles up a lethal concoction of congregational hostility—characterized by fault-finding, clutching, conflicting cliques, and clergy-targeted scapegoating. This is partly due to the fact that the local church is one of the few institutions remaining in our society where expression of emotions can any longer happen and have any impact, if only negative. These marginal churches result not only in the entropy of fatigued members wearied into absence but also in a depressive deterioration in clergy morale. Statistical successes as reported by megachurches tend to evoke in other pastors a sense of failure, often stirring resentment and jealousy over the influence and financial power that the leaders of these behemoths inevitably assert in denominational matters. These non-megachurch clergy are understandably vulnerable here, for no matter how hard they labor, the persistent decline in membership and finances inevitably takes its toll on vocational and personal self-confidence. Add to this the academic debt many bear, deflating salaries, increased time demands straining marriage and family relations, and uncertainty concerning the

99. Eagle, "More People, Looser Ties," para. 13.

future. In contrast, corporate success necessitates having enthusiastic sales personnel who are optimistic about the future.

An increasing number of articles in denominational journals indicates that this vulnerability in pastors has to do not only with depression but with unhealthy obsessions, forcing them to seek therapeutic help as never before. Vicar Samuel Wells characterizes today's clergy as being forced "to carry on in ministry and make the church function as if there were no God."[100] Sarah H. Wilson observes that the word mission, which is on the lips of most Christian leaders today, is "frequently a frantic response to declining membership or a thinly veiled borrowing from the business world, the better to market our ecclesiastical product."[101] Frantic would seem to be a well-chosen term for this situation. What else are we to make of the emergence in the Church of Sweden of drop-in church weddings and baptisms[102] offered in every major city and in many smaller towns? Each couple is given a twenty-minute premarital talk, chooses two favorite hymns and a song, goes to the altar with a priest and a musician, and in twenty minutes, it is finished.

This problem of facilities is impacting mainline seminaries as well, experiencing this same relentless demise characterizing the churches as a whole. Almost all of them are struggling with the drain of diminishing enrollments, making for unneeded buildings and increased maintenance cost. Indicative is the response of Saint Paul School of Theology in Kansas City. While its urban location was ideal in the 1960s for the social justice action/reflection mode of teaching that made it nationally known a generation ago, the board of directors judged this location an unmanageable liability. Strapped with costly security issues, aging and excessive facilities, decreasing student pool, and eroding investments, the response was to sell off their campus and relocate within an affluent suburban megachurch in 2013.[103] This required purchasing in one direction from the center a commercial office building for faculty offices, and in the other direction renting distance-library privileges and housing.

Likewise in Kansas City, the trustees of Central Baptist Theological Seminary in 2006 voted to sell the old inner-city campus and move to a smaller and more modern facility in the suburbs, citing as reasons millions of dollars in deferred maintenance, major revenue problems, and declining

---

100. Wells, "Ministry without God," para. 7.

101. S. Wilson, "Mission in Spite of Empire," para. 1.

102. Hicap, "Churches in Sweden," paras. 8, 13.

103. Hendricks, "New Plan Emerges," paras. 4, 11.

enrollment.[104] They placed their hope for survival through partnership with Korean Americans, refugees from Myanmar, and a school there. Their local clientele are persons already in ministry who have not been previously trained, for whom are being offered weekend or weeklong classes. Prestigious Union Seminary in New York has been forced to sell off development rights for some of its campus, so that building luxury condominiums could help raise $100 million for legally required repairs on its buildings.[105] Episcopal Divinity School in Cambridge, MA, is seeking its survival by bringing its assets into affiliation with Union Seminary.[106]

Similar transitioning is occurring with other seminaries. Baptist Theological Seminary in Richmond decided that total liquidation was their only option.[107] Two Lutheran seminaries in Pennsylvania are closing,[108] hoping thereby to slash costs and reverse years of declining enrollments of 24 percent since 2005. One of them indicated a projected yearly deficit of over $200,000. Unable to continue to eliminate faculty positions by attrition, they are escaping some of their obligations to tenured faculty by closing both schools and reopening as one seminary. Even so, in order to attract students who are put off by the specter of a student debt averaging over $30,000, they plan to reduce student costs to $15,000, but thereby exacerbate the total seminary deficit. Prestigious Andover Newton, the oldest graduate seminary in the US, has been a pioneer in training clergy. Yet it has been forced to sell its campus, reduce its faculty, lower overhead, and seek partnership with Yale Divinity School.[109] If this does not work, they will attempt "a lean, cooperative-learning model" in which much of the teaching would be in local congregations. In less than ten years, eleven independent seminaries have been forced to such a merger with larger schools.

Frank Yamada, the executive director of the Association of Theological Schools (the seminary accrediting agency), indicates that significant changes of this sort will likely happen in as many as eighty of the hundred mainline seminaries in this country. While most seminaries in the past regarded formation through residential community as indispensable, this model is quickly becoming unsustainable. As a result, in 2013, the Association of Theological Schools was prescient in granting permission for six theological schools to meet entirely online the requirements for the master of divinity

---

104. Tammeus, "Central Baptist Theological Seminary," paras. 6, 9.

105. MacDonald, "Housing Venture Roils Union Seminary," para. 4.

106. Union Theological Seminary, "Episcopal Divinity School," para. 1.

107. Union Presbyterian Seminary, "Legacy of BTSR," para. 2.

108. MacDonald, "Two Lutheran Seminaries to Close," paras. 4, 6, 8, 12.

109. MacDonald, "Andover Newton to Move," para. 7.

degree requisite for ordination, as well as doing so for professional master's degrees.[110] In 2013, Chicago Theological Seminary was the first to offer a completely online MDiv, attempting to reverse its yearly loss of $8 million yearly. The dean of one of these online seminaries defended this radically reduced model by indicating that seminarians can still participate in weekly chapel services at their computers. Other online seminaries require occasional campus visits for special events or workshops. In order to become further competitive, Claremont School of Theology offers its MDiv by reducing the traditional three-year residential degree to twenty-four months. By coupling extensive online teaching with some "intensive meetings," they claim to be saving $22,000 for each student. The justification provided by President Jerry D. Campbell is that since the church as a whole is changing, so must the way in which its leaders are educated. Meanwhile, a friend of mine recently resigned as professor of homiletics from his seminary post because he was convinced that excellent preachers cannot be formed online. Bexley Seabury Seminary (Episcopal) now sends a faculty person to each student's parish location, teaching students alongside their supervising pastor, congregational leaders, and interested parishioners. As the faculty admits, such experiments are "very fragile."[111]

Clearly these far-reaching changes in theological education are not being impelled by either theological or pedagogical creativity but simply by economics. Institutional survival requires intense competition for enticing a diminishing pool of students for filling a diminishing number of full-time pastoral openings. There would seem to be no alternative to this cost-efficient online educational technology. Thereby minimized is face-to-face interactive group engagement for theological, practical, sacramental, and spiritual formation, focusing more on knowledge proficiency than on functional competence. Consequently, it is highly unlikely that the seminaries will any longer provide the creative edge for church renewal as they have done in the past.

I have no desire to pass judgment on these varied ways in which the church is understandably struggling with its crisis. Instead, the intent is to identify the inevitabilities that are ingredients of the growing plight of being the church in this post-Christian world. Only by exploring the extent and causes for this diminishment can we face realistically the options that remain.

110. Dart, "Seminaries Expand Online Options," paras. 6–8.
111. Kennel-Shank, "Forming Priests among the People," paras. 5, 16.

Adaptation of the Product

Since the second century, Christian apologists have endeavored to make a case for belief through rational arguments, often in dialogue with philosophy. During the past two centuries, however, such efforts within liberal Protestantism have been quite different. Here, the inclination has been to adapt Christian beliefs to the modern mentality, accommodating Christianity to the tastes informing the modern cultural context. Academic efforts in this direction began in earnest with Friedrich Schleiermacher (1768–1834) and continued with such highly influential thinkers as Albrecht Ritschl and Adolf Harnack. Their writings largely reflected the rationalism, optimism, and individualism of Enlightenment philosophers such as John Locke, Immanuel Kant, and G. W. F. Hegel. A major intent was to discern a place for religion behind the prescientific worldview informing Scripture and faith, adapting kernels among the husks for modern appropriation. In the early twentieth century, however, theologians such as Karl Barth led a severe attack against such liberal accommodations, insisting that faithfulness to Christian revelation required a prophetic judgment by the church upon the idolatry of modern society. These neo-orthodox theologians insisted upon an either/or approach rather than a both/and one. Building upon their work, thinkers such as H. R. Niebuhr, Hans Frei, George Lindbeck, and Stanley Hauerwas continued this focus away from dealing with Christianity as an expression of religion in general to exploring its unique particularity, identifiable only through participation within its ecclesiological context. Christian theology needed to be church theology. With this insistence upon any external support as constituting compromise, what remained as the theological task was a phenomenological description of lived communal faith. Instead of proof, the invitation was to stand within the Christian community, gazing out upon the world from that unique stance, deplete of any efforts at making a case for entering in the first place.

Presently, however, church diminishment has intensified pressure for accommodation within the mainline liberal churches, continuing Schleiermacher's original intent of Christian dialogue with its "cultured despisers." Theo Hobson's book *Reinventing Liberal Christianity* is a plea for such a resurrection of liberal theology, but it also exhibits the dilemma in reopening this approach of accommodation. He admits that our present secular culture is in need of critique, having become shallow, atomized, and hedonistic. But therein is the dilemma. On the one hand, he acknowledges that only a free liberal society can provide "the proper modern context for Christianity," yet, on the other, only a "reinvented liberal theology" can provide any hope of substantial revival of "the cultural fortunes of Christianity in the West." In other words, society needs the leaven of Christianity for its renewal, while the cultural resources for regaining such a hearing are no longer available. Philosophy, once an intellectual ally in the struggle for meaning, has forfeited that enterprise, claimed by a scientific methodology that recognizes as valid only empirical verification, thereby denying as valid even the questions that religion attempts to address.

As a result, the contemporary focus in intellectually accommodating the Christian product to modernity has tended to center in Christology. Scriptural scholars who are attempting these apologetic efforts have been intent on providing an objective portrait of the historical Jesus, purged of the accoutrements of faith, replacing the church's religion about Jesus with the religion of Jesus, thereby offering a verifiable Jesus of history to replace the centuries-long Christ of faith. Albert Schweitzer's classic *Quest of the Historical Jesus* (1910) had been widely regarded as having ended such accommodation efforts. Just as the scriptural records concerning Jesus were inevitably couched within the dated constructional framework of his time, so it will be of any such attempts in our time, for strict objectivity is epistemologically impossible. Schweitzer anticipated what would become a dictum of postmodernism in insisting that evaluation occurs always through the filters of one's own preestablished mindset. Thus, his conclusion was that all efforts at adaptation through deconstructing the Christ of faith will inevitably say more about the scholar and his context than about any Jesus devoid of his. Schweitzer's conclusion was that Jesus is destined always to remain as "one unknown."[112]

It is somewhat surprising, then, that there has revived this effort at adaptation through a new quest for the historic Jesus. Central has been the work of such scholars as John Dominic Crossan, Marcus Borg, and Robert Funk, helping to establish the Jesus Seminar as an effort to establish a consensus among liberal scholars regarding what can objectively be known about the historical Jesus. The portrait tending to emerge is Jesus as a nonviolent moral teacher and healer. Presupposing a postmodern stance in which miracles are regarded as impossible, such accretions appearing in Scripture are dismissed as later additions or taken parabolically rather than literally. Borg draws a severe line between the Jesus of history, which he calls the "preresurrection Jesus," and the "post-resurrection Christ of faith."[113] The irony is that even if it were possible to extract the original teachings of Jesus that the original disciples actually heard, the truth is that with the death of Jesus they simply went fishing. It was over. Instead of being impelled to continue

112. Schweitzer, *Quest of Historical Jesus*, 403.

113. Borg, *Meeting Jesus Again*, 15–16.

his teaching, two disciples on the Emmaus road said it well: "We had thought he was the one . . ." (Luke 24:21). After 136 pages given to defending the stripped anatomy of his historic Jesus as being basically a teacher, Borg takes only three paragraphs to indicate what is left. Postmodernism insists that what one sees is determined by where one stands in order to look. Borg's accommodation presents an attempt to see what Jesus looks like from a vantage outside rather than within the church. For William Willimon, this effort is "the last gasp of modernity" to salvage any objective truth in support of a liberal Jesus,[114] being an accommodation of filtration by which the secularized postmodern mindset establishes in advance the parameters for determining the non-scandalizing truth behind the scriptural portrait. No longer do we have here an apologetic effort to make a case for Christianity by using mutually acceptable methods but a postmodern determination of what the Christian can legitimately believe. Instead of adaptation, the faith-stance of theologians whose vantage is within the church is far more likely to challenge the informing dynamic-driving modernity.

While these efforts at accommodation have primarily been within the academic community, for several decades candidates for mainline Protestant ordination have largely been taught by professors so inclined. But in time, books for laypersons appeared, such as the best seller J. A. T. Robinson's *Honest to God* (1963), which popularizes the attempts by the scholar Rudolf Bultmann to make Scripture more palatable through demythologizing it. Such efforts threatened many lay Christians by stripping away literal conceivability. Rather than doing much to convince the irreligious, its appeal has been more with those raised within a Christian environment, grasping for a way into partial retention, largely by a diminution of religion into ethics and by refocusing Christ the Savior into Jesus the teacher. In 1966 appeared the best seller *Situation Ethics* by Joseph Fletcher, removing from Christian ethics all principles, rules, dictums, and axioms, reducing morality to bringing love into each unique situation. Since this entails the end justifying the means, we must prepare to "sin bravely." The famed philosopher Alfred North Whitehead was quoted as a focus: "The simple-minded use of the notions 'right or wrong' is one of the chief obstacles to the process of understanding."[115] What we are left with is little reason for retaining Christian language to embellish an ethic of love.

All of these reactions of Christian liberalism raise the haunting question as to how much of Christianity's central uniqueness remains, sufficient for grounding gathered worship and instilling institutional loyalty.

---

114. Willimon and Borg, "Encountering Jesus," para. 2.
115. Whitehead, "Importance," lecture 1 in *Modes of Thought*, 1–27.

The consequences of such diminishments becomes evident in the widely used *Interpreter's One-Volume Commentary on the Bible*, composed of seventy contributions by acclaimed liberal biblical scholars, representing most mainline Protestant Churches. Focusing their liberal lens on once literally conceived biblical events, they tend to interpret them as projections from later dates and/or perceptions from within the cultural settings of dated mindsets. Thereby they sort out truth from the miraculous, corrected by archaeology, scientific plausibility, and commonsense. Again the question arises: "What is left?"

We can see the ecclesiastical results of such efforts at liberal accommodations in megachurch pastor Robin Meyers's *Underground Church: Reclaiming the Subversive Way of Jesus*. While Meyers claims for his liberal efforts a radical step forward in restoring the church as an alternative, what we are actually given turns out to be a softened version of the liberal social gospel approach of a century ago, tailored for suburbanites. Meyers offers us a domesticated religion *of* Jesus as a substitute for what he calls the traditional religion *about* Jesus. The resulting portrait is a nonviolent Sermon-on-the-Mount teacher who models a mercy ministry that Meyers regards as uniquely Christian. The radical megachurch manifesto that he proposes is actually not radical at all but an accommodation resembling a religiously trimmed humanism, forfeiting all sense of mystery for a love-initiated morality. Filtered through the sieve of scientific conceivability, Meyers discards beliefs as needless stumbling blocks to attaining faith. He finds little of consequence in the traditions that the church has lived through the centuries, regarding them as standing in the way of restoring what he discerns as being the ideals of the early church. Thus, what he advocates is the importance of being loving rather than being right,[116] following the "spirit of Jesus" rather than affirming transformation by any Holy Spirit. Nothing remains of the traditional characteristics of Christ as Redeemer, replaced by a moral Jesus who as a leveling accommodation appeals to modernity by his teaching and example. The usefulness of such a Jesus he sees in rendering persons more caring within a socioeconomic system that is not challenged—mitigating with love the local "hard edges" of capitalism. Meyers has morphed theology into ethics and the religion of Jesus into a belief-stripped nonviolence. The Christian residue provides much to doubt, with little to believe. Yet he insists that his approach is "subversive and dangerous," grooming persons who would be candidates for the "no-fly list." Actually, corporate America should welcome his efforts, for he is actually recruiting free volunteers to mend the tattered safety net that the system is shredding, thereby helping to mollify the

---

116. Meyers, *Underground Church*, 254.

stigma of its immoral structure. While we often hear the aphorism "I'm spiritual but not religious," Meyers takes this accommodation one step further, that the Christian needs to be moral but not spiritual.

Such accommodations of the Christian product for the sake of saleability tends to be a tempering of attitudes without much clear content, eschewing conversion for behavior modification. These appeals are more likely to appeal to persons who, while raised Christian, might find helpful a way of holding onto a vestige of faith, rather than attracting the unchurched into adopting an alternative way of living. In his *Kingdom of God in America,* H. Richard Niebuhr's characterization of liberal accommodation seems as valid today as when he wrote it nearly eighty years ago. The heritage of faith with which liberalism had started was used up, with an ever-diminishing capital. As a result, what he sees remaining is "a God without wrath [who] brought men without sin into a kingdom without judgment through the ministrations of a Christ without a cross."[117]

Kate Bowler in her *Blessed: A History of the American Prosperity Gospel* details how conservative Christianity in America has involved adaptation, especially in regard to the American Dream. It has incorporated upward mobility and unfettered consumption into promises of the gospel. By mid-twentieth century, evangelical and Pentecostal strands had helped to forge this born-again gospel of prosperity into a movement. National figures in this adaptation included Kenneth Hagin, Oral Roberts, T. D. Jakes, Joel Osteen, Gloria and Kenneth Copeland, Perry Noble, James MacDonald, Ed Young Jr., and Robert Schuller—gaining prosperity for themselves by preaching it as a promise for others. Prosperity-gospel preachers not only have created lucrative syndicated programs, but some own their own TV networks. What prosperity megachurches are providing is a religious ritualization for the secular gospel of free enterprise. Thus, only recently, rapper Kanye West announced as reward for his being a born-again Christian a $68-million tax refund check he just received.[118] But for persons whose personal experience has tarnished beyond religious repair the American Dream for them, other liberal churches provide coping skills by which they might be able to live with economic failure without questioning the injustices of their non-prosperity demise.

A telling example of accommodation appears in an email advertisement that I keep receiving. This apparently successful enterprise promises that 182 days "could totally transform your relationship with wealth and abundance." It will be possible "to live the life of your dreams all on online."

117. H. Niebuhr, *Kingdom of God in America,* 193.

118. Langlois, "Kanye West," para. 2.

Welcome to Spirit School—where Wealth Consciousness, the Divine Feminine, and Spirit merge, replacing "poverty consciousness," enabling one "to live at the level of wealth that brings you the most ease and joy in bliss consciousness." This new life identifies itself as "Spirit-led Magic." Magic, indeed, for there is no state in the US where a full-time worker at minimum wage can rent a one-bedroom apartment for less than 30 percent of one's wages—the benchmark set for housing affordability.

In her "Body in Motion" article, Carol Howard Merritt describes in appreciative terms a Sanctuary of the Arts, which is a "dance church" organized by two pastors. The congregation is described as "made up of an eclectic group of people, diverse in age, ethnicity, sexual orientation, and religious or nonreligious background." It is "a multifaith community, including some with no faith."[119] Such efforts suggest that there is a point at which adaptation of the product so draws the center off-center that what is left is hardly a shadow of itself. In their efforts at survival, we are arriving at a place where the churches are increasingly unclear about what the *sine qua non* of the gospel really is. While whatever sells is an appealing temptation when one is in survival mode, even if it might manage some success, the result is most often a Christianity that falls in upon itself. Our churches, much like our secular society, are tempted to defend themselves in a manner that threatens to sacrifice the very fabric that makes itself worth preserving. The Americanization of Christianity is proving to be a process of custom-tailoring diminishment.

Blank Slate, by Lia McIntosh and Jasmine and Rodney Smothers, epitomizes the shallowness of many such efforts as they explore for Christian use the correlation between the unique characteristics of the millennials and Generation Z, and why Facebook, Starbucks, Uber, Netflix, and Disney appeal to them. They insist that success in marketing with this generation entails focusing on "What's in it for me?" Thus, churches need to create new ways to compete for customers by making persons "feel better about themselves."[120]

These adaptive approaches to the church's plight pose a major question. In today's post-Christian world, is it possible any longer for the church to be both successful and faithful? The evidence is becoming strong that our efforts at confronting diminishment are failing not only regarding quantity but quality as well. What if that which is gospel no longer sells, and that which sells is no longer gospel?

---

119. Merritt, "Body in Motion," para. 13.

120. McIntosh et al., *Blank Slate*, 153.

Creative Advertising and Coming Attractions

If accommodating the product is becoming questionable both as to effectiveness and faithfulness, another corporate success strategy is that the packaging needs changing. Thus the national offices of most denominations have not been derelict in trying varied forms of advertising, from billboards to television messaging. More recently, however, these expansive and expensive efforts have largely been abandoned, deemed ineffective in reaching the advertisement-saturated unchurched. Instead, advertising is becoming more localized, encouraging newspaper notices that announce special events and time of services, especially when there is a seasonal change. Following the lead of secular media, some denominational publications are changing from a newspaper format to a glitzy feature story magazine. Typical is the *Missouri Methodists Magazine* effort in this direction, highlighting stories of church successes, youth rock concerts for Jesus, upbeat personalities, computer suggestions for better communication, local leadership training, innovations in mercy ministry, and foreign mission projects—focused for an overall youth appeal. But since its distribution is internal to the churches rather than including an outreach to the unchurched, it is primarily a positive attitude adjustment to counter depression over membership decline.

The megachurches are the ones more able to use the strategy of repackaging, advertising an appealing array of mall-like options: all kinds of groups for a diversity of purposes, specialized counseling focused on varied needs, coffee shop fellowship at convenient hours, extensive bookstore diversity for every spiritual taste, popular lectures and study groups on multiple topics, sports clubs and youth adventures, health clubs and fitness centers. But to provide such costly offerings necessitates locations with an affluent clientele.

Inventive was a church in Wilmington, NC, who offered "What Would Jesus Brew" contests, conducted in breweries willing to provide popular social spaces as a lure. One rector explained the rationale as an attempt "to introduce Christ or Christian community without churchiness getting in the way."[121] Other novel wrappings include drive-by communions and drive-through wakes. A recent phenomenon is the imposition of ashes on Ash Wednesday by strolling pastors at malls and on college campuses. Southern Baptists in Kentucky hold Second Amendment Celebrations in which guns contributed by local dealers are awarded as door prizes.[122]

---

121. A. Greene, "What Would Jesus Brew?"

122. Wolfson, "Ky. Baptists Lure New Worshippers," para. 1.

Another strategy recently disclosed is one by the fastest growing Southern Baptist megachurch—the staging of "spontaneous baptisms."[123] Within each of the services of this congregation of 14,000 members, fifteen persons are planted at strategic places, and at the right moment, in response to the invitation, they spontaneously come forward as a psychological inducement for others to join them in being baptized on the spot. What awaits them are dressing rooms, baptismal clothing, deodorant, and makeup remover. Another effort at repackaging is the vogue of renaming local churches so as to hide their denominational connection—hoping that New Life Community might be more enticing than First Presbyterian Church. Successful advertising requires drawing a clear connection between an acknowledged need and an effective product. Yet what is being exposed by such efforts is the church's lack of clarity about what it is they really have to advertise, accompanied by confusion as to any basic need that might be touched.

Supportive social relationships, family fun, youth adventures, fellowship suppers, rock band gatherings, mothers' day out, calisthenics at the family life center. . . Even if such packaging might attract, the churches must finally be about selling Jesus—but who is this Jesus who no longer seems able to be packaged directly for successful sale? While commercial ventures may thrive on competitive brands, competitive denominational packaging tends to discredit the product and confuse the members. Thus, efforts at innovative packaging are tending to reinforce the conclusion we have been drawing along the way, that the problem is much deeper than the attractiveness of messaging. In this post-Christian era, what we are witnessing is uncertainty by the churches regarding what is uniquely left to sell, for which there might remain some modicum of need in a potential clientele somewhere. Diminishment is reflecting a disconnect between product and buyer, rooted in a significant change in both.

Restoration of Taste

The church's success in the past has been grounded in there being cultural predilections to which appeal could be successfully made. Christian answers could be proffered as remedies for acknowledged concerns and sensed needs—illuminating meanings that had resonance in connecting hopes with results. But what must be recognized now is that these traditional answers no longer stroke questions that the vast majority of persons are any longer asking. In spite of ambiguity as to what questions might be implicit within society, they no longer seem to be touching anything

123. Bailey, "Megachurch Pastor," paras. 5, 7–8.

recognizable as authentically religious. What once was regarded as meaning is no longer regarded as meaningful, with nothing seeming to be left that needs Christian answers.

We have explored the church's strategic option of adapting the product to meet changed tastes. We have also examined the indirect strategy of employing nonreligious appeals to attract religious participation. There is a third option: an attempt to revive taste for what formerly sold. This strategy is mostly being attempted by the conservative wings of both Protestantism and Catholicism. They identify the primary factor in Christian diminishment as residing not in the product but in the change of taste in the clientele. This makes the church's task twofold. First, there is a need to restore the heart of the traditional product by removing the adulterations that have occurred through adaptation. Second, there is a need to restore the public taste for the product that formerly had appeal. The focus of such evangelism is on the clientele—promising, as previously noted, an afterlife for those with whom they have been successful in reestablishing a fear of hell. But as we will continue to explore, the intense this-worldly ethos of our post-Christian era cannot be halted or even significantly redirected. Thus, any success that these reactionary efforts might have is unlikely to be as an evangelistic outreach tool but a temporary reinforcement for already conservative Christians who are feeling threatened by the church's liberal wings. Actually, this effort is proving to be counterproductive, for it is exacerbating the rift within Christianity itself—between otherworldliness and the progressive focus on the Christian's this-worldly responsibilities as stewards of God's good creation. Furthermore, within society as a whole, such right-wing messaging is impelling the negative stereotyping of Christianity as such. While large billboards in my town shout promises about purchasable secular comforts and guaranteeing of dependable security, the sign in front of the local Assembly of God church declares: "Our one goal is getting to heaven." Haunting are the words of Jesus: "If salt has lost its taste, how can its saltiness be restored? It is no longer good for anything, but to be thrown out and trampled under foot" (Matt 5:13). Even if Christianity is somehow able to retain a hint of saltiness, of what consequence is it if a salt-free diet has become the modern lifestyle?

UNDERLYING CAUSES OF DECLINE

The postmodern era that is breaking in upon the church is unplanned, unsought, and unanticipated. Tragic events served to identify its commencing and its character. The Holocaust was an exposé of the darkness inhabiting human propensities, Hiroshima and Nagasaki birthed the ominous shadow of nuclear extermination, 9/11 terrorism launched a state of perpetual war against an invisible enemy, and the Japanese tsunami prophesized unprecedented catastrophes of a nature being strangled. Ours is a world in which things seem out of control, rudderless in an ethos bereft of certainty about anything, its values shattered into the subjectivity of rival ideologies, society splintered into bewildered selves isolated by competitive individualism, and its institutions invasively controlled by the greed of transnational corporate capitalism. The nonprofit Global Challenges Foundation put on its list nuclear war, climate change, and pandemics, projecting that across the span of one's lifetime, the average American is more than five times likelier to die during a human extinction event than in a car crash.[124]

On May 17, 2013, the Pentagon claimed that US presidents have the power to send troops anywhere in the world to fight whomever they regard as terrorists, whenever they want.[125] They based this potential for world domination on the Authorization for Use of Force bill passed by Congress the day after 9/11. Thereby was established an aggressive, addictive, and endless war mentality, a growing domestic militarization for internal security, and an expanding global arms market—kindled, sustained, and enforced by the US corporations for whom this dynamic is enormously lucrative. According to Brown University's Watson Institute, since 9/11, $6.4 trillion has been spent by the US on wars alone.[126] When the US performed a drone strike that assassinated Quassim Suleimani, defense contractor stock values immediately soared.[127]

Postmodern is the name for the disintegration of three fundamental premises that once characterized the optimistic Enlightenment of our past era. 1) No longer is reason regarded as able to transcend the particularities of any historical context in determining objective truth. 2) Nor is human experience any longer regarded as based on a common identifiable nature, no matter the context provided by society, culture, and civilization. 3) Neutrality of perspective is impossible for establishing any basic common agreements for the sake of establishing some common good. In heavy contrast to the past, our postmodern age is incapable of locating objective meaning anywhere, is despairing of belief in progress, is streaked by an awakened sense of the deep dark forces in human nature, and is overshadowed by diverse global propensities hinting broadly of apocalypse. As Vladimir

124. Meyer, "Human Extinction Isn't That Unlikely," para. 3.

125. "Astoundingly Disturbing," para. 1.

126. Watson Institute, "Costs of War," para. 1.

127. Fang, "TV Pundits Praising Suleimani Assassination," para. 12.

Nabokolv declares, "The word 'reality' is one of the few words that no longer means anything without quotes."[128] Karl Lowith concludes, "Our modern historical experience is one of steady failure."[129]

Further, there are widespread efforts by multiple governments to exploit this demise, as described in Peter Pomerantsev's *Nothing Is True and Everything Is Possible*. As a Russian TV producer, he experienced personally the Kremlin strategy of creating alternative realities, falsehoods, concocted theories, etc., not to persuade but to confuse—the aim being to foster an environment in which people give up on facts, convinced that you cannot believe anyone anymore. As a strategy, the Trump administration created "alternative facts" and "alternative truth," and wrote off mainstream media as "fake news"—the intent of which is to render truth unknowable. By the end of Trump's presidency, Mr. Trump had made 30,573 false or misleading claims—with nearly half coming in his final year.[130]

A key thesis being developed in this book is that, given this postmodern condition, efforts at reversing the steady decline of the church are not only ineffective, but no matter how innovative our efforts might be, at best they can only slightly and momentarily slow the impact of this postmodern secularizing dynamic. With its dynamic continuing to erode the underpinnings of Christianity, we are passing over a threshold into a post-Christian era that is irreversible. Not by modernizing our facilities to current tastes, not by adapting our product to society's likening, not by technologically updating the vehicles of our marketing strategies, not by restructuring our institutional models along lines of corporate effectiveness, not by accommodating our worship gatherings to reflect the transient likes of the present youth culture, not by supporting our theological content with postmodern thought patterns—none of these, nor all of them, will be able at best to do more than slow for the moment this pervasive irreversible dynamic of our sociocultural secular ethos. So erosively inconceivable for the postmodern mind is Christianity—and so undercutting of the basic motivations that once deemed Christianity relevant and meaningful—that not only is diminishment of the churches relentless, but even the survival of Christianity itself is in question. I draw this conclusion as a practicing Christian, deeply committed to the Christian faith, but who is being forced to conclude that survival of any authentic vestiges of our faith depends upon our honest recognition of the crisis we are facing.

128. Delbanco, "Getting Real," para. 1.

129. Curran, "Headed toward Christ," para. 3.

130. Kessler, "Trump Made 30,573 False," para. 2.

James K. A. Smith wisely identifies liturgies, whether sacred or secular, as that which shape and constitute our identities, forming our fundamental desires, and establishing our most basic attunements for engaging the world.[131] In short, liturgies are what rehearse us into being the kind of people we are. While within the Christian tradition liturgy is intentional and self-conscious, the present liturgies defining our society are largely unconscious, primarily the byproducts of the economic factors that are determining our social interactions. They shape our values, so that they in turn support and undergird the system's perpetuation and expansion. We will explore the reasons for believing that never before has a societal liturgy as ours been so permeating, relentless, and global. This corporate transnational-industrial-technological-security complex structures our societal/cultural environment, forges the nature of our interactions, determines our consciousness as the atmosphere we unconsciously breathe, and constitutes the manner in which we assimilate data and judge conclusions. As a market force, it seduces wants into needs, attractions into distractions, and endless trivia of choice into an illusion of freedom. Its dynamic instills an obsession with endless consumption, insists on the self-destructive axiom of limitless GNP growth, cultivates an insatiable passion for upper mobility, idolizes a dream world of materialistic meaning, drives a frenetic infatuation with activity, shadows leisure with guilt-suspicion, promotes an ardor for first appearances, atomizes society into a competitive individualism, measures values according to quantitative efficiency—all the while burrowing an entrapment in deficit living and enmeshing the whole in a militarism that promises false security. This not only defines our postmodern condition, but its self-feeding momentum establishes a vicious cycle of relentless escalation.

Sunday afternoons, from autumn to spring, on gridirons almost everywhere in this nation, we can participate in a microcosmic gridiron of liturgical rehearsal. From Thursday evening to Monday evening on TV, as an immense prop for the mandatory national anthem, a song about a victorious military battle, is the unfurling of an enormous flag almost the size of the football field itself, as fervent fans cheer from end zone to end zone. Emblematic of the militarized patriotism that has invaded even our sports, an honor guard representing our varied armed services stands in solemn attention as overhead swoop jets or, if particularly blessed, a stealth bomber. As the congregation sings this programmed unity of displayed power, the players of the violent conflict soon to happen are expected to stand dutifully in unquestioning patriotic devotion—under threat of lifetime suspension from the sport.

---

131. J. Smith, *Desiring the Kingdom*.

The Nuremburg trials (1945–1949) were a frightening disclosure, in which attempts were made to indict Nazi leaders for crimes against humanity. What was exhibited, in case after case, was that it was not really individuals that were on trial but a complex—a whole for which no one was personally responsible. Each individual had a prescribed task to do to the best of one's ability, with personal efficiency promising advancement within defined compartments, each part operating efficiently in an interlocking self-perpetuating whole for which no person or group was accountable or capable of controlling. Even in the Jerusalem trial of Adolf Eichmann (1961), Eichmann could defend himself as having no moral responsibility for the death camps, because he was simply carrying out efficiently and faithfully the bureaucratic project that had been assigned to him to accomplish. The banality of evil, it has been called.

This condition is distressingly analogous to our present secular/ capitalist complex, happening outside overall control by any person, group, leader, or even nation. Each entity defined by the whole is functioning within the purview of its own positioning, individuals motivated by their own competitive advantage, and each compartmentalized segment driven by profit efficiency, together bound economically in a self-perpetuating, self-defining, and self-rewarding dynamic. Each segment and each person performs a self-interested role in this composite whose overall direction is beyond the ability of any person or entity to determine, slow, or redirect. Corporations focus for their existence on creating global profits for their stockholders, their legal lobbyists are paid well to eliminate legislative regulations and controls, and the legislators themselves are bought off by needing to please their funding sources for the sake of reelection. The military with its own escalating budget pushes for increasingly efficient weapons in order to establish and maintain a world scene favoring US economic self-interests, while secret agencies such as the Central Intelligence Agency (CIA) are empowered without accountability to use whatever covert means are needed to undermine foreign leaders belligerent to our own self-interests. Professionals throughout the world do whatever is expected of them to gain financial promotion/recognition, while the rest are competitively dependent upon whatever employment is left, unquestioning lest they be fired. Zachary Karabell calls it a "fairy tale" to think that "we can halt this tide."[132]

Further alarming are the self-replicating and self-reliant technologies being created by and for this system. For example, in the Stock Exchange, key to our economy, 80 to 90 percent[133] of the volume trading is driven

132. "Fight over Obama's Trade Deal."
133. "Stockmarket Is Now Run," para. 10.

instantaneously by competitive computers that with their reactive algorithms are no longer humanly operated, making even expert predictions impossible. Also being developed are artificial intelligence weapons, so inexpensive to create that they are likely to mark a new level in the global arms race, capable of redesigning themselves instantaneously for guaranteed devastation. Even now, drone strikes remove the human element for the sake of the destructive equation. Growing use of artificial intelligence for efficiency in multiple fields is rendering conscience increasingly remote. Stephen Hawking and other famed scientists express alarm that if envisaging such systems is not halted, they could well spell the end of the human race.[134]

Never before has a dynamic of such power and breadth permeated human history so deeply, in which diverse elements have become so interlocked into a whole that any instrumentality outside of itself cannot viably challenge or render it accountable. Experts in varied fields, from Saul Alinsky to Reinhold Niebuhr to Henry Kissinger, have wisely insisted that effective change requires negotiation necessitated by countervailing powers sufficient to force a transcendence of the narrow self-interest of each. From the power of labor unions to that of Cold War nuclear deterrence, the viable strategy has been that of power neutralizing power into an impasse that forces negotiation. A further working assumption has been that the nationalism of each country was strong enough to control internal economic self-interest, so that the health of each nation would not be undermined. But even seventy-five years ago, Reinhold Niebuhr became alarmed by how this growing nationalism was actually functioning. The self-directing nationalism of each nation was not establishing a mutually beneficial bargaining table, but instead was creating an unbalanced competition that was bringing the ominous threat of ongoing war. Thus, this unstable and undependable condition was undercutting mutual deterrence. All that Niebuhr could proffer as a counterforce was an international cultural exchange of varied arts. So today we find ourselves having passed over a threshold in which a transnational economic dynamic is beyond control by countervailing nations. Instead, the nations themselves are being locked into subservience to this global complex. Consequently, even nationalistic loyalty is diminishing, as each nation is forced into a self-interested allegiance to the economic whole, sacrificing autonomy to an unbridled transnational capitalism.

Some years ago, I began to sense what was happening when my airplane seat companion turned out to be the wife of a corporate executive. After having spent a weekend with family in Phoenix, she was returning to Paris, where she and her husband, after having lived there for three years,

134. Clark, "Artificial Intelligence Could Spell End," para. 2.

had requested a corporate transfer in order to work for a time in Greece. She suggested that they were entertaining the possibility of retirement in Japan. Clearly their global-based corporate profession was providing a freedom of residence that removed all national loyalty. In fact, she even expressed freedom from loyalty to the particular company of their immediate employment. Their passport had become a corporate global citizenship. Wesley's motto, that "the world is my parish," is becoming a secular way of life for the affluent.

This ethos characterizing the corporate executive and his wife simply reflects what is true of the major corporations themselves. No longer is each rooted in a separate country with a self-interested concern for the stability of its national base, but having become global, possesses a transnational mobility that serves its own narrow economic self-interests. Cheap labor, availability of raw materials, politically exploitable markets, favorable taxation: these are the factors determining their choice of locations—temporarily. Such flexibility, in turn, provides corporations with enormous power to negotiate favorable concessions by exercising the threat to leave. Indicative of this economic power is the intense bidding recently between cities to acquire the new Amazon headquarters, offering staggering concessions in order to be the winner.[135]

This self-interested corporate control has become so invasive of the foreign policy of the many countries where these huge corporations are located that inevitable national conflict becomes built into the global dynamic. Competition for economic advantage bequeaths endless conflict, wiping away any viable interest in peace. The rationale for the war in Afghanistan that has been going on for twenty years received illumination when it was exposed that this country possesses mineral deposits worth $1 trillion.[136] To follow the oil deposits is to foretell the locations of military involvement and major conflicts. Weapon manufacturers, in turn, are making unprecedented fortunes, as evident in the present Mideast chaos, by arming countries in escalating hostility against each other. This self-interested economic dynamic has propelled the US during the last five years into being the number one exporter of weapons into ninety-six countries,[137] irrespective of human rights violations or war crimes. Illustratively, a $1.15 billion arms deal with Saudi Arabia was pushed by senators who received extensive campaign contributions from General Dynamics, a company that would greatly profit from

---

135. Miranda et al., "Here Are the Most Outrageous."

136. Mackenzie, "Donald Trump Eyes," para. 2.

137. "US Remains Top Arms Exporter," paras. 1, 10.

the sale.[138] Even though Saudi Arabia is involved in the brutal bombing of Yemen, legislators justified the sale by claiming that, otherwise, American workers in the extensive arms industries would lose their jobs. According to the Stockholm International Peace Research Institute, the US weapons industries has made exorbitant profits, with the world's total military expenditures for 2019 being $361 billion.[139] The US itself spends as much on weapons as the next eleven nations together.[140]

Such profitability has grown exponentially into an interlocking complex of industrial-technological-security industries that employ such huge numbers of persons that global conflict has become indispensable for their economic survival, as well as being indispensable for the perpetuation of our country's economic advantage. Corporate giants like Lockheed Martin, Boeing, General Dynamics, Raytheon, and Northrop Grumman thrive on global conflict for guaranteeing and enriching their profits, together receiving yearly $137.6 billion in militarily related contracts.[141] In 2019, 70 percent of Lockheed-Martin's sales ($37.8 billion) came from contracts with the US government.[142] Boeing employs twenty-four in-house lobbyists and twenty lobbying firms to influence legislators and government agencies on its behalf, spending over $15 million for lobbying in 2018.[143] During the Trump administration, Patrick Shanahan, who served as deputy secretary of defense, had previously worked at Boeing for over thirty years. National Defense accounts for over 50 percent of all discretionary spending, with Congress spending several times more money on the military than on education, energy, and the environment combined.[144] The $178 million that it costs taxpayers for one fighter plane would provide 3,358 years of college tuitions.[145] What we have is the military-industrial complex against which President Eisenhower graphically warned us—but which has expanded far beyond his fears, into a military-industrial-technological-security complex firmly embedded in Washington.

A century ago, we might have spoken with some hope about the secular humanism that was emerging among intellectuals in varied forms from

138. Kinzer, "Frustrating the War Lobby," paras. 6–7, 9.

139. Stockholm International Peace Research Institute, "Global Arms Industry," para. 1.

140. "United States Spends More," para. 1.

141. Macias, "American Firms Rule," paras. 6–10.

142. Best, "Lockheed Martin's Top Competitors," para. 1.

143. Zanona and Gurciullo, "Boeing's Congressional Base Frays," para. 5.

144. Tax Policy Center, "Briefing Book: Some Background," fig. 4.

145. Van Buren, "For $178 Million," para. 11.

the Enlightenment, evidencing a rational concern for the common good. We can even see traces of this in Alfred Marshall, one of the founders of modern capitalism. He insisted that there operates within the capitalist system an "economic chivalry" that would provide an internal transcendence over sheer greed. This "economic force of the first order of importance" is the "desire of men for approval of their own conscience and for the esteem of others."[146] Instead, what we see happening is that the enormous power of this economic system is severely refashioning conscience and esteem. Both are turning out to be remarkably malleable, as affluence is redefining them both. Enough is never enough to satisfy self-aggrandizement, and admiration is never ego-complete. As former President Obama observed, those with the luck of economic success no longer need the once-shared common arenas such as public schools, parks, and libraries, for they are abundantly cared for privately. In heavy contrast to the Enlightenment trust in reason to identify universal truths for the common good, we now recognize that what one sees depends on where one stands, and the place of one's standing is increasingly being determined by structured inequality. Self-interest is becoming all-determining.

Foreign columnists such as William Robinson are indicating that this economically impulsed dynamic is intensifying even within the so-called social-welfare nations, precipitating crises of such an unprecedented magnitude as to threaten ecological degradation, social deterioration, and increasing violence.

Norwegian editorial writer Jan Kjaerstad recently identified in *Aftenposten* this crisis as operative within his own nation, one that formerly prided itself in establishing an alternative between socialism and capitalism—by taking a portion from the rich sufficient to provide a decent level of services for all. Yet, as Kjaerstad laments, within several decades an oil boom has been replacing this commitment to the common good with a growing passion for the "omnipresence of profit." By instilling into each person a competitive drive to become rich, the previous core societal resources are being privatized, establishing an unequal society that is squandering the moral principles of equality, justice, and solidarity. The resultant economy is "poisoning our planet" through a passion for "consumer happiness" that is "gagging our collective conscience."[147]

Again, we must recognize that this economically driven ethos has not really been designed, planned, or chosen. It is emerging as the inevitable by-product of a global corporate capitalism that has taken on a life of its own. Characterized by materialism, hedonism, and consumerism, its dynamic compels a competitively individualistic milieu that renders

146. Marshall, "Some Aspects of Competition," 285.
147. *Week* Staff, "Norway: Drowning Our Ideals."

its populace fearfully reactionary toward change and unduly amenable to authoritative control, thereby serving as warrant for perpetuating the dynamic. What we will be showing is how the diminishment of religion in general and Christianity in particular is the inevitable result of this ethos, relentlessly evoking a lifestyle that defines the whole of our daily living. It provides our orienting perspective, our functional presuppositions, our operative attitudes, our unquestioned ideology, the imagery sifting our collective memories, and the impetus driving our emotions—coalescing as a disposition that defines who we are. The church's demise is the result of its corrosive impact, for although largely unchosen and often unrealized, we are being quietly and persistently socialized to live as if religious dimensions are no longer part of the defining equation.

This awareness came to me some years ago as a personal crisis. At midlife, I came to the shaking awareness that although I was an ordained professor of theology in a seminary that trains persons for vocations in church ministry, I was actually living my own life as a functional atheist. My comfortable lifestyle could well have been that of a decent agnostic, except for the habit of church attendance. While intellectually considering myself a Christian, I was living as if not. I could have been a cover-candidate for the American Dream—from coal mining poverty to a Yale PhD, I was living my respectable professional role within a whole that was relentlessly driving us all toward the cliff—antithetical to the direction and goal that should have been forthcoming from living a Christian calling. Is there much left of the Christian faith if being Christian is only peripherally different from being a good citizen in a post-Christian world?

An added difficulty is that many of us who are becoming serious about living out of a deep Christian commitment are having difficulty finding commonality with other fellow Christians, often finding them diametrically opposed to the stands to which we feel faith propelling us. Recently a good friend who as an evangelical Christian shared with tears that "as much as we both love Jesus, in all honesty I must tell you how much I disagreed with many of the issues you support." Out they came—death penalty, pro-choice, the military, Israel, climate change, etc. I was being encountered by a Christian whose lived faith rendered her the foe to much that flowed as cause from my faith. It is highly likely that watchers of the national conservative Catholic TV station EWTN, on the one hand, and readers of the *National Catholic Reporter*, on the other, would each leave the Roman Catholic Church if required to believe what the other holds. Given the decreasing commonality identifying Christians and the gaping spectrum of gospel implications, is there any real meaning left in lumping us all together? Have we come to the point where the label Christian is like identifying Republicans and Democrats as belonging to the same party?

CHAPTER TWO

POSTMODERN DIMENSIONS
OF THE DEMISE

The so-called new atheists are largely irrelevant, gaining their public notoriety mostly for attacking a dated theology with which serious Christians do not identify as being even close to what they believe. As we have been maintaining, the diminishment of both Christianity and the church is not so much a matter of rational choice as it is the result of a gradual and relentless corrosion, draining the *therefore* until there is little of the *so what* left. The church's diminishment is not necessarily the result of the churches doing things wrong, or insufficiently. Instead, a complex of factors has silently impacted our daily ethos until, as the Gallup polls consistently indicate, there is little difference between Christians and nonbelievers on basic moral issues. This momentous paradigm shift is so determining life in our post-Christian world that in multiple arenas such as business, the professions, social networking, sports, and television, we are being marinated into a world of divine absence. The desert temptations that attempted to lure Jesus away from his calling were trifold: the sins of power, prestige, and possessions. Yet these three *p*'s are the very motivations in which our society is rooted, that impel our basic institutions, that encourage our personal behavior, and that reward our actions. The church has never been at this point before—in which success as culturally defined has all the hallmarks of what Christianity has denounced as sin—both for society and for the individual. Church and society are unmistakable antagonists. To understand more deeply how this postmodern situation has become a post-Christian world marking demise for society and for the church, we will explore more deeply eleven crucial factors:

1. Elimination of Literal Conceivability

2. Counter-Christian Moral Ethos

3. Loss of Religious Sensitivity

4. Unfamiliarity of Religious Language

5. Accommodation of Religion as a Coping Supplement

6. Undercutting of the Veracity of Religious Authority

7. Power of Socioeconomic Control

8. Loss of Narrative Vision

9. Dissipation of Religious Familiarity

10. Deterioration of Religious Motivation

11. Forfeiture of Objective Truth

SCIENCE AND THE ELIMINATION OF LITERAL CONCEIVABILITY

Literalism and Locate-Ability

Scripture makes bold use of anthropomorphic imagery, gliding easily from earthly to angelic to heavenly realms, their literal conceivability making for successful communication with prescientific hearers. An exemplar of such images is Jacob's dream ladder, in which divine-human traffic goes on continually, in both directions. Altars dot the Old Testament landscape marking the abundant places where the Divine made appearances. Adam and Eve stroll with God in the cool of the evening. Jacob wrestles with a God so physical that he receives permanent hip dislocation. The psalms are filled with literalistic imagery for picturing God, as in Psalm 17, where reference is made to "God's right hand" and taking refuge "in the shadow of God's wings." In Psalm 68, God rides on the clouds, marches in the desert ahead of his people, has "thousands upon thousands" of chariots at his disposal, and possesses the "keys of death." In Psalm 104, God walks "on the wings of the wind" and makes lightning his servant.

Although there is a tradition in the Old Testament holding that humans cannot see God and live, far more frequent are accounts to the contrary. We are told of the seventy elders who went up with Moses to the top of Mount Sinai and "they beheld God, and ate and drank" (Exod 24:11). At another point, Moses is purported to see God's "back side" (Exod 33:21–23), and yet another declaration is that he met God "face to face" (Exod 33:11). Moses reported dictations of the law by God, at one point declaring that God did the actual writing in stone. Many are the biblical persons who encountered visible and talkative angels. The prophets testified literally to hearing God's voice as God gives concrete directives. Throughout Scripture, there is expressed the yearning "to seek the face of God, to encounter God face to face" (Ps 24:6) or lamenting "why do you hide your face?" (Ps 44:24).

The cosmological framework underlying such imaging is that of a physical dome called a firmament that encloses an earth sustained by pillars over the seas, containing holes through which the divine light shows forth as stars and water drops through as rain. God's dwelling place is in a heaven directly above the firmament, while beneath the earth is Sheol, the realm of the dead. With such intimate proximity, divine visitations are available for the asking. Thus, the New Testament writers in turn can easily conceive of Jesus descending to earth, visiting Sheol, and ascending visually back into heaven, sitting on a throne at the right hand of his Father, from which he will return on the clouds.

In the halcyon days of Christianity's medieval primacy, the church built physically in spectacular fashion on this literal understanding, encouraged by the need to communicate with a population largely illiterate. Traveling miracle plays rendered biblical imagery visible as dramas. Gestures and chants enhanced a mysterious language, and saints and sacred events were translated into the glowing immanence of stained glass portraiture, called the Bible of the poor. The details of the passion event were replicated in literal stations of the cross, physical pilgrimages made martyrs graphic, and labyrinths distilled sensuously the anatomy of the Christian life. Soaring Gothic heights rendered transcendence visible, while incense became the identifiable aroma of mystery as it lifted the prayers of the faithful into an arcane interplay of dark with light. Statuary of saints was so realistically carved that Protestants accused their display as idolatry.

Paintings were key in this portraiture of faith, with patroned artists drawn into experimenting with techniques for increasing the persuasiveness of visual literalness. As early as the fourteenth century, Giotto was revolutionary in creating the illusion of depth in proffering greater realism. In the fifteenth century, Piero della Francescca in his fresco *The Resurrection of Christ* masterfully portrayed the defeat of death by Jesus with all the persuasive vibrancy of a dramatically physical happening. In the sixteenth century, Leonardo DaVinci was without equal in capturing biblical scenes with a convincing realism. Perhaps the epitome of conceivability was reached in Michelangelo's Sistine ceiling and walls, as God is given the graphic literalness of an elderly grandfather, with Adam partaking of God's physical likeness. Here the distance between the fingertip of God and that of Adam, Divine and human, was almost imperceptible, as the moment of creation was given a conceivability that lasted for centuries. With Raphael, angels and humans frolicked together in a common arena. In Caravaggio's *Holy Night*, we behold the dazzling miracle of incarnation, and his *Doubting Thomas* leaves little uncertainty about the resurrection, as Thomas touches the literal wounds of Jesus. In Caravaggio's paintings, nature itself glowed with divine light, and his church ceilings and cupolas became marvels of illusion, opening up into the hues of heaven itself, as the legs of the heavenly hosts dangle downward for eager human contact. With Tintoretto, Jesus walks easily and naturally on water. With Rubens, the crucifixion becomes itself a visible spectacle of resurrection, as the sheer physical power of Jesus himself is beheld as defying death. In the sixteenth century, Grunewald's Isenheim triptych altarpiece portrays a gruesomely physical *Crucifixion*, standing in powerful counteraction with his *Resurrection,* which is itself an equally physical rendition of the risen Christ with the brilliance of convincing ecstasy. With El Greco, even nature itself shimmers with the visual immanence of the Spirit's upward yearning.

In the seventeenth-century Baroque age, Christian visual realism reached its climax. Giovanni Battista Gaulli painted the spectacular vaulted apse of the Jesuit Il Gesù Church in Rome, in which we seem to be gazing into heaven itself, ablaze with a divine radiance only slightly above the ceiling. Who would dare to be agnostic here, as architecture and painting merge theatrically with myriads of angels and saints overflowing every edge, as if the sheer weight of heaven is bursting through the ceiling, disclosing the very gates of God. As one critic describes this masterpiece, Gaulli's purpose was to "confuse and overwhelm us so that we no longer know what is reality and what is fantasy."[1]

Through such artistic expressions, the church established worship environments as faith-worlds so highly conceivable that Christianity was experienced as plausible, credible, likely, and believable. Even for persons not proximate to any of these masterpieces, or able to undertake a pilgrimage to any of them, the local churches, although with less artistry, likewise shaped the believers' literalistic ethos. Yet in our time, these aesthetic masterpieces that once shaped faith have become the domain of tourists rather than worshippers.

Theologians through the centuries have wrestled to forge sophisticated analogies by which to transcend literal imagery, as with the doctrine of *analogia entis* (analogy of being), in which divine and human, although

---

1. Gombrich, *Story of Art*, 330.

radically different, exhibit a recognizable likeness. In spiritual practices, while the kataphatic approach uses images from creation to point toward God, the apophatic approach renounces all imagery in order to contemplate nonconceptually the divine presence. Even mystics have hesitated to speak about their experiences, insisting that they were touched by a Mystery beyond all conceivability. Christian poets such as T. S. Eliot acknowledge that, even at best, words can only function as "hints followed by guesses"[2] for the sacred, inviting us to leave the literal world for an evocative one of metaphor and simile.

In a real sense, then, the history of Christianity has proceeded broadly on two parallel tracks. On one level are the theologians and educated ecclesiastical authorities who, as intellectually fluent, tend to understand Scripture and doctrine more figuratively, using typology, analogy, metaphor, and simile. On the other level is the domain populated by the majority of laity whose understanding remains more literalistic, with religious imagery conceived equivocally. Ironically, our postmodern world is similarly literal in the sense of being binary—either/or, off/on, true/false. But this yes or no is decided empirically by scientific verification, the result being that the literal faith-world of the laity can no longer meet the criteria for testable conceivability. Furthermore, the modern ethos is no longer attuned to the rich sophistication of language, without which religion is strangled.

During a recent visit, one of my daughters picked up my breviary, read a page, and gently responded, "Surely you don't believe this stuff." The issue was literalness. So regarded, no, I don't. We shared how literalistic was the imagery of the Christian world of her Sunday School upbringing. The language freely spoken and vigorously sung was of God's breath, hands, face, mouth, arms, feet, voice, tongue, and ears. "Breathe on me, breath of God," sang the hymn. The throne on which Jesus sat was at God's right hand, to which Jesus physically ascended. Angels were a dime a dozen. Heaven was up, hell was down. Earthquakes and violent storms were candidates for expressions of God's anger, and strange weather could evoke apprehension concerning the second coming. We trusted that prayer could interrupt natural law in favoring select persons and nations. We recalled a neighbor pounding on our door, trembling from having seen Jesus in her kitchen—as folks in the neighborhood gathered on our porch, sharing similar literal incidents, or stories of friends who had. This literalism was the assumed language of faith, and it is this conceivability that modernity is now severely undercutting.

2. Eliot, "Dry Salvages," in *Complete Poems and Plays*, 136.

Christian scholars have struggled for several centuries to determine what is left after acknowledging how deeply biblical imagery is dependent on the obsolete mythology of a physical three-tiered earth, with Jesus shaped by the dated culture of his time. In the early twentieth century, this liberal-conservative conflict became public with the publication of a series of tracts entitled *The Fundamentals.*[3] They insisted upon the infallibility of Scripture, with its literalism especially in regard to the virgin birth, miracles, bodily resurrection, physical ascension, and the second coming of Christ. Conflicts and denominational splits resulted during the rest of the century over fundamentalism. In response, mainline liberal Protestant seminaries routinely begin with a Bible 100 course intent on discrediting literalism by injecting a process of demythologizing. This made folks back home uneasy, frequently warning their ministerial candidate to not "let them take your faith away from you." This wariness focused on literalism. Often, I would hear students state about what they were being taught, "I wouldn't dare preach this stuff in my parish or back home; it would mean the end of my ministry." While some students resisted this liberal approach to biblical studies, most accepted it, creating tensions that could lead to a divorce between themselves and the laity they were called to serve.

But more than through direct theological conflict, membership diminishment happened through the quiet diminishment of literal conceivability as secular culture crept into the mindset of the laity. I remember well the disquiet in local churches after October 4, 1957, when Christians heard of Sputnik circling in the heavens. The shock was given words four years later when the Russian astronaut Yuri Gargarin, having returned from space, sarcastically opined that he had looked all around up there and there was no god to be seen. This event marked symbolically the crisis over spatial availability for literal religious imagery. The impact has continued to the extent that it now seems quaint to hear the Mormon persistence on a literal heaven on a physical planet habited by a physical God—out there somewhere. Likewise, peculiar has become the Jehovah's Witnesses' door-to-door *Watchtower* in which heaven is literally portrayed as the physical homecoming of families, where children who died young remain innocently playful, grandparents appear contentedly aged, and parents are always unblemishingly young. By recognizing this literalism as the Christianity in which our youth were raised, it is not difficult to understand our unoccupied pews. But also being diluted is the Christianity of older adults whose faith remains resting on literal conceivability.

---

3. Torrey and Dixon, eds., *Fundamentals.*

While in the past, divine inconceivability was largely regarded as the implicate of transcendence, today it functions primarily as evidence of divine nonexistence. Therefore, before the issue of scriptural truth or falsity can even be raised, the prior question is whether the biblical world is any longer even remotely conceivable. Does the realm of angels have any more substance than that of flying reindeer? Yet the churches continue to use this literalistic imagery, as in the prayer prefacing today's breviary readings in which our request is for God to "rend the heavens and come down!"[4] The accompanying Isaiah reading persists: "Look down from heaven and see, from thy holy and glorious habitation" (Isa 63:15).

To illustrate this profound contrast between how secularized citizens perceive the world and how Christians have traditionally done so, we need look no further than my coffee table. On it are several issues of the *National Geographic* that I regard as worth keeping. The cover of the July 2013 edition heralds cosmic violence with the words "Our Wild Wild Solar System." Amazing are the literal pictures accompanying this "new story of our solar system." The central article is entitled "It All Began in Chaos." The account convincingly describes it as happening nearly four billion years ago when a heavy bombardment of asteroids and comets hit the fledgling earth—and from these "extremely violent" collisions was created our moon. One scientist confessed to being dumbfounded by this recent research, acknowledging that he had grown up believing the solar system to be reliable and well-behaved, much like a clock.[5] Instead, what is being found is that our solar system was turned inside out during its infancy and experienced a raucous adolescence.

The Hubble telescope and its successors have been exploring the inconceivable global vastness that is without conceivable end. In 2017, a Nobel Prize in physics was awarded for detecting gravitational waves produced by the collision of two black holes a billion light-years away—and there are billions of such black holes. In 2019, a study by researchers in Australia and the US discovered evidence of a massive energy flare that tore through the heart of our galaxy 3.5 million years ago, so powerful that the blast could be felt 200,000 light-years away, lasting for perhaps 300,000 years.[6] Thus, no longer is there any location remaining for a loving Creator doing his fourth-day thing, nor can angry thunderbolts from a deity account for such cosmic violence. While creationists attempt to render this incongruity between biblical and modern understandings as being a debate between

4. International Commission on English in the Liturgy, *Liturgy of the Hours*, 1:594.
5. Irion, "It All Began in Chaos," 47–48.
6. "Not Long Ago," paras. 1, 4, 12.

two entertainable theories, it is the one characterizing the faith of most laity that is losing its conceivability. For good measure, in brazen refutation of the biblical six-day creation, the same *National Geographic* issue provided a tour by a robot named Curiosity of a rock strata on the surface of Mars that was formed four billion years ago.

This modern worldview is fast becoming publicly normative, with graphic imagery appearing on TV, in newspapers and magazines, and even in elementary grade school texts. Displayed with certainty is the beginning of the universe as a Big Bang happening 13.8 billion years ago from an unimaginably hot dense point a billionth the size of a particle. Recent findings by an Antarctic telescope have given evidence to a theory that even our subsequently expanding universe may just be one of a vast number of such creations that have spontaneously burst into existence.[7] One remembers how deeply the church was threatened by the Copernican theory simply for questioning the earth's centrality in our small universe. In fact, it was only in 1992 that the Papacy revoked its 350-year condemnation, in which Galileo was forbidden "to hold, teach or defend" the idea.[8] When he refused, he was forced to recant under threat of torture and imprisonment. Consider, then, the impact that this subsequent flood of scientific data is having on the literality of lay believers. In 2016, a South African super telescope still being completed had already discovered 1,300 galaxies in a tiny corner of the universe where only 70 had previously been detected.[9] Astronomers have opined that in the region of the universe visible from Earth, there are perhaps 100 billion galaxies. Each one has about 100 million stellar-mass black holes, holes with unimaginable energy.[10] NASA astronomers have suggested that the vast Milky Way is likely home for as many as 4.5 billion earths our size that orbit sunlike stars, with surfaces suitable for sustaining water and life.[11] In 2020, NASA's Chandra X-Ray Observatory detected another galaxy more than 12 billion light-years away that is likely hospitable to more than a trillion planets, ranging in size from the moon to Jupiter.[12] A radio telescope in Australia has gotten our first glimpse beyond the Milky Way, spotting 883 galaxies, with an average galaxy containing 100 billion stars.[13] Over nine years, the Kepler space telescope has identified billions of planets in our galaxy, estimating that

7. "NSF-Funded Researchers Say," para. 1.

8. Cowell, "After 350 Years," para. 2.

9. M. Strauss, "Powerful New Telescope," para. 2.

10. Van der Marel, "How Many Black Holes," para. 2.

11. Wall, "Four Point Five Billion," para. 2.

12. Strickland, "Astronomers Find Galaxy," para. 1.

13. Handwerk, "Hundreds of Galaxies," paras. 6, 10.

300 million planets resembling our own could be host planets that support life.[14] Understandably, then, an MIT computer scientist described the earth as a small rock orbiting an ordinary star on one of the spiral arms of a galaxy with hundreds of billions of stars—with there being at least tens of billions of similar galaxies in the known universe alone.

Space is staggering, in which more stars have been discovered than the combined sand particles on all the beaches of the world. In a landmark event, there was recently observed a cataclysmic collision of two neutron stars that took place 130 million years ago, so distant that the signal did not reach earth until August 2017.[15] In 2018, astronomers detected the most distant star ever seen, located 9.3 billion light-years away.[16] Consider the arithmetic: multiply the speed of light per second at 186,282 miles, traveling at the speed of 670,616,629 miles per hour, times 24 hours, times 365 days, times 9.3 billion years. This scientific portraiture has birthed an inconceivable enormity of space that is utterly beyond human imagination. Daily pictures from the Hubble telescope bombard us with a vastness that is easily accessed by any person with a computer. One cannot deny the erosive impact on believers that this graphic portrayal is having—of living on an earth which seems to be an unplanned afterthought, awash in billions of years of time, lost in the backwater of a Milky Way that is infinitesimally tiny, nearly lost within the infinity of ever-expanding galaxies. So much for an intimate homelike earth, embraced by a wise and loving deity who created it and its first inhabitants within a seven-day span, knowing the fall of each sparrow and numbering the hairs on every head (Matt 10:30).

If the church was shaken by the earth's eviction from its unique centrality in our solar system, how much more are believers being impacted by a universe of infinite space, in which the earth is likely to be far from alone in supporting life, with recent estimates being that there are at least 300 million potentially habitable planets in the Milky Way alone. Religious questions come flooding in. As one pundit put it, apparently Jesus will be kept quite busy making guest appearances. And if he doesn't visit them all, can he be regarded any longer as the unique and only Savior? Will we find Adams and Eves on each planet? If so, are there some couples who were able not to fall, making atonement and redemption irrelevant for them?

Not only is astronomy impacting Christian conceivability, but the undermining is occurring as well through discoveries in evolution. Less than a century ago, on July 1, 1925, the Scopes trial verdict rejected all teaching

---

14. Yeung, "There Are at Least," para. 3.

15. Kaplan and Guarino, "Scientists Detect Gravitational Waves," paras. 1–2.

16. Dunham, "Most Distant Star," para. 1.

about any evolution (289 SW 363). Yet twenty-five years ago, biologist Stephen Jay Gould received widespread acclaim for his *Wonderful Life*, in which he not only makes a convincing case for evolution but declares it to be the result of utter randomness and unpredictability. Humanity, he insists, is a sheer accident, deplete of any grand plan, rendering history a complete contingency. Evolutionary biologists largely accept as fact his position—in which there is no overarching plot, direction, or goal to evolution. When the brilliant Jesuit paleontologist Pierre Teilhard de Chardin endeavored to identify a strand of continuity within evolution that could provide meaning to it, his Jesuit order (in the early 1920s) effectively exiled him to China and forbade him to write.[17] Most of his works were not published until after his death in 1955. In 1962, the papacy issued a formal warning of the dangers presented by his writings. Their condemnation of him was literalism, focusing upon his unwillingness to ascribe to Adam and Eve a ready-made literal beginning to the human race. Scientific evidence is overwhelming that such a biblical understanding is no longer entertainable, with humans being newcomers in the slowly evolving scene. While Christian tradition has dated the creation of humans as occurring in 3124 BCE, human DNA recently found in Spain dates this emergence at 800,000 years ago, surpassing previous analyses by 400,000 years.[18]

Not only is instantaneous creation undermined but so is the traditional understanding of divine holistic providence. Evolution is not only painfully slow but involves a deeply bloody process of trial and error, dotting the historic landscape with numerous detours and abundant dead-end failures. Belief in God's providential overseeing is severely damaged by the discovery that the dinosaurs and two-thirds of living species were wiped out by a wayward asteroid, setting wildfires of tragic proportions. Recent research discloses that a massive bloom of microbial bacteria 250 million years ago may have started a chain reaction that raised large amounts of methane into the atmosphere, ultimately wiping out more than 70 to 90 percent of life on earth.[19] Known as the Permian mass extinction, this catastrophe can rival the methane hydrate that is presently being released in the Arctic due to global warming, likewise portending apocalyptic consequences. There have been five episodes of massive extinctions in the earth's 4.5 billion-year history. Colossal volcanic eruptions happening over 250 million years ago were part of the so-called Great Dying, a 60,000 year period in which 90 percent of sea creatures and 70 percent of all plants and animals were destroyed. Research

17. Gibson, "U.S. Nuns Haunted," para. 10.

18. "Oldest Ever Human Genetic Evidence," para. 1.

19. Dunham, "Methane-Spewing Microbe Blamed," paras. 2, 23.

at Stanford University indicates that, about 3.3 billion years ago, at least two massive asteroids thirty to sixty miles in diameter smashed into earth, boiling oceans for at least one year, with temperatures reaching 932°F, leading to the extinction of much of the primitive life-forms.[20]

Likewise, evolution leading to human emergence defies belief in its being led by God's benevolent providence, for it witnesses far more failures than successes. Nor can death any longer be regarded as a culpable judgment inflicted on an adventuresome first couple but from the very beginning has been woven into the fabric of all that exists. From multiple directions, then, what we are seeing is anything but a loving blueprint designed by a wise Creator God, with apt regard for the lilies of the field. And now we find ourselves on the verge of another extinction, this time by human causation. Scientists are predicting that within two generations, 50 percent of the species we now know will become extinct,[21] with the bird population in North America already having lost 2.9 billion birds over the last fifty years.[22] This morning's news reported the hottest month in human history, and while there is some conversation about allaying the tragedy through human action, nowhere is divine intervention seriously entertained or requested.

So here is our modern portrait: the Big Bang has forfeited any six-day creation process, any literal Eden has been eliminated as the locus for humanity's beginning, our earth floating in an infinity of empty space has vacated any physical heaven or dwelling place for God, an eventual burnout of the sun is replacing any second-coming ending, and our molten earth core has replaced the sulphur smell of hell. Thus far the empty pews are mostly reflecting the incredulous younger generations, but how much longer can the older adult church members continue to believe the literal physical imagery rehearsed in Scripture, liturgy, and hymnology? Thus, the major diminishment of church attendance is still to come, because a goodly number of present church attenders are still holding on to this growingly unstable literal Christianity. Most recent Gallup polls find that 68 percent of American Christians identify themselves as Christian, 30 percent of whom attend services at least weekly, 24 percent believe that Scripture is to be interpreted literally and 34 percent of whom identify themselves as "born again."[23] Of these "born agains," 42 percent believe in a creationism, in which the earth has existed for no more than several thousand years, which began as an instantaneous creation, with humans birthed as a ready-made adult couple.

20. Fessenden, "Asteroid Impacts," para. 2.
21. McKie, "Biologists Think 50 Percent," para. 2.
22. Fitzpatrick and Marra, "Crisis for Birds," para. 2.
23. "Religion," tables 2, 6, 8, 14.

Forty one percent of Americans believe that "Jesus will return to earth in the next forty years."[24] While six in ten Americans have come to affirm human evolution, a 2013 Pew Research Center poll indicates that 64 percent of Protestant evangelicals continue to believe that "humans have existed in their present form since the beginning of time."[25] These statistics are reinforced by a *Newsweek* poll finding that 45 percent of US Christians believe "the world will end as the Bible predicts, in a battle at Armageddon between Jesus and the Antichrist."[26] A survey by the Public Religion Research Institute and Religious News Service indicates that 49 percent of Americans believe that the biblical accounts surrounding Christmas are historically accurate.[27] A 2004 *Newsweek* poll finds that two-thirds of Americans believe in the literal historicity of the entire Christmas narrative.[28]

In the face of such abundant literalism, confronted by the relentless scientific impact that is assumed and being taken for granted by media and by educators, Christian conceivability will continue to undergo significant erosion. Just yesterday, the local newspaper ran an article detailing evidence of humanlike creatures having emerged approximately 2.5 million years ago. Apparently, it took 13.8 billion years for God to get around to scheduling the incarnation. With a number of ministers realizing that even questioning the virgin birth in their congregations would entail ministerial suicide, the future is bleak. Therefore, what tends to be occurring is a growing disconnect between the way in which the laity hears what is being preached and the way in which it is being homiletically used. Thus, an unburned Daniel and friends continue to be saved literally in fiery furnaces by a humanlike figure called God, who miraculously becomes their unburned companion as together they sing. While what the liberal preacher perceives is a pastoral parable, many of the laity hears it as a news report. Meanwhile, what is happening is that the secular-scientific mindset is quietly circumscribing for the laity what really is scripturally possible and impossible.

Illustrative of the price a literal Christianity is demanding appeared in a main article in the *Christian Century* (2013). The author confessed the difficulty in teaching Scripture, especially to young people, in any way approaching a PG rating, given the abundance of violence deserving of an R. This issue was further precipitated with the History Channel's series in which efforts at portraying biblical history literally encountered disturbing cases of

24. "Jesus Christ's Return," para. 1.

25. Liu, "Public's Views on Human Evolution," para. 6.

26. Woodward, "Way the World Ends," para. 3.

27. R. P. Jones, "Do You Believe," para. 2.

28. P. Smith, "Nativity Story Has Its Share," para. 6.

immorality, not only by humans but also by God.[29] This led the editor to conclude that no one should ever believe in such a god, one who "orchestrated and carried out death and destruction everywhere." Thus, if the only alternative to rejecting the whole Bible is that of picking and choosing, on the basis of what is this to be done? This brings us again to the postmodern mentality, in which the possibility of objective truth is denied, so that what appears to be true for some persons appears untrue for others, the difference depending on the subjective perspective that one brings to the data. This brought one of the series writers to declare the need to make clear, once and for all, that Scripture should no longer be understood as recording what God says. All that we can ever have are records of what various people have said about God, within their own dated context. This means no longer being confronted by the compelling authority of objective revelation. Scripture at best is an invitation to evaluate contrasting opinions according to whatever hermeneutic one personally chooses to use. Therefore, even as basic a statement as "Jesus loves you" is lacking in clear meaning. Is he still the one seated on a throne at the right hand of a grandfatherly God, whose love beams warm feelings, periodic instructions, and occasional miracles to special believers? Perhaps a question deeper than how many Christian believers are left is what is left for them to believe in our post-Christian world? How much longer can a literalistic Christianity survive this relentless scientific-secular erosion? This a new crisis point for the church.

Miracles and the Supernatural

While the secular/scientific mindset defining our time gives no spatial localities for Christian conceivability, it likewise permits no place for miracles. We are no longer permitted to live in a world where the breaking of natural law is woven into the fabric of our daily living. This modern axiom renders unacceptable any biblical world in which the sun stands still at a human command, streams flow backwards, seas are opened by the raising of a stick so that God's favorite people can walk through "dry shod," mass killings are perpetrated by angels, raisings of the dead are possible, bodies ascend above the clouds, weather is an index of divine moods, virgin births happen, and Jesus is portrayed as the miracle worker par excellence. Thus, these features once endemic to a vibrant belief are being filed away somewhere close in the status of black cats and the number thirteen. "Miracle" drugs heal ailments that once were the domain of evil spirits. One calls for an ambulance, visits a doctor, or schedules therapy, but few persons any

29. Buchanan, "History Channel's Violent God," para. 2.

longer would consider a faith healer or an exorcist. In our everyday activities, natural law is unquestioned. If an exception seems to have occurred, the working assumption is that such strangeness has a natural reason that will be discovered. In some churches, there remains a vestige craving for some exception—for a miraculous cancer cure, a statue that cries, a vial that rhythmically coagulates blood, a Marian visitation, an unbelievable cure at Lourdes. But this is desperate—that if only there can be one miracle among the thousands or millions of non-miracles, then there remains at least a thread on which to hang the possibility.

Formerly there were Christian efforts to squeeze God into the cracks of scientific ignorance, but this has proven counterproductive, for as scientific discoveries keep closing the cracks, the overall feeling is of religion's relentless retreat. Intercessory prayer for a miracle tends to be as a last resort, after medical terms such as terminal elicit desperation—just in case. Christians continue to use such phrases as "I'll pray for you," with any results now scientifically understandable in terms of the placebo effect. Increasingly becoming off limits is appealing to a God who reaches down to divert wayward trailer trucks from hitting the car of one's traveling friends. Even if a rare exception might appear to have happened, the gnawing question is where was such a God during the innumerable accidents where no divine intrusion happened?

Thus, what is occurring is a severe undercutting of the fundamental Christian concept of divine providence—the belief that God is in control of what happens. While we have seen this absenting cosmically and in terms of evolution, perhaps even more threatening to faith is the carnage threatening civilization. The threshold of our postmodern period was marked by tragedies: the Holocaust as the determination by one nation to exterminate a total race, the dropping of atom bombs with the capacity to obliterate humanity, and 9/11 as the shredding of security by the horror of universal vulnerability. Victims and gaping spectators cried out, "Where is God?" "Why me?" The laments of the psalmists are becoming documented accusations. While Scripture has abundant questioning as to whether God is sleeping, hiding, closing his ears, or temporarily absent, the accusation is never of nonexistence. Today the questioning increasingly implies the latter. Tragedies are so frequent that they exude arbitrariness. In Old Testament times, the working assumption was that the tragedies that happen to people, cities, and even nations relate directly to God's just judgment on punishable misdoings. But today, when deadly tornadoes recently swept across Oklahoma, widespread aid was offered and crowds attended funerals, but never was there expressed even a hint of communal penance and prayers for forgiveness—in total contrast to what the people of Nineveh did to avert such tragedy.

When several years ago a popular TV evangelist proclaimed that a particular natural disaster was because of God's judgment on gay persons, the reaction was one of ridicule. When occasionally it is stated that a tornado that wiped out a whole area left one family "miraculously" untouched, the image of a God involved in such bizarre picking and choosing is hardly helpful. Unappealing is a providence that likens God to a curtained Wizard of Oz with levers, deciding each morning the day's schedule of cancer deaths, suicides, and deaths by accident. The puzzling Jobian conundrum is becoming the unquestioned assumption—that there is no correlation between religious behavior and good fortune. In fact, empirical evidence might well suggest that the most faithful ones are those most likely to be creamed.

Commenting on receding religion, Mitchell Stephens writes, "God once was seen as commanding the entire universe and supervising all of its inhabitants—inflicting tragedies, bestowing triumphs, enforcing morality. But now, outside of some lingering loud pockets of orthodoxy, we have witnessed the arrival of a less mighty, increasingly inconsequential version of God."[30] Distant, indistinct, uninvolved. Even the skeptic Voltaire had at least reserved the domain of earthquakes and natural disasters to God. But the recent diminishment of religion refuses to recognize any divine causation to anything anytime. Prescient was the atheist poet Shelley in predicting that religion would not be overthrown but would "simply become disregarded."[31]

Bifurcation

We are exploring the dominant secularized consciousness, in which we all live, move, and have our being and how it is affecting the viability of the church and the future of Christianity. As we are seeing, the impact is not confrontational as much as it is quietly invasive and erosive. Thus, the current competitive ecclesiastical strategies are off focus, powerless to reverse this diminution of membership, finances, and influence. Furthermore, these efforts are tending to dilute the countercultural integrity of the Christian faith. For those attempting to preserve the integrity of faith, what tends to result is bifurcation. While the faith in which most of us cradle Christians were raised was a literal, locatable one, and while we regard ourselves as having become theologically sophisticated, the fact is that our faith continues

30. Stephens, "Commentary," para. 6.
31. Stephens, "Commentary," para. 14.

to be imaged by at least vestiges of literalism. When we pray, we continue to look up toward God, who persists at the edgings of our minds as having Michelangelo's grandfatherly profile. Left without conceivable location and feasible imagery, what else can we do? In struggling to live in a scientifically determined world while remaining within the church, whether we are conscious of it or not, we tend to live bifurcated lives, preserving a parallel Sunday morning world. Living in these bilateral worlds requires some variety of schizophrenic consciousness. We have on one hand the weekday secular world of cause and effect, predictability, promotion, and calculated income. In contrast, on the other hand, we live within the Sunday morning worshipping hour and the defining confines of an ecclesiastical building and its accoutrements—where our singing, gesturing, imaging, and languaging is a world where miracles are entertainable, where during the anthems the angels do sing. In hearing Scripture, God does look down from a heaven. Our hymns emit the intimacy of a garden-walking Deity, and a fatherly providence extends his gentleness to the lilies by the altar and the hairs of our balding heads. Without apparent cognitive dissonance, our Sunday mornings are permissively populated by talking snakes, volcanic gods, divided seas, abundant breakings of natural law, and a Galilean carpenter who not only walks on water but is presently sitting on a throne at his Father's right hand. In imagery, action, and attitude, this is a world apart, strange yet seemingly appropriate for Sunday mornings. But then comes Sunday afternoon football, drawing us into a contrasting world of blatant commercialism and violent competition—maybe three games of it. Thereby prepared for reentry, on Monday morning we slip into our assigned place in the weekly nonbiblical scientifically secular world. But how much longer can this split of belief and functional atheism continue to coexist in the living of it? You cannot live both, insisted Jesus.

This Sunday morning parallel world has a pervasive price, not only on Sundays. This bi-focusing separates the realm of private from public, home from occupation, church from state, otherworldly from this-worldly, internal from external. And while cradle Christians may have some impetus for preserving a remembrance of things past, such bifurcated strangeness has little appeal for those without a memory to placate. For the younger generation, a parallel religious world is beyond their ability to conceive, let alone enter—at least for any reasons likely to be religious. It simply is not their world, nor can it become so.

The psalmist echoed something of this dilemma for today's serious Christian when he remembered "the years long ago," rich with God's "wonders of old." He rehearsed in his mind the events of the Red Sea—dramatic with thunder, whirlwind, arrows of lightning, when "the earth trembled and shook" as God's actions were clearly marked as "God's favor for his faithful." But now the psalmist is forced to acknowledge a radically contrasting present, in which the abundant evidence points to God's absence. His is now a world in which God's love and compassion have apparently ceased, and God's promises have seemingly ended. His conclusion expresses our dilemma as well: "This is what causes my grief; that the way of the Most High has changed" (Ps 76:11).[32] In parallel fashion, when he is singing praises in the temple, all is well; but in writing from his stark weekday realization, the psalm can end only in nostalgia.

To anticipate, the church's dilemma leaves three basic options. First is to continue this schizophrenia of dual living as long as one can, practiced privately—likely motivated as recompense for some form of this-worldly failure. Second is to respond to some variety of the megachurch appeal that offers supplementation to current society in providing coping opportunities. Third is capitulation to some variety of success theology that intertwines religious reward with success in pursuing the American Dream. While formerly a case for God was attempted through the failed effort to insert divine activity into temporary gaps in the scientific world, the present strategy is an effort to find societal gaps into which the church might be inserted. These efforts focus on finding a way to still be religious, whatever that might turn out to mean. As we will explore, Christian faithfulness in the face of the destructive dynamic characterizing our post-Christian era can no longer be through coping or supplementation. It requires nothing less than the propheticism of an authentic countercultural alternative, faithfully disengaged so as to be "in but not of" our modern world. This cannot be accomplished through a bifurcation that clings to a previous conceivability, nor through a liberal theological accommodation that sacrifices the heart of the gospel. What is needed is a retranslation of the orthodox heart of Christianity into a way of living that has honest integrity in the face of the multiple limitations closing in upon the Christianity and church that we once knew.

COUNTER-CHRISTIAN MORAL ETHOS

In addition to the impact of the modern mindset upon the literal conceivability that the Christian world previously took for granted, another significant impact is the moral displacement that is happening. This is particularly injurious when the religious tend to be redefined in terms of morality, for the secular ethos is undermining the morality that was formerly informed with and supported by the church's teachings and authority.

32. Gelineau, *Psalms*, 137.

This is leaving Christianity, even in this arena, strangely irrelevant, disregarded, and replaced, reducing the moral impact of the churches, at best, to the status of a nagging wife. Even the Christian right is pulling back from its former strident insistence on an objective Christian morality, as when Russell Moore, the public voice of the Southern Baptist Convention, acknowledged that its vociferous condemnation of homosexuality, contraception, premarital sex, and marriage equality was driving away large numbers of younger persons for whom the church's positions were not even vaguely plausible, let alone humane.[33]

Indicative of this moral diminution was the 2016 presidential election and the administration of Donald Trump that followed. The result, according to Jeff Jacoby in the *Boston Globe,* was that the religious right has lost its moral credibility.[34] Trump represents in many ways the antithesis of Christian morals—brash; boastful; lying; narcissistic; driven by money, power, and fame; having had three wives; openly bragging about his infidelity and boasting of groping women's bodies—with himself being non-church attending. Yet the great majority of evangelical leaders continued to endorse him enthusiastically. Some have tried to justify his immorality by claiming that a flawed candidate is simply proof of God's mysterious ways, while several conservative Christians go so far as declaring him "God's Chosen One for our time."[35] What is becoming clear is that Christian ethics, whether from a conservative or a liberal orientation, now depends more on perspectives brought to Scripture rather than being extracted from Scripture.

We once knew the basic ethical behavior expected of the Christian, much of which had been supportively appropriated into the declared conscience of the public domain. But now there is no denying the incredible change in public ethics within our lifetime, as, for example, in sexual morality. When in 1922 my grandmother on my father's side died at an early age, my Aunt Elizabeth dropped out of high school to care for the five siblings. When six years later it was discovered that she was pregnant out of wedlock, she instantly became the black sheep of the family, was rejected by her church, made an outcast in the town, and in grief was soon buried in an unmarked grave. On my mother's side of the family, my Aunt Cleo, a revered public school teacher, had to leave the state when it became known that she was lesbian. In radical contrast, a 2020 Gallup poll[36] disclosed that 66 percent of Americans now believe it is morally acceptable to have a baby

33. King, "Evangelical Leader Preaches Pullback," para. 4.
34. Jacoby, "How Religious Right Embraced Trump," para. 1.
35. Scott, "Comparing Trump to Jesus," para. 6.
36. J. Jones, "Is Marriage Becoming Irrelevant," para. 6.

outside of marriage (up from 45 percent in 2001), 72 percent believe it is morally acceptable for unmarried people to have sex (up from 53 percent in 2001), while 66 percent regard gay relationships as morally acceptable (up from 40 percent in 2001).[37]

A respected television critic recently declared that romantic comedy is now dead. The plot of boy meets girl, boy marries girl, and they are happy ever after has become passé. It has been replaced by one-night stands craved or acquired, made interesting by the complexities of relationships that follow. Television keeps pushing the envelope of moral acceptability, reaching a point where it is difficult to find anything that is any longer risqué. Illustrative is the TV series *Girls,* acclaimed as a "boundary-breaking HBO comedy" that has won two Golden Globes and an Emmy. Its heroines are four women in their mid-twenties for whom explicit sex abounds. As one reviewer described it, "Hannah, a writer, seeks varied experiences with sex so that she can write about them. Jessa uses sex for power. Beautiful Marnie struggles to figure out what it might mean to be more than just a pretty girl, and Shoshanna sees her virginity as shameful."[38] In that series, nonmarital sex has become reduced to a required experience, something to check off the to-do list.

Another television example of this counterreligious moral ethos is the original TV series *Transparent,* about a Jewish family. The patriarch comes out, sharing his feminine identity with his children, and his/her hidden life of secret drags. The eldest daughter Sarah shares her affair with a married college girlfriend, keeping it from her husband. The middle son, in turn, has been sleeping with the family babysitter since he was in his teens and is now passionately involved with two women at the same time. Meanwhile a younger daughter is experimenting with both sex and gender identity, doing so with gleeful abandonment. Yet one reviewer calls this series "the least cynical" of many such shows. Not surprisingly, then, a recent report disclosed that over half of US teenagers have had sexual intercourse,[39] and in the social media, their boasting and fantasizing abounds. The Yale Alumni Magazine from my alma mater recently dealt with an on-campus scandal over rape. The moral stance suggested was that a "gentleman" should make sure that, before having sex, his date is "ready and eager."

There are a diversity of TV sex channels and websites providing hardcore pornography for every taste—pedophilia, homosexuality, bestiality, rape, and heterosexual creativity—resulting in millions of touches that have

37. Statista Research Department, "Moral Views," para. 1.
38. B. Jones, "What Girls Want."
39. Centers for Disease Control and Prevention, "Over Half of U.S. Teens," para. 1.

produced an enormous source of profit. Advertisements for kinky sex are readily available, with ads listed under entertainment that offer "sex flights" for "exploits with comely children." Without even a public ripple, British sex expert Helen Driscoll declared that robophilia, sex between humans and robots, will be considered the norm within the next fifty years.[40]

This loss of a Christian-formed sexual morality is also well evidenced in the cinema—as, for example, in the mainstream pornographic film, *Fifty Shades of Grey*. Interestingly, this smash hit was particularly popular in the religiously conservative South, where it led the nation in preopening ticket sales. While only a decade ago a motion picture with an R rating risked box-office failure, today it is a badge of appeal, as economically evidenced in the majority of currently successful releases. I consulted the review of films in the *Kansas City Star* on a random day, and of the thirty-one presently being offered, thirteen have an R rating, eighteen have a Parental Guidance rating, and there are none intended for General Audience.

This shift in moral attitudes not only significantly influences behavior, but it also desensitizes feelings. Video games, regarded by many pundits as the defining popular art form of the twenty-first century, are now played by three out of every four persons, or 244 million people in the US play video games,[41] 41 percent of whom are women.[42] Many of these games appeal to and in turn motivate a desire to perpetrate suffering, violence, and even extermination. Take, for example, *Grand Theft Auto V*, exhibiting immense popularity, having made 800 million dollars on the first day of its release. It is incredibly violent, with players committing highjackings, torture, and murder. While such incidents are explicitly and abundantly described in novels, movies, television, and lyrics so as to render us spectators of violence, these video games evoke participation in visual bloodshed. As advertised, "It is you who steals the car, beats up the prostitute, and pulls the trigger."[43] In one video, the participant actually perpetrates torture on a helpless victim. In another, one is made capable of simulating an amazing realistic massacre. Even in a seemingly benign popular TV show of competitive funny home videos, almost every submission involves someone getting hurt—specializing in children and small animals.

Violence has now become as attractive for box-office sales as is sex, portrayed as an inherent ingredient in our common day life. Indicative is the *Texas Chainsaw* 3D that opened a month after the Newtown

---

40. Parsons, "Ban 'Disturbing' Sex Robots," para. 8.

41. "More People Are Gaming," para. 1.

42. Yokoi, "Female Gamers," para. 1.

43. *Week* Staff, "Grand Theft Auto V," para. 2.

Elementary School tragedy, earning $23 million in the first weekend.[44] As the main character chops off the feet and hands of multiple victims, viewers with 3D glasses participate in the acts, rendered even more realistic by having simulated blood thrown in their faces—often with shrieking followed by applause. This popular culture shapes and forms who we are, and today's expressions are significantly post-Christian. The Christian morality that was formerly regarded as normative is now regarded as reactionary at worse and quaint at best.

In my youth, a few thin blue untitled booklets of timidly racy material were secretly available under the counter at the local pool hall, for those with the courage to ask. Today, the issue is not how to find what has now become heavy sexual stuff, but how can we and our children avoid it. As a boy, the entire sexual collection that my friends and I had consisted of two dirty comics and a well-thumbed coverless book by Henry Miller. My first intercourse was on my honeymoon. While I might confess to have preferred it otherwise, I was fearful of both pregnancy and hell. I suspect that my actions might have been different had I known about the birth control that is now being taught to youth in school, if the local theater had shown more than the Lone Ranger; or if my friends had been willing to defy the threat of hell. Condoms, once illegal, are now displayed in multicolored splendor with ticklers on Walmart shelves, next to the hand cream. Explicit magazines are publicly displayed at grocery store checkouts—complete with movie star disclosures of who is sleeping with whom, who is most likely to be involved in divorce due to a steamy affair, and photographs of pregnant bellies accompanied by odds as to who the father might be. An email last week from a friend in Florida illustrated how this secularly moral displacement is impinging upon the church. My friend, active in a Presbyterian church, reported that their pastor, single after a divorce, announced from the pulpit that Annette, a member of the congregation, would be moving into the parsonage with him. The spontaneous response was a standing ovation with "shouts of joy."

From the perspective of our present cultural ethos, the recent past appears quaint, as when Chaucer's *Canterbury Tales* was published in this country with "The Miller's Tale" removed because of mild sexual innuendo. Or when the Supreme Court banned James Joyce's *Ulysses* in 1933 for having sexual allusions, even though these are only discoverable for the few with infinite patience to search them out among the profuse verbiage. Interestingly, this ban was lifted by the Supreme Court the same year that Prohibition (1933) was repealed. Since then, countless explicitly sexual novels have been

44. Setoodeh, "Texas Chainsaw 3D," paras. 2–3.

published, populated with graphic scenes, even in the score of novels written by Catholic priest Fr. Andrew Greeley. In fact, these frank sexual novels have become so passé that current best-selling novels, in order to gratify the tastes of present readership, need to develop bizarre plots intertwining drugs, incest, sadomasochism, orgy, children, and torture.

There was a time when a sexual affair was sufficient scandal to end a political career, but no longer. Mark Sanford, the once disgraced former governor of South Carolina who lied about an Appalachian Trail trek to cover for an ongoing extramarital affair, was nonetheless elected to Congress.[45] More recently, New York Representative Anthony Weiner, who resigned after being caught tweeting lewd pictures of himself to women he didn't know, still was able to run for the mayorship of New York City.[46] A national political analyst concluded that sex scandals no longer have lasting impact on political careers, citing as evidence Bill Clinton, who in spite of the Lewinsky affair and a subsequent impeachment remains one of American's most beloved politicians. Eliot Spitzer, after his prostitution scandals, became a host on prime time TV.[47] Senator David Vitter, after his sexual exploits, was reelected in conservative Louisiana.[48] For those who in the public eye are caught in a really messy humiliation, the remedy of choice is a good lawyer and/or a creative public relations agent. Increasingly, any public morality left has its motivation not in a fear of God but in having one's image tainted. Yet in the age of President Trump, even this is difficult, with tasteless behavior being a subject of pride. Keith Wagstaff, writing in the *Week*, confirmed this paradox, that such scandals, rather than being a detriment, are becoming a positive instrument in providing name recognition.[49] In our society, in which a genuine sense of guilt is hardly ever confessed, what follows is a correlative diminishment of need for a religion of forgiveness.

While some vestige of conscience may remain in private morality, increasingly even this is being undercut by hypocrisy. In 2015, anonymous hackers published a massive trove of data containing private information about 33 million persons worldwide from the website of Ashley Madison. This website promotes itself as a prefidelity venue in which married people can find sexual partners in order to have an affair. Its market slogan is unabashed: "Life is short. Have an affair."[50] Josh Duggar, evangelical reality TV star, was one of

45. Camia, "Mark Sanford Wins," para. 1.

46. Wagstaff, "Name Recognition," para. 4.

47. Folkenflik, "Disgraced Governor Eliot Spitzer," para. 1.

48. Elliott, "David Vitter, Running For Governor," para. 1.

49. Wagstaff, "Name Recognition," para. 6.

50. Badham, "It Hurts," para. 4.

these millions who were "outed,"[51] as was a San Antonio police captain.[52] Yet the condemnation that resulted was not directed toward the immorality of such acts but that their right to privacy had been violated.[53]

Beth Jones, who teaches at the conservative Wheaton College, expresses this retreating moral role of Christianity in today's society as forcing the believer to live in "a world in which sexual autonomy is such a given that it's almost impossible to call any sexual encounter a poor choice, much less to imbue it with shame."[54] She concludes that today's operating dictum is that "consenting adults can do what they will." As Andrew Bacevich puts it, the former "people of 'thou shall not' have long since become the people of 'the whatever,' with obligations once derived from moral tradition now subordinated to claims of individual autonomy."[55]

What we are seeing here again is that the churches with their faith practices are not undergoing frontal attack, nor are they enduring intentional refutation or expressed ridicule. Nor is a counter-Christian morality intentionally being promulgated as a replacement. Instead, what is happening is that the secular moral ethos is becoming so assumed that it is being portrayed as functionally normative to modern life. In almost every portrayal within the media, religious practice is simply absent—not only as a major factor but even as a minor ingredient. Modern life as presented by the media is devoid of any practices, conversations, or even symbols reflective of Christianity. Therefore, what is therein assumed as normal is taking on the formative power of the normative. Adultery, recreational sex, drug use, divorce—on and on. Even polygamy is becoming acceptable, with 20 percent of Americans finding it "morally acceptable," up from 7 percent in 2003.[56] Such practices have become so much the way things are that they have largely lost their shock appeal, leaving the media little for titillation beyond the now popular vampirism, an occasional taste of cannibalism, and violent fantasies from other times and strange places.

The impact of all this is disclosing suspicion as insipient to our present individualism, rootedness in its competitive self-preservation. Studies reveal that a third of Americans can no longer regard other persons as

---

51. DenHoed, "Josh Duggar's Ashley Madison Problem," para. 1.
52. Landau, "Ashley Madison Leak," para. 3.
53. Badham, "It Hurts," para. 13.
54. B. Jones, "Jane Austen in California," paras. 5, 8.
55. Bacevich, "Under God," para. 5.
56. Newport, "Understanding the Increase," para. 3.

trustworthy,[57] and only 19 percent of millennials believe this.[58] Across all age groups, a web of paranoia and conspiracy mongering is rising. Children are trained not to trust adults. Air travel defines every passenger as a potential terrorist—with background checks, baggage searches, X-ray scanning, shoe removal, and toothpaste limitations.

Gun ownership, formerly intended for hunting and sport, has expanded significantly toward being a requirement for home protection. This growing fear is legitimizing the personal carrying of concealed weapons and the hiring of private guards for businesses, public institutions, schools, and even churches. In Missouri, the legislature easily overcame the governor's veto in approving the right of teachers to have guns in the classroom, at the same time lowering to nineteen years old the right to carry guns openly.[59] Fear is creating an upsurge in arms sales, illustrated by the fact that Smith and Wesson's profits doubled in the period following the San Bernadino mass shooting.[60] Ours is increasingly becoming an armed society, solidifying a morality of self-defense, with Stand Your Ground laws justifying murder if one feels threatened. Facebook groups create weapon bazaars for militia groups. Forty-six percent of the world's civilian-owned weapons are owned by Americans—nearly 393 million firearms—which is more guns than people, nearly 50 percent higher than any other country.[61] Forty-two percent of households possess at least one gun, with which we are killing each other at the rate of one hundred deaths each day. In 2019, there were over 39,000 gun deaths.[62] But March 2021 set all records in gun purchases, with the FBI indicating that it had conducted 4,691,738 background checks.[63] Interestingly, 50 percent of the nation's firearms are owned by 3 percent of the country's population,[64] mostly by men who are stockpiling weapons in fear of the future. Hate shootings are becoming almost normative, so that by 2015 there occurred the equivalent of one mass shooting each day,[65] becoming so commonplace that they are often regarded as not worth reporting in the media as news. During this same time that mass shootings killed 339

57. Rainie et al., "Trust and Distrust in America," para. 8.

58. Drake, "Six New Findings about Millennials," para. 6.

59. Associated Press, "Missouri Approves Concealed Guns," paras. 1–2.

60. Kasperkevic, "Value of Gun Manufacturers' Stocks," paras. 1, 15.

61. Ingraham, "There Are More Guns," paras. 1–3.

62. Centers for Disease Control and Prevention, "All Injuries: Mortalities," para. 4.

63. Knutson, "Gun Background Checks."

64. Ingraham, "Just 3 Percent of Adults," para. 1.

65. Silverstein, "There Were More Mass Shootings," para. 1.

persons in the US, police killed 4,355 persons.[66] As of May 2019, there are 699,977 registered machine guns in the US.[67] The NRA, not satisfied with their successful lobbying of legislators to pass laws permitting the carrying of concealed weapons, has turned their efforts to legitimize carrying of open firearms into public places, such as bars, restaurants, airports, and churches. Such permission would include military-styled weapons designed for mass destruction, with studies showing that the persons most desirous of display-ing such weapons tend to be those least responsible for having them. Once declared legal, illegality begins only after they are fired.

It is revealing that with the election of our first African American president, gun manufacturing in our country almost doubled, with 5.6 million guns produced in 2009 and 10.9 million in 2013.[68] Ironically, President Obama himself brokered and authorized the sale of more arms to foreign governments than any other US president since World War II.[69] Understandably then, Pope Francis, in addressing Congress, charged legislators with "culpable silence" for permitting such US arms sales, be-ing "shamefully drenched in blood."[70] President Trump pulled the US out of the nuclear disarmament treaty, authorizing development of nuclear weapons that are "useable" and working to create an additional branch of the military intent on arming space. As scientists search for evidence of planetary life in outer space, the media is responding with vivid episodes of galactic warfare—the unquestioned assumption being that aliens from outer space will be violently hostile to us, urgently needing for us to create instruments of obliteration rather than hospitality.

The Second Amendment guarantees personal possession of arms for the sake of participating in a militia whose intent is defense against foreign tyranny. Why, then, has our government become far more permissive, even encouraging expansiveness in interpreting this amendment? Firmin DeBra-bander suggests a clue drawn from Machiavelli's *Prince*, the classic manual for acquiring and solidifying state control of a society. The prince, we are told, can best evoke loyalty by permitting subjects to keep arms so as to feel empowered, willingly allying with the force and authority of the prince.[71] To deny that right would be to evoke them as enemies, while permission as a palliative is still insufficient to arm the populace with sufficient weapons to

---

66. Barton, "Cops Killed Nearly Thirteen Times," para. 1.

67. DeRoos, "ATF Releases the Number," para. 9.

68. Ingraham, "There Are Now More Guns," para. 9.

69. Hartung, "Obama Administration Has Brokered," para. 12.

70. Pope Francis, "Transcript: Pope Francis's Speech," para. 25.

71. DeBrabander, *Do Guns Make Us Free*, 109.

challenge the massive power of the prince. Thus, says DeBrabander, the gun lobby is thriving on a permeating ideology of fear, compelling belief that the possession of guns is necessary, which in turn elevates violence, that in turn intensifies fear, which escalates the demand for state control. It follows that fierce advocates of the Second Amendment are those most insistent on escalating the annual military budget—which amazingly tops $934 billion through September 30, 2021.[72] Fear fans the impetus toward fascism as an antidote for the growing feeling of impotence, with the specter of threat imaged in terms of terrorism, racism, immigration, or a lurking host of conspiratorial enemies, real, imagined, or intentionally invented. This welcomes a desire for stronger defense that encourages profits from greater global arms sales, resulting in a perpetual war condition that encourages the merger of state power with transnational corporate control.

A frightening aspect in this scenario is that, since its inception, more than 11,500 domestic law enforcement agencies have taken part in the 1033 program, receiving more than $7.4 billion in surplus military equipment[73]— including tens of thousands of machine guns; grenade launchers; seventeen mine-resistant armored vehicles; scores of M16 rifles; hundreds of silencers; 200,000 ammunition magazines; thousands of pieces of camouflage and night vision equipment; and even aircraft. The Federal Bureau of Investigation (FBI) is not only providing them with information gained by their own surveillance drones but has given them drones to provide their own surveillance. Heavily armed SWAT teams are deployed more than 50,000 times yearly. Underway is the development of a DNA database of everyone involved in virtually any crime. Since 2013, the FBI consolidated files on 100 million Americans into a single $1.2 billion database of which local police everywhere have access, in addition to a pooling of local, regional, and national databases.[74] They now have the capacity to jam cellular communications in any area of the nation. The Trump administration lifted all bans limiting the types and amount of such gear to be made available to local police, opening unfettered access to weapons of war for use on our streets. *Do Not Resist*,[75] awarded the Best Documentary Award in 2016 at the Tribeca Film Festival, opens with footage from the confrontation at Ferguson, MO, where police are graphically portrayed as if heavily armed Marines, complete with helmets, shields, weapons, and mine-resistant vehicles. The film's theme is how the War on Terror has resulted in the massive militarization of

72. Amadeo, "US Military Budget," para. 1.
73. Lee, "How Police Militarization Became."
74. *Week* Staff, "Biometrics Boom," para. 1.
75. Atkinson, dir., *Do Not Resist*.

America, from major cities to small towns, from brute force to sophisticated surveillance. Director Craig Atkinson stated as his intent to show how $40 billion of military equipment is being imparted without any stipulation as to its use or training as to how to use it.[76] His insistence is that we are in the midst of domestic warfare for which the police are being made the militant vehicle. In the process, First Amendment rights are violated, as SWAT raids and battering rams provide excitement with the latest novelties. Since 2016, police nationwide have shot and killed almost 1,000 persons each year, increasing from 961 to 1,021 in 2020.[77] After reviewing the videos of such occurrences, reviewer Ed Rampell was painfully forced to conjecture: "Is America the land of the free or a police state under the iron heel of the government, where resistance is futile?"[78] With the power of our military providing international support for the power of corporate socioeconomic self-interests, the evidence is strong that the police are correlatively becoming the domestic force for controlling resistance and revolt—with the mass media providing patriotic justification and conservative Christianity promising divine support. In 2019, an Alabama law allowed a megachurch to establish its own police force.[79] Once upon a time, Christianity had at its heart the leaven for nonviolence.

In procured secret CIA documents, torture has emerged as a standard procedure with political prisoners, in one case documenting by video the waterboarding of the same person 183 times, another 83 times.[80] When these videos were released to Congress, the reaction was simply a knowing nod. While torture formerly was almost universally condemned as immoral, roughly half of Americans now support it as sometimes "acceptable and necessary."[81] It has further been disclosed that the American Psychological Association secretly asked the CIA to develop a policy of ethics for use by their members in functioning within these detention and interrogation operations.[82] Meanwhile, "coercive interrogative techniques" are being taught to disciplinary personnel in public schools.[83]

The anomaly of Christians now supporting torture illustrates the powerful impact of modern society on Christianity. Our present I-me

76. Rampell, "Do Not Resist," para. 4.

77. *Washington Post*, "Fatal Force," para. 4.

78. Rampell, "'Do Not Resist,'" para. 12.

79. Aspegren, "Alabama Governor Quietly Signs Law," para. 1.

80. Human Rights Watch, "USA and Torture," fig. 1.

81. Delehanty and Kearns, "Wait, There's Torture in Zootopia," para. 1.

82. Risen, "American Psychological Association," para. 1.

83. Van Brunt, "Adult Interrogation Tactics in Schools," para. 1.

world is a far cry from the one in which we are called to be our brother's keeper. With competitive self-interest being society's primary motivation, biblical teachings advocating cheek-turning are no longer ideals but naivities. A pastor daring to preach a nonviolent, all-forgiving, enemy-loving, self-denying, second-mile walking Jesus, if not fired, would likely hear this response: "I know, pastor, but . . ." This *but* discloses a crucial factor in Christianity's demise. As a result, recent polls show that on moral issues, Christians and atheists exhibit little difference.

Based on extensive interviewing, Christian Smith and Hilary Davidson write in *The Paradox of Generosity* regarding the impact of our society's present "grasping posture" on the growing personal loss of meaning and purpose. Almost sounding biblical, while the poll found that there is a consistent correlation between generosity and well-being, the majority of Americans are on the ungenerous end of the scale.[84] Even among Christians who have traditionally tithed 10 percent of their income for helping others, only 2.7 percent do so any longer,[85] with 86.2 percent of Christians giving less than 2 percent. Although the surveyors offered no explanation for this anomaly, clearly the societal ethos in which we are immersed is severely undercutting the Christian stance that was formerly accepted without question—St. Paul's insistence that "no one should seek his own interest, but rather that of his neighbor" (1 Cor 10:24).

Another significant impact of this secularization process upon the churches is the traditional family unit, around which Christianity has historically centered. Formerly when young adults strayed from the faith, the working assumption was that when children were born, the family unit would return to the church. But having children today is postponed until later in life and with fewer in number. In fact, the traditional family is itself becoming increasingly rare, with baby boomers on a trajectory to have the highest lifetime level of divorce of any generation in US history.[86] The traditional household that once consisted of a married couple with several children has shrunk in the last forty years from characterizing 40 percent of the population to 19 percent—with children born to unmarried women having risen from 5 percent to 43 percent.[87] This is no longer the world that once provided supportive ambience for the church.

Further, as the church has been quietly elbowed from the public arena, it has attempted to make a final moral stand by focusing on bedroom

---

84. C. Smith and Davidson, *Paradox of Generosity*, 103–5.

85. C. Smith and Davidson, *Paradox of Generosity*, 101.

86. Moore, "This Is Why Baby Boomers," para. 2.

87. VanOrman and Jacobsen, "U.S. Household Composition Shifts," paras. 6, 16.

activities. Yet society is rendering this arena too as being private—even among believers. Thus, as we saw, not only Protestants but a significant majority of Catholics no longer agree with the church's official stand against such matters as abortion, contraception, gay marriage, and divorce, resulting in the church's moral authority being severely undercut by practice.[88] In 2019, the United Methodist church teetered on the edge of a hostile split over the issue of homosexuality.

The media's portrayal of modern life as devoid of religion is happening even when this is not the case. The recent motion picture *Forty-Two* is an example.[89] Christianity was a crucial factor in the lives of both Jackie Robinson and Branch Rickey in their courage to integrate baseball. Yet this crucial ingredient was totally eliminated in the motion picture, with the filmmakers justifying this omission to avoid any appeal to religion that might undercut the film's box office appeal.[90] Even when some religious aspect is occasionally portrayed, it is usually in the past tense or with a smiling sense of oddity.

Although Joseph Bottum in his *Anxious Age: The Post-Protestant Ethic and the Spirit of America* tends to confuse cause with result, he insists that "the single most significant fact over the past few decades in America—the great explanatory event from which follows nearly everything in our social and political history—is the crumbling of the mainline churches as central institutions in our national experience."[91] The question of cause and effect here is a false dichotomy, of whether the demise is rooted in church or in society, and whether the media is creative of modern culture or reflective of it. It is a cross-feeding vortex.

Therefore, we are living in a post-Christian time in which our culture no longer elicits, no longer is conducive to, and no longer portrays itself as compatible with Christian thinking, beliefs, and/or behavior. Emblematic is St. John the Baptist Church in Pittsburgh. After being closed and sold in 1993, it has recently reopened as the Church Brew Works.[92] It is now a restaurant with its own crafted beer, using the baptismal font for dispensing its brew—apparently without a raised eyebrow. In London, L'Oscar Hotel, reopened in a former Baroque-style church,[93] has been heralded as "boldly opulent," decorated with "decadent maximalism," and boasting a "Baptist

88. Lipka, "Majority of U.S. Catholics' Opinions," para. 4.
89. Helgeland, dir., *Forty-Two*.
90. Metaxas, "Jackie Robinson's Faith Missing," para. 3.
91. Bottum, as cited by Crocker, Review, para. 1.
92. "History," para. 4.
93. L. Ford, "L'Oscar Hotel Review," para. 2.

Bar with a cocktail named after a deadly sin," complete with "its own animalistic scent that is 'utterly seductive.'"

LOSS OF RELIGIOUS SENSITIVITY

National Public Radio picked up on the Pew Research Center's findings that at least one-third of present-day young adults no longer identify with any organized religion.[94] They conducted several interviews with representative millennials, intent on discussing why this demise of religion. I listened and confess being appalled. What I heard was a superficial floundering by young people raised in a nonreligious environment who were not only unaware of the viable religious options available but, even more crucial, were even alienated from the religious questions. They were conflicted and confused. Some admitted a fear of death, others were envious of the apparent comfort that religious people seemed to feel, and still others found somewhat appealing the idea of community. Almost all of them admitted that they prayed "in some way" when they were in trouble, were fearful, or felt vulnerable. But as they shared, what I sensed being cast over this whole scene was a vague maybe-ness about which it did not seem to matter much, one way or another. The god-question was absent, functionally irrelevant, with almost no awareness as to any difference either a yes or no decision might make. Sad.

What we see here may relate to today's functional separation of church and state. The image of a wall between the two as applied to public education conveys the untaught impact on students that one can know everything one needs to know while remaining totally ignorant about religion. Disregarded is the functioning of religion as a significant factor throughout history in almost every arena of the human enterprise. The working assumption is that while other subjects can be taught objectively, not so with religion. Religion is privatized, as an optional personal supplement for those so inclined, for use behind the Sunday wall. Without religion, what is really being taught in the public schools is secularism—formation in and preparation for a religionless life. For the Christian, such a posture is tantamount to teaching atheism. Any God who is optional or functions only in a separate religious sphere is no longer the God of Christianity. Faith is holistic, the spectacles of a person's overall perceptions, the determiner of value, the distiller of motivation, and the establisher of goals. To push faith into being a segment, an appendage, or an addendum is to reduce religion to what it is not. For the Christian, God is nothing less than the working premise of everything

94. Glenn, "As Social Issues Drive Young," para. 2.

that exists. Made optional, faith at best is reduced from the essential to the supplemental, the central to the peripheral.

Yet even more damaging in Christianity's diminishment may not be the rejection of its answers, but the minimization and loss of its underlying questions. Several decades ago, tensions between science and religion were rendered more hospitable by distinguishing the *how* questions of science from the *why* questions of religion. The describing of was distinguishable from the accounting for. Since then, however, the intriguing scientific discoveries regarding the what, where, and when have been permitted to stifle the *why* dimension into disinterest. The secular mind is becoming satisfied with description, so that the god-question that has haunted humankind from our inception is being lost or, at best, becoming a dispensable curiosity. The why is becoming no longer a recognizable conundrum, a trepidation, a resident ache. Consequently, mystery is becoming exiled, our concerns impounded within the perimeters of problems theoretically capable of solution. And so St. Peter Chrysologus's question applies well to our times: "Why do you ask how you were created and do not seek to know why you were made?"[95]

The anthropologist Bronislaw Malinowski, in his study of primitive tribes, came to draw a key distinction. Magic, as the precursor of science, is intent on producing calculated and verifiable results.[96] Religion, by contrast, is a universal phenomenon of value for its own sake, without any purpose beyond itself, as the human response to mystery. Yet, as Max Weber declared, ours is a desacralized world.[97] With the sacred swallowed into the secular, the cosmos forfeits its awe and the earth its mystery. Skies that once danced with stars are now leftover garbage from wayward collusions, composites of dust and ice doing their meaningless things in a cold and infinite emptiness. Actually, for 80 percent of Americans, light pollution blots out even the possibility of seeing the Milky Way in the night skies.[98] Wilderness is where RVs park for taking selfies to share with bored neighbors. Holy mother earth is sectioned off into lots to be bought, sold, and exploited for personal and corporate gain, while dirt is bagged for convenient tomato raising.

In conversations with several physicists regarding cosmic origins, I found it amazing that their projections backward into a mathematical

---

95. International Commission on English in the Liturgy, *Liturgy of the Hours*, 3:1563.

96. Malinowski, *Magic, Science and Religion*, 38.

97. Spencer, "Complicated Legacy," para. 11.

98. Greenfieldboyce, "Light Pollution Hides Milky Way," para. 1.

convergence point as the instant of the Big Bang were sufficient for them. There was no mystery left, no evocation of awe, for theoretical constructs describing the way things are were all that they needed, with nothing remaining for pondering. But for theologians through the centuries, no matter how completely things may be analyzed and described, the religious dimension remains as the question of questions: "Why something rather than nothing?" There is primal mystery in the sheer fact that anything *is*, that life *is*—herein is the gnawing endemic to the religious mind. Either one is awestruck by existence or one is not—and this contrasting deportment makes all the difference. If a person is satisfied simply by learning how things work, something very primal has been forfeited.

If our great-grandparents were to enter today's society, they would be transfixed above all by the mystery of it all. Olympics happening in Russia are inexplicitly snatched from the air for viewing on a screen in one's living room, in a box providing 150 channels from which to choose. Airplanes traveling near the speed of sound can deposit persons anywhere in the world. Satellites sweeping infinite space send back wondrous cosmic portraits through the air. A smartphone in one's pocket provides not only communication with almost any place in the world but can respond within seconds to questions about the whole of human knowledge. Computers provide unlimited access to limitless information, a voice on a dashboard provides kindly directions to wherever, e-readers can access whole libraries, and medical miracles range from heart transplants to noninvasive laser surgery. Our ancestors would be awestruck, utterly speechless. Yet, ironically, we who are bombarded by such mysteries are being desensitized to their mystery. Instead of birthing humility through our ignorance over how such these things can possibly work, instead they precipitate in us the arrogance of expectation. Breakthroughs are in daily demand and innovations are simply expectations—as the humbling why disappears into an arrogant shrug of why not. In the process, what is lost, in T. S. Eliot's words, is "the One who knows how to ask questions."[99]

Even though the heavens that the psalmist beheld would be dwarfed by the unending expansiveness of the space that we can presently behold, nevertheless he delighted in morning and evening and shouted glory. Yet the sun, moon, stars, rain, wind, night, mountains, and oceans—these are now managed with a five-minute evening TV weather report. Thus, once again, what we are discerning in our present religious diminishment is not really alternative beliefs or even disbelief, but a forfeiture of the mindset that

---

99. Eliot, "Choruses from 'The Rock,'" in *Complete Poems and Plays*, 103.

once grounded religious sensibility, without which not even the religion questions any longer make sense.

Our society is experiencing now what contemporary philosophy has been insisting upon for several decades—that no questions can be regarded as valid that cannot be verified by the empirical method. Therein is dislodged and dispensed the questions that have intrigued and shaped cultures from the time of our human emergence. For the Christian, even if answers cannot be known with certainty, it is in struggling with the questions that we are rendered authentically human. Since what one is able to perceive depends on what one is drawn to ask, the heart of Christianity's demise is not that persons today are experiencing the presence of God's absence but not even sensing the absence of the absence. T. S. Eliot lamented that we have lost wisdom in knowledge and, in turn, lost knowledge in information[100]—and thereby we acknowledge as valid only those yearnings that are capable of being materialistically filled. Jean Paul Sartre once lamented: "It is very distressing that God does not exist, [for] if God does not exist . . . man is forlorn."[101] This is an honest atheism by a person who struggled mightily with the god-question. In contrast, our culture is the one about which T. S. Eliot prophesied—of having "left God not for other gods" but for "no god"—and "this has never happened before."[102]

Openness to the religious dimension has often happened through an awakening to finitude—to the awareness of one's contingency, to the radical dependence of being sustained in each instant by that which one is not, but which must be, or we would not be. Using the analogy of electricity, normalcy involves the availability of light by the flick of a switch, heat by thermostat, and refrigeration by automatic control. This arrangement we simply take for granted—until the ice storm strikes. Suddenly there is nothingness—darkness, cold, bewilderment. "Where did the power go?" It didn't go anywhere; it simply is no longer, and that which was, is not now. So with us. The ontological argument for God is not a proof but is an explication of the consequence of experiencing this radical contingency. In sensing everything as radically and intrinsically dependent for its existence, it follows that there must be a That whose existence is necessary, a *sui generis* Other which cannot not be. To deny this sustaining Reality would be to deny one's own existence. The *why* is the reverse side of the contingent *that*, sensed with a correlative gratefulness. Either one senses this defining condition, or one does not. Our society is one that does not—becoming an insurance culture in which one can purchase

100. Eliot, "Choruses from 'The Rock,'" in *Complete Poems and Plays*, 96.

101. Sartre, "Existentialism Is a Humanism," 290–91.

102. Eliot, "Choruses from 'The Rock,'" in *Complete Poems and Plays*, 108.

security against every contingency. In the process, ontic dependency is drained into a self-sufficiency of fact, reducing death from a disclosure of finitude to a postponed inconvenience.

In their book *Self-Deception, False Beliefs, and the Origins of the Human Mind*, Ajit Varki and Danny Brower develop the intriguing thesis that humans have become the most successful of creatures because of our ability to deny reality. The evolution of consciousness brings us no evolutionary advantage if it is permitted to awaken us to the distressing fact of our contingency, that we are doomed to die, which would awaken a terror that would make us fail in the struggle for survival. Therefore, continued existence has necessitated that humans develop "neural mechanisms for denying reality." Totally disregarded in their analysis is the kinship between this awakening into finitude and the emergence of religion. Nevertheless, their research is insightful in perceiving a significant correlation between today's increasing "cultural mechanisms for denying reality" and the diminishment of that sensitivity in which religion has been birthed and has nourished. Indicatively, a number of recent polls are disclosing that well over half the persons interviewed tend to reduce religion to morality—to doing the right thing.

In contrast, recent research is disclosing the profound role that religion has had from the beginning of our human emergence. Previous theories surmised that religion emerged when, at the end of the Ice Age, the opportunity for domesticating plants and animals occurred, giving rise to permanent agricultural settlements, in which religion then emerged as an aid in social cooperation and control. Yet quite different is the evidence emerging from a far earlier civilization, some 11,600 years ago, at Gobekli Tepe[103] in southeastern Turkey. Found are sculptured pillars placed in a circle, each weighing as much as sixteen tons. Strongly implied is that people first began to assemble for religious reasons, establishing social units around sacred sites. Primitive nomads began building holy places for rituals that could give expression to their emerging capacity for symbolization. Significantly, at the Gobekli Tepe site, several decades after the huge circle of pillars had been created, it was buried and a new circle complex created. This process of building, covering, and recreating suggests that their meaning was not in the accomplishment but in the creating itself—as a ritualistic act of worship. Religion was birthed in an emergence of wonderment, marking the human differentiation from the natural world, budding into sacred rituals that provided a spiritual locus for this emerging self-conscious transcendence. Rather than resulting after the human emergence, religion seems to have been a grounding impetus in the emergence of human self-consciousness

103. Curry, "World's Oldest Temple," paras. 7, 12.

itself. Religion is causal rather than consequential. The famed Canadian atheist photographer Mark Schacter found himself obsessed with photographing places of worship. He wisely discerned: "Even an ardent atheist can look at a house of worship and see the signs of an invisible human longing that is common to us all, believers and unbelievers alike."[104] It is this loss in modern society that is causal in Christianity's decline.

I remember as a boy sitting on our back porch with my dog, as I looked in wonder at the golden rising of a full moon. I pointed my dog's head toward it, guiding his eyes so that he could enjoy what was mesmerizing me. It was to no avail. Stars, moon, sunrises, sunsets, even flowers, all these emblems of beauty for me were utterly impossible for him. He simply could not see them, and thus for him they did not exist. It is not difficult then to imagine the dawn of human emergence happening when for the first time someone looked up and actually saw the starry skies, feeling something—mystery perhaps, certainly awe. Primal stirrings, yearnings deeper than the need for food or anything physical—the innate hunger for meaning. Modern society's separation from nature, its splintering of community by individualism, in becoming obsessed with possessions and status and power—all of these are eating away at that primal sensitivity of being the earth's humble guests and its reverent stewards. Tyler Nordgren has explored the impact on us of light pollution, which eliminates exposure to the heavens. Almost totally lost, he laments, is the amazement of the night skies that from the beginning has claimed us in commonality with our race.[105] Sadly irredeemable is this loss of primal sensitivity in determining what it means to be human—a loss happening so gradually that we are unaware of the tragic deficit.

The vastly accelerated life pace of modern society is likewise extracting its toll in the church's diminishment. It is significantly shrinking our sense of the present, swallowing it up in the not yet. This modern lifestyle contrasts greatly with the one that Jesus taught, the intense experience of living the depth of each *now* for its own sake, taking "little thought of the morrow." Today's multitasking lifestyle, motivated by efficiency for future recompense, undercuts the mindful depth intensity of living in the present. A 2018 study disclosed that fully 95 percent of teens have access to a smart phone, and 45 percent say they are online "almost constantly."[106] It is not a stretch to extrapolate that the average American is consumed by technology. Researcher Andrew Sullivan concludes that we have gone

104. Ribiat, "Quote of the Day," para. 1.

105. Nordgren, *Night Sky*.

106. Monica Anderson and Jiang, "Teens, Social Media," para. 2.

from looking up and around to constantly looking down[107]—into an artificial reality. This entails a distraction and diversion from breadth and depth. Oriented by the modern consumer mindset, the attitude toward religion is likewise becoming pragmatic: "What's in it for me?" And measured by such modern values, the honest answer is *nothing*. Thus, a crisis for the churches resides in the question of what appeal is left for our severely narrowed selfie age, when the authentic value of Christianity is not instrumental but intrinsic, for its own sake.

UNFAMILIARITY OF RELIGIOUS LANGUAGE

I remember vividly as a youth the experience of participating in the cancerous dying of a family friend. He was an engineer by trade and an enthusiastic Sunday School teacher by choice. As his disease advanced and he sank into delirium, from the reservoir of his memory poured out visionary biblical language and narrative. He communicated with the saints as the friends he would soon embrace, sang with the angels around the incensed throne of God, reached his arms toward the opening heavens just beyond the ceiling, readied to greet him as "a bride adorned," as he shed tears he knew God would wipe away soon. In peace, Christ came for him. This was narrative as lived—one increasingly lost for most persons.

When I was a child, my mother nightly read to me from *Hurlbut's Story of the Bible*, until Abraham, Moses, Samson, David, Mary, and Jesus became my daily friends. So it was for even the most uneducated of medieval monks, required to memorize all 150 psalms in Latin so that they could be pondered at heart's length during their labors, thereby enabled to "pray without ceasing." Even the simplest of peasants was likely to know by heart the Lord's Prayer, Rosary, Apostles' Creed, Salve Regina, Ave Maria, Gloria Patri, Jesus Prayer, Angelus, Confiteor, Agnus Dei, etc.—with accompanying gestures. They had as walking companions the saints such as Gregory, Augustine, Scholastica, Jerome, Martin, Anthony, Catherine, Benedict, Bernard, Cecilia, and Francis, hospitably available for intercessory help as needed. During the Reformation, such devotions came to include as well the catechism, meal prayers, and daily family Bible reading. In the coal mining community of my ancestors, biblical verses were so memorized that daily conversation was sprinkled by the stately prose of the King James Bible and the language of the church. Even after seventy years, my memory still has on call the psalms learned to acquire glued stars on a Vacation Bible School chart. Yet no longer

---

107. A. Sullivan, "I Used to Be," para. 16.

can we assume today that persons have even the Lord's Prayer or the Twenty-Third Psalm as memory deposits.

Before our modern period, to be educated meant exposure to the humanities—to history, literature, the arts, and religion. Thus, public education provided multidimensional encounters with key figures who in various fields had struggled with meaning. Today, however, the relentless socioeconomic dynamic is seriously questioning any value for the liberal arts and, in so doing, even doubting the usefulness of a college education, when what is needed is skill training for specialized employment. Public education is being privatized by establishing charter schools that divert public school funding into schools not subject to local voter control, where teacher unions are undercut. While in the last twenty-five years charter schools have drained $4 billion of public funding intended for public education,[108] even worse, "more than 35 percent of charter schools funded by the federal Charter School Program (CSP) between 2006 and 2014 either never opened or were shut down, costing taxpayers more than half a billion dollars."[109] This privatizing is further funded by corporation-based foundations intent on privatizing all of education, so that, in a deep sense, the market is determining what is needed in order for a person to be educated. One consequence, according to Sarah Mervosh (*New York Times*), is that schools primarily serving students of color receive $23 billion less in funding than White schools, despite serving the same number of students.[110] In addition, voucher programs in twenty-nine states are rerouting more than one billion dollars yearly of taxpayer money to private schools,[111] including religious ones that believe that Scripture provides the only correct biology, geology, and cosmology. Largely controlled by wealthy donors, the result is that these schools refocus education toward proficiency training with measurable learning outcomes. Much of this corporately financed reform focuses on creating a common curriculum, with a clear self-serving bias. This privatizing signals that educational institutions are succumbing to corporate interests, resulting in the sacrifice of critical thinking and the loss of motivation for social change. Emphasis is upon market values rather than democratic ones and on grooming self-interest rather than concern for the common good. School choice has been made a vehicle of market forces, in which failing schools in poverty areas are simply closed or transitioned into redefining the goal of education as being job training.

108. V. Strauss, "New Report Finds," para. 10.

109. V. Strauss, "Report: Federal Government Wasted," para. 1.

110. Mervosh, "How Much Wealthier," para. 1.

111. Pudelski and Davis, "Public Loss Private Gain," 2.

A considerable amount of this public funding has encouraged the emergence of a charter school business complex served by lobbyists having close connections with corporation interests, such as the conservative American Legislative Exchange Council. Large chains of charter schools are being funded and controlled by corporate foundations such as the Bill and Linda Gates Foundation, the Walton Family Foundation, and the Koch brothers. Their operating concept is that schools need to operate as if they are private business firms, with the bottom line being measurable benefits, costs, profits, and results. These charter schools are largely exempt from state regulations, being controlled by independent boards. The result, according to research columnist Dustin Beilke, is that the agenda of the federal Department of Education matches well that of the billionaire-funded anti-public-school pro-privatization movement that is promoting much of the misinformation about the "failure of public education."[112]

In her *Death and Life of the Great American School System*, Diane Ravitch traced this slow dying of the public schools through privatization. The curriculum that has emerged focuses on memorization for testing, thereby driving authentic learning from the public schools, with many dedicated teachers leaving the system in frustration. No longer are students encouraged to think for themselves and to appropriate learning into their own search for purpose and meaning. Instead, they are submitted to a stifling and pressurized environment of competitive and aggressive individualism. Focus on science and mathematics pushes the humanities from the classroom, questioning the utility of such fields as art and music—those dimensions without which the imagination tends to wither. Pennsylvania legislator Brad Roae has even gone so far as to propose eliminating all grants for students who "study poetry or some other pre-Walmart major."[113] Critics liken his proposed spending cuts to "a medieval crusade against the arts, culture, and learning."

Southern states are adopting their complex of charter schools through voucher inducement that is, in effect, establishing fashionable segregated schools. The first step in this transition from public education was to grant vouchers for children with special needs. Next was developed a voucher plan for children in schools with low test scores. Finally, everyone receives a voucher under the banner of school choice—with racial and economic segregation now an established fact. The *Detroit Free Press* reported that Michigan taxpayers are pouring nearly $1 billion a year into charter schools over which there is no oversight as to how the money is

---

112. Beilke, "Obama Administration Enables Billionaire Takeover," para. 27.

113. Sterling, "Roae Responds," para. 2.

being spent or who is doing the teaching. As a result, charter schools that have had poor records of achievement continue unchanged.[114] In a follow-up article, we learn that in Milwaukee, the mother of voucher-funded experimentation, private schools are showing no improvement over public schools. In Ohio and Louisiana, charter school results are even worse, leading to the conclusion that there is no demonstrative evidence that the privatizing mechanics of market choice are resulting in improved education, even when judged by their own criteria.[115]

One of the consequences of this educational morass is the surge in home schooling. In conversations with parents who have chosen this option, the reasons usually given focus on the stifling common-core testing mentality that they see robs students of the passion for discovery, creativity, critical thinking, and values learning, suffocating in a competitive disciplinarian environment that undermines mutual exploration. This understandable disdain for the inferior education being provided by public schools is a self-feeding dynamic. As students withdraw, there is a lessening of available funding, and as public school budgets and support services diminish, the result is an escalation in which two million US children are now being home schooled. Furthermore, an unschooling approach to home schooling is gaining popularity, in which the children determine what and when and how much they will study.

In higher education, the value of the humanities is being seriously diminished. In 2014, only 6.1 percent of bachelor's degrees were in the humanities, the lowest level since statistics on college majors began being kept in 1948.[116] With the growing economic need for colleges to compete for students, non-endowment colleges are increasingly offering online courses for part-time students whose appeal is specialized vocational improvement. Even as accomplished an economist as Bryan Caplan, in his *Case Against Education: Why the Educational System Is a Waste of Time and Money*, goes so far as to call for the privatizing of all education, rendering college degrees rare among the non-wealthy. He insists that only one in twenty persons really needs a four-year college education, with the other nineteen persons needing instead a market-value schooling that prepares them for the diverse roles needed by the economy. Reflecting this approach, corporations are beginning to provide their own "college-level" training for potential employees, eliminating liberal arts classes as an unnecessary waste. Over 4,000 companies worldwide have now created in-house corporate universities with

114. J. Dixon, "Michigan Spends $1B," paras. 1, 7.

115. Higgins, "Can School Vouchers Give Kids," paras. 4, 23, 25–26.

116. Jaschik, "Shrinking Humanities Major," para. 4.

their own faculty and curriculum, training employees narrowly in success-ful techniques of the market.[117] Likewise, in higher education, the market is undermining professors whose tenure once guaranteed the right of critical speech and freedom for challenging research, replacing such positions with nontenured part-time teachers who have low pay, minimal benefits, and no job security, often with nonaccredited credentials.

This dynamic within education is symbolic of our society as a whole, as detailed in Yale professor Anthony Kronman's book *Education's End: Why Our Colleges and Universities Have Given Up on the Meaning of Life*. He in-sists that institutions of higher education have always been some of the few places where the meaning of life can be explored in an organized way. But no longer are they providing forums "for the exploration of life's mystery and meaning," for being embraced by the "question of what living is for." His lament is that no longer does this vision occupy a "central and honored place" in the curriculum of most colleges. Instead, present-day learning is functioning narrowly within the field of one's choice, promising success in personal escalation toward the mythical American Dream. The search for meaning once evoked by the perennial questions is dissolving into unques-tioned economically defined goals.

Education so defined in terms of a useful curriculum that is testable according to informational competence and devoid of imaginative out-stretching: this is the vacuous world in which the church now finds itself struggling to breathe. Current language is literal, strong on denotation, and suspicious of connotation. It establishes an ethos of digital off/on, with computer processing devoid of maybes, hunches, and shadowed innuendo; immune against the imaginative subjunctive power of *if only*; serving rather than questioning the status quo by eliminating formation in critical think-ing. Thus, as we have seen, when Scripture is approached with this literal mentality, it becomes too strange for entry. In heavy contrast, the world of believers is one of graceful and rhythmic flow, where poetically, animals do talk; angels appear to the imagination; the sky has holes that leak rain; there is an Eden of poisoning fruit; God speaks out of a volcano; and the dead can rise. But within a literal society in which only a literal Christian-ity can be considered, faith is fated to relentless diminishment. In contrast to the mentality of present society, the countercultural world of Christian existence is shaped by the drama of worship, its syntax is that of music, its truth the aroma of incense, its Eucharist the choreography of ballet, and its impetus a language of the poetic heart. Entrance into it is enabled by those touched by a Bach aria, a Shakespeare sonnet, an El Greco landscape, and

117. "Keeping It on Company Campus," para. 4.

a Barlach sculpture. It is the world in which Hamlet exists at the depth of soul struggle, Melville's white whale swims the oceans of unredeemed anger, and Beethoven's final quartets dance the courage of yearned commitment. The humanities are faith's prelude, yet these are the entrees that modern education is closing down. Plato insists that the search for meaning begins in wonder, reaching toward that which only the poet can touch. So it is, Walter Brueggemann states, that, when one engages the Bible, one must "read, speak, and think as a poet."[118] Beliefs function as symbols of a reality that transcends empirical knowing, a realm where a waged commitment alone can render objections immune, where song is the favored medium of expression, and where the poetic whets the imagination.

The philosopher Ludwig Wittgenstein insisted early in his career (*Tractatus Logico-Philosophicus*) that modern binary language renders meaningless the domain of religion. In his final work (*Philosophical Investigations*), however, he came to recognize multiple functions of language—as in giving orders, play-acting, cursing, greeting, and praying. Thus, he asserts, religion for both the ancient shamans and modern priests rests on the language of ritual, a distinctly legitimate mode of linguistic behavior. He muses on why the primitive rain dance, usually regarded as done in order to cause rain, always occurred during the rainy season. Thus, the dance is more plausibly understood not as causal but as a ceremonial ritual celebrating rain with thanksgiving. Thus ceremony, rather than being a minor part of human life, is so major that humans can almost be regarded as ceremonial creatures. He illustrates this by declaring that a person can hold to the Christian belief in a final judgment and still not be Christian. The fullness of true belief hinges upon a steadfast ultimate life decision that celebrates life as existing under an inescapable moral imperative, however one might wish to name it factually. Instead, ours has become a society almost incapable of experiencing ceremony, our major holidays having largely lost their ceremonial reason for being. What is left is called partying, with tailgating often surpassing in significance the game itself. Foreign today is the psalmist's proclivity to "lead the rejoicing crowd into the house of God, amid cries of gladness and thanksgiving, the throng wild with joy" (Ps 41:5)[119]—for its own sake.

In my local county newspaper, a woman recently wrote a letter to the editor challenging an article by a local atheist who had ridiculed a literal portraiture of Scripture as if he had demolished Christianity. She patiently explained that just as childhood involves a rich daily interaction of fiction and fantasy, so in growing up we dare not write off everything that is not literal.

---

118. Moss, "Dance in the Dark," para. 14.

119. Gelineau, *Psalms*, 82.

We need to be exposed to interactions opened by metaphor (e.g., that God is a rock or an eagle, yet not so), by simile ("like a shepherd, God leads," while not being a shepherd); through parable ("there was once a man who had two sons . . ."); as hyperbole ("cut off your offending hand"); as figurative language ("stand up and come to our help"); as dated material (stoning to death or owning slaves); and as pre-Christian writings (bashing foreign babies against a rock). What she was wrestling with was this dilemma in which for today's binary mind the poetry of Christianity appears ludicrous, no longer able to envisage a God "who makes the clouds his chariot, who walks on the wings of the wind" (Ps 103:3)[120] and for whom "the hills sing with joy and the trees clap their hands" (Isa 55:12 NRSV). Poetry is the language of Christianity, music its sound, dance its gesture, drama its liturgy, story its conveyor, and bread and wine its taste—wrapped in a blessed imagination. In contrast, literalism deflates the imagination, doctrines evoke weariness, rules call forth regimentation, and domestication is rewarded.

Calligraphy once embellished words with visual beauty, as in the ancient hand-scribed biblical manuscripts. But now students no longer know even how to write in simple script. Through texting, the beauty of language is shriveled into a minimal subject with verb, typed with aborted spelling. Language clipped of its metaphorical depth and denied the thickness of similitude is no longer hospitable to religion. Thus, in a society where persons are no longer being born into an environment rich with the imagery of religious language, where the normative mindset is deplete of sumptuous modes of language, they are starved out of a parlance in which Scripture can become Pascal's "language of the heart."[121]

ACCOMMODATION OF RELIGION AS A COPING SUPPLEMENT

However one might come to terms with a water-walking Jesus, the heart of being a Christian is *metanoia*, a reorientation in being, in which one sees through the eyes of God by incorporating the mind of Christ. This conversion is radical, for it so changes a person that society's competitive lures lose their appeal. Instead, the Christian truly does want to love the neighbor as oneself, does foster community over the self, does desire a healed soul over material rewards, and does acquire a sacrificial concern that the marginal and rejected no longer go empty away. Put in eight words, Christian faith is about *loving as one has been loved by Christ*. But this is a heavy

120. Gelineau, *Psalms*, 181.

121. Pascal, *Pensées*, 127.

sell in our society whose dynamic is self-promotion—the very opposite of losing oneself in order to find it.

Through the centuries, Christianity's sale pitch has been variations on this theme of self-reward. We find in the gospel of Matthew that the motivation for relinquishing this-worldly benefits is in order to receive a far greater compensation in an otherworldly post-life. Thus even a life of severe persecution can be promoted as joyous: "Rejoice and be glad, for your reward is great in heaven" (Matt 5:12). Therefore, "fight the good fight of faith and win the price of eternal life" (Titus 2:1). Pascal's wager distills this approach—that enjoying this short life of worldly pleasures is no match for forfeiting them in wagering for the reward of eternal life. Yet, as we will explore later, in our present this-worldly ethos, heavenly compensation is no longer much of a selling commodity for relinquishing the American Dream. Furthermore, even if one would make such a wager, from the Christian perspective, loving in order to get is a contamination of loving because one is loved.

But as our secular society is increasingly outstressing its population in ways economic, social, and psychological, religion as reward is finding some re-entry, as offering an inner support in order to make it through the night. Much of the spirituality emerging today is of this variety, offering inner peace as a coping mechanism for persons disheartened by failure in reaping much of what the materialistic dream promised. But a Christianity that helps a person cope can be legitimate only if the society in which one is immersed is commensurate with Christian values and goals. Since this is not true of today's society, such coping tends to prostitute faith as a means for supporting indefensible ends.

Certainly, Christianity must support individuals in their personal struggles. Yet I remember the painful day when our local church social justice group came to the realization that in tutoring inner-city students we were actually helping them survive in a system not intended for their good—encouraging them to submit, obey, and resign to it, undercutting motivation to protest for change. The silent corrosion occurring within modern society is exposing the heresy of a Christianity relegated to a coping means for shoring up a society with which it should be fundamentally at odds. Offering the Christian faith as a tool for personal subsisting without challenging society's counter-Christian dynamics is betrayal. Once again, failure is made the fault of the individual rather than the consequence of structured inequality.

Illustrative of this accommodation for the sake of coping is evident in how the spirituality named "mindfulness" is being mainstreamed. Scientific research done upon monks disclosed that contemplation actually alters the structure of one's brain.[122] Psychologists are using such mindfulness to help depressed clients function more productively within their work-obsessed, frantically busy, and lonely lives. The Pentagon, in turn, began experimenting with how such mindfulness might make soldiers more focused and increasingly resilient in battle.[123] General Mills has created a meditation room in every building of its headquarters complex.[124] So it is in many Silicon Valley complexes, such as Twitter, where mindfulness meditation is an "in thing." Google sponsors mindfulness programs and has installed labyrinths at their worksites. Mindfulness has been co-opted by entrepreneurs for profit, issuing a flood of apps and conferences promising efficiency of focus through breathing and bodily sensation. Such secularized spirituality is attempting to provide for individuals a temporary respite from their addled past and a discounting of future consequences, enabling living in the present—not for its own sake but for greater efficiency. This helps explain how and why persons can be spiritual but not religious. Separating the two makes available a coping mechanism that sequesters and domesticates the Christian faith, avoiding metanoia. Roger Owens and Anthony B. Robinson, in their essay "Dark Night of the Church," pose well this condition. The church, called to be a community worshiping the God of Jesus Christ, finds itself immersed in a socioeconomic culture that worships rival gods.[125] Therefore, it is heretical for the church to claim any longer that it is Christian if it finds its niche within the religious marketplace by mirroring and/or providing coping skills in support of our socioeconomic ethos.

UNDERCUTTING OF THE VERACITY OF RELIGIOUS AUTHORITY

Theologians such as Wesley and Calvin craved assurance—that their faith was certain and thus their salvation assured. Wesley sought this through personal experience and Calvin more through external signs of being favored. For centuries, Catholics have sought certainty in the Aristotelian-Thomistic proofs for the existence of God, then drawing the implication that an existing God would establish a church to provide authoritative certainty about faith and morals. But in our postmodern world, where certainty about anything is being severely undercut, faith as well is being drained of both proof and assurance. So dispossessed, individuals are

122. Smuga-Otta, "Physician-Monk Leads Stanford Doctors," para. 4.

123. R. Armstrong et al., "Bio-Inspired Innovation and National Security," 163ff.

124. Gelles, "Mind Business," para. 2.

125. Owens and Robinson, "Dark Night of Church," para. 20.

cast into a wilderness of options, left to gamble on whatever modicum of personal meaning each can scavenge. As a bulwark against this invasive subjectivism, the church has insisted on making varied claims to authority. In Puritan days, this often happened unconsciously because the clergyman was the most educated person in town; but today's preachers are often moderately educated in comparison with other professions. The response of the Catholic Church was been to declare as infallible papal pronouncements on matters of faith and morals. Yet to the once effective declaration that the pope says so, the current response is likely to be *so*? Thus, despite the official Catholic stand against homosexuality and gay marriage, only 31 percent of US Catholics agree.[126] Despite the ecclesiastical stand against abortion, 56 percent of American Catholics support it in some or all cases.[127] Despite the official stand against artificial birth control, 24 percent of abortion patients identify as Catholic, the largest religious group represented.[128] The Shriver Report finds that 73 percent of Catholics believe that you can be a good Catholic and have an abortion. Despite the attempt by the papacy to place the ordination of women beyond debate, the Shriver Report finds that 88 percent support having women priests.[129]

The most cataclysmic affront to ecclesiastical authority, however, has occurred through the vivid disclosure of widespread priestly misconduct with minors, compounded by extensive denials and concealments by authorities on all levels. This impact intensified when *Spotlight* won an Oscar for the best motion picture of 2015, rooted graphically in the *Boston Globe's* investigation into clergy sex abuse.[130] Powerfully portrayed, as one critic put it, was the "immensity of betrayal" and the "misplacement of trust." Even more devastating for the Catholic church was the detailed disclosure of vast clergy molestation in Pennsylvania.[131] Vivid descriptions made clear that this scandal can no longer be disregarded as involving a few exceptional cases. Uncovered was a vast network of immorality, with priests passing on to incoming priests the names of sexually vulnerable youth. Furthermore, it has been disclosed that in Catholic seminaries, homosexual subcommunities function as a widespread intimidating force in clergy formation.[132] Thus, while previous polls rated clergy near the top in trustworthiness,

126. Diamant, "How Catholics around World," fig. 1.

127. Fahmy, "Eight Key Findings," para. 5.

128. Jerman et al., "Characteristics of U.S. Abortion Patients," para. 2.

129. Hart Research and Echelon Insights, *Shriver Report Snapshot*, 7.

130. T. McCarthy, dir., *Spotlight*.

131. "Attorney General Shapiro Details Findings."

132. L. Greene, "Critics See 'Gay Bullying'," para. 1.

recent polls rank them near the bottom, just above used car salesmen.[133] While a clergy collar formerly established authority, for many of us now it evokes a sense of embarrassment, if not shame. To this wide distrust, even disrespect, of clergy and the church, add the skeptical attitude of today's young people toward all authorities and public institutions, and the implications for Christian diminishment are clear.

This undercutting of religious authority, however, is not only self-caused by the churches but is becoming endemic to modern society itself. Conservative Stephen L. Carter, Yale professor of constitutional law, in his *Culture of Disbelief: How American Law and Politics Trivialize Religious Devotion*, has convincingly displayed how society's secular ideology is undercutting religion's authority, not so much through hostility as through trivialization. Religious convictions and motivations are being treated as private hobbies, as something one might choose to do in one's spare time—in contrast to religion being what defines the whole life of the believer. Toleration is a way of no longer taking faith communities seriously, regarding beliefs as arbitrary and unimportant. The general tenor of First Amendment interpretation through the years by the Supreme Court has become that of protecting the state from the church, in contrast to Carter's insistence that separation of church and state was meant to protect the church from the state. It was intended to guarantee freedom for the church to resist the existing order whenever it needs to be challenged. The American founders depended on such a tension, expecting the church to contend with the moral arrogance of a government ruled by an oligarchy of experts. Yet instead of expecting religion to function in this moral check and balance, present-day courts are tending to reflect society as a whole in regarding religion as primarily a personal matter, resenting any effort for it to be a serious voice in the public debate. Public school curricula reflect this bias, failing to teach the important role that religion has played upon the crucial dimensions of history. With religion tolerated rather than respected, believers feel pressured to bracket their convictions, splitting off a part of themselves as believers from the rest of their living. Recent conservative appointments to the Supreme Court have not significantly altered this situation but are giving support to conservative policies that happen to agree with Christian right-wing conservative ones. Meanwhile, Carter critiques the churches for becoming involved in a Faustian bargain by which, to gain advantages of such lucrative advantage as tax exemption and federal funding, the churches are willing to relinquish their responsibility for influencing government in terms of the common good. This approach supplements the political exploitation of the conservative

133. Jackson, "Seven People Christians Trust More," paras. 4, 16.

churches for electoral advantage. Yet religion, which is to be a focus in the human search for ultimate meaning, is in particular need of being heard "in a world steeped in materialistic ideologies." Instead of the churches assuming this role of external moral critic and alternative source of values and meanings, believers are being circumscribed and infected by society's rival secular definition of normative living. In his farewell address in 1796, George Washington insisted on "religion and morality as indispensable supports" of democracy, warning against the assumption that "morality can be maintained without religion."[134] Yet this is our situation today.

Christianity cannot function as a societal moral authority if at its heart there is no transcendence of the ethos dominating today's competitive market society. Otherwise, believers and churches are easily co-opted, as is happening in right-wing Christianity, in which the attempt at refinding a modicum of authority is resulting in having its integrity exploited for the sake of political influence. Mainline churches, fearful of further membership loss, are intimidated from serious involvement in controversial political issues. Meanwhile, many of the churches are supplementing the government's failures by supplying basic human needs for its citizenry, as with food pantries. But in so doing, the churches are really making more tolerable the structured injustices that they should be challenging prophetically. Christianity can be true to itself only if it serves as a counterweight to the dynamics of modern society—resisting external efforts to brush it off as fanaticism and internal ones encouraging domestication. The real diminishment that the church needs to fear is that of losing its faithfulness to the God whose authority transcends that of the state. Yet with the church's present obsession with resisting the dynamic of diminishing numbers, it is unlikely that she will attempt the hard sell of rendering each believer a potential martyr.

134. Washington, "Washington's Farewell Address."

CHAPTER THREE

CAPITALISM, SYSTEMIC INEQUALITY, AND LIVING THE CONSEQUENCES

We have been disclosing the multiple dimensions of modern life that are impinging on both Christianity and the church in forcing their inevitable diminishment. We turn now to the related dynamic that with its multiple dimensions is propelling society to its own relentless demise. These dual diminishments are deeply intertwined, and the fate of the church is at stake.

Henry Giroux expressed boldly as logic the conclusion toward which our documentation is moving: "It's easier to imagine the death of the planet than it is to imagine the death of capitalism."[1] The deaths of both are causatively related, and drastic are their implications for the church. Free market capitalism is becoming so universally invasive as the world's informing ethos that it is controlling our major institutions, at the cost of destroying our planet. Key to understanding this oncoming tragedy is that there is no longer any nation, structure, or anything outside this dynamic that has sufficient power to effectively rival, challenge, deter, or block it so as to bring it to accountability. Never before has such controlling power been so expansive, centralized, and innate in impacting society's institutions and controlling the mindset of its populace. So self-consuming is the direction of this uncontrollable dynamic that, as Wolfgang Streeck concluded in his book *How Will Capitalism End*, capitalism is on the verge of internal collapse, bringing down society with it. Thus it is essential for the church to understand its own diminishment in terms of this relentless demise.

---

1. Moyers, "Henry Giroux."

John Adams, our second president, maintained that "democracy never lasts long. It soon wastes, exhausts, and murders itself. There was never a democracy that did not commit suicide."[2] James Madison, our fourth president, provided in his Federalist Paper No. 51 a rationale: our fallen nature. If we were angels, he said, no government would be necessary; if angels were in charge, no controls on government would be necessary.[3] But given our human condition, how can the government be forced to control itself? His solution, as adopted, was to create a government structured by three branches, each holding the other two in compliance so as to serve the common good. But today, with all three being controlled by a relentless socioeconomic dynamic intent on fostering the power and wealth of the affluent, what then? Adams's dire view is becoming prophecy.

FREE ENTERPRISE

Free market capitalism is a system in which the means of production, distribution, communication, and exchange are largely owned privately, with minimal governmental control. Democracy, on the other hand, involves a government determined by its people, either directly or through elected representatives, rooted in freedom understood as an equality of rights, opportunities, and treatment for every citizen. What is happening in our time is that corporate capitalism so controls our elections with massive financial contributions for electing our representatives that they, in turn, are bound to propose and support legislative bills and deregulations that favor corporate self-interests. Thereby the celebrated democratic value of freedom is contorted into meaning unregulated control for an oligarchy of the affluent. In 2018, winning a seat in the US House of Representatives required on average a campaign spending of $2 million, and winning a Senate seat cost $15.7 million.[4] Indicatively, a majority of the members of the 116th Congress are millionaires, with many of the rest likely to join the wealthy 1 percent after leaving office through prestigious lobbying positions in corporations they have favored.[5] While our system is a democracy in name, it is fast becoming a plutocracy in functioning. Between 2010 and 2018, at least 10,000 bills submitted to state legislatures and Congress have

2. Adams, "From John Adams to John Taylor," para. 2.
3. Madison, "Federalist Papers No. 51," para. 3.
4. Evers-Hillstrom, "State of Money in Politics," para. 2.
5. Evers-Hillstrom, "Majority of Lawmakers," para. 2.

actually been drafted by industry groups and other special interests—2,100 of which have become law.[6]

Capitalism, once regarded basically as an economic theory, has so expanded in its practices that it is impacting almost every aspect of contemporary society. This intertwining, in turn, is establishing a new reality—the corporate transnational-industrial-technological-security complex, an amalgam whose dynamic is self-feeding and self-perpetuating, each part efficiently, albeit unintentionally, playing its role in moving the whole toward the self-destructive cliff of societal collapse. Key in this ethos is a competitive individualism of winners and losers, in whole and in all its parts, lured by promise of the three *p*'s: possessions, prestige, and power. These are so proffered as societal rewards for unquestioned compliance that they have come to control our basic motivations. Yet they are what Christianity has declared to be the primal temptations called sin. These lures are so powerful in seducing our human nature that even Jesus had to undergo forty days and nights of desert struggle with the magnetism of these three temptations. And even when he emerged victorious so that Satan left him, it was only "until an opportune time" (Luke 4:13). What we will examine is how this permeation of postmodern life is dissolving the motivations and goals that once drew persons to Christianity.

In 1975, during a church-sponsored visit to Cuba, I had a telling conversation with Raúl Castro. He shared how he and Fidel had been raised in parochial schools, becoming especially impressed by Jesuit teachers who focused on the social conscience of Jesus. After the successful revolution against the corrupt American-supported Batista regime, Raúl said "we expected the full support of Cuban Christians in creating a new society commensurate with these Christian values." Instead, what happened was that a huge majority of Christians left, lured by the capitalist promise of making it big in the United States. Many who remained, ironically, formed enclaves of subversion, attempting to undercut the vision of equality that the Castros were striving to establish. "Had the church been faithful to the Jesus of the New Testament, this could have been a Christian revolution." For Raúl, capitalism appeals to the worst of human motivations, forging and rewarding a selfish, grasping, and competitive individualism. In contrast, he described the Cuban socialist vision as intent on nurturing the best in human nature, encouraging an altruistic *we* of cooperative equality, team functioning, mutual sharing, and social responsibility. He concluded: "I would rather commit my life to that vision and fail, than to be part of

---

6. O'Dell and Penzenstadler, "You Elected Them," para. 4.

the greedy capitalist mindset and succeed. And I would think that you as a Christian would have the same commitment."

While we are in basic agreement, the difference may be one of strategy—whether to function from the optimistic stance of nurturing the best in our human nature or the pessimistic one of controlling our worst tendencies. The US experiment, now heavily under judgment, has attempted to link both. As Reinhold Niebuhr maintains, the human capacity for justice makes democracy possible, but our inclination to injustice makes democracy necessary.[7] Raúl Castro posed well the crisis in which serious Christians find themselves: how to be faithful while living in a system driven by an unregulated passion for maximizing profit for the few while demonizing the multitude of losers, intent on appealing, promoting, and legitimizing the worst side of our human nature. Central is the enticement that modern society fosters in each person to seek the American Dream, presented as universally accessible for each person willing to work hard enough to attain it. Thereby we are socialized to regard failure as the fault of the individual—when, in reality, the enormous resultant inequalities are structurally predetermined. Thus our intent in this chapter is to exhibit how this dynamic is diminishing the church as it is likewise undermining our society. In response, what we will be proposing is to distill a minimalist essence of belief capable of functioning as a base commitment for establishing a faithful core within each church, freed from obsession with success in order to function as a remnant prepared to outlast the demise of our society.

CORPORATE INCOME AND POVERTY

The statistics on wealth inequality vary slightly, depending on the source, but the overwhelming impact is clear. The richest 1 percent presently possess more than 20 percent of our nation's earned income,[8] the highest level since 1913 when the government instituted a federal income tax. Corporate profits in the United States rose 27 percent to $2.02 trillion in the third quarter of 2020. It was the sharpest increase in corporate profits since the first quarter of 2009, even though the economy was recovering from the coronavirus pandemic shock.[9]

Even though the economy is always changing, the overall trend can be illustrated in the New York Times 2018 report that "paychecks lag as profits

7. R. Niebuhr, Children of Light, 40.
8. Stebbins and Comen, "How Much Do You Need," para. 1.
9. "News Stream," in Trading Economics, "United States Corporate Profits," para. 3.

soar, and prices erode wage gains."[10] In the three years after the 2008 financial crisis, 95 percent of the economic gains went to the top 1 percent.[11] The 99 percent are making less than they did in 1989, and since 2000, the gain within the 1 percent has been fivefold. The top 1 percent has captured 49 percent of the new income generated since 2009.[12] The top one-tenth of the 1 percent now owns as much wealth as the bottom 90 percent. The Census Bureau reported that 34 million persons in 2019 lived in poverty.[13] The richest 400 Americans now have more wealth than the bottom 150 million persons combined. Over the past several decades, the top 1 percent of Americans have taken $50 trillion from the bottom 90 percent.[14]

On and on goes the data. During the last major financial crisis in 2008, huge Wall Street banks received more than $700 billion in financial aid from the Treasury Department and more than $16 trillion from the Federal Reserve, simply because they were "too big to fail." During this time, the 25 top hedge fund managers made enough to pay the salaries of 158,000 kindergarten teachers.[15] Glaring is the portraiture of CEOs who with arrogance purged of embarrassment boast of outlandish salaries. The amount of pay increase that the US Treasury approved in 2012 for executives at firms that received federal bailouts was $6,162,208.[16] In 2019, the biggest US corporations set records for CEO pay, surging to $21.3 million, growing from 1978 by 1,167 percent.[17] Presently the top 5 percent now control 67 percent of our nation's wealth.[18] Interestingly, more than a third of financial service professionals making more than half a million a year said that they have witnessed or have firsthand knowledge of wrongdoing in the workplace, and 23 percent suspected their colleagues of wrongdoing. Interestingly, a recent study identified CEOs as among the highest of occupations to attract psychopaths.[19]

Before the Reagan administration (1981), taxes were progressive, so that the greater the corporate assets, the larger the percentage of taxes to support the common good. In 2013, the oil industry alone made $93 billion

10. P. Cohen, "Paychecks Lag as Profits Soar," paras. 8–9.

11. Cronan, "Some 95 Percent," para. 4.

12. Sepeda-Miller, "Bernie Sanders Says 49 Percent," para. 4.

13. United States Census Bureau, "Income, Poverty," para. 3.

14. Hanauer and Rolf, "Top 1 Percent of Americans," para. 2.

15. Bump, "Twenty-Five Top Hedge Fund Managers," para. 5.

16. "Harper's Index" (2013), para. 38.

17. Mishel and Kandra, "CEO Compensation Surged," para. 1.

18. Ingraham, "Richest 1 Percent," para. 15.

19. Dutton, Wisdom of Psychopaths, 162.

in profits, yet its leaders lobbied for additional tax breaks.[20] It is typical that the largest corporations pay no federal income taxes for years past. In fact, in 2018, ninety-one companies in the Fortune 500 had an effective tax rate of zero or less, paying no federal taxes.[21] With the 2017 GOP tax reform package, the tax code became even more intentionally skewed in favor of corporations and the rich. According to the National Association for Business Economics, despite rosy predictions otherwise, 6 percent of the tax cut was used to increase hiring, and only 10 percent was used for investment in the business.[22] Individuals now pay income taxes up to 37 percent, which is 76 percent higher than the corporate rate.[23] This tax reform is working well only for the affluent, with the richest 1 percent reaping an average of $33,000 in tax breaks, while the poorest receive only $40.[24] The effective tax rate that American corporations actually pay averages 11.3 percent instead of the official 21 percent the bill enacted, which is far less than the repealed 35 percent rate.[25] US corporations have been so successful in reducing their tax rates to historic lows because they have such lobbying power that they are virtually writing themselves out of the tax code. In fact, there are so many loopholes in the present tax code that lawyers are able to render legal this totally irresponsible corporate situation. As a result, the wealthy who make $20 million on investments pay a lower tax rate than plumbers and teachers. In 2018, for the first time in our history, billionaires paid a lower tax rate than the working class.[26] Forty-one companies in the S&P 500 paid no taxes in the twelve months prior to July 19, 2020,[27] due to a combination of tax credits and aggressive accounting. In fact, in 2018, almost sixty companies in the S&P 500 had negative tax rates, obtaining rebates despite billions in profits, for example: Amazon—1 percent tax rate, John Deere—12 percent, Delta—4 percent, Eli Lily—9 percent, General Motors—2 percent, and Netflix—3 percent tax rate.[28]

With this loss of tax resources, the national debt is soaring. The debt is a record $27.9 trillion, with the budget deficit in fiscal 2021 projected to

20. Beans, "Despite $93 Billion in Profits," paras. 1–2.

21. Pound, "These Ninety-One Companies," para. 3.

22. Frazee, "Did Trump's Tax Cuts," para. 2.

23. Tax Policy Center, "Briefing Book: Key Elements," table 1.

24. Stein, "Richest Americans," para. 1.

25. Sherman, "Incredible Shrinking Corporate Tax Rate," para. 2.

26. Ingraham, "For First Time in History," para. 1.

27. Krantz, "Tax Free," para. 2.

28. Matthew Gardner et al., "Corporate Tax Avoidance," table 1.

be $2.3 trillion.[29] Although we are reaching a point of collapse in US cred-itworthiness, this escalation is relentless, for the socioeconomic dynamic demands it because of its built-in obsession with growth. The national debt is now larger than the size of the entire US economy, equaling 102 percent of the country's gross domestic product[30]—ever increasing as self-serving politicians feed upon the fear of its populace for justification, certain that the self-serving media will provide a positive spin.

The three wealthiest persons in the US (Jeff Bezos, Elon Musk, and Bill Gates) together are worth close to $500 billion.[31] The Center on Budget and Policy Priorities explains some of the tax breaks available to the wealthy but not to the typical taxpayer:

> Consider Jeff Bezos, the founder of Amazon. The company's filings with the Securities and Exchange Commission (SEC) show that he receives an annual salary of $81,840, which is subject to ordinary income taxes each year. As founder, howev-er, Bezos owns a significant share of Amazon stock. The value of Bezos's Amazon holdings grew by more than $100 billion over the last decade, making him the world's wealthiest person. This $100 billion in income is only taxed when—or if—Bezos decides to sell some of his stock. This ability to defer tax on one's primary source of income effectively makes the income tax largely voluntary for most of the income that people like Bezos receive, unlike for the salary income that middle-income people live on. Bezos sold Amazon shares worth roughly $6.3 billion between 2009 and 2018, according to SEC filings, but the tax code ignores the rest of his $100 billion gain. Thus, his tax bill on a decade of stock sales likely was about $1.5 billion, or less than 1.5 percent of his increase in wealth due to the appreciation of his Amazon stock.

> Wealthy owners of profitable corporations can choose to *never* sell their valuable stock and therefore avoid paying tax through-out their lives. If they need access to large amounts of cash, they have plenty of options besides selling their shares. Larry Ellison, CEO of Oracle and one of the world's richest people, pledged a portion of his Oracle stock as collateral for a $10 billion credit line. In other words, he can borrow up to $10 billion, and if he fails to repay the debt, the bank can seize his Oracle shares. This lets him obtain cash without selling his shares; thus, he avoids

29. J. Cox, "Deficit Projected at $2.3 Trillion," para. 1.
30. Heeb, "National Debt Set," para. 1.
31. Moskowitz, "Ten Richest People in World," para. 1.

paying taxes, and the stock can continue growing in value. Though he must pay interest on the debt and eventually pay back amounts borrowed, this is often a much cheaper strategy than selling stock and paying capital gains taxes, particularly when interest rates are low.[32]

A study of 25,000 major taxpayer subsidies over the last two decades indicates that the subsidies are going primarily to extremely wealthy, politically connected conservative conglomerates.[33] They, in turn, are the most powerful voices in pressuring the government to cut help for the poor, elderly, unemployed, and underemployed, in almost criminal fashion propagandizing the myth that the plight of the non-rich is their own lazy fault.

The intertwined dimensions of this structured inequality are making desperate the plight of the average American. In 2019, there were 34.0 million Americans living below the poverty level, which is 10.5 percent of the population.[34] By 2014, Americans at the poverty level spent 56 percent of their income on food and housing.[35] Prior to COVID-19, the number of children in poverty was at 14 percent, involving 10.5 million children.[36] Among American men, the top 1 percent in income will live fifteen years longer than the poorest 1 percent, and with women the wealth gap regarding longevity is ten years.[37] In a report on the well-being of households between 2018 and May 2019, the Federal Reserve found that if a person suddenly had to come up with $400, four in ten Americans would have difficulty covering such an expense.[38] This is living on the edge.

Race is a significant factor in this gross inequality, for, according to the Institute for Policy Studies, by 2050, the median White family will have $174,000 of wealth, while Latino median wealth will be $8,600 and Black median wealth will be $600. The median Black family is on track to reach zero wealth by 2082.[39] Research by the Federal Reserve Bank of St. Louis indicates that a middle-aged African American with a graduate degree has roughly the same odds of becoming a millionaire as a middle-aged White American who

---

32. Marr et al., "Substantial Income of Wealthy Households," paras. 17–18.

33. Sirota, "No, Really, You Didn't," para. 4.

34. Semega et al., "Income and Poverty," fig. 7.

35. Schanzenbach et al., "Where Does All Money Go," fig. 1.

36. Thomas and Fry, "Prior to COVID-19," para. 2.

37. Chetty et al., "Association between Income," para. 6.

38. "Dealing with Unexpected Expenses," in Board of Governors of Federal Reserve System, "Report on Economic Well-Being," para. 1.

39. Collins et al., "Dreams Deferred," 4.

has completed only high school.[40] The death rate for Black infants is twice that of infants born to non-Hispanic White mothers.[41] Before the coronavirus pandemic sent the US economy into a recession, child poverty was at 14 percent, the highest of any developed country; and among African American children, it was nearly twice that at 26 percent.[42]

According to the *National Geographic* (2014), one-sixth of all Americans do not have enough to eat.[43] In 2016, one million persons in twenty-two states lost their food aid (SNAP) because of stricter rules governing them.[44] Forty-two percent of children born to poor families will still be in poverty as adults[45]—a higher percent than in any other developed country. Understandably, then, the Stanford Center on Poverty and Inequality gives the US the grade of *poor* when compared with other nations,[46] expressing particular concern for our tattered safety net and the structural obstacles for escaping poverty. In 2018, the UN rated the US as worst among developed countries in regard to youth poverty, infant mortality, incarceration, income inequality, and obesity, estimating that forty million persons now live in poverty.[47] The Urban Institute (2019) found that one-fourth of the people in the US who are living in poverty receive no help from food stamps, nutritional programs, subsidized housing, cash benefits, or childcare assistance.[48] Yet one-third of these have an income of less than $13,000. On any given winter night in the United States, there are 567,715 homeless persons, one-fourth of whom are children.[49] One-third of these are living in unsheltered places such as parks, cars, under bridges, and in abandoned buildings. Of the total, 37,085 are veterans, and 219,911 are female. While 6 percent of the general population suffers from serious mental illness, 25 percent of the homeless do.[50] Unbelievably, there were 187 cities that in 2014 made homelessness some form of crime.[51]

40. Stilwell, "What Are Your Odds," para. 7.

41. Taylor et al., "Eliminating Racial Disparities," para. 1.

42. Thomas and Fry, "Prior to COVID-19," para. 2.

43. McMillan, "New Face of Hunger," para. 7.

44. Bolen et al., "More Than 500,000 Adults," para. 1.

45. Fass et al., "Child Poverty and Intergenerational Mobility," para. 2.

46. Stanford Center on Poverty and Inequality, "State of the Union," 7–8.

47. Alston, "Extreme Poverty in America," paras. 3, 7.

48. Jan, "Thirteen Million People in Poverty," para. 1.

49. "State of Homelessness 2020," para. 1.

50. "Two Hundred Fifty Thousand," para. 1.

51. Bauman et al., "Housing not Handcuffs," 9.

In the meantime, the wealthy have been successful in pressuring congress to cut $8 billion in food stamps—an allotment averaging only $4.50 a day, two-thirds of which benefits children, the elderly, and the disabled.[52] The coronavirus pandemic has left millions of families without stable employment. More than forty-two million people, including thirteen million children, may experience food insecurity,[53] which the US Dept. of Agriculture defines as a lack of access to "enough food for an active, healthy life."

Of the new income being created by our economy, 95 percent of it has been going to the top wealthy echelons, with 3,592,054 American households (2.8 percent of all households) in 2020 having crossed the threshold into this top echelon, measured by having over $5 million in assets.[54] And still the *Wall Street Journal* continues the mantra of the wealthy being "subjected to unfair hatred by the 99 percent," even using the theme of Holocaust to describe the plight to which the wealthy are being subjected.[55] Yet CareerBuilder reports that 78 percent of full-time US workers live paycheck to paycheck.[56] One of the harsh consequences of this condition is that, as seen in Missouri, exploitive payday loans have risen by 350 percent in 2018, charging an average rate of 452 percent, with the legal maximum rate being 1,950 percent.[57] There are presently more payday loan store fronts than McDonalds or Starbucks.[58] Estimates place at twelve million the number of Americans forced each year to borrow with payday loans to tide them over until the next paycheck, while many of those who don't borrow, refrain out of fear that creditors and/or the IRS will electronically empty any meager savings that they might have. In order to maintain their accustomed consumer level, an increasing number of persons are being forced into debt, with household debt in 2019 topping a record $14 trillion—$9.6 trillion in mortgages, $1.5 trillion in student liability, and credit card debt increasing by $46 billion.[59] Beginning a decade ago, as wages stagnated and inflation eroded purchasing power, credit cards made their ubiquitous appearance. According to the Federal Reserve, credit card debt in the US hit a record high of $1.1 trillion in February 2020.[60] Corporations have aggressively distributed credit cards,

52. Peterson, "How New Farm Bill," para. 1

53. Feeding America, "Facts about Poverty," para. 1.

54. "How Many Millionaires," para. 5.

55. T. Perkins, "Progressive Kristallnacht Coming," para. 1.

56. Z. Friedman, "Seventy-Eight Percent of Workers," para. 1.

57. Kite, "James Takes On," paras. 1–2.

58. J. Bennett, "Fast Cash and Payday Loans," para. 2.

59. Marte, "U.S. Household Debt," paras. 1–4.

60. Luthi, "Credit Card Debt Continues," para. 1.

with even high school students being lured with cards, so that, from an early age, millions are becoming trapped by debt, many of whom are unable to pay even the interest, let alone any of the principal. A 2018 NBC News survey indicated that three out of four millennials in the US are in debt of some kind; a quarter of persons eighteen to thirty-four years old are more than $30,000 in debt; and 11 percent owe more than $100,000.[61] Relatedly, the big four banks (J. Morgan Chase, Citigroup, Wells Fargo, and Bank of America) made an astonishing $11 billion in overdraft fees in 2019.[62] Consequently, nearly three-quarters of Americans die in debt, each leaving an average outstanding balance of $61,554—credit card debt being the highest single item, with an average unpaid balance of $4,531.[63]

Susan George, in her *Shadow Sovereigns: How Global Corporations Are Seizing Power*, describes graphically how big banks, large insurance companies, and asset management firms have formed an interdependent network of global financial and corporate global control. Her conclusion is that they have so taken over the American economy, supplanting even manufacturing, that when they went down during the recent depression, they took with them 105 of the country's largest domestic products. At the nineteenth annual climate talks in Warsaw (2013), corporate lobbyists flooded the gathering, and, for the first time, the event had corporate sponsorship.[64] Domestically, more than 30,000 lobbyists and professional interest counselors are presently employed in various dimensions of the US government so as to ensure increased corporate deregulation and control. There are presently eleven lobbyists for every member of Congress whose express task is that of reducing corporate tax legislation.[65] We have reached the point where transnational corporations have the power to significantly determine public policy, writing favorable bills and bartering votes for their passage.

Economic theorists are drawing dire conclusions concerning the vast inequality that is resulting from this powerfully engineered corporate control of both society and government, in which the common good has succumbed to the self-interest of the wealthy. Thomas Piketty, in his *Capital in the Twenty-First Century,* declares that this relentless dynamic that is propelling such inequality is fated to "continue to soar"—until the whole cannot hold, folding back destructively upon its parts. The church must grasp the full human consequences resulting from this dynamic. Not to do

61. Arenge et al., "Poll: Majority of Millennials," paras. 1–3.

62. Ziv, "Banks Reaped $11 Billion," paras. 1–2.

63. Digangi, "Americans Are Dying," paras. 1, 4.

64. Goodman with Moynihan, "Corporate Lobbyists Flood," para. 3.

65. M. Wilson, "Analysis," para. 3.

so means for Christians a loss of soul, in which obsession with ecclesiastical survival entangles the church even more deeply as a supportive participant in this moral/spiritual crisis. How tragic if, as one pundit concludes, the only possibility for significant change is the quite unlikely one, that the rich suddenly get a conscience.

THE MIDDLE CLASS

The middle class has previously been the stable center of American society and of the church. Yet corporate control is vaporizing the middle class, bequeathing to the US the highest level of economic inequality of any developed country, with the gap increasing. Consequently, our cities are in crisis, bewildered as how to meet basic human needs.

Significant are recent disclosures about the underbelly of Amazon's rapid growth, heralded as a miracle in capitalistic success.[66] It operates on what is called "purposeful Darwinism," a severe version of the cult of efficiency. For its white-collar workers, the expected work week is an efficient eighty-four hours, with no excuse for poor performance. As a result, attrition is high and the breakdown of employees frequent, placing machinelike efficiency before the needs of its employees. Yet, it is reported, this unhealthy atmosphere is actually good in comparison with blue-collar workers who in the warehouses endure "bad working conditions, pay, and prestige." Yet such circumstances are not unique to Amazon, for they tend to characterize the modern workplace—that is, long hours, escalating stress, and no extra pay for overtime. In many factories, "robot overlords" of artificial intelligence log how long it takes each worker to do particular tasks, automatically firing those who do not perform at maximum rate. The real problem, concludes Louis Hyman of the *Los Angeles Times*, is that "for decades, in ever more insidious ways, employers have made workers disposable."[67] Fifty-six percent of US workers over fifty have lost long-time jobs before they were prepared to retire. According to Brigid Schulte of the *Washington Post*, 70 percent of those receiving public assistance in order to survive are employed.[68]

The result of this fragility of the middle class is that the US now has the highest level of inequality of any developed country, with the gap increasing.[69] Partly responsible is the tsunami of economic and cultural globalism that during the past twenty-five years has swamped the working class, taking

66. Kantor and Streitfeld, "Inside Amazon," para. 4.

67. Hyman, "Opinion," para. 1.

68. Schulte, "Trump's New Rule," para. 5.

69. Disilver, "Global Inequality," para. 1.

away jobs and dignity. Since 1979, the US has lost seven million manufac-turing jobs,[70] in part due to outsourcing to China and Mexico through trade agreements. For example, in 2016, Nabisco's Chicago bakery of iconic Oreo cookies shut down the Oreo line of products, laying off half of the workers and moving some of its production to Salinas, Mexico.[71]

The middle class is sliding toward third-world status. In her *Squeezed: Why Our Families Can't Afford America*, Alissa Quart identifies the rea-son as being that the deck is stacked. In the past twenty years, middle-class incomes have stagnated, while the cost of middle-class living has increased 30 percent. Indicatively, at least ten million Americans have lost their homes in foreclosure since 2008.[72] Statistics released in 2018 predict that 40 percent of middle-class persons will face poverty by the time they reach the age of sixty-five.[73] With decreased money available to spend in America's consumer-driven economy, the vicious cycle will force greater strictures for efficiency.

We are an economically frightened country. As previously mentioned, four out of ten Americans live from paycheck to paycheck.[74] A study by the Institute for Policy Studies discloses that 58 percent of Americans have less than $1,000 in their savings and checking accounts combined,[75] and 25 percent of renters spend more than half of their monthly income on rent.[76] Further, significant under-employment is becoming a permanent feature of our economic system. With corporate taxes being radically di-minished and the national debt rising at a reckless rate, social welfare ex-penditures are being severely threatened. In President Trump's proposed 2020 budget, while privileges for the wealthy increased, Medicaid was slashed by $1.5 trillion, Medicare by $845 billion, and Social Security by $25 billion. Fear was increased.

Furthermore, polling of the full-time employed discloses the alarming degree to which workers are weary, overworked, depressed, and burned out. While employee productivity has increased 21.6 percent between 2000 and 2014, wages have increased only 1.8 percent.[77] Almost gone is the once-normal 9 to 5 work hours, for with such technology as smart phones and

70. Harris, "Forty Years of Falling Manufacturing," para. 1.
71. Trotter, "End of an Era," para. 2.
72. Shalby, "Financial Crisis Hit," para. 2.
73. Menard, "Almost Half of Middle-Class Americans," para. 2.
74. Mullen, "Four in Ten Workers," para. 2.
75. Reich, "Jaw-Dropping Realities," para. 1.
76. Passy, "Rent Is Too Damn High," para. 2.
77. Bivens and Mishel, "Understanding the Historic Divergence," para. 7.

email, employees are expected to be available around the clock. Due to heavy workloads, more than half of employees are having to leave vacation time unused. Burnout is responsible for at least half of employee attrition.[78] Add to this the pressure of a growing number of persons who need more than one job in order to survive. A RAND study indicates a vicious cycle involved in this milieu—that Americans who simply cannot afford to do so, are nevertheless spending $150 billion a year on illegal drugs, such as heroin, methamphetamines, cocaine, and marijuana.[79] Four point five percent of American employees tested positive for one or more destructive drugs in 2019, an all-time high.[80] The rate of alcohol consumption has grown even more, with 12.7 percent of Americans being alcoholic.[81] In 2018, more than 155,000 Americans died from alcohol-related causes and drug-induced fatalities (67,367)—the highest ever. A record number of 70,980 Americans died of overdosing in 2019, an increase of 4.6 percent over the previous year.[82] An alarming reaction to this depression is the deadly opioids drug epidemic, begun with aggressive pharmaceutical marketing that intentionally lied to doctors that it would become a problem for only 1 percent of users. More than 191 million opioid prescriptions were dispensed to American patients in 2017, with wide variation across states.[83] In 2016, more than 11.5 million Americans reported misusing prescription opioids in the past year.[84] The overdose rate since 1999 is up, and the death toll (70,980) is far greater than even American fatalities in the Vietnam War, making drug overdose the leading cause of death for persons under fifty. The downward trend in life expectancy within the poor and middle classes has drugs and suicide as primary factors. The conclusion drawn by Mona Charen of *Truthout* is that "we're facing not so much a drug problem as a heartbreak problem."[85] With it, "for a great swath of our population, the family structure has broken down amid rampant divorce, children are being raised out of wedlock, and young men are unable to find jobs that support a family." Even the conservative *National Review* is forced to portray this crisis as an anomaly—that even though the US is one of the richest

78. Montanez, "Burnout Is Sabotaging," para. 1.

79. Midgette et al, "What America's Users Spend," para. 3.

80. Steele, "Positive Drug Tests," para. 2.

81. Ingraham, "One in Eight American Adults," para. 1.

82. "Fatal Drug Overdoses," para. 4.

83. Centers for Disease Control and Prevention, "Prescription Opiods," para. 2.

84. Centers for Disease Control and Prevention, "About CDC's Opioid Prescribing," para. 3.

85. Charen, "Why Are Americans So Sad," para. 11.

and most powerful nations on earth, it is the one most "wracked with grief and despair."[86] Deborah Hasin's research suggests the likely cause for this tragic situation being the increasing number of persons who "feel pessimistic about their economic chances," and thus with drugs attempt to kill the pain.[87] According to a 2018 Gallup poll, only 34 percent of Americans feel engaged or inspired at work, while 53 percent say they have "checked out" at work, and 13 percent say they are actively disengaged.[88] A 2019 poll found Americans the most stressed-out people in the world, with 55 percent indicating having experienced "a lot of stress" the day before. In contrast, the global average was 35 percent.[89]

While the present is bleak for many, the future is even bleaker. Nearly half of the Silicon Valley technology experts interviewed by the Pew Research Center had a dystopian view of the future, especially indicating how robots will eliminate many present blue- and white-collar jobs, with no new sources of employment replacing them. The predicted future is one of "widespread unemployment, deepening inequality, and the likelihood of violent uprisings."[90] A study by researchers at the University of Oxford estimates that 47 percent of US jobs are at risk of automation, and that the largest impact will be on retail salespersons, with a 92 percent chance that their jobs will be automated over the next twenty years.[91] According to a study by Citigroup, up to 30 percent of employees in the US banking industry are likely to lose their jobs to new technologies over the next ten years.[92] Using Nobel Prize winner Arthur Lewis's model for appraising developing nations, economist Peter Temin concludes that, based on the degree of inequality, the US has regressed to the status of a "developing nation."[93] Illustratively, household debt in the US now stands at $14.35 trillion, with over 60 percent of households worried about finances.[94]

An Associated Press survey in 2013 indicates that four out of five US adults are struggling with joblessness, are near the poverty level, or have been reliant on welfare for at least part of their lives.[95] In chairing a panel

86. French, "Make America Live Again," para. 20.

87. Aubrey, "With Heavy Drinking," para. 6.

88. Harter, "Employee Engagement on Rise," paras. 1–3.

89. Ray, "Americans' Stress, Worry," paras. 1–2.

90. A. Smith and Anderson, "AI, Robotics, and Future," para. 4.

91. Osbourne and Frey, "Automation and Future," para. 1.

92. Egan, "Thirty Percent of Bank Jobs," para. 3.

93. Farand, "US Has Regressed," para. 1.

94. Albright, "Average American Household Debt," fig. 1.

95. Yen, "Exclusive: Four in Five," para. 1.

with African American leaders in 2015, President Obama declared that the "ladders of opportunity" once promised to Blacks are being dismantled, and now it is happening for poor Whites as well. His conclusion: "It's hard being poor. It's time-consuming. It's stressful."[96] The new jobs that have emerged since the last recession are those paying on average 25 percent less than those they have replaced, coupled with stagnant wages and vanishing mid-level jobs. A study by Princeton and Harvard economists determined that 94 percent of the ten million net new jobs created between 2005 and 2015 were either temporary or contract-based, not traditional 9 to 5 positions.[97] Researchers at the University of California at Berkeley found that even among families with frontline US manufacturing jobs, one-third needed help from government safety-net programs such as food stamps and Medicaid.[98] The majority of low-wage workers earn so little that they must rely on public assistance program to make ends meet. Eleven million or 14 percent of children in the US live in poverty.[99] Twenty-two thousand babies died in 2017 before their first birthday, with Black babies dying at double the rate of White, Asian, or Hispanic babies.[100] A 2019 Gallup poll shows that thirty-four million Americans had a family member or friend die in the past five years because they could not afford medical treatment, and 23 percent (58 million) indicated inability during the past year to pay for medication that their doctor deemed necessary.[101]

Employee pay in the US is now down to the smallest share of the economy since the government began collecting wage and salary data sixty years ago, while corporate profits constitute the largest share of the economy since then.[102] With the median living wage for households being $67,690 in 2021,[103] just about 50 percent of American households fall beneath this level.[104] Public school unpaid meal debts have reached $10 million.[105] A 2019 study by Kaiser Health News predicts that, in ten years, over half of middle-class Americans over seventy-five years of age will not be able to afford rent even for assisted living or pay their medical

96. Grossman, "Obama: Defeating Poverty," para. 2.

97. Ceniza-Levine, "Ninety-Four Percent of New Jobs," para. 1.

98. Jacobs et al., "Producing Poverty," 3, 9.

99. Haider, "Basic Facts about Children," para. 1.

100. Lakhani, "America Has Infant Mortality Crisis," para. 3.

101. Witters, "Millions in U.S. Lost Someone," paras. 1, 3.

102. P. Cohen, "Paychecks Lag as Profits Soar," para. 1.

103. Borden and Davis, "How Much Money You Need," para. 6.

104. Congressional Research Service, "U.S. Income Distribution," 11.

105. Forde, "Other Student Debt," para. 1.

expenses.[106] Meanwhile, in the last decade, the wealthiest four hundred Americans have doubled their financial worth.[107]

A 2019 report by Michael Hout quantifies what many millennials have been experiencing for years—that it is increasingly difficult for young people "to climb the economic ladder and achieve more than their parents."[108] Those in the bottom 50 percent make an average of just $16,000 a year, while the wealthy top 1 percent average $1.3 million, giving their children enormous economic advantage, one that is widening every year.[109] David Leonhardt in the *New York Times* declares that "for Americans under the age of forty, the twenty-first century has resembled one long recession."[110] Since 2000, Leonhardt says that, the median net worth has plummeted for every age group under fifty-five. In contrast, the Walton family of Walmart fame now owns more wealth at $247 billion than the bottom 40 percent of Americans,[111] growing in 2019 at $4 million every hour, while Walmart sales soared to $514 billion[112]—and yet Walmart only recently agreed to raise wages for some workers, while maintaining an $11 starting wage.[113] In capitalist circles, they are celebrated as the model of free market success.

As wealth and income rise to the top, not only does greed swell but so does political power. The Republican response to the pressure of the wealthy is to reduce taxes even further for the rich, defund programs for the poor, fight unions and collective bargaining, pressure for the median wage to continue dropping, oppose a minimum wage, and fight any limits to campaign contributions and spending. They propagandize widely the image of the poor being shiftlessly lazy, refusing to work—while the truth is that there are twelve unemployed persons for every ten job openings,[114] while high-paying middle-class jobs are being outsourced through free trade agreements. Robert Reich, former US secretary of labor and now professor at Berkeley, indicates the result as being "an increasingly lopsided economy, more entrenched wealth, further deterioration in the quality of living for many, and an increasingly corrupt democracy."[115]

106. Knight, "In Ten Years," para. 1.
107. Zeballos-Roig, "Staggering Amount of Wealth," para. 1.
108. Hout, "Social Mobility," 31.
109. Long, "U.S. Inequality," paras. 2–3.
110. Leonhardt, "Fleecing of Millennials," paras. 1, 4.
111. "Number One Walton Family."
112. Pesce, "Walton Family," paras. 1, 4.
113. Kay, "Walmart CEO Says," para. 1.
114. Gould, "Job Openings Surged," para. 2.
115. Reich, "Labor Day and Election," paras. 9–10.

All of this data not only documents the harshly deteriorating economic condition of the middle class but discloses as well in this class a deepening corrosion of lifestyle. Christianity insists that humans are deeply social creatures, bound together in mutual commitment to the common good. But in radical contrast, our postmodern society is shaping a society in which individualism is the defining human posture, casting persons out on their own to survive in Darwinian competition, dissolving social connectedness. Forced to function as a conglomerate of singulars, we volunteer less, entertain less, marry less, and have fewer close friends and fewer children. The Census Bureau in 2018 illustrated the degree to which the life of Americans is increasing solo. Twenty-eight percent of all US households are composed of a single person, the highest level in our history.[116] Fifty-three percent of the time we eat breakfast by ourselves and eat lunch alone 45 percent of the time.[117] According to health insurer Cigne, loneliness has reached an epidemic level, ranking in the US alongside smoking and obesity as major threats to public health.[118] It was reported that 44 percent of those interviewed indicated that their relationships with other persons are not meaningful, and 27 percent confessed that they feel that no one knows them well. Generation Z (ages eighteen to twenty-two) were the loneliest of the group.[119] Since loneliness increases with aging, this is an ominous finding. Social media is not providing much help, with editors of this survey summarizing the feelings they found: "Ten thousand Facebook 'friends' cannot equal one live person." Their prediction was that, by 2020, depression will be the second most prevalent medical condition in the world. A 2019 study warned of "troubling generational health patterns for millennials," involving depression, hyperactivity, and type 2 diabetes, pointing towards a higher mortality rate than the preceding generation.[120] All of this was true even before the radical isolation caused by the coronavirus.

Relatedly, in his 1979 best seller *The Culture of Narcissism: American Life in an Age of Diminishing Expectations* (1991) and in his *Minimal Self* (1985), Christopher Lasche identified narcissism as the primary psychic malformation that capitalism afflicts on its citizens. It establishes a culture of competitive individualism, in which the pursuit of happiness is pushed to the dead end of self-preoccupation. As a result, Christian Smith in his *Souls in Transition* (2009) identified our present generation as one that has difficulty finding

116. "U.S. Census Bureau Releases," para. 5.
117. Ferdman, "Most American Thing," paras. 5–6.
118. Tate, "Loneliness Rivals Obesity," para. 4.
119. Polack, "New Cigna Study," para. 3.
120. R. Miller, "Millennials Are Less Healthy," paras. 4–5.

any objective reality beyond itself—submerged in fluidly constructed private networks of technologically managed intimates and associates.

Thus technology is turning out to be an amplifier of humanity's worst traits. According to 2015 research that analyzed multiple studies of the online phenomenon,[121] researchers found that a median of 23 percent of teens report being targeted. There were consistent associations between exposure to cyberbullying and increased likelihood of depression. Researchers believe that the more persons are involved in media interaction, the angrier people become.[122] Instead of creating the predicted global community of peace, love, and understanding, the US and the Western world are splitting into angry factions spewing vitriol and insult. The more one's internet contact, the more irritated one is inclined to be, avalanched by contrasting ideas, habits, and attitudes, in a faceless interaction inviting anti-social sadists to inflict psychic pain. Relevantly, an AAA Foundation study discovered that four out of five US drivers experienced road rage at least once in the past year, with 90 percent feeling threatened by such aggression.[123] Half of this belligerence occurred as hollering at other drivers, tailgating them, cutting them off, keeping them from changing lanes, or honking at them in fury. Eight million drivers have gone so far as intentionally to ram other cars, even leaving their own car to threaten the other driver. Fifty-six percent of fatal car accidents, killing an average of 40,000 Americans yearly, involved such aggressive driving.[124]

While one might expect despondency to be greatest among the aging population, actually it is the eighteen to twenty-two-year-old age group that rates highest in this sense of loneliness. Even so, the Centers for Disease Control and Prevention identify that among thirty-five to thirty-nine-year-olds the suicide rate rose more slowly than for any other age group.[125] From 2006 to 2014, the suicide rate in virtually all age groups has increased 2 percent annually.[126] In 2015, it hit a thirty-year high, surging 24 percent in the last fifteen years.[127] In 2018, 48,344 Americans committed suicide, with 1.4 million more attempting it.[128] Among veterans who have fought to defend our way of life, because of that way of life, eighteen

121. Pappas, "Social Media Cyber Bullying," paras. 1, 6.
122. Moskalenko, "Why Social Media," para. 1.
123. Gross, "Nearly 80 Percent of Drivers," paras. 1–3.
124. Insurance Information Institute, "Facts Plus Statistics," para. 1.
125. Centers for Disease Control and Prevention, "Suicide among Adults," table 1.
126. S. Curtin et al., "Increase in Suicide," para. 2.
127. Tavernise, "U.S. Suicide Rate Surges," para. 2.
128. "Suicide," table 2, fig. 8.

of them commit suicide daily, 1.5 times more than civilians of that age bracket.[129] More Veterans have killed themselves than have died in the wars in Iraq and Afghanistan combined.[130] Suicides among our active troops have surged to a record high.[131]

Researchers are not surprised that the dramatic rise in US suicides likewise correlates strongly with economic conditions.[132] Even among the adequately employed, this fracturing of well-being is occurring, with a recent poll indicating that 46 percent of Americans are deeply worried about losing their jobs.[133] Such economic troubles cultivate social isolation, which in turn causes family breakdown.

Finances are not the only basic cause for depression. As David Graeber portrays in his *Bullshit Jobs: A Theory*, a large share of today's workers regard themselves as engaged in performing pointless tasks. Thus, what is increasingly being raised even within our work force is the haunting human question: "What difference does my life make?"

Snopes, a fact check website devoted to debunking fake news, has identified how this confusion is being reinforced by the alarming degree to which our society is being impacted by such media as Facebook. Doctored photos, conspiracy theories, phony stories by propagandists and pranksters—these have led journalist Michael Tomasky to opine that with "another five or ten years of this, we will have a class of millions of citizens who get 'news' only from fake sources."[134] Furthermore, in 2021, Reporters without Borders ranked the US as forty-first out of 180 countries in press freedom.[135] What then is one to think?

On and on goes this plummeting from multiple sides that is diminishing the middle class. Our power brokers are dismantling public schools in poor and middle-class neighborhoods, blocking health care for all, destroying our environment for immediate profit, sickening our food, and endangering our water—certain that the manipulated media will cover up their irresponsibilities. Exhaustive research by the Environmental Working Group concludes that Americans have up to 420 carcinogenic chemicals in our bodies.[136] To prevent all regulations, the pharmaceutical industry spends

129. Shane, "Suicide Rate among Veterans," para. 3.
130. Beynon, "After Years of Failure," para. 11.
131. Vanden Brook, "Suicide Rate," para. 1.
132. Collins and Cox, "Bad Economic News Increases," para. 1.
133. Jaimungal, "Most Young Americans," para. 3.
134. Tomasky, "At Snopes," para. 12.
135. "World Press Freedom Index," para. 1.
136. Environmental Working Group, "Pollution in People," para. 3.

far more on public marketing, physician advertising, and congressional lobbying than it does on research and development[137]—thereby being able to establish enormous markups. Catalyst Pharmaceuticals is now charging $375,000 annually for a medication that for years had been available to patients for free.[138] The new drug for Hepatitis C costs $1,000 per pill, demanding $84,000 for the full treatment.[139] In 2016, US doctors and hospitals were awarded $8.18 billion by drug and medical device companies.[140] The largest health insurance companies saw $913 billion in revenue in 2019,[141] greater than the profits of even the biggest tech companies.

Naomi Klein, in her *Shock Doctrine: The Rise of Disaster Capitalism*, documents the depth and breadth of this sweeping capitalist complex that Christians are facing—extending from the privatization that is rendering public institutions vehicles of profit, to the economic management of nations that is effecting regime change when a country defies our corporate interests. This dynamic, coupled with multinational corporation tax-evasion, is forcing a tax burden on the middle class, increasing personal expenditures for normal services, escalating our enormous national debt that benefits the wealthy, and minimizing any safety net for the growing number of the working poor. Battered and diminishing is the middle class, that huge segment of our population that once constituted the stable base in which the church was comfortably anchored.

THE AMERICAN DREAM

The American Dream has been operative in some form almost from the beginning of this country. While functioning as an incentive for different persons in different ways, basically it is the belief that this nation uniquely nourishes hope for everyone that if they work hard enough, anything is possible. It is significant, then, that a 2020 poll indicates that only 54 percent of US adults think the American Dream is attainable for them.[142] For the first time in our history, the present generation is doing worse than their parents. In fact, Robert Putnam, in *Our Kids: The American Dream in Crisis*, declares that the American Dream has become a lie. No longer does success depend on how hard one works but is increasingly determined by where one is born

137. Swanson, "Big Pharmaceutical Companies," para. 3.

138. Daugherty, "Sanders Asks Why," paras. 1–2.

139. Gokhale, "Same Pill," para. 5.

140. Silvestrini, "Drug and Device Companies," para. 1.

141. Payne, "Top Health Insurers' Revenues," para. 1.

142. Ballard, "In 2020," para. 3.

and to whom. Thus, for example, it is now eight times more likely that a child born into a wealthy American family will earn a college degree than a child from a low-income family.[143] Class is now the primary determinate of a person's chance for success—with student loans for the non-rich topping $1.7 trillion as of February 2021, with $122.2 billion in default.[144] Today's young Americans, compared with their counterparts a generation ago, are less educated, less prosperous, less likely to own a home, less politically potent, and less socially and economically mobile. Putnam's conclusion is that we are becoming "two Americas"—one in which prosperity is all but guaranteed by birth and the second in which even hard work and talent are not enough to overcome the odds.

Mark Karlin of *Truthout* draws the implications, that the American Dream has become "nothing more than an advertising slogan to sustain the oligarchy and elect opportunistic politicians."[145] This appraisal is documented in Noam Chomsky's documentary film *Requiem for the American Dream,*[146] illustrating as intractable the inequalities endemic to our present socioeconomic society. The wealthy tend to ridicule pundits who are critical of this enormous inequality, accusing them of fostering class conflict. But billionaire Warren Buffett honestly and smilingly confesses, "Actually it is class warfare. And it's my class, the rich class, that is making war, and we're winning."[147] His billionaire investor son, in being interviewed about the conflict between capitalism and humanism, draws the bottom line: "You can't have both."[148]

Even conservative economist Robert Samuelson, in the *Washington Post,* is forced to conclude that this vaporizing of the American Dream is "killing us." As he sees it, the rising death rate for American White persons is resulting in a self-inflicted "death by despair."[149] American culture is forging its citizens to define meaning in terms of achieving economic success, promising that the reward will be a deep sense of accomplishment, self-worth, and well-being. What happens, then, when this striving falters and fails, when individuals find that, for them, the American Dream is unattainable? We are programmed to regard such failure not as the injustice of a society with its intentionally structured inequality, but as a judgment

143. Luhby, "Rich Are Eight Times Likelier," para. 1.

144. Z. Friedman, "Student Loan Debt Statistics," paras. 1, 5.

145. Karlin, "It's Time to Call," para. 7.

146. Hutchinson et al., dirs., *Requiem for American Dream.*

147. B. Stein, "In Class Warfare," para. 6.

148. Flanders, "Peter Buffett: Big Philanthropy," para. 1.

149. Samuelson, "Is American Dream Killing Us?" para. 5.

upon the individual as the consequence of his/her own inadequacies, incompetencies, and basic unworth. Thus, tragically, a growing number of Americans are "becoming hostage to unrealizable hopes," thereby becoming severely bruised and wearied to the edge of pointlessness. It is telling that over the past eight years, even before the pandemic hit in 2020, Google search numbers for *anxiety* have been steadily increasing,[150] and, since then, they have skyrocketed.

Urgent then is the need for the church to understand how her own diminishment interrelates with our socioeconomic system that favors an oligarchy of wealth, strategically managed by a plutocracy that controls not only the basic decisions defining society's agencies but manipulates our mindset so as to guarantee public support for a way of life that is no longer providing us with meaning. What Christianity has to offer is diametrically opposed to the life that is being forced upon us by this structured inequality, both as means and as end. We are at the point where spiritual metanoia dare no longer be divorced from societal metanoia. They are integrally related, both as means and end. Yet Christianity is becoming so intertwined with this collapsing American Dream that it is increasingly difficult to disentangle the heart of the gospel from its phantasm. "The poor tell us who we are," says Phillip Berrigan, "and the prophets tell us who we could be."[151] And I would add, the rich tell us who we have become—as when JPMorgan Chase executive Jamie Dimon declares that any tax on the wealth of the wealthy "vilifies successful people."[152]

GLOBAL POVERTY, DISEASE, AND UNEMPLOYMENT

In 2013, Alex Berezow in the *Week* identified poverty as the number one threat to humanity.[153] "Food Not Bombs" is our menace. Over 600 million persons globally go hungry daily,[154] while the US consumer expectation of unblemished produce results in half of the vegetables and fruits produced being thrown away.[155] Around 770 million (13 percent) persons in the world do not have access to electricity.[156]

150. Kecmanovic, "Could Our Efforts to Avoid," para. 2.
151. Dear, "School of Prophets," para. 6.
152. D. Strauss, "JPMorgan Chief Jamie Dimon," para. 2.
153. *Week* Staff, "Biggest Threats to Humanity," para. 1.
154. Reid, "Five World Hunger Facts," para. 1.
155. Goldenberg, "Half of All US Food," para. 1.
156. "SDG7: Data and Projections," para. 1.

Widespread infectious diseases are becoming increasingly resistant to multi-drug-resistant bacteria. In 2015, calculated predictions concluded that unless unlikely drastic actions are taken to curb this excessive use of drugs, antibiotic-resistant bacteria will become a bigger killer than cancer, killing over ten million persons yearly.[157] Superbugs are already killing over 700,000 persons a year. As researcher Jim O'Neill insists, "If we don't solve this problem, we are heading toward the dark ages." As if this predicted tragedy were not threat enough, DARPA (the Pentagon weapons research agency) is a major investor in gene-driven explorations, in which insects are engineered to spread untreatable diseases, and seeds are being designed for sowing in enemy countries so as to suppress or destroy food crops through release of a single engineered organism.[158]

Furthermore, the global marketplace has so changed that reliable economic forecasts indicate that there will never be nearly enough jobs for the world's rising unchecked population. Having a reserved unemployed labor force as buffer against employee demands has always been a systemic ingredient endemic to capitalism. The World Bank sees this job unavailability as being so severe that with more than one billion young people entering the global labor market during the 2015–2025 decade, only 40 percent will be able to find employment among jobs that currently exist.[159] Adding the corporate enthusiasm for robots and new forms of cost-saving automation, this relentless unemployment spells inevitable calamity.

ENVIRONMENT AND CLIMATE CHANGE

One of the most frightening aspects of this escalating global corporate control is its repercussions on the environment, especially evidenced in climate change. Al Gore has been prophetic in insisting that "now, more than ever before, we are reaping the consequences of our recklessness."[160] He cites as evidence Superstorm Sandy that crippled New York City and large areas of New Jersey, the drought that periodically is parching more than half of our nation, the flooding that has inundated large swaths of Australia, and the rising seas that are threatening catastrophe for millions around the world. An international team of scientists recently published a study arguing that we are at the end of the Holocene epoch that began some 12,000 years ago,

157. "Global Antibiotics 'Revolution' Needed," paras. 3, 5–6.
158. Kupferschmidt, "Crop-Protecting Insects," para. 1.
159. "Addressing Youth Employment Crisis," para. 1.
160. Gore, "Four Hundred PPM," para. 2.

with our planet tipping into a new age they call Anthropocene.[161] This means that, with human infrastructure now covering half of the earth's surface, we have become our own geological agent—poisoning our ecosystem, as with things like plastic, aluminum, concrete, fertilizers, radioactivity, fossil fuels, and water diversion by dams. In 2019, one-fourth of the world's population was already under "extreme water stress;" by 2025, half of the world's population will be living in water-stressed regions.[162]

According to the National Oceanic and Atmospheric Administration (NOAA), in January 2020, the temperatures on Earth and in the Northern Hemisphere had become the highest in recorded history, probably since human life began.[163] Carbon pollution is reaching historic highs, with carbon dioxide in the atmosphere having passed the milestone level of 417.1 parts per million, with the NOAA reporting this as the highest month ever recorded.[164] It is the richest 10 percent of the world's population who is responsible for producing half of these record deadly emissions.[165] Carbon emissions from fossil fuels alone have set a record of 36.8 billion tons in 2019.[166] A UN study disclosed that 90 percent of the world's population now lives in areas of dangerous levels of air pollution, resulting in seven million deaths annually—making it one of the leading causes of disease and death.[167] More than 90 percent of the world's two billion children breathe air so toxic that their health is at serious risk, resulting in the death of 600,000 children yearly. As a result, the UN declared climate change to be a global health emergency, birthing not only disorders from the heat and cold themselves but exacerbating issues such as mosquito-borne disease, food and water-borne illness, respiratory and allergic disorders, malnutrition and starvation, and crises in mental health. Furthermore, research indicates that the rate of this climate change may so outpace the ability of key staple crops like rice, corn, and wheat to adapt that the result will be widespread famine.[168]

A crucial component in this ecological demise is described in an emergency edition of the World Wildlife Fund's (WWF) *Living Blue Planet Report*, reporting a 49 percent decline in marine vertebrate populations between

161. Carrington, "Anthropocene Epoch," paras. 1, 15.

162. Davidson, "Water Stress Could Affect," para. 1.

163. "January 2020 Was Earth's Hottest," para. 1.

164. "Rise of Carbon Dioxide," para. 1.

165. "Carbon Emissions of Richest," para. 3.

166. Mooney and Dennis, "Global Greenhouse Gas Emissions," para. 2.

167. "Nine out of Ten," para. 1.

168. Physicians for Social Responsibility, "Climate Change and Famine," 1, 4.

1970 and 2012, with numerous fish species being 75 percent wiped out.[169] With billions of people reliant on fish for their main source of protein, this dynamic toward lifeless oceans will be tragic. The crisis is likewise occurring as well with animals as seen in another report by the WWF indicating that the global wildlife population has plummeted by 68 percent between 1970 and 2016.[170] Furthermore, up to one million plant and animal species are facing extinction due to human influence,[171] immersed in an epoch in which 75 percent of all species will likely vanish.[172] A massive extinction of essential insect species is likewise happening.[173] Every six seconds, a football-field size of irreplaceable rain forest is being destroyed,[174] with fires intentionally ravishing the rain forests of Brazil. Already, there are 500 percent more pieces of plastic in the oceans than there are stars in the Milky Way; by 2050, there will likely be more pieces of plastic than fish in the seas.[175] In New York State alone, the plastic bags discarded each year would be enough, if tied together, to stretch to the moon and back thirteeen times.[176] Yearly, up to thirteen million metric tons of plastic waste are dumped into the oceans, this rate predicted to double by 2025. The result is the killing of wildlife, ravaging of coral reefs, and contamination of our entire food chain. Half of the Great Barrier Reef has died since 1995.[177]

Unless a significant cut in poisonous emissions happens soon, our sea level is predicted to rise fifty-three inches by 2100—threatening half of the world's 7.5 billion people living within sixty miles of a coastline.[178] Experts predicted in 2018 that, within thirty years, this flooding from sea level rise will threaten 311,000 US coastal homes.[179]

A 2018 World Bank report concludes that already 143 million persons are climate migrants, attempting to escape from sea level rise, crop failures, and water scarcity.[180] Commenting on the migrant crisis at our southern border, *Truthout* columnist Michael Galant identifies as its cause

169. Campbell, "Ocean Fish Populations Cut," para. 1.
170. Almond et al., "Living Planet Report 2020," 5.
171. Leahy, "One Million Species at Risk," para. 1.
172. Neuhauser, "Seventy-Five Percent of Animal Species," para. 1.
173. Carrington, "Plummeting Insect Numbers," paras. 1–2.
174. Spring, "Two-Thirds of Tropical Rain Forest," paras. 1, 7.
175. Johnston, "How Plastic Is Damaging," para. 5.
176. Curtin, "Let's Bag Plastic Bags," para. 3.
177. "Great Barrier Reef," para. 1.
178. McVeigh, "Sea Level Rise," para. 3.
179. Union of Concerned Scientists, "Underwater," 5.
180. Parker, "One Hundred Forty-Three Million People," para. 1.

the global system of economic exploitation that forces workers to leave their homes.[181]

While New Orleans reported lower temperatures than Anchorage,[182] on January 1, 2018, in Aberdeen, SD, the mercury plunged to minus 32°, breaking a ninety-nine-year record.[183] The temperature reached 122.4° in Pakistan on April 30, 2018, the highest ever recorded for that month anywhere in the world.[184] The Thwaites Glacier in the Antarctic, approximately the size of Florida, if it collapses as predicted, will raise our sea level by two feet.[185] Scientists predict that one-third of the glaciers in the Himalayas will melt by 2100.[186] Research published in January 2021 indicates that 1.2 trillion tons of ice and snow from our glaciers are melting each year.[187] In 2018, scientists found that the seas are heating up 40 percent more than a UN panel estimated five years ago.[188] The Atlantic Ocean current that helps regulate global climate is the weakest in 1,600 years.[189] Meanwhile, the temperatures at the North Pole surged above freezing in the dead of winter, with February temperatures in 2018 some days reaching fifty degrees above normal.[190] With melting permafrost come lethal implications, not only of methane released but also fifteen million gallons of mercury, twice that present in the rest of the earth.[191] Climate change has even caused the North Pole itself to take a sharp turn to the east.[192] Environmentalist and author Bill McKibben calls the 2019 UN scientific report on biodiversity "as depressing a document as humans have ever produced."[193] UN Secretary-General Antonio Guterres draws the bottom line: that because efforts to address the global climate crisis have been "utterly inadequate," the "point of no return is in sight."[194]

181. Galant, "Honduran Labor Fight," para. 4.

182. Rice, "Baked Alaska," para. 4.

183. Associated Press, "New year Brings New Lows," para. 5.

184. Astor, "Hottest April Day Ever," para. 1.

185. M. Taylor, "Antarctic 'Doomsday Glacier,'" para. 10.

186. Quackenbush, "Third of Himalayan Glaciers," para. 1.

187. Mooney and Freedman, "Earth Is Now Losing," para. 2.

188. Pierre-Louis, "Ocean Warming Is Accelerating," para. 2.

189. Berardelli, "Atlantic Ocean Circulation," para. 1.

190. Meyer, "Parts of Arctic Spiked," para. 3.

191. Welch, "Melting Arctic Permafrost," para. 13.

192. Hall, "NASA: Earth's Poles Are Tipping," para. 1.

193. Lyons, "Gene Lyons: 'We're Doomed,'" para. 3.

194. Parra and Jordan, "UN Chief Warns," para. 2.

We are now on track that, by 2050, we will witness a climate unseen on earth in fifty million years, which climatologists warn will have catastrophic consequences. A dire report by the UN Intergovernmental Panel on Climate Change (IPCC) warned in 2018 that the world has only a dozen years left to cut greenhouse emissions before catastrophe strikes.[195] In 2019, the IPCC used all available data and refined modeling techniques to explore the consequences for not interrupting the increasing rate of heating the planet.[196] A comparable study in 2019 done for the Trump administration was simply scrapped. Meanwhile, a record twenty-two weather and climate disasters have cost the US more than a record $22 billion in 2020, demolishing all previous records.[197] This cost will continue to escalate as our financial deficit climbs out of control.

Global corporate interests are increasingly involved in the fight for dwindling raw materials, with our military perpetrating widespread intimidation and violence on behalf of these self-interests, as in oil and gas resources, mining, logging, hydropower, and agribusiness operations. Despite the absurdity, it is indicative that, after centuries of indifference, President Trump proposed purchasing the island of Greenland, as melting is disclosing an abundance of raw materials.[198] Likewise, the thawing of the Arctic area is uncovering a vast trove of untapped resources, so that Secretary of State Michael Pompeo recently upset a meeting of the eight Arctic States by indicating that the era of cooperation is over, with serious competition beginning—for the area is now "at the forefront of opportunity and abundance."[199] In anticipation, US Special Forces and Marines in Alaska are training for cold-weather military operations.[200] Part of the corporate perjury in renouncing climate change involves the killing of environmental activists, killing them at the rate of almost four per week in 2017.[201] Forty-five percent of the world's hundred largest companies have been vigorous in obstructing climate change legislation. Many of the other companies who are not themselves involved are members of trade associations that are involved.[202] According to Sierra Club reports, fossil fuel companies have spent nearly $2 billion in climate change denial, outspending climate activists ten

---

195. Watts, "We Have Twelve Years," para. 1.

196. "Choices Made Now Are Critical."

197. A. B. Smith, "Twenty-Twenty U.S. Billion-Dollar Weather," para. 2.

198. Salama, "President Trump Eyes a New Real-Estate Purchase," para. 2.

199. Hansler, "Pompeo: Melting sea ice presents 'new opportunities,'" para. 2.

200. Decker, "Cold Weather Training," para. 2.

201. Watts, "Almost Four Environmental Defenders," para. 1.

202. DiBenedetto, "NGO: Forty-Five Percent," para. 1.

to one.[203] There are 172 climate-denying members of the 116th Congress.[204] Multiple members of Congress have investments in firms they are supposed to regulate. Documents, followed by interviews, disclose how Exxon, one of the world's largest oil company deniers, actually knew clearly that what they were doing was heating the planet disastrously, yet, for decades, they organized campaigns of disinformation and denial.[205] Since the Paris Agreement in 2015, the world's five largest oil and gas companies have spent over $1 billion on misleading campaigns and on lobbying related to climate change.[206] Volkswagen was exposed for installing sophisticated software in eleven million of their vehicles from 2009 to 2015 in an effort to rig emissions testing. After a hearing before a US congressional committee, the president of VW identified the issue as simply a communication problem rather than an ethical matter.[207] Then we have Dupont, who created Teflon with its dangerous cancer-causing component called C8, knowingly exposing millions for decades.[208] Collusion between federal regulators and Duke Energy, North Carolina's largest electric and gas supplier, resulted in a massive coal ash spill coating seventy miles of the Dan River with 60,000 tons of sludge that will take at least two years to clean.[209] In the face of possible congressional regulations, their corporate plea was: "Instead, trust us."

An interview with Helena Norberg-Hodge illuminates her thesis that the "globalized monoculture is consuming the planet" as she shows how the structure, dynamic, and scale of our global economy is the underlying cause of this ecological crisis[210]—having such control that it is blinding us from seriously facing climate change, with a built-in rapacity for deadening any motivation to act yet. Steve Fraser, in his *Age of Acquiescence: The Life and Death of American Resistance to Organized Wealth,* investigated this blindness to the "auto-cannibalism" of our economic-cultural dead-end dynamic. The puzzle for him was how there could be so little resistance to our frightening condition, in which "wage income is stagnant or falling, infrastructure is crumbling, social mobility is declining, resources once considered the 'commonweal' are being privatized, consumer debt is exploding, work weeks are longer, more children are in poverty, middle-class neighborhoods are

203. Rauber, "All the Environmental News," para. 5.
204. Negin, "Corporations Should Stop Funding," para. 5.
205. Hall, "Exxon Knew about Climate Change," para. 1.
206. Folley, "Top Oil Firms," para. 1.
207. Argenti, "Biggest Culprit," para. 1.
208. Kelly, "Teflon's Toxic Legacy," paras. 3, 7.
209. Deike, "Duke Energy Announces," para. 1.
210. Polychroniou, "Interview with Helena Norberg-Hodge," paras. 1–8.

shrinking, life expectancy is declining, use of convict labor is growing, and no mandated paid maternity-leaves."[211] His answer, as we have been discerning, is that this dynamic itself has been successful in shifting responsibility for failure away from systemic inequality, lodging it instead in personal ineptness. As we will be exploring further, this groomed false consciousness is guaranteeing an imperviousness to the whole. An apt analogy for this corporate myopia is one we referenced previously—the Nuremburg trials, in which each person in the Nazi complex had a defined task to do, received apt compensation for unquestioned efficiency, and thereby was uninvolved with the whole, either as means or goal. Thus no one was really responsible for the whole or its consequences, for the narrow self-interest of each gave a self-perpetuating dynamic to the whole.

INEQUALITY AND CHRISTIANS

The Census Bureau has disclosed that the present gap between haves and have-nots is the highest in the fifty years of its tracking.[212] The dynamic driving the world into the consequences of this tragic wealth inequality dare never be acceptable to serious Christians—no way, ever. Therefore, the church and Christians must confess their own guilt for participating in any such system that supports, fosters, grooms, and thrives on such inequality. Faced with the specter of world hunger, we are greatly complicit—not only for what we do and fail to do, but for where we live, what we drive, for whom we work, what we consume, what we wear, and thus, in an unfortunate sense, who we are. If there is a God of judgment, as I believe there is, no nation will survive that is rooted in a socioeconomic system in which so few are gaining so much, while so many are losing the little they have. Surely under divine judgment is our nation's insatiable global economic colonialism, self-righteously camouflaged with the pseudo-image of the US being the world's avatar of benevolence, democracy, and peace. As columnist Glen Ford insists, "When American rulers say that they are defending US national security against all potential enemies, what they really mean is that they are defending the prevailing capitalist order against any social movements that might oppose it anywhere on earth."[213]

Yet the church, with its life-and-death struggle for survival, is being co-opted in support of this dynamic, and in some quarters is even being used intentionally in its defense. Many Christians who try to minimize

---

211. Westbrook, Review of *Age of Acquiescence*, para. 8.

212. Telford, "Income Inequality in America," para. 1.

213. Glen Ford, "US Funds 'Terror Studies,'" para. 9.

their involvement still envy this lifestyle of self-indulgence, ambition, envy, consumerism, and greed, finding vicarious identity through TV celebrities, rock stars, sports heroes, sitcoms, and talk shows—all rooted in the pursuit of wealth. Christianity's primal temptation, declares Ronald Rolheiser, is to succumb to this societal corrosion. Symptomatic is how easily President Trump was able to capture conservatives connected with the Christian prosperity movement, a form of evangelicalism that celebrates the accumulation of wealth as a sign of God's blessing. At a recent gun show, one of the most popular T-shirts for sale had a picture of a gun and a Bible with these words, "Only These Two Are Needed." Yet there is hope appearing in Christians who are becoming haunted by the awareness that serious faithfulness must entail the radicalness of countercultural living. It is these persons to whom we will be appealing.

It is helpful to refer again to when the United States began its radical experiment in freedom, when President John Adams acknowledged the risk, for "there never was a democracy that did not commit suicide."[214] In a letter to James Madison (1785), Thomas Jefferson warned of the pernicious effect of concentrated wealth in this regard, insisting that "enormous inequality produces so much misery to the bulk of mankind."[215] His solution was a "geometrical progression" of taxes on the wealthy. Yet this is precisely what is being undone, and this nation has reached the point where the narcissism of competitive individualism has expanded into an impulse of corporate greed that is self-perpetuating, dissolving the regulations that might once have established some accountability. The genii in the bottle has been released, and we are reaping the destructive consequences. All experiments are tested in terms of their fruit, and this is the severe testing that is now occurring—determining if John Adam's prediction of suicide is true.

214. Adams, "From John Adams to John Taylor," para. 2.
215. Jefferson, "To James Madison from Thomas Jefferson," para. 2.

CHAPTER FOUR

THE POWER OF SOCIOECONOMIC CONTROL

CAPITALISM

In this chapter we will show how ingredients within our present socioeconomic system are bringing our society to inevitable collapse, having heavy implications for the church. Updating the work of Adam Smith, Milton Friedman and the Chicago school of economics are supporters of a closed loop theory in an effort to give economic factual objectivity in our modern age of subjectivity, insisting that free enterprise is a scientific system guaranteeing that individuals acting on their own self-interested desires will inevitably create maximum benefits for all. So understood, whenever anything goes wrong in practice, the reason must be that the market is not permitted to be truly free, solvable through a stricter and more complete application of free market fundamentals. Friedman insists that profit maximization for the benefit of stockholders is and should be the defining motivation and goal of corporations, which he calls "share value."[1] Thus, the defining duty of every corporation CEO is to increase the profits and stock prices for that firm. Adam Smith, in his *Wealth of Nations* (1776), rested the feasibility of his capitalist theory on the "invisible hand" that would guarantee that each person seeking his own interests would serve society's interests as a whole. This thesis might have had some credibility in a pre-industrialized time, birthing the American Dream, in which by working hard and competing fairly, each person would either succeed or fail through personal laziness. Yet, in practice, this system sharply rewards certain types of behavior while penalizing others, necessitating that a person either get with the program by internalizing its values or fail. After studying a number of mass shoot-

1. M. Friedman, "Friedman Doctrine," para. 33.

ings, Adam Lankford, a University of Alabama criminal justice professor, concluded that it is the American Dream that is actually contributing to the frequency of these killings.[2] As hard work increasingly does not produce wealth and success for the masses, millions of persons are being pushed to the margins of society, where they feel cheated, emasculated, and hopeless, taking their own lives or threatening the lives of those on whom they project their pain.

Further, talk of a free market has in practice become a misnomer, for when unfettered by regulation, the market becomes increasingly controlled by fewer and fewer large corporations, with their monopolies undercutting competition. Capitalism is an evolving system, and it is increasingly evident that the destructive features of its evolution are not the result of pure capitalism being tainted by external interference. They are the inevitable consequence of idolizing the system. Free market economics have never functioned freely, but always in practice reflect the existing power arrangements intent on exacerbating their power. Those who hold power will bend both the formal and informal rules that determine how markets will operate so as to maximize their own profit. As if in confession, Thomas Friedman has admitted the damning reality that the hidden hand of the market "needs the hidden fist of the military."[3] As a result, journalist Conor Lynch concludes that "it is not the state who has corrupted the corporations, but the corporations who have corrupted the state."[4] The corporate goal of pure capitalism is unrestrained self-interest. In appraising this situation, Pope Benedict XVI declares that the "exclusively binary model of market-plus-state is corrosive of society."[5]

Privatization is a code word for this minimizing of governmental regulations so as to eliminate both accountability and competition, substituting private profit for the common good. Privatizing prisons, for example, means employing prisoners by corporations at slave wages, while raising nonprofit costs by inserting high corporate profit. Privatizing water supplies is creating an intentional profit-controlled scarcity of global proportions. Privatized Genetically Modified Organisms (GMO) are designed to monopolize seed sourcing for corporate profit. Public lands are being functionally privatized through deregulation so as to legalize exploitation, such as fracking, which contaminates water supplies with billions of pounds of cancer-causing chemicals. There are an estimated 137,000

2. *Week* Staff, "America's Killing Contagion," para. 3.
3. Ahn, "Open Fire and Open Markets," para. 14.
4. Lynch, "America's Libertarian Freakshow," para. 12.
5. Pope Benedict XVI, *Caritas in Veritate*, 78.

privatized wells that from 2005 to 2015 released over five billion pounds of poisonous hydrochloric acid yearly.[6] This growing impetus for privatization is a concerted effort to eradicate the remaining vestiges of responsibility for the common good, which are being negatively referenced as entitlements. Libraries, fire stations, public schools, prisons, post offices, HeadStart, welfare, social security, legal aid, Medicaid, police—all of these and more were once regarded as the shared responsibility of all taxpayers for the sake of all citizens. Yet each of these is presently being pressured toward privatization, as profit for the few. The American Legislative Exchange Council (ALEC) is a group of wealthy persons committed to such privatization, presently focusing their power on local issues, such as privatizing public schools, weakening teacher unions, and lowering teaching standards. Their overall conservative agenda is updated every five years and has been dedicated to barring local governments from limiting short-term rentals, calling for a constitutional convention to limit federal spending, mandating cities and states enforce immigration laws to crack down on sanctuary cities, passing Stand Your Ground legislation, reducing the liability of companies facing asbestos claims, reducing taxes, and removing regulations, among other things[7]—meanwhile contributing millions of dollars to elect like-minded people to public offices and appointed positions. Despite the US having the safest air travel in the world, efforts are being made to remove air traffic control from the authority of the Federal Aviation Administration (FAA), giving it to a private corporation, transferring to it the 38,000 federal employees (80 percent of the FAA's workforce), and giving billions of dollars worth of air traffic controller equipment to this private body.[8]

About 53,000 US private contractors were in the Middle East in 2019, compared with 35,000 US troops, hiding the real cost of military actions.[9] The pretext of needing to reduce the national debt is widely used to justify such privatizing of public services, but researchers conclude that this has instead led to a glut in spending by the military. More than half of the defense budget in 2019, $370 billion, was spent on all the contractor efforts, from weapons to services.[10] In 2017, there were over 1.1 million private security guards, compared to 666,000 police officers.[11] On and on goes this dynamic—selling off public housing, privatizing state-owned properties, shrinking social services,

6. Ridlington et al., "Fracking by the Numbers," 4.

7. Y. Sanchez and O'Dell, "What Is ALEC?" paras. 13ff.

8. Halsey, "House Republicans Move Ahead," paras. 1–2.

9. Horton and Gregg, "Use of Military Contractors," para. 4.

10. Peltier, "Growth of 'Camo Economy,'" para. 1.

11. N. McCarthy, "Private Security Outnumbers Police," para. 2.

advocating inequitable flat taxes, and blocking minority and women's rights. Margaret Thatcher made their understanding clear: "There is no such thing as society. There are only individual men and women, and there are families."[12] So defined, what follows is the elimination of social welfare and collective responsibility, so that the purpose of education, for example, is the acquisition of the skills necessary for keeping corporations competitive in the global economy. Consumerism has thoroughly infiltrated our educational systems, the goal being to maximize the student's marketability. Education is becoming a business and students its customers.

In radical contrast, Professor Robert Reich of the University of California describes a viable society as one rooted in mutual benefits and duties as visibly embodied in public institutions such as public schools, libraries, transportation, hospitals, parks, museums, recreational facilities, and universities.[13] These are mutual responsibilities to be assumed by the taxpayers, progressively so, with the affluent being able to help pay for those less able. Instead, the intent of today's corporately managed dynamic is the privatization of all public institutions, from education to drinking water to prisons. The result is an engraved individualism, in which persons are responsible for purchasing everything for themselves, including all that was once regarded as a public good and a mutual right.

What is becoming increasingly clear is the fatal illusion endemic to our capitalist system: it is not true that a self-regulating market will guarantee that the competitive selfishness of each person will produce the common good of all. Yet it is this myth that continues to be taught by many of our business schools, insisting that the primary duty of every corporation is to create growth return for investors, indifferent to the consequences. In reaction, the church must come to recognize the extent to which this self-feeding myth is at profound odds with the Christian understanding, minimally at two key points. 1) The very nature and purpose of life is fatally corroded when a society is motivated by and in turn socializes its citizens into competitive individualism, self-indulgent possessiveness, and materialistic reasons for being. 2) The human condition is such that when humans are left free to their own designs, we will inevitably become competitively and arrogantly destructive. Consequently, without enforceable regulations independent of the dynamics of the economic system itself, what John Kenneth Galbraith calls countervailing power, the persons in command will rationalize their self-serving corporate rapaciousness, unhampered by thoughts of too much or going too far. Telling was the disclosure during the last major recession

12. Thatcher, "Margaret Thatcher," para. 7.
13. Reich, *Common Good.*

that we had reached the point where certain corporations had become so powerful that they were too big to fail, forcing huge expenditures from the public domain to keep afloat the wealthy private domain lest they take us all down with them. Ralph Nader draws the conclusion: "The world has never seen such an ingenious power-concentrating machine as the modern, global corporation."[14] Yet the church in its struggle to survive is being tempted to offer salable versions of Christianity as a coping spirituality for losers and a theology of plenty for winners and wannabes.

A DEFINING MOMENT—9/11

This socioeconomic system is functioning with such protective insularity that its dynamic is rendering unstoppable the demise of our society as we know it. In spite of how 9/11 has been packaged by the media, it was in fact a harsh symbolic judgment upon our nation. It was a dramatic eruption of reactionary anger to the global price our nation's corporate greed is extracting from two-thirds of the world's population and from the earth itself. Yet instead of recognizing this event as identifying the US as foe, we have been propagandized into conceiving ourselves to be the innocent victim of an external foe—thereby believing that our national survival depends on an all-out war against terrorism. So perceived, the rest of the world becomes regarded as potential foes. This false consciousness perpetuates a permeating fear, one that exacerbates widespread militant aggression and, at the same time, effects forfeiture of those core rights and values that would render our society worth preserving. This aggressiveness against an abstract enemy generates in turn significant counteraggression terrorist groups as foes. Groups such as al-Qaeda, formerly present only as small groups in small weak countries, have been hyped by our military-industrial complex into becoming safe opportunities in which to generate corporate profits through massive expenditures. Conflict and war are proving to be highly lucrative for corporations. By stimulating fear in our citizenry, the predatory nature of their global outreach is cloaked by promising security against an untrustworthy world. This war against terrorism has plunged us into involvement with seventy-six nations, establishing Afghanistan as the longest war in US history, at a cost of over $2 trillion.[15] Since 2001, the conflicts waged by the US have caused over 800,000 deaths, 335,000 of whom were civilians, and displaced over twenty-one million persons because of the violence unleashed. Yet behind this cloak of national security, in almost every nation

14. Nader, "Food Science," para. 1.

15. "Latest Figures," in Watson Institute, "Costs of War."

in which we have a military presence, an underlying motivation involves oil, gas, precious metal, and ingredients or opportunities deemed important to our nation's economic self-interest. By identifying our nation's corporate economic self-interests, we can identify where there is US military involvement. As a US general classically admits, "I spent most of my time being a high class muscle-man for Big Business, for Wall Street and for the Bankers. In short, I was a racketeer, a gangster for capitalism."[16]

It was the violent events of 9/11 that solidified, expanded, and justified these global tentacles of corporate capitalism. I was at my monastery on that day. The abbot received urgent calls with the theme: "Quick, get to a television set—it's terrible." Not having a television, we went to the guest house, and with the retreatants sat through frightful repetitions of the Twin Towers demise. The initial response by all of us was disbelief, followed with most persons expressing a reflexive intertwining of fright with revengeful anger. What was happening in that room that morning proved to be reflective of what was happening nationally. A bewildered President Bush spoke for most Americans as he mumbled to the nation, "I do not understand why anyone would ever want to hurt our country." I felt very alone, unwilling to risk expressing my feelings out loud: "What took them so long?"

This could have been our national moment of truth, birthing the beginnings of confession and penance—or at least a luminal awaking regarding the destructive impact of our nation on much of the world. Instead, the mass media focused the populace on symptoms rather than causes, on being victim rather than perpetrator. The irrational fear that quickly arose and subsequently intensified has justified a defensive aggression fed by an obsession with security. On September 16, 2001, Barak Obama's pastor Rev. Jeremiah Wright preached these words: "The stuff we have done overseas is now brought back into our own front yards. America's chickens are coming home to roost." In March 2008, after an investigation by ABC News discovered these words, there created an almost hysterical backlash, from which then presidential candidate Obama was forced to distance himself.[17] Yet on *Meet the Press*, Tom Brokaw challenged the nation to look at the roots of rage occurring in the Islamic world against us, citing as one illustrative cause our indiscriminate use of drones.[18] He called for our accountability in finally confessing "the presumptuousness of the US."

Retired lieutenant general and former head of the Defense Intelligence Agency Michael Flynn confessed that without the Iraq war there

16. S. Butler, "Smedley Butler on Interventionism," para. 5.

17. Ross and El-Buri, "Obama's Pastor," para. 9.

18. Sirota, "Cronkite Moment," para. 4.

would be no ISIS[19]—which is especially tragic since the invasion was itself justified by intentionally skewed intelligence. Joby Warrick, in his *Black Flags: The Rise of ISIS*, establishes that the rise in terrorist groups has largely occurred from warfare waged in far-off lands by our spies, Special Forces, and robotized killing machines. Mark Mazzetti, in *The Way of the Knife*, concurs, citing that in 2015 alone the US used at least 23,144 bombs and missiles, hitting at least 22,000 targets in Iraq and Syria alone, with the Syrian conflict resulting by 2018 in 500,000 deaths. For over a decade now, the US has been intent on encountering terrorism through bombing, invading, and occupying, killing hundreds of thousands and causing tens of thousands of casualties. As a result, such countries as Iraq, Afghanistan, Syria, Yemen, and Libya are now chaotically vengeful. Since 2001, our war in Afghanistan has cost the US more than $2 trillion, the lives of more than 2,400 personnel, and the wounding of more than 20,000 troops, with tens of thousands of them scarred by PTSD.[20] Hours before a round of Afghanistan peace talks were scheduled to begin, the US dropped its most massive non-nuclear bomb ever, the 21,600 pound "mother of all bombs"[21]—intent, ironically, on destroying the complex of tunnels that in the 1980s the CIA built to fight against Russia.

Why this deep Mideast aggression? It actually began long before 9/11, as when in 1953 the US with Britain staged a coup in Iran, overthrowing the democratically elected Prime Minister Mohammad Mossadegh. Newly declassified CIA documents disclose that this violent behavior was designed to preserve Iran's rich oil fields under the control of Western corporations.[22] This intent to preserve Iran's cheap oil and high profits accounts as well for other blood-for-oil adventures, such as Kuwait. Secret British government memos also link the US invasion of Iraq with oil reserves.[23] What 9/11 provided then was overt justification for what our country has long been about covertly. This aggression, in turn, has created fertile ground for recruiting enclaves of retaliatory vengeance against the US, such as ISIS. In 1982, Israel, with the support of the US, invaded Lebanon, purportedly to destroy the PLO. But the result of the extensive bombing and killing, especially of civilians, was the evoking of angry Shiites to take up arms and become terrorists. Consequently, former Israeli Prime Minister Ehud Barak was brought

---

19. Ferner, "Former Military Chief," para. 1.

20. Almukhtar and Nordland, "What Did U.S. Get," para. 2.

21. Hogan, "What We Know," para. 4.

22. Allen-Ebrahimian, "Sixty-Four Years Later," para. 3.

23. Bignell, "Secret Memos Expose Link," para. 7.

to confess: "It was our presence there that created Hezbollah."[24] He added, "They weren't there when we came, but they were certainly there when we left." Hezbollah's professed purpose is to undermine US self-interests in the region. "Follow the oil" has been a reliable mantra for understanding US foreign policy. Corporate economic strategy and our country's foreign policy have become so interdependent as to be virtually indistinguishable. Follow the lucrative locations of gas, oil, and corporately needed raw materials, and these will intersect with US military presence. Baffling for me was the dynamic between Israel, Gaza, and the US until exposed were the Palestinian offshore oil reserves.

Expressing his personal anger, journalist Ted Rall (2013) struck out at what he called "our mystified national cluelessness." "Why do people blow up our embassies," he asked, "bomb our ships, fly planes into our buildings, try to blow up their shoes and their underwear in our planes? They do it in part because we can't imagine why anyone would want to do such a thing."[25] But a person "would have to be blind not to understand why Muslims are enraged at the US: Gitmo, drones, propping up dictators, Palestine, Abu Ghraib, Afghanistan, Iraq, the list goes on and on." Under the self-professed right of exceptionalism, the US has expanded the Monroe Doctrine globally, attempting through military intimidation to suppress all dissent to our economic interests.

To understand the intensity involved in this tragic self-feeding vicious cycle, we need only scrutinize how our aggression appears to its victims. Nick Turse, in writing *Kill Anything That Moves: The Real American War in Vietnam*, researched the National Archives and discovered that My Lai was only one of many atrocities perpetrated in Vietnam. Our crimes included mutilations, murders, tortures, assaults, rapes, and intentional civilian slaughter. To increase body counts, reward competitions were developed for our soldiers as incentives. Abuse of children was done for amusement. Millions of gallons of chemical defoliants were dropped to poison the earth, along with using lethal gases, napalm, cluster bombs, and anti-personnel rockets. More tons of explosives were dropped on Vietnam than were used in all of WWII—on a country the size of Connecticut. Some who have experienced this carnage firsthand have identified it as an "American blood lust for profit." Understandably then, many of our troops returned with PTSD so severe that more than 60,000 veterans committed suicide in just a ten-year period, between 2008 and 2017.[26] The US suffered about 58,000 fatalities

24. Conan, "Who Is Hezbollah?" para. 5.

25. Rall, "If We Learn Geography," para. 3.

26. Margaritoff, "More U.S. Veterans," para. 3.

over the course of the Vietnam War, which lasted from 1955 to 1975. The newly created psychological term for describing what has been happening to veterans is *moral injury*.

I once took solace in the fact that the US withdrawal in defeat would surely end our involvements in anything like Vietnam again. Naïve. Instead, our government began a $65 million propaganda campaign to alter America's image before the world, painting our involvements as honorable, even as noble adventures. And although such adventures have resulted in the death of three million Vietnamese, Cambodian, and Laotian peasants, along with 58,262 Americans, General Westmoreland celebrates the Vietnam War as "an overwhelming success" for it was an "opportunity to test our latest weapons and tactics."[27]

MILITARIZATION

Fear, stoked by paranoia, is guaranteeing that this global aggression will increase—justifying corporate self-interest in supporting, defending, and determining these massive military expenditures. Fear is creating an ethos in which Americans are willing, even eager, to sacrifice the very rights on which this country was founded, in return for security. This establishes perpetual wars, for terrorism has no clear or definable foe and thus has no basis for marking any final victory or even measuring success. Since the *they* exists potentially anywhere, our military presence everywhere is necessary—as yesterday's friends become today's enemies, until tomorrow. Reflective of this ethos is the testimony by the director of national intelligence before the Senate Select Committee on Intelligence (2014), declaring that the annual worldwide threat assessment prepared by the intelligence community "filled him with dread."[28] Yet it has been discovered that the Pentagon paid a United Kingdom public relations firm $540 million to run a top-secret propaganda program creating false videos of terrorists in Iraq.[29] In *America's Addiction to Terrorism*, Henry Giroux documents the degree to which terror has become a central part of our national nervous system, functioning as a major organizing principle of our society. So much is this the case that an article in the *Christian Century* (2016) debates not only the desirability of permitting guns at worship services but the wisdom of pastors wearing guns in the pulpit.[30] In

27. Ketwig, "Fiftieth Anniversary Commemoration," para. 3.

28. M. Cohen, "James Clapper," para. 1.

29. Garcia, "US Government Spent," para. 1.

30. Childress, "Guns in the Pulpit," paras. 6–9.

fact, so as not to offend parishioners, it is reported that some churches now have signs reading, "Guns Welcomed Here."

Consequently, fear is intensifying public support for a Pentagon budget exceeding even the rapacious demands of the military itself, extravagantly providing far more money than they can even use—propelled by corporation propaganda, contributions to legislators' campaigns, and electoral advantage in providing pork-barrel jobs for constituents. This dynamic of expansive profitability is such a driving force that, here again, economics and US foreign policy are becoming indistinguishable. This was brought home to me personally when a friend at church told me that he was employed by the State Department, which accounted for his frequent overseas trips. I asked him about his responsibilities. "I help to create markets."

Another way in which corporations are gaining enormous control is through trade pacts. Two of these that have been pushed recently are the Transatlantic Trade and Investment Partnership and the Trans-Pacific Partnership (TPP), both of which are the largest pacts ever. Carefully inspected, however, these pacts have less to do with trade and far more to do with corporation control, with the countries involved surrendering their sovereignty to a transnational dynamic that exacerbates competitive inequality. The US and the eleven countries involved, already controlling 40 percent of the global economy, are attempting by pact to so enlarge this corporate power that they can challenge the rules, laws, and court rulings of any country simply by suing governments in private corporation-run tribunals set up by the UN or the World Bank. This dynamic is creating transnational corporations capable of minimizing global environmental regulations, trade unions, human rights, and personal safety nets. One critic of the TPP calls it "a united alliance of exploitative multinationals." Multiple critiques declare it to be the first and foremost salvo fired by global corporations against national sovereignty and against democracy itself. The intent of the pact is to function as a Bill of Rights for international corporations, significantly limiting the ability of governments to control their transnational economic behavior. Veteran journalist Mark Anderson identifies the goal of such agreements as keeping the world safe for supranationalism and the rigged species of capitalism that keeps the rich, rich, and the poor, poor.[31]

A 2019 report by the Stockholm International Peace Research Institute[32] states that total global military spending is up 76 percent from the post-Cold War low in 1998. The United States, China, Saudi Arabia, India, and France led the world in military spending, accounting for 60 percent

31. Mark Anderson, "Trans-Pacific Partnership," paras. 30–32.
32. Schwartz, "Global Military Expenditures," paras. 1–4.

of the total expenditures in 2018. US military spending keeps increasing, reaching $649 billion. The US is "by far the largest military spender in the world," accounting for 36 percent of the total, spending almost as much as the next eight countries combined. China, which came in second on the list, spent $250 billion.

Even six decades after WWII, fear justifies the continuation of 300,000 American troops stationed overseas (35,000 in Germany; 55,000 in Japan; 12,000 in Italy).[33] There are 800 bases in 80 countries, with 83 installations in South Korea alone.[34] Our military is operating in 177 countries,[35] providing assistance to 73 percent of the world's dictatorships.[36] The *Defense Monitor* identifies the Pentagon as involved with 641,000 contractors in 196 countries, helping to arm and train 180 of these countries.[37] Our troop strength of 476,000 active army[38] soldiers graphically illustrates the security intent of patrolling the world for our economic advantage.

The war in Iraq has cost the taxpayers over $2 trillion,[39] much of this going to US corporations as profits that escape financial responsibility regarding taxes. With this kind of revenue, the corporation pressure for perpetual war is enormous. In 2010, private contracts awarded without competition amounted to over $140 billion.[40] The largest windfall went to Richard Cheney's former firm, a total of $39.5 billion in Iraq-related contracts.[41] In 2017, Lockheed Martin received $50.7 billion in US government contracts, while Boeing received $23.4 billion.[42] Marc Ash, in *Reader Supported News*, states perceptively the destructive dynamic. "From South America to Asia, from Africa to the Artic, the USA is using its might to procure for powerful, privately held corporations what for them are vital national resources."[43]

It is this extravagance that permits the Pentagon to be notoriously lacking in accountability, as in the $21 trillion audit failure reported by Lee

33. N. McCarthy, "Trump Plans," paras. 1–2.

34. Benjamin et al., "Military Spending," para. 4.

35. "Chart of the Week" in Desjardins, "U.S. Military Personnel Deployments."

36. Whitney, "US Provides Military Assistance," para. 4.

37. Hartung, "Pentagon's War on Accountability."

38. "Military Personnel," para. 1.

39. Cachero, "US Taxpayers," para. 1.

40. Weinberger, "Windfalls of War," para. 8.

41. Fifield, "Contractors Reap $138bn," para. 5.

42. Stebbins and Sauter, "These Thirty Companies," paras. 34–35.

43. Ash, "TPP: Case for Treason," para. 3.

Camp.[44] A Reuter's investigation (2013) into the US Navy expenditures found similar irregularities.[45] For example, in 2016, a Department of Defense inspector general found that the Army could not adequately explain $2.8 trillion in adjustments made in accounting procedures and could not identify $6.5 trillion spent that year.[46] A 2021 report by Citizens against Government Waste detailed incidents of financial disarray in the Department of Defense.[47] One disclosure of unaccountable spending was the disclosure that the Pentagon spent $22 million in 2018 for lobster tail.[48] Finally, Congress required that the Pentagon produce a financial audit by September 30, 2017, only to be told that such an audit "will take a couple more years." The Pentagon suppressed an internal study that uncovered $125 billion worth of bureaucratic waste, exposed by the *Washington Post*, that found that the Pentagon was spending nearly a quarter of its $580 billion annual budget on overhead.[49] Even more, the *New York Times* reported that the US has lost track of more than 750,000 of the 1.45 million assault weapons, machine guns, and other firearms that were provided for security forces, militias, and police in Iraq and Afghanistan alone.[50] Research discovered that many of these lost weapons were being sold by online arms dealers. The military has already spent $1.5 trillion on a controversial F-35 fighter jet that went down in the ocean during testing—a program that has already cost double its estimated price. On April 26, 2016, then-Senate Armed Services Committee Chairman John McCain (R-Ariz.) called the F-35 program "both a scandal and a tragedy with respect to cost, schedule, and performance." On January 14, 2021, then-acting Defense Secretary Christopher Miller labeled the F-35 a "piece of [expletive]."[51] Each littoral combat ship is costing taxpayers more than double the $220 million that was predicted.[52] The Army's Future Combat Systems program experienced a 76 percent cost growth before being abandoned.[53] The Navy's projection that its then-seven Zumwalt-class destroyer fleet would cost $16.4 billion was off—by a stunning $12.1 billion,

44. Camp, "Pentagon Failed Its Audit," para. 3.

45. Paltrow, "Special Report," para. 13.

46. Paltrow, "U.S. Army Fudged Its Accounts," para. 2.

47. "Department of Defense" in Citizens against Government Waste, "Critical Waste Issues," para. 13.

48. Manchester, "Transparency Advocate," para. 7.

49. Whitlock and Woodward, "Pentagon Buries Evidence," para. 4.

50. Chivers, "How Many Guns," para 7.

51. Kennedy, "F-35 May Be Unsalvageable," paras. 2, 5.

52. Grazier, "Littoral Combat Ship," para. 2.

53. Grazier, "Smaller Budgets Will Result," para. 5.

before being halted after launching just three of the planned thirty-two ships.[54] On and on goes the extravagance, as over the last sixty years, these ever-increasing defense expenditures have established a military-industrial complex with enormous power to control our foreign policy and set governmental priorities to its own advantage—made affordable by severely cutting our domestic social programs. Yet, unbelievably, the International Monetary Fund (IMF) indicates that in recent years the US has spent more on subsidizing fossil fuels than on defense.[55]

This obsession with corporate profits is further reflected in congressional indifference to our roughly 14,000 gun homicides yearly—in stark contrast to only one hundred domestic terrorist deaths since 2015,[56] even though there are presently over a million persons on the US terrorist watch list. This indifference is related to the enormous escalation of US weapons sales abroad. In 2020, the US approved over $175 billion in weapons sales globally,[57] reaping enormous profits for the related arms industries, such as Lockheed, Boeing, General Dynamics, and Raytheon. In 2019, the US Navy awarded its most expensive shipbuilding contract ever to General Dynamics, at $22.2 billion.[58] In spite of Saudi Arabia's notorious human rights violations, the US has become their primary weapons supplier. How are we to understand that, although it was from Saudi Arabia that the 9/11 hijackers came, yet we are now providing nuclear capability by constructing dozens of nuclear plants for them? It is understandable by remembering that this is a nation famous for its oil abundance. Appraising this dynamic, former President Jimmy Carter declares that in the eyes of the world "America is the number one war-monger."[59]

Given how enormously lucrative global conflict is for American corporations, intensification of fear becomes both stimulant for and justification of the extensive growth of defense industries. This is so much so that 50 percent of our national budget is now going to related matters. With enormous government contracts at stake, powerful lobbying by major corporations sees to it that this war dynamic continues to take on a life of its own. Infectious fear within the American public is so extensive that it is not surprising that poll data suggest that the fear of terrorism has shown

54. M. Thompson, "U.S. Navy's Titanium 'Tin Can,'" paras. 39, 7.

55. Ellsmoor, "United States Spend," para.1.

56. O'Harrow et al., "Rise in Domestic Extremism," para. 3.

57. Everstine, "U.S. Approved More," para. 1.

58. Gregg, "Navy to Pay $22 Billion," para. 1.

59. Daley, "America as No. One Warmonger," para. 12.

little sign of waning in the United States[60] and likely will remain a major part of life for the foreseeable future. Such intertwining of fear with enormous defense expenditures is creating a lethal dynamic. With democracy functioning as a euphemism for free market capitalism, dictatorships are quite acceptable, for they are able to guarantee US advantage in attaining materials and acquiring markets.

With this dynamic fueling international competition for control of diminishing raw materials, the consequence is a reckless indifference to pollution, climate change, and ecological destruction. With governments deeply at the service of an economy intent on the rich becoming richer, the operating value dynamic is that enough is never enough. With profit being the sole determinant, it is inevitable that the poor will become poorer and the middle class will continue to shrink. In an internal memo, the FBI acknowledges that protecting corporate interests is roughly equivalent to "ensuring national security."[61] Thus, the serious Christian must struggle at conscience depth about participating in a dynamism that is thrusting over 9 percent of the global population into extreme poverty (150 million by 2021, making less than $1.90 per day) or 40 percent of the global population (3.3 billion) living on less than $5.50 per day.[62]

This complex is intertwined as well with a neo-liberal foreign policy in which aggressive military threats are strongly favored over the use of diplomacy. Not surprisingly, then, in our country's relatively short life, we have been involved in ninety-three wars, big and small.[63] The war in Afghanistan alone, our longest foreign conflict, has already cost US taxpayers over two trillion dollars, with several hundred billion projected even if the majority of troops might be officially removed. Such conflicts are pushing our national debt to unsustainable heights, costing taxpayers $345 billion in yearly interest alone.[64] These war-expenditures have become so massive in our overall US economy that peace would bring economic collapse; and yet to continue such expenditures will entail economic bankruptcy.

In addition to this staggering economic cost is the cost paid by our troops in maintaining this global empire. After ten years of war, the tally by International Physicians for the Prevention of Nuclear War indicates 1.3 million casualties in the conflicts of Iraq, Afghanistan, and Pakistan.[65] It is likely that

60. Mueller and Stewart, "Public Opinion," para. 1.

61. P. Lewis and Federman, "Revealed: FBI Violated," para. 7.

62. "COVID-19 to Add," paras. 2, 9.

63. "List of Wars."

64. Congressional Budget Office, "Federal Net Interest Costs," 2.

65. International Physicians for the Prevention of Nuclear War, "Body Count," 15.

half of the 2.7 million veterans of the Afghanistan and Iraq wars are struggling with physical or mental health problems.[66] A Pew Research poll in 2019 found that a majority of US veterans say the wars in Iraq and Afghanistan were not worth fighting (64 percent and 58 percent respectively).[67]

Woodrow Wilson's slogan intent on characterizing our foreign policy was "making the world safe for democracy." What this has come to mean is that US-controlled corporations are militarily guaranteed the security of global advantage, with democracy meaning any country with a market economy in which the US is free to exert dominance. Often, Islam is identified as our enemy, making one wonder how much this might relate to Islam's opposition to usury. The media characterizes US foreign aid as being benevolent contributions to poor countries for poverty relief and improvement of their standard of living. In reality, much of it goes to purchase weapons from US dealers at heavy profit, in turn supporting autocratic leadership guaranteeing US advantage. In the largest grant the US has ever made, the recent aid package to Israel provided $3.8 billion a year over the next ten years to buy weapons from US companies, an increase from $3.1 billion annually given in the previous decade.[68] Of the half trillion dollars spent between 2003 and 2012 in Iraq, only 5.4 percent was supposed to go to development projects such as improved water and food availability.[69] Much of the rest went to warlords, criminalizing the state into becoming one of the most corrupt in the world. Indicatively, a senior director of the National Security Council in 2015 was appointed head of the US Agency for International Development,[70] exhibiting the deep links between US foreign aid and military involvements. The head of the US Central Command in charge of secret operations in Africa identifies that continent as being "the battlefield of the future"—because of oil and other raw material discovered there. According to General Thomas Waldhauser, US troops are conducting 3,500 exercises, programs, and engagements per year in secret missions all across Africa, averaging ten missions per day.[71] An extensive secret drone operation is now centered in Djibouti at a cost of $14 trillion, with supplemental drone centers in Ethiopia and Kenya, while US ships are deployed off the coast of East Africa.[72] Special Forces and covert agents in Libya are following a similar pattern. Illustrative

66. Watson Institute, "Costs of War: US Veterans," paras. 1–2.
67. Igielnik and Parker, "Majorities of U.S. Veterans," para. 2.
68. Morello and Eglash, "U.S. and Israel Reach Agreement," para. 3.
69. D. Francis, "How U.S. Lost Billions," para. 2.
70. Cooper, "Obama Nominates Gayle Smith," para. 10.
71. Turse, "US Military Is Conducting," para. 1.
72. Turse, "Target Africa," para. 2.

of what is occurring is our paradoxical deployment in the Democratic Republic of the Congo. While it is one of the wealthiest countries in the world, a majority of its citizens live in extreme poverty, hunger, and disease—so harsh, in fact, that one in seven infants dies before the age of five. Yet our grants are going not to alleviate such poverty but to guarantee US access to this wealth. In 2017, US Special Operation Forces increased to an all-time record its deployment in 149 countries,[73] which involves 75 percent of the nations on the planet—establishing treaties to defend 69 of these countries.[74] In 2018, the US had Special Operations in more countries than in which we have ambassadors.[75] It is not hard to believe that, using drones, the military has the capacity to kill anyone anywhere at any time. As if in proof, the Pentagon admits to deploying spy drones over the United States.[76] DARPA, the Pentagon's research agency, is submerging unmanned platforms in the open seas to increase the capability of launching drones anywhere with minimal detection.[77] Furthermore, plans are being made to use marine organisms as underwater spies to track naval traffic and to create genetically modified plants to act as environmental sensors.[78]

In previous centuries, the worldwide British Empire ruled overtly through residential colonialism and extensive naval dominance. It has since been replaced by the American Empire, which rules by economic control and manipulation, military intimidation, and covert operations. This empire has transcended national economic self-interests, now functioning globally. Corporate headquarters have become fluid, functioning in whatever countries provide maximum tax-exemptions, minimal commercial regulations, lowest labor costs, and most affordable technological expertise. John Perkins in his *New Confessions of an Economic Hit Man* describes convincingly how "corporate colonialism" functions as an empire. Why, for example, is North Korea's nuclear belligerency a problem for the US and not China? The answer is economic hegemony, masked by a fear-induced willingness to risk even nuclear conflict for commercial advantage.

Establishing peace is the publicly expressed goal of our foreign policy, reflecting an ideology popularly expressed in the *Star Wars* trilogy—the ego-passion of Darth Vader intent on establishing order through one dominant power. The publicized dictum is that without the American Empire as

73. Turse and wombatman1, "U.S. Special Operations Forces," para. 4.

74. A. Taylor, "Map: U.S. Is Bound," para. 7.

75. Toft, "U.S. Has Special Forces," para. 2.

76. K. Howell, "Pentagon Admits," para. 1.

77. Newdick, "U.S. Navy's Submarine-Launched Aerial Drone," para. 1.

78. Gabbatiss, "US military Wants," paras. 1, 14.

peacekeeper, there would be world chaos—even though transnational economics see to it that no enemy states pose any real military threat to the US. In almost every case where conflict is erupting, the US is already operative there. While the press continues to convey our aggressive foreign policy as benign and justifiable, recently released documents going back as far as 1973 show that the assassination of Salvador Allende, the democratically elected president of Chile, was backed and orchestrated by direct US involvement.[79] In October 1983, under Ronald Reagan, Grenada was invaded. The US is known to have been involved in the 1988 Guatemala genocide, the 2002 coup against the democratically elected government of Venezuela, and the 2009 coup against the Honduran democracy, among others.[80] The present Central American crises are largely because the US is backing repressive regimes for economic advantage—illegally funneling weapons into regions to enable internal suppression, resulting in swelling crime rates, aggravated poverty, and enormous inequality. It is no secret that President Trump's oppressive actions against Venezuela are related to their having the largest oil reserves in the world. Even as far away as the Ukraine, the CIA and FBI served as consultants long before the conflict there with Russia.

It is important to understand what US "consultations" can be like. In Pakistan, the CIA conducted a fake polio vaccination campaign in order to gather DNA in their efforts to capture Osama Bin Laden—and when discovered, the reaction was a violent and widespread distrust of the US.[81] Wherever the US consults, whether the intent is to support or to undermine depends on how our country's economic interests dictate, with such issues as dictatorships and human rights being of minor concern. Research done by political scientist Dov Levin of Carnegie-Mellon University comes to the conclusion that, between 1946 and 2000, the US attempted to influence eighty-one elections[82] in forty-eight countries—using such tactics as leaking damaging information, creating propaganda, delivering large cash sums to one candidate or party, and, in some cases, actually running presidential campaigns. Deeply involved in these operations has been the CIA, an agency whose original task was intelligence gathering but which has arguably become the most powerful institution in the US. With its huge budget hidden from public scrutiny, there are no limits on its covert machinations. All such incursions, even if discovered, become morally justified, as fear regards them as necessary for subduing the invisible foe called terrorism. As corporate

79. Bonnefoy, "Documenting U.S. Role," para. 3.

80. Associated Press, "Before Venezuela," para. 19.

81. McNeil, "C.I.A. Vaccine Ruse," paras. 1–2.

82. Levin, "Partisan Electoral Interventions," 94.

competition increases for the world's markets and its diminishing raw materials, increased violent intervention is almost guaranteed.

INTERNAL SECURITY

The fear infecting the US citizenry not only justifies exerting controls within other nations but is defensively alive within our own borders. Since 2015, more than $20 billion has been spent for border security,[83] more than the equivalent of eight border patrol agents for every mile of the Mexican border.[84] In fact, according to the Transnational Institute, privatization has created a powerful border-industrial self-perpetuating economic complex.[85] The Department of Homeland Security has installed a $1 billion airport facial scanning program in nine major airports.[86] Under development is e-skin, which makes one's skin a computer display with the power of a smartwatch, receiving and emitting information anywhere, anytime.[87] The US Customs and Border Protection has almost as many planes as the Australian Air Force and more boats than the Russian Navy.[88]

The infamous border wall, part of which has already been built, has cost on average $26.5 million per mile,[89] with some remote areas in Arizona costing as much as $41 million. Meanwhile, the Immigration and Customs Enforcement agency has become a fully deputized well-armed national police force operative throughout our country, an illegality that we have never experienced before. This fear of invading violent hordes is not only rendering such enormous expenditures acceptable but is fashioning a populace acquiescent to an unprecedented expansion of governmental powers, a sacrifice of personal rights, and an invasion of privacy. Indicatively, a recent poll discloses that Americans are more concerned about security than about jobs and economic inequality.[90] Still, in spite of our total national security budget topping one trillion dollars each year, fear has not subsided. Top corporations spend millions to protect the world's richest people. For example, Apple spends $457,000 yearly to protect their CEO, Amazon and Oracle

83. Amoros, "This Chart Shows," table 1.

84. Valverde, "Has Number of Border Patrol," paras. 4, 8.

85. T. Miller, "More Than a Wall," 27–28.

86. Nixon, "Facial Scans at U.S. Airports," para. 1.

87. "Highly Sensitive Tactile E-Whiskers," para. 1.

88. United States Customs and Border Protection, "Air and Marine Operations," para. 3.

89. S. Sanchez, "Terminating Border-Wall Contracts," paras. 14, 3.

90. Horowitz et al., "Most Americans Say," para. 2.

each spend $1.6 million, Google spends $1.2 million, and Facebook's costs for security and travel for CEO Mark Zuckerberg are $23 million, which includes a security detail 24/7.[91] Our society presently employs more private security guards than high school teachers.[92]

In addition, fear encourages trepidation about internal unrest, violence, and uprisings, eliciting a tough-on-crime mentality that is permeating our justice system, setting all kinds of records for domestic incarceration, at a cost exceeding $1 trillion yearly.[93] One in nine state government employees work in corrections.[94] We have more persons in prisons than we have in colleges; during the past thirty years, we have spent more for prisons than for education.[95] Even so, prisons are increasingly crowded, with the rising cost used to justify elimination of most rehabilitation programs. Research by Cornell University discovered that one out of two US adults has had an immediate family member imprisoned for at least one night, and one in seven has had an immediate family member imprisoned for at least one year.[96] One in twelve minors has a parent who is in or has been in a prison.[97] One in fifty-eight US adults was under some form of community supervision at the end of 2018.[98] As many Americans have criminal records as have college diplomas, totaling one-third of all adults. The consequences of conviction can be lifelong, with the potential of being denied student loans, college admission, food stamps, public housing, and/or the right to vote.

The US is the world's leader in incarceration, with 2.2 million housed behind bars,[99] seven times the incarceration rate in all of Europe. Although having only 5 percent of the world's population, we now have 20 percent of the world's prison population.[100] This per capita rate amounts to more than Russia, China, and Iran combined. One in seven prisoners is serving a sentence of fifty years or more.[101] Observers make clear that the US is incarcerating African Americans at a rate six times that of South Africa

---

91. Hamilton, "Bulletproof Panels, Private Jets," paras. 6ff.

92. Hart-Landsberg, "Security Guards Outnumber," para. 2.

93. Spade, "New Study Indicates," para. 1.

94. Liptak, "One in One Hundred," para. 15.

95. V. Bauman, "Incarceration vs Education," para. 4.

96. Weiner, "Almost Half of U.S. Adults," para. 1.

97. Gotsch, "Families and Mass Incarceration," para. 1.

98. Kaeble and Alper, "Probation and Parole," para. 1.

99. "Criminal Justice Facts," para. 1.

100. Wagner and Bertram, "What Percent of U.S.," para. 5.

101. "Facts of Life Sentences," para. 1.

during Apartheid.[102] The odds of an African American man going to prison are greater than that he will go to college, get married, or join the military. Across the country, some 80,000 prisoners are held in some form of forced isolation on any given day.[103]

The National Research Council roots this condition in what fear has done to our criminal justice system, advancing pressure for governmental social control at the expense of social justice. This has created an extremely profitable prison-industrial complex. Fear is profitable—in this case, through the privatizing of prisons. The Nashville-based Corrections Corporation of America (now CoreCivic) has floated a proposal to prison officials in forty-eight states, offering to buy and manage public prisons at a "substantial cost savings" to the states. In exchange, the states must guarantee a 90–100 percent occupancy rate for at least twenty years and be given millions of dollars in federal income tax breaks.[104] The profitability of privatized prisons impels pressure for an increase in the number of prisoners, for lengthier sentences, and for a higher rate of recidivism. Furthermore, the impetus to increase profits by incarcerating more persons at less cost intensifies inhumane treatment. Profit has replaced rehabilitation.

This privatized corporate industry employs extensive lobbyists to push legislators and the judiciary to pronounce harsher prison punishments for an expanding number of crimes. This profit dynamic has resulted even in exorbitant phone rates charged for prison calls, with attempts now being made to exploit for profit all email and messaging availabilities. In many states, deprivation of even minimal hygienic items is forcing prisoners to compete for prison jobs that produce goods and services for private corporations at slave wages. In Arizona, the infamous anti-immigration legislation of 2010 was drafted in large part by private prison companies.[105] This incarceration industry has now reached $5.1 billion in yearly profits, with little public accountability for the contracting process.[106]

Marie Gottschalk, in her *Caught: The Prison State and the Lockdown of American Politics*, discloses how the penal system has abandoned any real attempt at rehabilitating inmates, rendering prisons largely repositories for society's unwanted—the poor, uneducated, undocumented, addicted, mentally ill, ethnics, and political activists—run by for-profit companies motivated to keep the growing prison population imprisoned for as long as possible. Not

---

102. J. Greenberg, "Kristof: U.S. Imprisons Blacks," para. 19.

103. Fenster, "New Data: Solitary Confinement," para. 1.

104 McGlothlin, "Arizona Tops in Guaranteeing," para. 1.

105. L. Sullivan, "Prison Economics Help Drive," para. 13.

106. "Correctional Facilities Industry," para. 1.

surprisingly, a recent study discloses that there are ten times more mentally ill persons in prisons and jails than in state psychiatric hospitals.[107] Here, once again, what we are finding is how fear supports and even encourages a destructive self-feeding dynamic, in which a growing number of persons are being regarded as undeserving of dignity, of being beyond reform, and thus as vulnerable for exploitation and expendable for profit.

THE COMMON GOOD

Perhaps up to half a century ago, there was evidence of legislative concern for the common good. In 1935, there were adopted Social Security and the Works Progress Administration, Civilian Conservation Corps, Soil Conservation Act, Wagner Act (labor rights), National Industrial Recovery Act, Fair Labor Standards Act, and the Agricultural Adjustment Act—with tax rates of 94 percent on the rich paying for these creative ventures. In 1944, F. D. Roosevelt provided a vision called the Second Bill of Rights—intent on assuring for all citizens the right to a job where each person could earn enough to provide adequate food, clothing, education, recreation, home, and medical care and be provided for in times of unemployment, accident, aging, and retirement. The GI Bill of Rights, passed after WWII, elevated opportunities for lower- and middle-class Americans. In 1964, President Johnson's war on poverty was followed by the Civil Rights Act, Voting Rights Act, Food Stamp Act, Medicare, and Medicaid. These too were largely paid for by taxes, even though the top tax rate was reduced to 70 percent. But during the Reagan presidency, the tax rate was significantly decreased to 50 percent and, in 1988, to a startling 28 percent. With President Clinton, the top tax rate was raised to 39.6 percent for those whose income topped $1.2 million. Throughout this period, the GOP kept predicting economic catastrophe, but instead the economy did well, with the Clinton era attaining a balanced budget and unemployment reaching a thirty-year low. But beginning with President George W. Bush, tax rates for corporations and the wealthy were again cut, coupled with significant budget reductions for agencies whose concerns had been for the common good. Even though poverty increased to 14.3 percent in 2009, conservative efforts persisted in establishing even greater tax cuts for corporations and the rich, thereby intensifying economic inequality. Privatization further undercut or eliminated taxpayer-supported agencies for the common good, such as libraries, post offices, clean water, fire prevention, and national lands and parks. Such diminishment is being justified as not being economically feasible.

107. M. McCarthy, "US Jails," para. 1.

A further factor in fracturing the common good has been the escalation of overt racism. Hate groups began rocketing to an all-time high with the election of our first African American president. Politicians seeking election are no longer subtle in stoking fear with bigotry, establishing race as an electoral and organizing tool. So-called active hate groups have risen from 457 in 1999 to a high of 1020 in 2018.[108] Corporate capitalism, in turn, is co-opting these conservative and rightist fear groups under the banner of personal freedom, encouraging opposition to all governmental regulations as being repressive. In so doing, ironically, the economic self-interests of the fearful are undermined.

This dynamic is also causing a number of persons and groups to project their fears onto conspiratorial plots. One such target is the Trilateral Commission, which in truth is an international discussion group of 390 members founded by David Rockefeller and Jimmy Carter to encourage cooperation between countries of North American, Europe, and Japan.[109] The United Nations is also under suspicion. Various hypothetical global elites are likewise suspected of sabotaging American sovereignty by attempting to establish a one-world socialist government that will crush the freedom of the iconic White self-made male. Ever wilder conspiracy myths such as QAnon are dividing even families with fear and paranoia. January 6, 2021, marked a frightening advancement of this dynamic to an internal domestic level, in which a violent insurrection was aimed at overturning the government itself—-guaranteeing a rapid advance in centralized autocratic control of society. What such conspiracy theories actually accomplish is concealing the real conspiracy—the dynamic of global capitalism that is establishing its one-world rule through a plutocratic oligarchy intent on imposing its self-interest through multiple strategies in controlling individual nation-states, economically, politically, socially, and culturally.

In order for the common good ever to be a significant ingredient in any democracy, there must be a willingness to establish a significantly graduated system of taxation, thereby able to modify the inevitable inequality endemic to the free market system. Therefore, it is alarming to discover how giant corporations are using their control in multiple ways to undercut their responsibilities for the common good. One way this is being done is through inversion, in which corporation profits are advanced by scorning national loyalty and relocating their corporate headquarters overseas in order to gain write-offs, minimal regulations, and the lowest tax rate. For this, a corporation legally names as its corporate headquarters the subsidiary that provides

---

108. Southern Poverty Law Center, "Year in Hate," 4.
109. Blessing, "Trilateral Commission," para. 1.

the best profitable advantage. This tactic discharges tax responsibility for contributing to the common good of the nation that fostered its origin and continues to be its primal market. Pfizer, for example, considered escaping $35 billion in taxes by renouncing its US citizenship.[110] Others who have made the move include Burger King, Budweiser, Purina, Nestle, Frigidaire, and Lucky Strike.[111]

The massive leak of 11.5 million documents (the Panama Papers) in 2016 from the Panamanian law firm Mossack Fonseca produced a shocking revelation of how the rich and powerful from numerous countries are using a network of shell companies, money laundering, and tax havens to hide billions of their taxable wealth—with the CIA implicated in these schemes in ways that, if not outright criminal, are highly questionable. Among these documents are linked seventy-two current or former heads of state, as well as numerous wealthy actors and sports figures. Many of the world's top banks helped clients do shady business with this Panamanian law firm, together constituting what one critic labels "greed of gargantuan proportions." In fact, Brooke Harrington in the *Atlantic* claims that this Panama firm is "just part of a web of legal corruption that reaches virtually every country in the world."[112] In 2020, the Tax Justice Network estimated that $8–$35 trillion had been placed in offshore tax havens, of which the Panama Papers were only one piece.[113] Oxfam indicates that the fifty largest American companies, making $4 trillion in profits from 2008 to 2014, kept a quarter of this income outside the US by using more than 1,500 subsidiaries in tax havens, costing the US $111 billion yearly in lost tax revenue.[114] This amounts to an estimate that, in 2016, US corporations hid $1.4 trillion in offshore tax havens.

Back home, the state of Delaware has more anonymous corporations than it has residents, with a nondescript two-story building in Wilmington being the official home of Apple, American Airlines, Coca-Cola, Walmart, and dozens of other Fortune 500 companies. The states of Nevada, South Dakota, and Wyoming have joined this lucrative scam by passing laws that make it easy to establish anonymous shell corporations. Meanwhile, in response to the proposed Medicare For All plan, corporations scoff: "Who will pay for it?"

---

110. Merle, "Giving Up," para. 1.

111. Morris, "Ten Iconic US Companies," paras. 5ff.

112. Harrington, "Panama Papers," para. 13.

113. Shaxson, "Could Wealth in Tax Havens," para. 5.

114. Davies, "US Corporations," paras. 8–17.

A further tactic that undermines the common good is outsourcing. Since NAFTA was instituted over twenty-five years ago, the transfer of American jobs to cheap foreign markets has been a leading export. In the first decade of this century alone, America lost 56,190 factories, an average of fifteen each day,[115] leaving millions of working-class Americans jobless, deflating the wages of less-educated workers, forcing a downward spiraling of the middle class, and launching a blighting of our cities. The only protection that such free-trade pacts actually provide is for highly paid professions. The World Bank, in which the US is a determining participant, is a key player in this global dynamic, effecting land grabs, mass displacement, exploited labor, and dependent debt—all in the name of establishing economic solvency. According to Oxfam, the majority of the World Bank's investments in Sub-Saharan Africa go to companies with offshore accounts.[116]

Another part of this relentless global corporation dynamic is the increasing hierarchy of monopolistic mergers and acquisitions, intent on undermining competition as a dynamic of regulation. Such transactions totaled $1.9 trillion in 2014, up 73 percent from the previous year. In 2020 were recorded mergers and acquisitions totaling $2.8 trillion.[117] This escalation has been widespread in diverse fields, from railroads, through oil, then airlines, followed by brewing and food processing, then prisons, and now media and health care. Megahealth insurers Aetna and Anthem bought out megahealth insurers Humana and Cigna. Heinz purchased Kraft. Four airlines now control 70 percent of all domestic air travel. Expedia and Priceland control nearly all travel booking. Ten giant corporations control virtually everything we buy, by owning, marketing, and distributing the products of most other companies, thereby providing the public with the illusion of real choice. Monsanto controls 80 percent of the genetically modified US corn market and 93 percent of the genetically modified soy market.[118] In merging with Bayer in 2018, they are now the world's largest supplier of seeds and pesticides, owning a quarter of the global business, even though their weed-killing products increase the risk of cancer by 41 percent.[119] Such hierarchical supremacy also grants the power to create artificial scarcity to justify irrational cost increases. Many major corporations no long produce anything but instead establish brands to authenticate products made cheaply overseas in poor working conditions, with some of these giant international

115. Gerard, "Who Is Killing American Manufacturing," para. 4.

116. Mis, "World Bank Invests," para. 1.

117. Rudden, "Value of M&A Transactions," para. 1.

118. Kaldveer, "U.S. and Monsanto Dominate," para. 1.

119. Gillam, "Weedkiller 'Raises Risk,'" para. 1.

companies becoming more powerful than the internal workings of producer nations themselves.

Such mergers create a tax advantage. For example, in 2016, the US auto parts supplier Johnson Controls renounced its corporate citizenship by merging with Ireland-based Tyco International, thereby taking advantage of Dublin's lower corporate tax rate. Yet this very company had received $149 million in tax breaks between 1992 and 2009 from the state of Michigan alone, indirectly gaining $80 million from the auto bailout.[120] Perhaps not coincidentally, in 2015, Johnson Controls had to pay a $3.75 million penalty to Michigan and give up its tax-exempt status at the plant because it failed to create the 400 new jobs promised when it received a $75 million tax break. Yet, in spite of the low tax rate presently operative in the US, corporations are able to achieve single-digit effective tax rates by having corporate lawyers exploit the innumerable loopholes built into the tax code.

Further, in a manner almost out of control, large corporations now have the power to force cities into auctions by competing with concessions and tax breaks to lure their plants and headquarters. In 2018, the bidding to entice Amazon to locate a headquarters in New York and northern Virginia resulted in an offer of at least $4.6 billion in taxpayers' subsidies, to be drawn from funds designated for health care, education, and infrastructure.[121] Yet, in 2017, Amazon had made profits of $5.6 billion without paying a penny in federal taxes[122]—while many of its workers were forced to rely on food stamps, Medicaid, and housing subsidies. A further strategy for minimizing corporate taxes is what is called earnings stripping. After a corporate headquarters is moved overseas, it then borrows large amounts of money from its American subsidiary, the interest from which is used to offset its taxable earnings.

Also happening is the upsurge in philanthropic foundations. One of the best known is the Bill and Melinda Gates Foundation, with astonishing assets of $49.8 billion (2019). While such foundations are useful in improving corporate public relations, even more are they a method for escaping taxation, with their grants escaping almost all accountability and oversight. Together they form what is called philanthrocapitalism, which is intent on issuing grants that promote the self-interested virtues of corporate capitalism. Such promotion focuses as well on such self-interested issues as industrial agriculture, private education, private health care, and the adoption of genetically modified patented seed systems with chemical

120. Sorkin, "Tidal Wave of Corporate Migrants," para. 11.

121. Dayen and Cohen, "Amazon HQ2 Will Cost," para. 1.

122. Henney, "Amazon Earned $5.6B," para. 1.

fertilizers that undermine the sustainability of small-scale farmers. Even with issuing generous grants, the Gates foundation still is not able to give away its money as fast as its unearned income is accumulating. Such tax-avoidance through philanthropy accounts for the 2015 86,000 private grant-making foundations, doubling those operative in 1993.[123]

With such an avalanche of tactics for minimizing corporate responsibility, the result is the economic inability of society to provide for the common good. As a result of this absence, there is a diminishing of expectation by our citizenry that the common good should be an essential part of society's responsibility—thereby erasing not only their expectation but any motivation to demand it. Fostered is an unfortunate alternative orientation, with multiple dimensions. 1) The meaning of personal life is defined in terms of economic success, enabled through acquisition of possessions, prestige, and power. 2) Private property is an unquestioned determinant, thereby rejecting common and collective ownership in favor of privatization, regarding raw materials and the control of production and distribution. 3) The individual rather than the community is regarded as being the defining unit, rendering personal initiative and competitiveness normative rather than cooperation and team endeavor—emphasizing rights over duties. 4) Profit maximization is made the focusing goal of the economy, thereby rendering labor, environment, and politics as means for economic gain, inevitably favoring the affluent few. 5) Quantity is valued over quality, maximizing compulsive consumption with an ever-changing plethora of gadgets, gimmicks, and styles, designed for a quick replacement that squanders resources and guarantees massive waste. 6) Short-term gains are placed ahead of long-term benefits, as people become oblivious to consequences. 7) Work defines the purpose of life, making leisure a waste of time.

These replacement values have the power to infect Christianity as well, especially in permitting the power of privatization to replace concern for the common good with undue focus on the private life of a person. In contrast, authentic Christian existence is fundamentally communal. Therefore, in contrast to the present mentality, in which each individual is forced to compete in an attempt to earn life's essentials, Christianity insists that the fundamentals for being human are deserved by each person by the simple fact that he or she exists and that humans should learn how to act in responsible thankfulness. The Christian is pro-life from birth to death, with the common good trumping individual freedom. All persons are entitled to a living wage in terms of meaningful labor, sufficient for acquiring affordable housing, adequate health care, quality education, leisure time,

123. Aswell, "Thirty-Four Grant Statistics," para. 5.

healthy food, and a clean environment, with special care for the disabled and age and a guarantee of freedom for all in worship, association, and speech. The contrary is in violation of Christ's kingdom, which is at hand in foretaste and promise. Therefore, although unfortunately necessary, the churches should not need to provide food cupboards, clothes closets, and free meals—for, in fact, they are judgments upon a society that is failing its responsibilities for the common good. Therefore, for churches to meet symptoms without awareness of the underlying causes is a form of betrayal. Thomas Aquinas may have been wiser than his times when he insisted that the common good is more divine than individual perfection.[124] Likewise, the Second Vatican Council insisted that the work of the church is to be that "of restoring and enhancing the dignity of the human person, of strengthening the fabric of human society, and enriching the daily activity of [all] with a deeper meaning and importance."[125]

POLITICAL CONTROL AND
THE KOCH BROTHERS

What is becoming clear is the commanding power of corporate control that is invading almost every vital dimension of our society. Investigative journalist Jane Mayer, in her *Dark Money: The Hidden History of Billionaires behind the Rise of the Radical Right*, documents convincingly how an elite group of the extravagantly wealthy has been able to create this enormous power, financing pro-privatization and pro-corporate agendas that through financial contributions are manipulating both political parties. During the 2016 election cycle alone, the professed goal of their network was to spend $889 million on candidates who favored their self-interests, which would allow their political organization to operate at the same financial scale as the Democratic and Republican Parties.[126]

Brothers Charles and David Koch, billionaire industrialists, became icons in this momentum. Their father, Fred Koch, was a founding member of the ultraconservative John Birch Society. After running unsuccessfully on the Libertarian Party ticket, Fred with David took another tactic—that of using nonprofit organizations to funnel deliberately untraceable money not only into electoral campaigns but into other vehicles of influence such as think tanks, universities, and media outlets. This magnetic financial

124. Maritain, "Positions of St. Thomas," para. 16.

125. International Commission on English in the Liturgy, *Liturgy of the Hours*, 4:403.

126. Confessore, "Koch Brothers' Budget," para. 2.

availability has helped draw the Republican Party into a hard right turn. Additionally, they engaged in support for a secretive data and technology company to improve voter turnout and election results.[127] Also disclosed are front groups, including the Koch brothers and corporate ties with the tobacco industry, that planned and engineered formation of the Tea Party as their means of gaining political control.[128] Further, the Koch brothers funded the Bundy land seizure agenda,[129] a coalition of anti-government activists and militants desirous of seizing and selling off public land and national monuments. They have also blocked solar initiatives at every point and maneuvered multimillions into fighting electric vehicles. They mounted significant lobbying pressure on Congress in 2017 for lower corporation taxes, while personally profiting $1 billion each year.

Having reaped a fortune from fossil fuels and other environmentally exploitive practices, the Koch brothers have spent at least $88 million in financing nonprofit groups vigorously intent on removing all environmental regulations, denying climate change, and ridiculing all scientific evidence for it. They have also blocked climate change action in state legislatures, funding the work of such reactionary organizations as the American Legislative Exchange Council, the American Energy Alliance, and the State Policy Network. Also drawn into this powerful compilation are the Charles Koch Foundation, the David H. Koch Charitable Foundation, the Cato Institute, the Heritage Foundation, Americans for Prosperity, and the Mercatus Center—all mouthpieces for corporate control, providing data, strategy, and financing for nurturing a right-wing radicalism that serves the self-interests of the rich elite. Their approach is quite visible in the support they provide for the Grassroots Leadership Academy, which is intent on training "foot soldiers . . . to fight for freedom and against progressive policies and false narratives of the left."[130]

One of their tactics is to provide funding for think tanks at institutions of higher education, such as a $5 million grant made to Arizona University. Charles Koch himself has given $108 million to 366 colleges and universities from 2005 to 2014, intent on funding "free market academic centers."[131] The Koch brothers have been particularly successful in interfering with university admissions, governance, curricula, and faculty freedom—endeavoring to convert universities into vehicles of free market principles within a

127. Henderson, "Kochs Help Republicans," para. 2.
128. Nesbit, "Secret Origins of Tea Party," para. 7.
129. Lee-Ashley and Rowland, "Koch Brothers," paras. 1–3.
130. Armiak and Bottari, "Kochs' "Grassroots Leadership Academy,"" para. 12.
131. Kotch, "Koch Brothers Are Using," para. 2.

determining culture of competitive individualism. Recently disclosed is the heavy involvement of the Charles Koch Foundation in determining student admissions and faculty appointments at George Mason University.[132] Further, David Koch attained membership on the boards of top science museums, even on the decision-making board of the Smithsonian's Natural History Museum, funding the Hall of Human Origins. Only heavy pressure by well-known scientists was able to force him from the board of the American Museum of Natural History.

In spite of independent studies showing that the Veterans Administration has been outperforming the rest of the US health sector, Concerned Veterans for America, a creation of the Koch network, manufactured scandal as a way of dismantling and outsourcing the VA's health services to the private sector.[133] Furthermore, David Koch was on the board of the Reason Foundation, which insists on privatization as the solution to water problems, such as the lethal situation in Flint, Michigan. The stated goals of the Koch brothers are unabashedly self-serving: deregulating corporate controls; privatizing public institutions and programs; eliminating safety nets, ranging from food stamps to Medicaid; and rejecting any response to climate change. In other words, the impetus is to exacerbate without conscience the corporate dynamic threatening this nation. This is being accomplished, on the one hand, by an integrated network hidden as philanthropy, leaving behind only a minimal money trail. On the other hand, this is being done by such tactics as denying voter rights, influencing and controlling politics with dark money, and packing the courts.

In addition to this national strategy, Gordon Lafer traces this takeover on a statewide level in his *One Percent Solution: How Corporations Are Remaking America One State at a Time*. Lafer shows how state legislations are being controlled by the best-funded and most powerful political forces among the US corporate lobbies. At a private donor retreat in early 2018, the Koch brothers pleaded for upwards of $400 million to protect Republican majorities in Congress—60 percent more than they spent in 2016.[134]

As the true work of the Koch Brothers is being increasingly discovered, so is coming to light a second powerful and secretive group of rightwing ideology: the Bradley Foundation. Presently focused in thirteen states, it has as its focus corporate control of the economy through destruction of labor unions; privatizing of public services; governmental deregulation; and funding of conservative think tanks, candidate recruitment, controlled

132. E. Green and Saul, "What Charles Koch," para. 6.

133. Mundy, "VA Isn't Broken, Yet," para. 4.

134. Mui, "Conservative Koch Brothers' Network," para. 2.

media outlets, and advocacy groups. In 2015, this group began rivaling the Koch family in giving grants—$49 million compared to $58 million.[135] The Bradley Foundation also contributed heavily to higher education, supporting conservative professors and academic centers dedicated to free market economics, including such schools as Harvard and Marquette. What is happening also is the morphing of education into a commodity, with universities serving as its supply corporations and students its consumers.

It is indicative of this amassed power and influence that eight years after the onset of this country's second largest financial crisis, big banks have been forced to pay $200 billion in federal and state fines, yet not a single top Wall Street executive has been held personally responsible for any wrongdoing. JPMorgan Chase was fined $13 billion for fraudulent sale of mortgage-backed securities, yet not one person was charged with any crime[136]—as profits continued to mount to three times what they had been before. Furthermore, even the fines that were levied will be dramatically diminished through the use of tax cuts and multibillion-dollar insurance payments from the government through the FDIC. Former coal executive Don Blankenship was sentenced in 2015 to only one year in prison and a mere $250,000 fine for conspiracy in violating mine safety rules, resulting in the deadliest US mine explosion in four decades. Up to 75 percent of the fine that may or may not finally be imposed on British Petroleum for the largest oil spill in history will be tax deductible, meaning that US taxpayers will foot most of the bill.

Even the benign-sounding US Chamber of Commerce has been a powerful vehicle of corporate control, investing millions of dollars in fighting public healthcare, financial reform, climate change, and efforts at closing corporate tax loopholes, primarily by influencing legislators, courts, and elections. According to the Sunlight Foundation, a small cadre composed of 1 percent of the top 1 percent of the population contributed more than $1.6 billion[137] to political campaigns in 2012, and likely provided as well the lion's share of the $350 million in campaign dark money. Such dynamics will intensify, for recent estimates are that corporations are reaping $760 in return for every $1 invested in political campaigns.[138]

This ability of multinational corporations and banks to become so deeply involved in choosing elected officials is due in part to the *Citizens United*

135. Kotch, "Documents Reveal," para. 8.
136. Cohan, "Jamie Dimon's $13 Billion Secret," para. 1.
137. Drutman, "Political 1 Percent," para. 10.
138. Bonifaz and Cohen, "There's Never Been," para. 2.

ruling by the Supreme Court.[139] It struck down previous contribution limits, opening the flood gates for each person to contribute up to $3.6 million in federal campaigns for each election cycle. The dramatic result has been that election spending by groups has increased from $5 million in 2000 to $6.5 billion in 2016,[140] giving the wealthy enormous manipulative power.

Further, by upholding restrictive voter identification laws,[141] the Supreme Court has permitted states to keep as many as 600,000 people from voting, mostly poor and minorities. Political gerrymandering is extensive, while ideological groups are attempting to control state, county, and local judicial elections by forcing candidates and incumbent judges to act like politicians, raising money for campaigning, even from those likely to appear before them in court. Hacking attempts into our voting systems is making the systems' reliability questionable, with the FBI providing convincing evidence of foreign influence in the 2016 presidential elections. Zachary Roth, in his *Great Suppression: Voting Rights, Corporate Cash, and the Conservative Assault on Democracy*, discloses the thoroughness with which such compromising efforts are finding success. As a result, the US electoral system is increasingly questionable, due primarily to voter suppression, dark money, and gerrymandering of voting districts.

The dictionary definition of democracy is "a form of government in which the supreme power is vested in the people and exercised by them under a free electoral system."[142] What then is left, given the enormous corporate control of elections, legislation, media, telecommunications, banking, energy, and foreign policy, in a web beyond control? George Monbiot, in *How Did We Get into This Mess*, carefully documents some of this impasse that we are exploring. During a nationally syndicated radio broadcast in August 2015, former President Jimmy Carter declared that the United States is now an oligarchy in which "unlimited political bribery" has created "a complete subversion of our political system as a payoff to major contributors."[143]

In *The Market as God*, Harvey Cox rightfully expresses alarm over the rights that have been awarded in granting personhood to corporations. These include such matters as trial by jury and immunity from double jeopardy, thereby sacralizing the market with all the accoutrements of a

---

139. *U.S. Reports*, Citizens United v. Federal Election Commission, 558 U.S. 310 (2010).

140. Ingraham, "Somebody Just Put Price Tag," para. 1.

141. *U.S. Reports*, Crawford v. Marion County Election Board, 553 U.S. 181 (2008).

142. "Democracy," in Barnhart and Stein, eds., *American College Dictionary*, 322.

143. Schwarz, "Jimmy Carter," para. 1.

religion—serving not as society's servant but its master. Their unabashedly self-serving goals, as clearly expressed by the Koch brothers, are that of de-regulating government controls over corporations, privatizing public insti-tutions and programs, minimizing safety nets, and rejecting all responses to climate change. Without conscience, this corporate dynamic has come to define economically our national self-interest. Pope Francis calls this a deification of the market.[144] In its struggle for survival, the church is find-ing itself fighting against a rival deity.

SURVEILLANCE

Another destructive dynamic that is developing in reaction to the fear of terrorist otherness is a surveillance complex that renders George Orwell's *Nineteen Eighty-Four* portrait a kindergarten version. A central expression is the National Security Agency (NSA), with its heavily fortified massive data-gathering center completed in 2013 outside Salt Lake City at a cost of almost two billion dollars.[145] It occupies more than a hundred thousand square feet of space; houses 17,000 employees; and has so many computers that the heat they generate requires 1.5 million gallons of cooling water each day. It is designed to function as a series of near-bottomless databases, stor-ing endlessly all forms of communication, including the contents of private emails, text messages, phone conversations, and Google searches made by every American and what will be made for the next five hundred years. In addition, there is an unbelievable assemblage of personal data trails, such as parking receipts, travel itineraries, bookstore purchases, and what is called digital pocket litter. There is sufficient capacity to store over one hundred years worth of such data, with considerable space left over. Technology journalist Andrew Leonard characterizes this facility as "designed to know everything there is to know about *us*."[146]

    In addition, the NSA has an enormous headquarters in Fort Meade, MD, as well as a new $1 billion facility at Fort Gordon, GA, this one focus-ing on Mideast intelligence. There is one in Hawaii for Asian intelligence and additional major facilities in Texas and Colorado, whose foci are un-clear. The NSA is now building a quantum computer capable of cracking in record time encryptions presently used to protect banking, medical, busi-ness, and government records around the world. The agency handles 29.2 petabytes of communication data daily, which is 2,990 times greater than

144. Pope Francis, *Laudato sì*, para. 56.
145. Carroll, "Welcome to Utah," para. 5.
146. Leonard, "NSA Doesn't Like," para. 6.

the total texts in the Library of Congress. In 2017, the NSA collected 534 million phone call records and text messages made by Americans, triple what was gathered in 2016.[147] Presently, over one billion phone calls daily enter the NSA data repositories, and 200 million text messages are being harvested each day across the globe. The agency has admitted to having implanted hacking software for surveillance in millions of worldwide computers under the automated code name TURBINE, having now attained the capacity to read computer radio waves without detection. A top-secret document discloses the NSA's ability to hack covertly into personal computers on a mass scale by using automated systems that bypass human oversight.[148] The *Washington Post* indicates that the NSA has direct access to Google, Facebook, Apple, and other internet giants, creating daily from such mobile devices an estimated 2.5 quintillion bytes.[149] This connection with the nine leading US technology companies supplies the NSA on request with emails, online exchanges, chats, videos, and search queries of specific foreign users. The Foreign Intelligence Surveillance Court has found evidence that the FBI violated the rights of millions of Americans by improperly searching the data gathered by the NSA.[150] In 2015, it was a revelation that a top-secret document from a decade earlier disclosed that Google for Voice was transcribing and indexing US citizens according to their verbal conversations.[151] In 2018, in spite of protests and resignations by its employees over artificial intelligence contracts with the Department of Defense, Google declared that the company is not responsible for how its technology will be used. The ACLU has filed a lawsuit against the "dragnet acquisitions" that the government is performing with Verizon, charging such action as "akin to snatching every American's address book, along with annotations detailing whom we spoke to, when we talked, for how long, and from where . . . thereby is revealed a wealth of detail about our familial, political, professional, religious and intimate associations."[152]

In fact, companies are now legally compelled to participate in such activities, gagged from revealing their participation. Even so, we do know that Yahoo has scanned hundreds of millions of accounts at the behest of the NSA, and the FBI, in 2015, secretly built a software program that scanned all customers' incoming emails for US intelligence agencies. AT&T was paid more

147. Savage, "N.S.A. Triples Collection of Data," para. 1.
148. Gallagher and Greenwald, "How NSA Plans," para. 2.
149. Cha, "Big Data," para. 4.
150. Goitein, "How FBI Violated Privacy," para. 3.
151. Gonzalez and Goodman, "Snowden Documents," para. 1.
152. Fuchs, "ACLU Sues Government," para. 4.

than $10 million by the CIA for one year of overseas investigations[153] and has routinely provided information on all 80 million of its customers. A recent report discloses that AT&T has developed, marketed, and sold spying equipment at a cost of millions of dollars of taxpayers' money.[154]

Edward Snowden disclosed the degree to which such global surveillance involves not only intelligence gathering but now an extensive network of industrial espionage. Now that the NSA has the capacity to record and keep 100 percent of all telephone calls made in all countries, even in-flight wi-fi at 30,000 feet, a top-secret presidential directive was issued to senior NSA officials to create a list of potential overseas targets for cyber-attacks. NSA claims to have this hacking capacity to disable all foreign computer networks, with the US Cyber Command employing more than 6,000 hackers.[155] Such surveillance has expanded globally, with the US partnering with at least four other countries in establishing a database of shared intelligence—with the United Kingdom, Canada, Australia, and New Zealand. In 2013, at latest public count, this spying has been on thirty-five world leaders.[156] A year later, it became known that as many as 122 world leaders were in the database.[157] Facebook is working with the Israeli government to suppress Palestinian voices in the social media sphere by deleting specific accounts.[158] After three nights of protests in early 2018, the Iranian government easily blocked Instagram and Messaging apps.[159] Andy Greenberg details the frightening capabilities of the Russian cyberwarfare unit in his *Sandworm: A New Era of Cyberwar and the Hunt for the Kremlin's Most Dangerous Hackers.*

Since 2002, the government has fingerprinted all foreign visitors, collecting 300,000 fingerprints a day.[160] After much denial, the FBI and CIA have finally admitted that, for six years, they have been collecting millions of phone records and commuter records daily from American citizens, the declared goal being "to track everyone's actions through surveillance of all communications." The technology is now available for automatically pairing computers with video cameras in order to identify people by their faces. The CIA is funding Skincential Sciences, which markets skin care products,

153. Savage, "C.I.A. Is Said," para. 1.

154. Lipp, "AT&T Is Spying," para. 10.

155. "Fully Staffed," para. 1.

156. Ball, "NSA Monitored Calls," para. 1.

157. Pengelly, "NSA Listed Merkel," para. 4.

158. Greenwald, "Facebook Is Collaborating," para. 3.

159. Frenkel, "Iranian Authorities Block Access," para. 2.

160. Thales, "DHS's Automated Biometric Identification," para. 4.

in order to collect DNA.[161] Furthermore, the CIA has a hacking tool called Dumbo that allows manipulation of Microsoft's Windows, webcams, microphones, and other devices from thousands of miles away.

Such hacking capabilities, however, are matched by foreign powers, so that cyber attackers have breached the Pentagon, State Department, and White House, and have stolen the personal data of an estimated half of Americans through attacks on banks and tech companies such as Yahoo. Such invasions can potentially target every aspect of our lives that depends on an internet connection. Furthermore, a cyber attack on the electric grid would not only shut down the electricity of millions of Americans but would close multiple services such as water supplies, cell phone towers, trains, and airport landing technology.

The NSA has not only been creating such surveillance capabilities internally but for the past two decades has been licensing its technology to private businesses. With these existing contracts involving hundreds of companies, they in turn are lobbying for significant expansion of the NSA's budget regarding research and surveillance expansion. Recently, a massive $7.2 billion army intelligence contract was awarded to NSA and its multiple private contractors as part of the unfolding air war in the Middle East.[162] This intimate relationship between the NSA and its multiple corporations has developed to the point that global spying is now a pervasively profitable complex. Thus, for example, documents released by WikiLeaks in 2016 disclosed the degree to which the NSA has been spying "on behalf of big oil."[163]

It turns out that the NSA's internet surveillance program (PRISM) is not even government built but has been constructed by Silicon Valley, whose self-interest in turn is to lobby for the NSA's expansion to meet its ongoing appetite for profitable innovation. Noam Cohen, in *Know-It-Alls: The Rise of Silicon Valley as a Political Powerhouse and Social Wrecking Ball*, ends the book by concluding that Silicon Valley leaders are preparing a society in which personal freedoms are near obsolete and governmental regulations limiting surveillance will wither away.

Clearly, the NSA has created a massively opaque spying complex that is even more secretive than the CIA. The only oversight that the NSA receives is largely by former lobbyists for NSA contractors and other intelligence insiders.[164] Although the Foreign Intelligence Surveillance Court is supposed to provide accountability, in 2015, it approved every surveillance

161. Fang, "CIA'S Venture Capital Arm," paras. 2–3.

162. Shorrock, "Who Profits," para. 1.

163. Vibes, "Wikileaks Documents Show NSA," para. 1.

164. Fang, "Lobbyists for Spies Appointed," paras. 1–2.

request requested by US authorities.[165] In fact, the court ordered Verizon to give the NSA "daily, ongoing records" of all domestic and foreign calls.[166] On July 18, 2013, NSA officials appearing before a congressional panel justified their gathering and analysis of phone records and online phone records that were beyond what had previously been disclosed.[167] Going back to 1950, a Senate Select Committee chaired by Sen. Frank Church investigated abuses of intelligence gathering by the FBI, CIA, and NSA—only to have much of their critique classified. In 1975, Church said of the NSA: "I don't want to see this country ever go across the bridge [of abuse] . . . . I know the capacity that is there to make tyranny total in America, and we must see to it that this agency and all agencies that possess this technology operate within the law and under proper supervision, so that we never cross over that abyss. This is the abyss from which there is no return."[168] When he delivered this forewarning over forty years ago, he never dreamed the extent to which this power for tyranny would grow and how severely the abyss would be crossed.

While the stated goal of the NSA is "to eliminate all privacy through global surveillance," it is likewise the precondition for totalitarian control. Information is power, and whoever holds vast amounts of information about us has determining power over us. A hint happened in 2018, when the Trump administration deployed a supposedly unblockable alert system on all cell phones.[169] Julia Angwin, in *Dragnet Nation: A Quest for Privacy, Security, and Freedom in a World of Relentless Surveillance*, documents how our culture of fear is rendering this expansive dynamic of surveillance inevitable. In justifying installation of cameras in heavily active areas of all cities, the logic given was that "in the age of terrorism, an unfettered right to privacy can also mean the ability 'to commit terror' in broad day-light and escape." By 2021, over one billion surveillance cameras will be in use, a 30 percent leap from those in use in 2019.[170]

A feature story in *National Geographic* (2018) estimates that in addition to the 2.5 million surveillance drones presently in use, there are more than 1,700 satellites monitoring our planet.[171] The surveillance from these drones is shared with local police. Researcher Chloe Combi is quoted as surmising: "One of the signs of true wealth and power may end up being

165. Volz, "U.S. Spy Court Rejected," para. 1.

166. Greenwald, "NSA Collecting Phone Records," para. 2.

167. Zengerle and Zacaria, "NSA Head, Lawmakers Defend," para. 1.

168. Bamford, "Agency That Could Be," para. 31.

169. Fung, "Cellphone Users Nationwide," para. 9.

170. Lin and Purnell, "World with Billion Cameras," para. 2.

171. Draper, "They Are Watching You," 41.

that privacy will become a commodity only for those who have the serious money to buy it. For everybody else, the world really will be a stage, with all the people on it self-consciously playing their role."[172] The FBI is deeply involved in such surveillance. In 2014, FBI Director James Comey lobbied Congress to require electronic manufacturers to intentionally create security holes that would guarantee government access to every US cell phone and computer.[173] In March 2017, Comey declared in a speech that he no longer believed that true privacy will ever again be possible,[174] disclosing as an example that during his presidential campaign, candidate Obama was under extensive surveillance.

Presently, the estimated number of names added to the FBI's criminal registry each day is 10,000 to 12,000, with one in three Americans presently in the FBI's criminal records database.[175] The agency even possesses a surveillance program in which, by gathering data about high school students, the FBI calculates the propensity of each student for violence. The Associated Press discloses (2015) that the FBI operates an air force of low-flying planes that crosses the country carrying video and surveillance technology, hidden behind thirteen fictitious companies as fronts.[176] These planes have been spotted circling for hours over Houston, Chicago, and Boston. Among the host of surveillance innovations being created is a tattoo recognition technology that, according to the Government Accountability Office,[177] using a face-recognition data base system, contained 411.9 million images in 2016. Microsoft Research is advertising a technology that can read the facial expression of individual persons in a massive crowd, quickly analyzing the emotions of each. An iris scan of a crowd can be done at the rate of fifty persons per minute. One of the largest such projects is the FBI's $1 billion Next Generation Identification project, focusing on correlating fingerprints, iris scans, facial recognition, and all other detection technology.[178] Indeed, the variety of FBI techniques used to identify and charge over three hundred suspected rioters at the Capitol on January 6, 2021, is broad and pervasive: "license plate readers that captured suspects' cars on the way to Washington; cell-tower location records that chronicled their movements through the

172. Draper, "They Are Watching You," 54.

173. Sanger and Apuzzo, "James Comey, F.B.I. Director," para. 1.

174. Shen, "FBI Director James Comey," para. 1.

175. Novak, "One in Three Americans," para. 1.

176. Gillum, "FBI behind Mysterious Surveillance," para. 1.

177. United States Government Accountability Office, "Face Recognition Technology," 48.

178. United States Government Accountability Office, "Face Recognition Technology," 2.

Capitol complex; facial recognition searches that matched images to suspects' driver's licenses or social media profiles; and a remarkably deep catalogue of video from surveillance systems, live streams, news reports and cameras worn by the police who swarmed the Capitol that day."[179]

In December 2017, Facebook proposed using facial recognition technology on all its users and then updated its usage in 2019.[180] Amazon has offered its own version, called Rekognition, for use by law enforcement agencies—in spite of heavy civil rights protests that accuse it of becoming an instrument of mass surveillance. More than half of all American adults are already in facial recognition databases. Facebook can now recognize people based on their hair, body, shape, and posture. A group of researchers from the University of Cambridge has trained an algorithm to identify people even when those people are wearing disguises.[181] In 2014, it was disclosed that the Drug Enforcement Agency has recorded billions of American calls without warrant.[182] Since 2006, the Department of Defense has been developing the ability to detect the unique rhythms of a person's heartbeats from considerable distance, even through walls.[183] At least fifty law enforcement agencies have radar that can, so to speak, see inside homes.[184] It is no longer surprising that there already exists a surveillance program that is scouring billions of citizen data points, including arrest reports, property records, commercial databases, deep web searches, and social media postings, calculating each citizen's threat level in terms of color-coded scores.

George Orwell in his prophetic *Nineteen Eighty-Four* fantasized about the possibility of visual surveillance through telescreens that would not only communicate government propaganda but would in turn transmit to the government every sound and visual image in the room where the TV was placed.[185] In 2011, Verizon filed a patent application for just such a capacity—a two-way TV that would transmit particularized ads in response to whatever the watcher was doing and using at the time. A patent was denied, but, more recently, Google TV applied, insisting that the technology exists and nothing can stop its inevitable use. A flood of surveillance opportunities have opened through unencrypted smart gadgets, with hackable instruments including TVs, thermostats, refrigerators, and security cameras. Futurist Ray

179. Harwell and Timberg, "How America's Surveillance Networks," para. 10.

180. O'Flaherty, "Facebook Confirms," para. 1.

181. Reynolds, "Even Mask Won't Hide," para. 1.

182. Ackerman, "DEA Sued over Secret," para. 2.

183. Rawnsley, "Follow Your Heart," para. 1.

184. Heath, "New Police Radars," para. 1.

185. Orwell, *Nineteen Eighty-Four*, 182.

Kurzweil opines that by 2045 we and our computers will have so merged that there will be little separation.[186] Since the internet is already controlled by five colossal firms for whom computers are totally accessible to surveillance, we shall become as we are known. Until recently, Facebook specialized in social media, Amazon in e-commerce, and Apple in hardware. But Apple's recent streaming services marks the beginning by each to gain total domination and thus complete control, the only choice being which giant corporate overlord will be in charge of one's digital tyranny.

This self-feeding and self-perpetuating surveillance dynamic has escalated so rapidly that it has become a lucrative multibillion-dollar security/surveillance industry—one in which the multifaceted relationship between governmental intelligence agencies and its outsourced private defense contractors is such that the dynamic is beyond regulation or control. For example, the global biometrics industry alone has a yearly revenue of $36.6 billion and is expected to double in five years.[187] The inability of Congress to pass even minimal commonsense legislative restrictions against these multiple invasions of privacy witnesses, once again, to the growing powerlessness of democratic institutions to counter effectively the consequences that are resulting from the intertwined fingers of fear and economic control.

This surveillance dynamic has now expanded into cyber security, needed as hacking techniques have extended, for example, into sending commands through the internet-connected entertainment systems installed in new cars, thereby able to control major functionings of the vehicle, from brakes to transmissions. Experts predict that, in the near future, such attacks will so disable cars that restoration will require ransom. Further alarming is the prediction that, by 2020, fifty billion devices will be connected to the web so as to make them hackable—controlling a host of arenas such as house locks and the house's internal equipment, as well as locks on medical devices. According to an early 2014 report by HP Security Research, 70 percent of these smart gadgets have serious security flaws.[188] Such vulnerability appears to be unstoppable, as the number of such innovations capable of invasion is projected to soar, creating a self-expanding industry. Additionally, these breaches cost global businesses $3.5 trillion in 2015. These costs are predicted to rise to $10.5 trillion by 2025.[189]

One attempt at preserving some modicum of security is encryption, scrambling information that needs a password for unscrambling. In response,

186. Reedy, "Kurzweil Claims," para. 2.

187. Burt, "Biometric Systems Market," para. 1.

188. *Week* Staff, "Brief Guide," para. 5.

189. Morgan, "Cybercrime to Cost World," para. 2.

FBI Director James Comey and US Deputy Attorney General Sally Quillian Yates appeared before a Senate Committee in 2015,[190] insisting that national security required that they be given a master key to everyone's digital life—whether it be email, text, video chat, or any other format. Otherwise, they argued, terrorists cannot be stopped from planning and executing an attack in our country. William Bradford, assistant professor at the US Military Academy at West Point, argued that even attacks on the home offices and media outlets of academic scholars should be legitimate.[191] Reports from controversial authors, in turn, charged that paragraphs kept disappearing from the computer manuscripts they were writing.

The Federal Communications Commission voted to strike down net neutrality, citing reasons that since have been shown to be indisputably false. Yet on October 1, 2019, a federal appeals court largely upheld the FCC's cancelling of net neutrality rules.[192] This will open the door for a handful of multibillion dollar corporations to exert increased control—a power they have long sought through lobbying—to censor persons and content. The FBI is fighting with Apple to acquire a master key with which to search iPhones for terrorists. While ultimately succeeding without Apple's help, the FBI argues that not only is there legal precedent for this, but the Constitution actually provides authority for searching anything—bedrooms, cars, diaries, financial records, even body cavities, when probable cause exists. Yet our government insists that there is no reason for concern, because much of this potentially damaging information is safe, being classified as top secret. Yet, in reality, there are an estimated 1,400,000 Americans who have top-secret security clearance. In addition, more than 4.9 million persons, many working for private companies, have some level of access to classified US government information. Additionally troubling is the discovery that police across the country, are using their databases for "romance, in granting 'favors' for friends, using information for business benefits, and spying on their neighbors."[193] Of the 33,900 surveillance applications made by the government to the Foreign Intelligence Surveillance Court from 1979 through 2012, 99.97 percent were approved.[194] In practice, the National Defense Act of 2014 almost guarantees governmental authority to exert surveillance on everyone it chooses, largely in the manner it chooses.

190. "Deputy Attorney General," para. 26.
191. Ackerman, "West Point Professor," para. 3.
192. Romm, "Appeals Court Ruling Upholds," para. 1.
193. Associated Press, "Curious Cops Snoop," para. 1.
194. Perez, "Secret Court's Oversight," para. 3.

This obsession with security-surveillance began seriously with the war on drugs in the 1980s. Dawn Paley, in her *Drug War Capitalism*, exposes, however, that the focus was not so much on preventing drug trafficking as it was on setting in motion a violence-centered policy intent on broadening the reach of global capitalism. With the 1033 Program, this control became domestic as well, with the federal agenda being that of allowing sale of discount weapons, supplies, and munitions to local police departments. This expansiveness continued with the massive infusion of new resources by the Department of Homeland Security, entering us into the war on terrorism phase. This militarization with accompanying surveillance then expanded even further into the war against crime, reshaping the self-image of the police from that of community peacemakers into high-tech urban warriors. The focus has become that of quelling unrest, protests, and change. The tragedy in Ferguson, MO, illustrates how police departments have embraced that mentality, functioning as if occupying soldiers in enemy territory dealing with counterinsurgents. During the year following Ferguson, 605 armed vehicles have since been sent to key cities intent on repressing dissent.[195]

More Americans were killed by police violence in 2015 (1146) and in 2016 (1091) than by ISIS; the total is double the highest number ever reported by the FBI in any single year.[196] In larger communities, control rooms with over fifty surveillance monitors are connected to hundreds of sweep-cameras stationed throughout the city, with further access to the cameras placed in schools, local businesses, and on officers' bodies. They also have access to private databases as well, thereby making available such technological capacity as locating vehicle license plates nationwide. The Drug Enforcement Administration is using license plate reader technology to build a complete database. These license plate scanners are able to take photos of the driver and all passengers. Homeland Security is vigorously promoting the issuing of national license plates as part of its tracking system. The software called *Beware* claims to have the capacity to access instantly a person's potential for violence, using all available data to provide a score.[197] Programs such as *Media Sonar* are available to scan social media and *Stingray* for cell phone collection. Policing technology is widely available to police departments, both urban and rural communities. Yet, ironically, TV shows featuring high-tech crime investigators are highly popular, apparently helping to assuage our underlying fear of their power.

195. K. Bennett, "Three Hundred Sixty-Five Days," para. 5.
196. Swaine and McCarthy, "Young Black Men Again," para. 3.
197. Jouvenal, "New Way Police Are Surveilling," paras. 13, 17, 36.

Former US Director of National Intelligence James Clapper and former Attorney General Eric Holder were caught in demonstrable lies about the extent of their surveillance programs.[198] It was also discovered that even the *Washington Post* has ties with the CIA, since Amazon has a $600 million computing contract to keep the CIA secrets.[199] The newspaper is owned by Jeff Bezos who is also the main stakeholder of Amazon. The FBI can now secretly activate any computer's webcam and view a room without turning on the indicator light.[200] Under present rules, the megadata program permits not only collecting a suspect's email, phone calls, and correspondence but can also do the same for everyone in the target's address books, plus their address books, and also their address books.

Such permissiveness regarding social/governmental surveillance has paved the way for corporation surveillance. Work arenas are now being carefully watched and intimidated. Office work involving computers is now open not only for scrutinizing content but for logging even keystrokes to determine productivity. A survey done by the American Management Association found that at least 66 percent of US companies monitor employees' internet use, 45 percent log keystrokes, and 43 percent track their emails.[201] In Amazon, warehouse workers wear wristbands that record their speed and efficiency.[202] Hospital nurses wear badges that document their varied practices. The conclusion drawn by the American Management Association is that "privacy in today's workplace is largely illusory."[203] Such invasion is even being used to provide evidence that a worker is contemplating quitting or exploring other job openings, thereby justifying that worker being fired. The penchant for increased productivity guarantees that broadening and intensifying surveillance will be a permanent fixture of capitalism—with *trust* the value most at risk in terms of employee morale.

Randolph Lewis, in his *Under Surveillance: Being Watched in Modern America*, details the exhausting implications that constant badgering within this surveillance environment has on workers. In 2018, Walmart became involved, acquiring a patent for an audio surveillance technology that measures workers' performance, even listening in on conversations with customers.[204] Simply knowing that one may be being watched guarantees

198. Lawson, "Did Intelligence Officials Lie," paras. 10, 12.

199. Solomon, "Why Washington Post's New Ties," para. 3.

200. Chan, "FBI Can Secretly Turn On," para. 1.

201. *Week* Staff, "Rise of Workplace Spying," para. 2.

202. Yeginsu, "If Workers Slack Off," para. 12.

203. Ribitzky, "Active Monitoring of Employees," para. 15.

204. McGregor, "What Walmart's Patent," para. 1.

restrictive conformity. Experts predict that the next tech revolution in this arena will likely be batteryless computers the size of three stacked quarters that by drawing power from wireless base stations can provide employees with compulsory wearables, sensors, and smart cards. With such surveillance and tracking capability, Shoshana Zuboff, emerita Harvard business professor, in *The Age of Surveillance Capitalism,* declares that we are being pushed "ruthlessly" toward a future in which every action and decision will be directed—thereby "destroying society."

Orwell's fearful portrait of a controlled environment in *Nineteen Eighty-Four* seems quaint when compared with how much farther our present surveillance dynamic has come. And there is no basis for thinking that there will be any turning back—if for no other reason than the profits that will be forthcoming from creating innovative practices such as fingerprints to start cars, voice recognition to verify accounts, iris scans to replace passwords, and medical records produced by facial scanning.

Early on, the Obama administration promised to substitute for this extensive shroud of secret surveillance a policy of total transparency. It never happened, as the attempt itself was so drawn into this relentless vortex that the administration actually set records in the opposite direction. While serious freedom of information requests were denied a record of 8,496 times in 2013, a 57 percent increase over 2012, that denial was doubled during President Obama's first year in office.[205] Such a reversal of intent illustrates the inability of even the presidency to halt the dynamics we are exploring. As a result, journalist Chris Hedges declares that we are in the "last gasp of American democracy" as this intrusive web of surveillance controls our lives by obliterating all privacy.[206] The frightening power that comes with such technology is enormous, so that the president, for example, now has the ability and authority to shut down all internet and phone services with one motion. Even more frightening is the research presently being done into how genetic predisposition can be tapped so as to sway public opinion.[207] Research by neuroscientists exploring the molecular mechanisms of memory and learning[208] might have implications for acquiring the ability to preserve, erase, and modify personal recollection.

An even more alarming aspect of this socioeconomic control is the growing technological capacity to determine human destiny itself. Edward O. Wilson, a dual Pulitzer Prize-winning biologist, sketches this out in his

---

205. Medsger, "Our Government Is Always Hiding," para. 2.

206. Hedges, "Last Gasp of American Democracy," para. 1.

207. Bartels, "Your Genes Influence," para. 1.

208. Bergland, "Mystery of How Memories Form," para. 6.

Meaning of Human Existence. The velocity of such technological change is such that we are on the threshold of abandoning the natural selection process through which humans have emerged thus far. Instead, we now have the capacity to direct our own evolution by volitional selection, redesigning our human nature into whatever form we wish it to be. While this power is presently being explored in an effort to correct genetic diseases, once this is accomplished, Wilson predicts, the next explorations will deal with longer lives, enlarged memory, better vision, less aggressive behaviour, and superior athletic ability, in an endless shopping list. Equally troubling is the who, what, and why of such determinations.

So posed, all Wilson can propose for mitigating this inevitability is the promotion of the humanities rather than the sciences in arenas where such determinations will be made. But in suggesting that philosophers, historians, and artists be placed in charge seemingly evidences little awareness on his part of where the power actually resides in our present society. What is obvious is that such decisions will inevitably result from the self-serving motivations of those in power. These ruminations are not hypothetical, for a select group of researchers, lawyers, and entrepreneurs met behind closed doors at Harvard Medical School to contemplate building a complete set of DNA from scratch, thereby creating a designer human being.[209] The timetable set by geneticist George Church for completing such a venture was ten years. The operative mantra of all such technology is this: "If it can be done and it will be profitable, it will happen."

A further technological apocalypse has been posed by Israeli academic Yuval Noah Harari, predicting in his *Homo Deus* that the human brain will increasingly outsource mental and communicative activities to computers. He then explores this growing technological dependency in terms of its heavy political implications. In the world that is emerging, he insists, the ruling class will be those who understand algorithms and biotechnology, resulting in a dictatorship that will process this control centrally, using technology to "construct a total surveillance regime that will follow every individual all the time, even tracking what is happening inside your body." He insists that such transhumanism is inevitable—given the dependence of our economic system on constant growth, the innateness of our human desires, and our fear of death. Regardless of any positive results that this technology of enhancement might hold, he insists that it dims in comparison with how a small minority of extravagantly wealthy and powerful persons will inevitably exert this "ruthless control" over the masses. The result will be the rise of an elite caste of modified superhumans in fusion with artificial intelligence

209. Creighton, "Harvard Scientists Hold Secret Meeting," para. 1.

and super-intelligent computers that will thereby have the potential to dissolve democracies and establish a global dystopian police state.

The term *military-industrial complex* was used sixty years ago to characterize the growing threat to our society. But what we are increasingly seeing is that it has expanded into a military-industrial-technological-security-surveillance complex. Its control is frightening. In his article "Chilling Effects: Online Surveillance and Wikipedia Use," Oxford University professor Jonathon Penney provides convincing evidence of how its momentum has become a vicious cycle. The fear that creates the surveillance state in turn breeds fear, conformity, and restricted expression, which in turn escalates fear. This outsized fear grooms us to accept as axiomatic that "the end justifies the means." Nonetheless, a 2019 Pew Research Center poll[210] discloses that a majority of adults are at least somewhat concerned about how much data is collected about them by companies (79 percent) and by government (64 percent). Sixty-six percent of Americans say that the potential risks of data collection outweigh the benefits of government collecting data. But only 20 percent read the privacy policies before agreeing to them. Forty-nine percent say it is acceptable for government to collect data about all Americans in order to assess potential terrorist threats, while only 31 percent say it is unacceptable. In heavy contrast, however, on the thirtieth anniversary of having invented the World Wide Web, Sir Tim Berners-Lee deeply lamented how it is now being exploited by "surveillance capitalism, electoral manipulation, and cybercrime."[211]

MEDIA AND FALSE CONSCIOUSNESS

Karl Marx predicted the demise of capitalism by identifying the internal dynamic endemic to that economic system. As he diagnosed it, the inevitable increase of exploitive inequality and rising unemployment would reach a point where the severe conditions would force a revolt sufficient to overthrow the system. He did acknowledge that false consciousness could be a mitigating factor, in which the perception of the exploited would be blurred as to the real cause of their plight. He believed this could be overcome by organizing the workers. A fatal flaw in Marx's diagnosis, however, was one he could never have anticipated: that the managers of this global inequality could come to own and to control an expansively ingenious communication technology with multimedia networks whereby to filter information so as to groom false-consciousness. News becomes slanted, fake news inserted, and

210. Auxier and Rainie, "Key Takeaways," paras. 3, 8–10.
211. Thornhill, "Boldness in Business Person," para. 3.

sifted out are events and stories that might reflect badly on those holding economic power—namely, the affluent owners of the media, their advertisers, and those whose political power favors the rich. Furthermore, Marx could never have imagined that elections could become so dependent on enormous expenditures of wealth that are needed to purchase sufficient media coverage to be campaign competitive. This in turn makes candidates beholden to wealthy donors, in turn favoring them with self-serving legislation. With the Supreme Court's decision to grant corporations the right to unlimited campaign contributions, the maneuvering of the media and elections toward the corporate agenda became inevitable. In the 2012 elections, congressional and presidential candidates and their supporters raised and spent $6.2 billion dollars. The total amount spent for the 2016 elections was over $6.5 billion,[212] with the bulk of this money coming from the richest one-half of 1 percent of the US population. More than 3.2 million Americans contributed to federal candidates in 2020, the federal elections themselves costing $14.4 billion.[213] Super PACS alone spent $2.1 billion in the 2019–2020 election cycle,[214] while small donors accounted for 22 percent of the campaign fundraising.[215]

Furthermore, while the working assumption has been that our legislators reflect the population they represent, for the first time in our history, more than half the members of Congress are millionaires. More than two-thirds of the members of Congress who began in 2017 and left January 3, 2019, now have lobbying-related jobs,[216] guaranteeing that a corporation-friendly voting record while in office will be a subsequent pathway to a lucrative position within a wealthy corporation. Thus this revolving door between legislators and corporate executives blurs the distinction. Corporations are now spending more money yearly on lobbying legislators ($2.6 billion) than taxpayers spend on funding Congress ($2 billion).[217]

More prophetic than perhaps he realized, former Chief Justice Louis Brandeis is purported to have said, "We can have democracy in our country, or we can have great wealth concentrated in the hands of a few, but we can't have both." Indicatively, a study by Professors Gilen and Page of political inequality in America concludes that US voters have nearly zero

212. Ingraham, "Somebody Just Put Price Tag," para. 1.

213. OpenSecrets.org, "Twenty-Twenty Election to Cost," para. 1.

214. OpenSecrets.org, "Twenty-Twenty Outside Spending."

215. Briffault, "Election 2020 Sees Record," paras. 1, 10.

216. Zibel, "Revolving Congress," para. 1.

217. Drutman, "What We Get Wrong," para. 14.

impact on national policy.[218] Instead, they claim, the "scandalous contributions" that "buy legislators" are nothing less than legitimated bribery, tendering as subterfuge Lincoln's image of a government of, by, and for the people. Little did Will Rogers realize the depth of his quip: "We have the best Congress money can buy."

Our country's founders were clear that an informed electorate is essential for a functioning democracy, with a free press the instrument of guarantee. While the power of the news media once provided the populace with a check and balance within the political scene, this has drastically declined. With today's newspaper industry plummeting in readership and thus revenue, what is being forfeited is the investigative reporting that formerly probed behind the scenes and stories, speaking truth to power as a significant counterforce in accountability. *Harper's Magazine* reports that the US newspaper industry has lost 240,700 jobs since 2000.[219] Indicative is the Newark *Star-Ledger*, once New Jersey's regional powerhouse with its 350 journalists, eliminated 240 jobs between 2008 and 2014.[220] Since 2004, more than 1,800 newspapers have closed.[221] With newspaper survival depending upon reversing the diminishing advertising revenue, the news is being rendered noncontroversial, sanitized in favor of potential advertisers. Attempts at attracting new readers has meant shifting the focus to local sports, social events, and feature stories about celebrities, spiced with the diversionary excitement of accidents, fires, and killings. As one editor confessed to me, "We are no longer about news but entertainment." Information about the larger world scene, if it appears much at all, is tucked away on page 19. As another editor put it, "I survive financially by functioning as a lobbying organization for hire." Indicatively, public relations specialists outnumber journalists six to one;[222] by 2029, PR jobs are expected to grow 7 percent, with journalistic employment shrinking by 11 percent.[223]

Another way in which newspapers are attempting to survive is through consolidation by buying rivals. For example, in 2019, Gannett merged with New Media Investment Group and, now under the Gannett name, owns over 260 dailies or one in five newspapers.[224] In 1983, 90 percent of the American media was controlled by fifty companies, but in 2020, 90 percent

218. Gilens and Page, "Critics Argued," para. 1.
219. "Harper's Index" (2018).
220. Boehlert, "What Shrinking Newsrooms Mean," paras. 1–2.
221. Hare, "More Than Eighty-Five Local Newsrooms," para. 5.
222. Tanzi and Hagan, "Public Relations Jobs Boom," para. 2.
223. United States Bureau of Labor Statistics, "Occupational Outlook Handbook."
224. Tracy, "Gannett, Now Largest," para. 2.

of the media is controlled by only six corporations, owned by the affluent 1 percent.[225] People are becoming increasingly dependent on television for their news, and here too the dynamic is basically the same—but with the distinction between news, entertainment, and advertising even further blurred. Sinclair Broadcast Group, the largest owner of television stations nationally, reaches 40 percent of US TV households, a total of 193 television stations nationwide.[226] The owners of Sinclair require that all their stations run conservative commentary on national topics, even providing mandatory scripts and requiring that certain main media news stories be called fake news. The chairman of the board told presidential candidate Trump in 2016 that his company was there "to deliver his message."[227] Such mergers as Time-Warner and AT&T are creating enormous centralized media control. Not surprising, the Koch brothers were interested in entering the media arena. Fox News became the house organ for the Trump Administration, silencing unfavorable news, distorting facts, using fake pictures—and thereby becoming, according to reporter Jane Mayer, both "his shield and his sword."[228] President Trump watched it obsessively and strategized almost daily with Rupert Murdoch, its owner. Without Fox, the report reads, "neither George W. Bush nor Trump would have been elected." Such a vehicle is unprecedented in the US, resembling the state-run news channels characteristic of dictators and communist nations. My cousin, who grew up with me as a sister, now believes Fox News to be the only reliable news source, insisting that all other channels propagate fake news. As a result, the two of us now live in different worlds. Meanwhile, researchers at the University of Oxford found that the number of countries whose governments have political disinformation campaigns has more than doubled to seventy-six in the past two years.[229]

In reflecting the self-interested corporate position of owners and broadcast executives, what the public receives is a uniformity of information on everything from national security to the social safety net, with the slant of false consciousness almost assured. Furthermore, public opinion is shaped to nurture listeners to be spectators rather than participants, let alone activists, often groomed to vote unknowingly against their own self-interests. In 2018, the CIA's Office of Public Affairs released information concerning the frequency with which it had "provided support" for films,

225. Louise, "These Six Corporations Control," para. 4.

226. Chang, "Sinclair's Takeover," para. 1.

227. Savransky, "Sinclair Chief to Trump," para. 1.

228. Mayer, "Making of Fox News," para. 4.

229. University of Oxford, "Social Media Manipulation," para. 1.

TV series, documentaries, and even novels.[230] Reflective of the sophistication of this media involvement, a partnership headed by Twenty-First Century Fox, the Rupert Murdoch-controlled company that owns the Twentieth Century Fox movie studio, the Fox television network, and Fox News Channel, purchased *National Geographic*.[231] All of this is a far cry from what our country's founders regarded as indispensable for democracy's working.

Conservative radio talk shows are replacing progressive ones in central locations such as Los Angeles, San Francisco, Detroit, Seattle, and Portland. The result is that right-wing personalities have a nine to one advantage over those with a more liberal orientation. The anger they express and encourage is never directed toward the system in which the listener is victim, but focused on ways that divide, blaming some other—whether the scapegoat be Muslims, immigrants, Black or brown people, the poor, the gays, or unions. Indicative was the presidential race of 2016, when hatred was evoked and fanned by an angry candidate who himself was one of the wealthy controllers against which emotions should have been turned. Conor Friedersdorf identified thirty of these focused grievances fed by the daily drumbeat of rage, paranoia, and race-tinged hatred—as on Fox News, conservative talk radio shows, and right-wing websites. As former President Obama surmised, the angriest people in America are those without a clue about what is actually going on. Ironically, while the Republican Party favors the self-interest of the wealthy, only 2 percent of Republicans earn more than $250,000 yearly.[232]

Even with such a media system as the Public Broadcasting System, with its reputation for objective reporting, it turns out that it has been receiving secret financing from billionaire activists intent on pushing their political interests. *Sesame Street*, after forty-five seasons on public TV, has been financially forced to relocate to HBO in order to survive. While previously its fictional environment faithfully depicted the grittier neighborhoods of the working-class poor, its channel relocation has entailed gentrification.[233] To claim a wealthier clientele, its new environment is suburban, and it has been significantly redesigned into reduced time segments for suburban kids with shorter attention spans. Perhaps the symbolic apex displaying the economic power involved in corporate advertising is the celebrative extravaganza called the Super Bowl. The fete lasts for days in costly preparation mounting toward the game, with tickets selling for

230. Secker, "ClandesTime 157," para. 1.

231. Farhi, "National Geographic Gives Fox," para. 3.

232. Kingsbury, "Big Data: Not-So-Wealthy Republicans," para. 1.

233. Suiter, "After Fifty Years," para. 13.

astronomical prices, TV records being set for global audience and profit, short commercials costing millions of dollars vying for competitive creativity—and for those without an appetite for football, tons of fireworks at the halftime show sparkle a costly celebrity into spectacle.

Silicon Valley giants such as Facebook, Apple, and Google are intensely involved in becoming dominant distributors of news, over which there is almost no control as to accuracy. Four out of ten Americans get their news from Facebook.[234] The risk of manipulation is high, with software readily available that can superimpose one person's face onto another person's body and can manipulate voices, thereby creating fake videos in which anyone can be viewed as saying anything that is desired. Furthermore, algorithms can now provide for each viewer what is predetermined to be best for that person, exercising significant editorial control in balancing profit with the information provided. Such capacities have brought Jeffrey Herbst of the *Wall Street Journal* to acknowledge that the determiner of these choices will have a profound effect "on the quality of our democracy."[235]

Not only are we being socialized by the media into a cloaked acquiesce to the way things are, but we are being groomed into glamorizing the controlling rich and powerful as our hope chest role models—rendering the 99 percent not angry at the 1 percent but envious of them. We are tutored to idealize who they are, what they wear, where they live, what they drive, and with whom they are having their latest affairs, establishing their flaunted affluence as an index to happiness. Even in sports, wealth and role models have become indistinguishable. Understandably then more Americans than ever before are undergoing cosmetic surgery, with 18.1 million surgeries done in 2019. According to the American Society of Plastic Surgeons, breast augmentation continues to be the top cosmetic surgical procedure and has been since 2006.[236] The present rage is rear end transplants that have increased 252 percent since 2000, which surgeons understand as due to the influence of celebrities like Kim Kardashian and Nicki Minaj who manifest ample posteriors. Even with men, plastic surgery is becoming more common, imitating the successfully famous. The power of false consciousness is unmistakable when both oppressors and oppressed take on the same appearances, dreams, and values, differing only as to where they are on the ladder of feigned promise.

In researching for her book *Living Faith: Everyday Religion and Mothers in Poverty*, sociologist Susan Crawford Sullivan was amazed to find that

---

234. Shearer and Matza, "News Use," para. 6.

235. Herbst, "Algorithm Is Editor," para. 14.

236. American Society of Plastic Surgeons, "Plastic Surgery Statistics Report," 5.

the poor women whom she interviewed never used social injustice to account for their plight. Instead, the cultural ethos is so powerfully and variedly rehearsed in our culture that the only explanation these women could entertain for their plight was an individual one. In blaming themselves, they reflected the widespread media-caused blindness to the systemic web in which they were caught. Illustrative of this dynamic is a recent cartoon portraying a couple watching a movie entitled "The World of Wall Street." One panel is entitled "What we should be thinking," in which the expected response to watching the film is "what a bunch of greedy morally reprehensible, prison-worthy crooks." A second panel is entitled "What we are really thinking." The inner thought of the man is: "Nice car! Hot babe!" And the woman: "Cool yacht! Awesome party!" What is happening is a version of brain washing as a growing media worship of gaudy wealth and fame, in which celebrity demigods dominate every field, from cuisine to medicine. The result is a super class, amassing increasing wealth and power as the country's middle class is losing theirs, yet evoking not angry resentment but a controlling envy. The mythical icon of success so persists, ironically, that this lack of anger toward the rich is because we have been socialized to regard them as the ideal.

Strongly operative here is the persistence of bootstrap hope—that anyone who tries hard enough can succeed, operating on the assumed illusion of a level playing field for all. Not so, for the poor are destined to limited success, if any at all, fated by multiple factors such as inadequate housing, broken families, insufficient nutrition, inferior education, depressing environment, unavailable health care, biased justice systems, and limited role models. In contrast, the 2019 college admission scandals disclose the illegal measures to which wealthy parents are willing to go in advantaging their children. Yet even the legal advantages available to wealthy offspring are enormous, as in having special tutors, coaches, college counselors, ghost writers, and hefty institutional gifts to navigate smoothly the channels into privileged universities and favored positions beyond. The reason why proposals to place restrictions on the wealthy get so little traction is that when the ship comes in for the non-rich, they would not want those restrictions to apply to them, too.

This lure of the mythical American Dream that has intersected with the myth of the rugged individual has become so engrained that millions of persons daily defy common sense in challenging preposterous odds, lured and seduced by the $40-billion-a-year gambling industry. The depth of this enculturation is displayed in the epidemic proportions that gambling has taken, especially among the poor, who can least afford being so entrapped. Research by the business school of Carnegie Mellon finds that most persons who gamble do so with a desire to improve their finances.[237] Thus, the greater the poverty rate, the higher the lottery sales—representing for millions the only perceived opportunity for changing their lives as catching the tail of the American Dream. Since lotteries depend on the poor and on gambling addicts for much of their revenue, forty-five states and the District of Columbia actively promote lottery gambling as the fastest way to get ahead. Although the chance of winning the Powerball jackpot is 1 in 292,201,338,[238] there have been lines of persons waiting to play, motivated by the fantasy of getting rich quick. Half of all Americans have played the lottery, with sales in various forms of gambling in the states totaling $30 billion in 2017.[239] In contrast, those whose income is below $30,000 spend an average of $412 per year, while those whose household income is greater than $75,000 spend $105 per year on state lotteries.[240] Sales come from primarily the poor and uneducated, in the hope of getting out of poverty. Indicatively, during the most recent economic depression, sales spiked. They are regressive taxes on poor people, in that a ticket costs relatively more for a poor person than a rich person. Even so, the majority of Americans resist taxing the rich, because they have been socialized to believe that they too will one day join their ranks. Advertising depicts winners in stretch limousines, counting stacks of money, dressed as classy folks in evening gowns and tuxedos, sipping champagne in partied mansions.

While in 1960 only Atlantic City and Nevada had casino gambling, today casinos operate in every state, in addition to state lotteries, Powerball, and now internet gambling.[241] More is spent on state lotteries alone than on sports tickets, books, video games, movie tickets, and recorded music combined. Even assisted living centers and local churches are organizing outings to casinos. Yet, in reality, as one person who made it big on the lottery laments, "I had to endure the greed and the needs that people have, as everyone tries to get you to release your money to them." In fact, studies indicate that lottery winners are disproportionately likely to wind up bankrupt or have their lives ruined in various ways by the sudden wealth.[242]

Marx was basically accurate in predicting the increasing inequality endemic to capitalism. Thus, as a Russell Sage Foundation study discloses, the net worth of the average American has dropped 36 percent from 2003

237. Haisley et al., "Subjective Relative Income," 19.
238. Adamczyk, "These Are the Odds," para. 2.
239. Urban Institute, "Lotteries, Casinos, Sports Betting," para. 5.
240. Kline, "How Much Are Americans Spending," para. 6.
241. Bourie, "Casinos by State," para. 1.
242. *Week* Staff, "Inside America's Lottery Addiction," para. 4.

to 2013, while that of the ninety-fifth percentile has grown by 14 percent, diminishing the middle class and swelling the ranks of the poor.[243] The Institute for Policy Studies discloses that, since 2012, US taxpayers have subsidized more than $2 billion in executive bonuses for the nation's largest banks.[244] In 2013, the median compensation of CEOs passed $10 million for the first time.[245] In 2019, the average compensation of the CEOs in the 350 biggest companies was 320 times that of the average worker.[246] In 2014, seven of the thirty largest US companies paid their chief executives more than the firms paid in federal taxes—Boeing, Ford, Chevron, Citigroup, Verizon, JPMorgan Chase, and General Motors.[247] Presently, CEOs are earning 257 times more than the average employee in their corporations, with employee wages stagnant or dropping. Between 1978 and 2018, CEO compensation has grown 940 percent, while typical worker compensation has risen only 12 percent during that time.[248] In 2016, the one hundred American CEOs with the largest retirement nest eggs had a total of $4.7 billion in their company retirement accounts—equal to the combined retirement savings of the bottom 116 million Americans or 41 percent of the country's families.[249] A generation ago, such behavior would have been utterly unacceptable, subject to the weight of public ridicule, as the Great Depression was on the verge of revolt. But the present reversal from what Marx predicted is due to the expansiveness of false consciousness, largely the result of the mass media.

Robert Reich (2020) provides three additional reasons for passivity regarding this gross, unjust inequality. First, the working class is paralyzed by fear of losing their jobs if they organize or even complain, apprehensive that others such as immigrants will gladly take their place for lesser wages. Without job security, unemployment is a constant threat against effective dissent. Second, it is difficult for employees to understand their situation when retaining their jobs and gaining any salary increase are dependent on their not understanding. Thus, while one might think the situation ripe for union organizing, workers are being widely socialized to believe that unions are a significant factor in creating their tenuousness. Third, college students who in the past have often been a major factor in social unrest are presently so laden with debt that they dare not risk anything that would damage their

243. Pfeffer et al., "Wealth Levels, Wealth Inequality," 1.

244. Sarah Anderson and Pizzigati, "Executive Excess 2016," para. 4.

245. Greenblatt, "Median CEO Pay," para. 2.

246. Mishel and Kandra, "CEO Compensation Surged," para. 1.

247. Drawbaugh, "Seven Big U.S. Companies," para. 1.

248. Mishel and Wolfe, "CEO Compensation Has Grown," para. 1.

249. Sammon, "One Hundred CEOs," para. 2.

resumés, blight their credit ratings, or create negative data discoverable in future background checks. They find themselves in an intensely competitive upper-level job market in which, even if employed, they will likely be at a lower level than that for which they have been educated. College students owe more than $1.7 trillion in student loans, with student debt having increased during the past decade by 102 percent.[250] As of September 2020, defaults are at 6.5 percent, and the average student loan debt for the class of 2019 is $28,950.[251] Starting salaries, when available, have dropped 10 percent in a decade. In 2020, 50 percent of millennials live with their parents after college, adding pressure to the already unstable family unit.[252]

A consequence of this economic crisis on many Americans is a growing cynicism about the government, as Americans despair not only of its ability to effect significant change but even its willingness to do so. Just 20 percent of US adults say they trust the government in Washington to "do the right thing" just about always or most of the time.[253] No longer is this dissatisfaction focused on particular politicians or even on a specific party but on Congress as a whole, with ratings of all major societal institutions never being so low. Elections give little hope for change.

Another important feature of this growing false consciousness is the attitude being groomed regarding leisure. At least as far back as Aristotle, an unquestioned assumption has been that a significant reason for working is to acquire leisure. Ironically, this is no longer so. In fact, our society is being programmed in the opposite direction. Benjamin Hunnicutt, professor of leisure studies at the University of Iowa, traces (1996) how this yearning for leisure had impelled the early twentieth century into envisaging "a golden age of leisure." It was expected that the economy would so grow that everyone would be able to experience the fullness of life outside the economic order itself, in a good life characterized by familial and communal togetherness and common activity. Marilyn Gardner, staff writer of the *Christian Science Monitor*, chronicled how utopian books appearing during this period projected a six-hour work day as soon realizable.[254] George Bernard Shaw predicted in 1900 that by 2000, people would need to work only two hours a day—and only ten hours a week in order to receive the basic necessities.[255] In the early 1930s, a bill for a thirty-hour work week failed in Congress by only

250. Hess, "U.S. Student Debt," paras. 3–4.

251. Hornsby, "Student Loan Debt Statistics," para. 7 chart.

252. Z. Friedman, "Fifty Percent of Millennials," para. 4.

253. "Americans' Views of Government," para. 1.

254. Marilyn Gardner, "Elusive Search," para. 2.

255. Bregman, "Solution to Just about Everything," para. 12.

a narrow margin. In this new era, life would be defined by creative leisure. How utterly ironic it is, then, that the advent of automation and robots that should be welcomed as hastening Shaw's dream is in fact a severe threat. In 2019, the *Week* suggested that fifty-four million Americans could lose their jobs due to automation and artificial intelligence in the next ten years.[256] The analysis included an Oxford University study in 2013 that concludes that 47 percent of American jobs are at "high risk" of automation within two decades and offered a warning by futurist Martin Ford that the pace of automation is no longer linear but exponential. For every robot, 6.2 jobs are lost.[257] Furthermore, predictions are that since transnational corporations are constantly building state-of-the-art high-tech production facilities for the sake of cost efficiency, quality control, and speed of delivery, the future elimination of millions of jobs promises a grim future. The prophetic irony is that in contrast to this tragic portrait, under an alternative system of production and distribution, this dynamic would be cause for great celebration—for by diminishing the amount of labor while providing adequate wages, significant leisure time would result for all.

How this great reversal from society's former leisure vision happened was that wealthy persons such as Henry Ford and his ilk recognized that this dynamic would result in reversal of expansive wealth for the rich. Thus, around the turn of the century, he and a host of businessmen spoke out passionately against the vision, and books with titles such as *The Threat of Leisure* by George Cutten have continued into the present. Their argument was that people should be taught to work not for acquiring additional leisure but for affording expanding goods and services. They were highly successful in promoting this lure of consumption—so able to demean leisure that it has become equated with laziness. Doing nothing is now cause for guilt. Emerging was what Professor Hunnicutt calls "the new economic gospel of consumption."[258] Instead of yearning for time to be more human, for what Christians would call the fullness of life, time was economically captured by doing for the sake of increased having. Not only was time drained of leisure, but curtailed were places associated with it, such as front porches, parks, and even living rooms. "Time is money." Thus, as the nineteenth-century essayist Thomas Carlyle presaged: "Every

---

256. *Week* Staff, "Will You Lose Your Job," para. 1.
257. *Week* Staff, "Will You Lose Your Job," para. 2.
258. Hunnicutt, *Kellogg's Six-Hour Day,* 4.

idle moment is treason."[259] In heavy contrast, St. Polycarp insists, "The source of all evil is the desire to possess."[260]

Sadly, Hunnicutt draws this conclusion: "Work emerges as something very close to a religion, answering the traditional ultimate questions, such as who are you, and questions of identity. It is the way we find meaning in life."[261] Consumerism has been so instilled and rehearsed into each of us that doing has become an idolatrous obsession, instilling in us the passion of never having enough—thereby assuring an ever-expanding gross national product that guarantees massive wealth for the wealthy through the drivenness within the rest of us. Not to be doing is to experience guilt, but church involvement requires leisure time. This dilemma for the churches is further exacerbated by the increase of women being forced into the work force—up from 35 percent in 1950 to 57 percent in 2020.[262] Since churches depend on volunteers—and, in the past, these volunteers have largely been unemployed homemakers with discretionary time—the implications for the church are clear.

Facebook's first president, Sean Parker, has publicly expressed regret for having designed social media platforms and apps that are exploiting our vulnerabilities so as to hopelessly hook us.[263] Average adults check their phones fifty to three hundred times daily. Ellen McCarthy of the *Washington Post* identifies the reason why breaking this addiction to the omnipresent cell phone is so difficult—simply because we no longer know how to be idle.[264] Harvard and University of Virginia researchers found that nearly half of the participants in their study preferred to give themselves an electric shock than to sit for fifteen minutes alone with their thoughts.[265] Yet Whitehead identifies religion as being alone with the Alone, with "what the individual does with his solitariness."[266] The implications for Christianity are clear.

An acclaimed wealth management advisor chastises any public resentment against the wealthy this way: "To revile the rich is to revile the American Dream"; the affluent should be our role models.[267] Billionaire investor Leon Cooperman insists that resentment would "squash the American

259. Singh, "Time to Smell Roses," para. 6.

260. International Commission on English in the Liturgy, *Liturgy of the Hours*, 4:319.

261. Hunnicutt, *Kellogg's Six-Hour Day*, 119.

262. "Women in the Workforce," para. 6.

263. Silverman, "Facebook's First President," para. 3.

264. E. McCarthy, "Breaking Up," para. 14.

265. Sample, "Shocking but True," para. 16.

266. Whitehead, "Religion in the Making," 484.

267. P. Sullivan, "All This Anger," para. 9.

Dream."[268] With this understanding instilled, citizens are reduced to customers within an economy dependent upon voracious consumers. Daniel Bell, in his *Economy of Desire: Christianity and Capitalism in a Postmodern World*, powerfully critiques our capitalist system "for the ways it deforms human desire and so warps relations with oneself, others, and God." Our economy is focused not on serving human ends but on subduing the population into "the service of capital ends."[269] This tragic situation resides in the fact that the health of our economy is not measured by factors such as how many persons have adequate health care, a living wage, reasonable housing, or clear water—that is, by concern for providing the greatest number of persons with what is needed in order to be human. The economy is not regarded as a means, but as an end, a thing to be served, taking on a life of its own, so that the daily health of the stock market is now an organic ingredient of the morning news. It is as if it were an organic something that needs ongoing health care, daily checked for stabilized blood pressure, and its GNP given the correct degree of medication to guarantee ever-rising profits. Economic growth has become an axiomatic theme, likened to a human organism in which failure to grow is tantamount to sickness. Thus, since the market is not intent on producing human solutions, the work of economists is, for example, to prescribe modest inflation as a necessity, regarding it as a healthy sign that consumer credit has passed the $3 trillion mark and total household debt has escalated to $13 trillion. They view the willingness of persons to borrow as a good omen and even regard personal savings as an economic liability. But no fear, for one-third of Americans are unable to save anything anyhow, and 68 percent are spending more than they earn—thereby making for a "healthy" economy.

It is imperative to realize what this healthy means—that 25 percent of all adults have no emergency funds at all, and 12 percent of Americans would not be able to pay a $400 emergency bill.[270] By 2030, the nonworking citizens who will be dependent on the employed will exceed 70 percent.[271] Nearly half of the US labor force has no retirement plan,[272] and, by 2035, persons over sixty-five will surpass those under eighteen, a national first.[273] Meanwhile, consumptive craving is giving rise to captive borrowing. According to the *Wall Street Journal*, US household debt tied to credit

268. Sandler, "Billionaire Leon Cooperman," para. 7.

269. Bell, *Economy of Desire*, 26.

270. Rosenbaum, "Millions of Americans," para. 5.

271. *Week* Staff, "Graying of America," para. 3.

272. "Nearly Half of U.S. Families," para. 4.

273. Overberg and Adamy, "Elderly in U.S.," para. 1.

cards, mortgages, student loans, and car loans rose in the third quarter of 2020 to \$14.35 trillion.[274] One hundred years ago, Sherwood Anderson in his classic novel *Winesburg, Ohio* gave us fair warning, graphically portraying his characters against the background that he recognized as "the beginning of the most materialistic age in the history of the world . . . when the will to power would replace the will to serve and beauty would be well-nigh forgotten in the terrible headlong rush of mankind toward the acquiring of 'possessions.'"[275]

This driving passion for growth based on consumption is unsustainable. With the world's population projected to be 10 billion by 2050 and 12.3 billion by 2100, the lifestyle of the typical American projected onto the world's population will destroy the planet. This consumerist dynamic is such that, for example, air conditioning, once a luxury for whom much of the world was without, is now being installed at the rate of 700 million new units yearly.[276] While some help could be forthcoming by de-growing our economy to the lifestyle level that thirty- or even twenty-hour-per-week jobs could provide for all, the economic dynamic that has been set in motion will never permit this to happen. False consciousness has rendered time a commodity to be measured chronologically by the clock. Thus since "time is money," all of our activities must be productive, evoking guilt for activities not measurable as if a salable commodity. To anticipate, in acute contrast to all of this, Christianity is rooted in holy leisure, in spending time participating with God in Sabbath rest and joyful playfulness for its own sake. While this ideal is increasingly strange in today's world, there is something exhilarating in confronting life's absurdities with faith's seemingly absurd wager in which even a bowl of strawberries with cream can become an extravagant hint of resurrection. As Thomas Merton insists, worship and prayer, when measured productively, are useless, a total waste of time—and so is God, and sunrises, and birds singing vespers at every sunset. Christianity is rooted in the delicious ache one feels as a V of geese honks south in the fall, or waves break relentlessly against the shore, or one becomes lost in a Mozart symphony. They are all instrumentally useless, good for nothing but for their own intrinsic sake. And to render them useful is to squander them—as in using a Beethoven Sonata to quiet a dentist's drilling. If one makes love with one's spouse and then rolls over, saying, "Honey, what good did that do?"—the marriage is over.

274. Harrison, "American Consumers Shun Plastic," para. 2.
275. Sherwood Anderson, *Winesburg, Ohio*, 45–46.
276. Mooney and Dennis, "World Is About to Install," para. 6.

Sabbath symbolizes the Christian's ability to do nothing and feel no guilt. In contrast to society's obsession with doing, the Christian's doing is laced by the holy leisure of worship, when everything is declared off limits except imaginative ways of romping with God in the wonders of creation's seventh day, anticipating the eighth. Being a Christian is a glorious way of existing intrinsically, living out the goal of evolution's intentionality, liturgically acting out as eucharistic exchange the drama in which everything that exists is being called to participate in the becoming of God. This involves pure faith, wagering qualitatively on life for its own sake, purged of self-serving. It involves love as intention and worship as thankful response to the sheer gift of existing, marinated in the evolving seasons of mystery. The fact that all of this sounds foolish to the modern mind witnesses to why the church is in diminishment. In a real sense, this modern realization that Christianity is, in fact, useless is at the heart of the church's demise. Yet, as we will explore, this recognition can be the entrée into a postmodern Christian spirituality.

Douglas Rushkoff, in his *Present Shock: When Everything Happens Now,* provides a further clue concerning this clash between modern consciousness and that of the Christian. Our culture has become characterized by "hyper distraction" or "digiphrenia," which Rushkoff identifies as how our technologies and media force us into multitasking. By dissipating us into being various places at the same time, intent on varied things, there is established a presence contrary to any spiritual sense of the word. Rushkoff identifies it as "a frantic convenience," a "desperate immediacy," a being "always-on urgency."[277] In contrast, Jesus insists on living fully in the now by refusing to let it be drained by preoccupation with past, future, or any other distraction. Focusing through purity of heart entails immersion in the rich giftedness of each moment—living in but not of the world. In contrast, our culture positions us to be of the moment but not in it, with a nowness in which we feel "distracted, peripheral, even schizophrenic." An onslaught of multiple demands for our immediate attention dissipates the pregnant presence of each now. Symptomatic is the present fad of mindfulness as a response to this dilemma but with little awareness of its systemic cause and thus its real solution.

The multidimensions of this false consciousness, then, are key in diverting us from understanding the nature of the systemic complex in which we are caught and by which we are being shaped. Controlled by and for the wealthy, the rest of us are socialized to locate the problem within ourselves as losers. But, as we have indicated, Pope Francis understands this dynamic

---

277. Rushkoff, *Present Shock,* 97.

clearly and thereby is intriguing many while angering the rich. In his *Joy of the Gospel*, he locates our crisis firmly within the dynamics of the system itself, scoffing at any trickle-down theory of free enterprise economics, declaring it to be a "cruel fiction." He declares as utterly immoral the "idolatry of money" and "the globalization of indifference," judging as foolhardy any "crude and naïve trust in the goodness of those wielding economic power."[278] Speaking directly to government officials, money managers, and board members of multinational corporations, Pope Francis casts disdain on our present system, in which "the income of a minority is increasing exponentially as that of the majority is crumbling." Worship of the golden calf has found a new and heartless image in the cult of money within the dictatorship of an economy "lacking any truly humane purpose." Therefore, sinful is any defense of this absolute autonomy of the marketplace and its financial speculation. Over against all this, the Pope's passion is on the dignity and worth of every individual, insisting that when this axiom is disregarded, there can be no peace. Journalist Richard Smith draws the same conclusion: "We have a stark choice. We can save capitalism or save human civilization. But there is no possible future that contains both."[279]

Yet as salutary as Pope Francis's courageous declarations are, they have an unintended sadness. They make clear that there is nothing external to this global economic tsunami that has the power to change its course, or even bring significant blunting—only a charismatic pope whose power is that of teaching and of example, basically to a Church that, by so doing, he is dividing. The value of this unexpected papal emergence, at best, was in challenging all the church to refrain from domesticating the heart of the gospel—a gospel that demands such a reordering of one's life perspective that it is a conversion from the dynamics by which our society is defining the meaning of life.

Nowhere has Pope Francis's witness emerged more clearly than in his amazing encyclical letter *Laudatio sì* (*On Care for our Common Home*). Here he takes his criticism beyond the confines of the church and the individual to address with alarm the whole of the human race, identifying as culprits those who act as if they were "lords and masters" of the world, "entitled to plunder her at will." In defiance of our cultural ethos, he declares that "less is more." "A constant flood of new consumer goods can baffle the heart and prevent us from cherishing each thing and each moment."[280] In contrast, he submits a Christian spirituality in which growth must be marked by

---

278. Pope Francis, *Joy of the Gospel*, 46–47.

279. R. Smith, "Beyond Growth or Beyond Capitalism," para. 44.

280. Pope Francis, *Laudatio sì*, 162.

moderation and inflated appetites purged into being happy with less. This lifestyle of spiritual detachment from much of what we now have, he identifies as having been modeled by monasticism. It is a way of living that "is essential now for our very survival on the planet." True, and yet there is a deep pathos in his prophetism—for the dynamic of modern culture is so diminishing the appeal of monasteries that they are presently disappearing as rapidly as the churches. With deaths far exceeding novices, the global survival of monasticism is in serious jeopardy. In my own Trappist order, two-thirds of our monasteries are regarded as precarious. Thus, Pope Francis is intensely right in insisting that the "ecological crisis is a summons to internal conversion,"[281] insisting that nothing short of a transformation of lifestyle will do anything more than treat symptoms. Yet while realism makes it unlikely that this will happen, it discloses how essential this conversion is if Christians are to be Christians and Christianity is to be worth surviving. More apt than ever, St. Paul insists: "Do not be conformed to this world, but be transformed by the renewal of your mind . . ." (Rom 12:2). By *world*, he does not mean rejection of God's creation but purification from a socioeconomic culture such as ours. A balanced life perspective marinated in wonder and hyphenated by silences is utterly at odds, says Pope Francis, with modernity's "profound imbalance that drives to a frenetic riding rough-shod over everything."[282]

In the face of this false consciousness that insists our ecological crisis is a hoax, Pope Francis discloses how systemically it is linked with the plight of the poor. Therefore, Christians dare no longer retain their own false consciousness of regarding faith as pertaining only to religious matters. Christianity is a total perspective regarding the whole planet, calling humanity into responsibility for its own survival by replacing "consumption with sacrifice, greed with generosity, wastefulness with a spirit of sharing, and asceticism which entails learning to give, and not simply to give up."[283] This transformation of lifestyle involves not only individuals but demands the transforming of our means of production and consumption. "The divine and the human meet in the slightest detail in the seamless garment of God's creation, in the last speck of dust of our planet."[284] Thus, there is an inseparable bond "between concern for nature, justice for the poor, commitment to society, and interior peace."[285] Perhaps never before has there been

281. Pope Francis, *Laudatio sì*, 158.

282. Pope Francis, *Laudatio sì*, 164.

283. Pope Francis, *Laudatio sì*, 8.

284. Pope Francis, *Laudatio sì*, 9.

285. Pope Francis, *Laudatio sì*, 10.

made more clear this antithesis between the ethos impelling our society and the one necessary for our survival, rooting our global crisis systemically in a corporate capitalism that is profoundly counter-Christian in nature. Yet his witness is making just as clear how helpless is our plight. On the one hand, our culture is shaping us into blindness regarding the need for such a transformation; on the other hand, we are being drained of the Christian resources that could ground such a transformation. The irony is that changing our basic structures depends on a radically changed consciousness on the part of the people, who are being shaped into a false consciousness that serves the wealthy—who have the power to resist anything that challenges their self-interest. Furthermore, if the churches were to preach seriously this holistic conversion into the mind of Christ, it would be so contrary to the dynamic impelling today's society that it would alienate the affluent, on whom the churches are dependent for physical survival. Actually, what we really have is a dual false consciousness, in which a significant majority do not understand themselves as being systemically exploited by the rich, and the rich, ironically, do not regard themselves as being exploiters.

The election of Donald Trump marked a threshold in this dynamic, entering us into a new age, as some pundits put it. The French ambassador to the US declared Mr. Trump's election as marking when the world "was collapsing before our eyes."[286] After eight years under a Black president, then threatened by the possibility of a woman president, and consequently threatened by an ethnic invasion, what divisively erupted was a reactionary passion to restore White male authority with its accompanying entitlements. "Make America Great Again" is the cry to reclaim the American Dream, restoring an imaginary past with a rosy portrait of former family stability regained by repulsing the governmental controls that threaten our freedom. Fear is establishing a composite of resentment laced with anger, thereby enabling support of an angry sycophant who is actually undermining the voters' own self-interests. Ronald Brownstein in his recent article in the *Atlantic* identifies Mr. Trump's campaigning for reelection as "running on fear," focused on warning rural Whites and evangelicals that "the American way of life" is in great peril, and "only he can shield them."[287] The irony is that Trump, the self-proclaimed consummate businessman who boasts of his enormous wealth, dwells in a world radically different from his base. Those living in 86 percent of the counties that voted for Trump have an annual income that is less than the collective $2.3 billion net worth of his

286. Agerholm, "Donald Trump Wins," para. 1.
287. Brownstein, "Trump Settles," paras. 4, 9–10.

twenty-seven closest aides, advised by a cabinet that is the wealthiest in US history.[288] This is false consciousness.

On the evening before president-elect Trump's inauguration, I mused as to where this global economic tsunami was taking us. This is the prediction I wrote. "During the term ahead there will likely be huge tax cuts for the rich; further shredding of the safety net for the poor; significant increase in military spending; further militarizing of the police; eroding of the First Amendment and enhancement of the Second; vigorous denial and delay regarding the human causation of climate change; diminishment of corporation regulations; undoing of Dodd-Frank banking reforms; further undercutting of the Affordable Care Act; minimizing clean energy controls and environmental protections; and opening public lands further for private drilling, fracking, and deforesting." Like a fulfilling prophecy, almost all of Trump's choices for cabinet and agency posts had a history of opposition to the very responsibilities for which their posts were intended. Instead of serving as watchdogs, these were the very persons in need of being watched. Trump's corporatocracy was composed of 150 former lobbyists. In 2016, when my newly elected Republican House Representative was asked what she planned to do in Washington, she angrily retorted, "I'm not going there to do anything, but I plan to undo a lot." We have entered the era of decentralization, privatization, and deregulation, in which power is possessed not only by a plutocracy but an oligarchy. In *A Theory of Imperialism,* Utsa and Prabhat Patnaik conclude that we have reached the point where any nation refusing to serve international capitalism risks economic collapse, with its insolvency guaranteed by capital flight. As long ago as the 1930s, the Frankfurt School was predicting that the mass media and the cinema industry would create the foundation for "a totally administered society" that would undermine lethally the structures of democratic society.

ECONOMIC CONTROL AND
CONSERVATIVE CHURCHES

In his *One Nation Under God: How Corporate America Invented Christian America,* Kevin Kruse describes how evangelical reformers in the nineteenth and twentieth centuries excoriated capitalism as inconsistent with the mandates of the New Testament. Famed evangelist Charles Finney, for example, saw a Christian businessman as an oxymoron, basing his case on capitalism's elevation of avarice over altruism. William Jennings Bryan, as well as social gospel theologians such as Walter Rauschenbusch, vigorously

288. Bump, "Eighty-Six Percent of Trump Counties," paras. 1–2.

attempted to protect workers from the ravages of unbridled capitalism. Yet within the past century, this situation has reversed—so much so that Jerry Falwell could insist that "the free enterprise system is clearly outlined in the Book of Proverbs."[289]

Other books tracing this conservative reversal of economic ideology are Darren Dochuk's *From Bible Belt to Sunbelt*, Jeff Sharlet's *The Family* as a study of the Fellowship Foundation, and Bethany Moreton's *To Serve God and Wal-Mart*. A key turning point was the advent of Franklin D. Roosevelt's New Deal, seen as posing a serious challenge to capitalism. In response, the National Association of Manufacturers enlisted friendly clergy on behalf of a campaign called Christian libertarianism. Congregational minister James Fifield, called the "apostle to millionaires," developed a comparable version entitled Spiritual Mobilization, a prosperity gospel base on a free market reading of the New Testament. Norman Vincent Peale and J. Howard Pew became influential personalities befriended by wealthy sponsors, financed to spread this evolving message into widely popular ministries. What emerged was a prosperity theology in which Christianity became interpreted as condemning all socialistic expressions, such as a minimum wage, Social Security, and benefits for veterans. Heavily groomed was a fear of communism. Kruse describes how a number of these reactionary parallel movements converged during the Eisenhower administration, during the administration of the only president to undergo baptism while in office. A month before his inauguration, Eisenhower stated that American democracy "makes no sense unless it is founded in a deeply felt religious faith." He made a point of opening his meetings with prayer and instituted such innovations as the National Prayer Breakfast. Billy Graham, a key personality during this time, gained an access to the White House that lasted through multiple presidential terms—holding that even labor unions were unchristian. Congress, in the meantime, provided support for this version of Christianity by inserting "under God" in the Pledge of Allegiance, insisting that religion is the foundation of America, and attempted to have the United States designated as a Christian nation. Although Eisenhower left office with a warning against the power of the military-industrial complex, he had in fact solidified the accommodation of Christianity with capitalism. And in the early 1960s, public school prayer provided the benediction.

By the 1980s, this strange fusion of Christianity and free market capitalism had become normative among conservative denominations, with Christian nationalism being a powerful movement in the political landscape. The religious right continues to draw significant energy from resentment

289. Balmer, "Doing Something for Self," para. 1.

over the felt loss of this Christian hegemony characterizing Eisenhower's America. Whatever intrigue might have been involved in this clergy cooptation, financial support for the wedding came from a who's who of Fortune 500 names—James L. Kraft, J. C. Penney, Harvey Firestone, Conrad Hilton, J. W. Marriott, Walt Disney, Charles E. Wilson (General Electric), and Robert W. Boggs (Union Carbide). Expecting a return on their investment, they received it, as evangelical Christianity and free market capitalism underwent a mutual baptism. This evangelical/fundamentalist coup continues to the present, as with the Koch brothers providing funding for the Christian far right. When I served recently as an election judge in my county, the polling place where I was assigned was a small rural Baptist church. On the wall, handprinted on newsprint for the children to memorize, was a threefold pledge of commitment to the flag of the United States, the Christian flag, and the Bible—in that order. Thomas Merton once predicted that the marriage of fundamentalist religion and advanced capitalism would produce "the greatest orgy of idolatry the world has ever seen."[290]

The Catholic Church has undergone its own version of this intertwining of conservative Christianity with free market capitalism. In addition to wealthy backers, conservative Catholic Christians have their own media empire with EWTN; evangelical academic expressions in Steubenville University and Ava Maria University; affiliate groups such as the Knights of Columbus, the Legionaries of Christ, and Regnum Christi; church-related institutions and agencies such as Catholic University's Busch School of Business, the Napa Institute, the Acton Institute, the Ethics and Public Policy Center, and the Chiaroscuro Foundation; and journals such as *First Things*.

CONCLUSION

To summarize, in this chapter, we have described how the powerful control of modern society by corporate capitalism is operating, unguided by any overarching plan, design, or rational intent. Instead, each segment, motivated competitively by a common rapacity, is converging into a relentless dynamic, bequeathing a destructive inevitability to the whole. This driving ethos, in turn, is rooting in us a craving for commercialized goods and services, expanding our wants into ever-expanding needs—devaluing that for which a price cannot be charged. As far back as 1966, Professor Caroll Quigley of Georgetown University, in *Tragedy and Hope*, warned that the far-reaching dynamic of financial capitalism is "nothing less than to create a world system of financial control in private hands able to dominate

290. Fox, "On the Fiftieth Anniversary," para. 12.

the political system of each country and the economy of the world as a whole."[291] In 1992, Francis Fukuyama, in his book *The End of History and the Last Man,* affirmed that history's termination will happen in the complete triumph of the capitalistic economic system at the global level. In 2013, Chris Hedges, in a collection of interviews named *The Death of Truth,* declared this to have already happened: "The world has been turned upside down. The pestilence of corporate totalitarianism is spreading rapidly over the earth. The criminals have seized power."[292] As a way of doing this, our news has become packaged so as to entertain; on television, competitive survival teams provide adventure; multiple channels offer venues of voyeurism, violence, and third-grade silliness; and even poker has been made a spectator sport. We obsess on iPhones, determining values by likes and *tbh*'s scored on Snapchat, circumscribed by the world of Instagram, Twitter, and VSCO. The content of political platforms is shaped by polls, candidates are chosen by popularity ratings, campaigns are financed by K Street, political correctness evokes mockery, national security justifies preemptive strikes, massive eavesdropping provides control, torture has become an acceptable interrogation technique, and establishing a strong military is code for corporate profits. Hidden behind the groomed image of patriotism is the aggrandizement of the military as heroes in establishing world peace, while in truth the intent is as guarantor of market superiority for our global economy. Prisons, surveillance, massive debt, implanted identification, GPS—these are but a few of the growing instruments of economic incursion and control. Political power concentrated in the hands of moneyed interests will continue to escalate its advantage through tax cuts, tax loopholes, corporate welfare, free-trade agreements, anti-union legislation, and a minimizing of any safety net—in indifference to any common good. Robert Reich, in his essay "Global Capital and the Nation State," described this dynamic by giant corporations as "holding governments and citizens up for ransom while sheltering their profits in the lowest-tax jurisdictions they can find."[293] "It is not, in the end, simply Assange or Manning they want. It is all who dare to defy the official narrative, in exposing the big lie of the global corporate state."[294] A recent global WIN-Gallup poll asked: "What country is the greatest threat to peace?" The United States won by an overwhelming margin, receiving three times more votes than

---

291. Quigley, *Tragedy and Hope,* 324.
292. Hedges, "Interview with Julian Assange," para. 54.
293. Reich, "Global Capital and Nation State," para. 1.
294. Hedges, "Interview with Julian Assange," para. 54.

second-place Pakistan.[295] Yet in our own country, false consciousness cloaks this, all the while hiding the stranglehold corporate power has in turning our lives into a profit-making enterprise.

The world-renowned physicist Carlo Rovelli in his international best-seller *Seven Brief Lessons on Physics* concluded in this manner: "I believe that our species will not last long . . . . The brutal climate and environmental changes that we have triggered . . . especially since the public and political option prefers to ignore the dangers that we are running, hiding our heads in the sand . . . I fear that soon we shall also have to become the only species that will knowingly watch the coming of its own collective demise, or least the demise of its civilization."[296] It is impossible to know which aneurism within this dynamic will burst first—climate change, nuclear disaster, food shortage, contamination of potable water, poisoned environment, mega-epidemic, economic collapse, or cyberwar. While we might stagger through one crisis, maybe even two, the effect will be relentlessly cumulative, as the systemic dynamic of socioeconomic competition escalates into the violence of naked survival. The four horsemen of the apocalypse have arrived, identifiable in terms of economy, ecology, media/surveillance, and war.

295. Bennett-Smith, "Womp!," para. 1.

296. Rovelli, *Seven Brief Lessons*, 77–78.

CHAPTER FIVE

LOSS OF NARRATIVE VISION AND DISSIPATION OF RELIGIOUS FAMILIARITY

Almost every society has had at least one journey narrative that provides its undergirding meaning. Homer in his *Odyssey* created the Grecian theme of searching for home. In the ancient *Epic of Gilgamesh,* the hero travels to the ends of the earth searching for a solution to his mortality. The Abraham story distills the divine promise of a special people traversing to a promised land, a narrative nurturing three major religions and their resident nations. The Jews remain a distinct people as long as they celebrate their Passover from slavery into freedom. Christians do so by celebrating the crucified and resurrected Christ as threshold into a new heaven and new earth. England has its legend of the Knights of the Round Table and the Quest for the Holy Grail. Spain has its Don Quixote in pursuit of the impossible dream. Dante both reflected and undergirded medieval Europe with his *Divine Comedy*, wherein humankind, awakening in an obscure wood, journeys toward paradise. Closer to our time, Martin Luther King Jr. coalesced a movement with a dream, paralleling Moses's vision on Mount Nebo and the Jesus-vision of transfiguration, portraying the narrative arc of the universe as being long but bending toward justice.

Yet Israel betrayed Moses's narrative, substituting for it the false promise of a golden calf. Martin was murdered by his own nation, avoiding his martyrdom by honoring his birthday. The muddy boots of our country's founders are being exposed, and our modern poets and novelists lament our culture's loss of any grounding story with which they can gain traction through engagement. Poking in his own country's embers, C. S. Lewis speaks longingly of the medieval model that once informed Western culture[1]—a narrative envisaging the universe as an ordered whole, its meaning radiant, as the pieces were knitted together by an internal telos and baptized in an external promise. Back then, humans were created in the image of God and, through struggling with their fallenness, became eligible for redemption. History's pilgrimaging was a religious narrative.

In a deep sense, ours is a post-Christian world because no version of the Christian narrative any longer functions as our society's defining story, with the church's diminishment reflective of this loss. Samuel Beckett's tragic-comedies image our society in humored pathos, awaiting a Godot who will never come. T. S. Eliot describes our cultural narrative as an unraveling, its demise to be marked not even with "a bang but a whimper . . . as London Bridge is falling down."[2] The pilgrimage of James Joyce's *Ulysses* is a one-day plotless circle much like every other day, perforated by the disruptive clatter of the past. As one character muses, "It is an age of exhausted whoredom groping for its god."[3] Franz Kafka, the master mythmaker, provides the final translation of the narratives he composed for our time: "The meaning of life is that it stops."[4] The novelist Rebecca West provides her distillation by proposing this tombstone epitaph for the human race: "It seemed like a good idea at the time."[5] Don Share and Christian Wiman, in *The Open Door*, collected what they regarded as the best of modern poetry from the past hundred years. In contrast to the powerful metanarratives of the Miltons and the Dantes, Wiman finds the modern narrative to be "fragments anxious about their origins."[6] Thus, as the Christian narrative is being winnowed into chaff by the modern ethos, the serious Christian is forced to blow on the ashes of its past to determine if there is still the glow of a narrative upon which a courageous remnant might find worth in wagering.

A case can be made that our country's nonindigenous origination was laced with versions of a defining narrative serving as a mission statement, told and retold in its various forms in rehearsing our reason for being. The Puritans are often perceived as establishing a colony called to be a religious haven for the faithful. William Penn fostered Pennsylvania as an ideal pacifist colony. Georgia offered a citadel where criminals could

---

1. C. S. Lewis, *Discarded Image.*

2. Eliot, "Hollow Men," in *Complete Poems and Plays*, 59.

3. Joyce, *Ulysses*, 204.

4. Schlicke, "Meaning of Life," para. 1.

5. Glendinning, "Talk with Rebecca West," para. 5.

6. Share and Wiman, eds., *Open Door*, 1.

rebuild their lives. The poem at the base of the Statue of Liberty deems this a nation serving as respite for exiles, welcoming the "tempest-tost" to our shores. Lincoln spoke eloquently of our nation as being rooted in a narrative about freedom, for which our soldiers at Gettysburg did not die in vain. World War I was sold to our country as a visionary narrative of making the world safe for democracy. H. R. Niebuhr in his *Kingdom of God in America* names the theme of kingdom as the explicit and implicit vision by which our country drew upon the Old Testament narrative of God calling a special people to be "peculiarly his own."

However noble, hypocritical, or destructive such narratives may have been, they did provide our nation with a narrative sense of calling. The Old Testament narrative from which this visioning tends to draw, however, itself underwent radical change. Originally, Israel believed that God chose them to be prosperously favored, so that God drove out the indigenous people from their own lands so that his chosen people could inherit through violence a land flowing with milk and honey. "I will spread prosperity to her like a river, and the wealth of the nations like an overflowing stream" (Isa 66:12). As promised, God "subdued peoples under us, and nations under our feet" (Ps 47:3). But through tragedies, the script began to be rewritten. An awakening came that the special call by God was not for prosperity and self-aggrandizement at all, but for living out a narrative in which, through teaching and example, Israel was to offer a vision as a promise for all nations. "I have given you as a covenant to the people, a light to the nations" (Isa 42:6). This revised narrative focused on serving rather than being served, committed to the common good—measured by treatment of the hungry, imprisoned, naked, widow, and orphan. "No more shall there be in it an infant that lives but a few days, or an old man who does not fill out his days" (Isa 65:20). In seeing this narrative being lived out, the nations "shall beat their swords into plowshares, and their spears into pruning hooks; nation shall not lift up sword against nation, neither shall they learn war anymore; but they shall sit every one under his vine and under his fig tree, and none shall make them afraid . . ." (Micah 4:3–4). This, O God, is how "your way may be known upon earth, your saving power among all nations" (Ps 67:2 NRSV). The Christian narrative expanded this narrative, obviating divisions between Jew-Gentile, rich-poor, male-female, and friend-enemy.

While there are hints that such a narrative might formerly have fed our country, instead of maintaining the biblical reversal, it reverted to Israel's original tainted interpretation—the promise of favored prosperity. The name now being used for this narrative is exceptionalism. Mushy to its core, its outer face retains the semblance of a unique mission—fighting to establish and preserve democracy throughout the world, the reward for which is an exceptional prosperity. While this narrative is being battered abroad, it continues to function in this country, but as subterfuge, hiding, justifying, and welcoming the exceptionalism of a favored plutocracy, by clutching onto some semblance of a missional narrative. Yet, in practice, it is becoming even further inverted, as fear causes increased division between the we and the they. Meanwhile, the loss of trust in our government reflects a suspicion of narrative loss. Functionally rudderless without a moral tiller, what is left is an attitude more than a vision. Several decades ago, we used the language of paradigm shift. But now what is happening is more like a narrative perforation.

Bereft of a defining narrative may help explain our present obsession with memoir. Even if a person's life involves mostly disappointments and failures, at least in retelling it, one might instill a hint of narrative. Understandably, then, the *New York Times* book review section recently characterized our times as the Age of Memoir.[7] Marooned in a sinking present, we are left to recall an ambiguous *once was* as a slight compensation for a shredded future. Our narrative loss may explain as well our current obsession with genealogy, seeking recompense in an unknown past for an unpromising future. This could account also for the present penchant within homiletical theory for storytelling rather than proclamation.

Life is a search for meaning—for a narrative with power sufficient to shape positively the present, evoking a commitment sufficient to embrace the future. Since Christianity is no longer providing society with such a narrative structure, intriguing is Elizabeth Kolbert's *Sixth Extinction: An Unnatural History*. Her study of our present wrecking of both earth and sky fits previous convolutions through history. Her grim conclusion from past narratives of extinction is that the earth has survived them before and is likely to endure one more—but without us. Her narrative theme is that we are on the edge of the earth's sixth extinction, a catastrophe that has so begun that there is no undoing. She roots the dynamic of this narrative in the "habits of greedy consumption," bearing an uncanny likeness to the narrative of original sin.

Variations on this narrative of extinction are appearing frequently on television, often as a post-apocalyptic narrative. After a devastation, a remnant is left to eke out a marginal existence. Yet almost never does a moral judgment operate as reason for the demise, nor is meaning found through repentance and transformed behavior. The narrative causes most often given reflect three options: 1) apocalyptic self-destruction by an internal enemy; 2) galactic invasion from without; 3) zombie cannibalism as we eat

---

7. Jamison and McGrath, "In Age of Memoir."

each other. In these narratives, what is being sensed, but not prophetically posed, is the shadow side endemic to the dynamic defining our modern way of living. Robert Joustra and Alissa Wilkinson, in their book *How to Survive the Apocalypse: Zombies, Cylons, Faith, and Politics at the End of the World*, disclose that an amazing number of these apocalyptic expressions have a "distinct sense embedded in them that this social order can't last—that we are, in fact, near the end of something."[8]

There is currently a movement called the American Redoubt (meaning fortress) operating in an area of the Pacific Northwest that includes Idaho, Montana, Wyoming, and eastern parts of Washington and Oregon.[9] It is rooted in a certainty concerning the end of the world as we know it. Their alarm is expressed through an online radio station called Prepper Broadcasting Network. Although most of them are "conservative God-fearing Christians," it is significant that the various catastrophes against which they are preparing themselves are all human caused, their narrative stripped of divine judgment. Thus, they no longer rely on divine aid but on their own preparedness through employing survival techniques.

These varied apocalyptic shadows that are being sensed, however, are far from fantasy, for we have been on the verge of an apocalypse numerous times. In 1961, a US Air Force B-52 bomber broke up in midair over North Carolina, dropping two Mark 39 hydrogen bombs with payloads 260 times more powerful than the bomb dropped on Hiroshima.[10] Three of its four safety mechanisms failed, but, just in time, a final low-voltage switch engaged, preventing the killing of millions, with fallout having reached as far as New York. This is only one of 1200 acknowledged accidents between 1950 and 1968 involving nuclear weapons.[11] Joseph Gerson, in his *Empire and the Bomb*, identifies thirty occasions since Hiroshima and Nagasaki in which US presidents have prepared for or threatened to initiate nuclear war. From 1962 to 1977, it is alleged that the US set the launch codes at every nuclear missile silo to 00000000[12] so as to increase the rapidity with which nuclear missiles could be launched. Newly released reports indicate how, during the Cuban missile crisis, we were frighteningly close to nuclear warfare, far closer than previously imagined.[13] In *The Doomsday Machine*, Daniel Ellsberg concludes that we have thus far avoided annihilation by

---

8. Joustra and Wilkinson, *How to Survive Apocalypse*, 60.

9. "American Redoubt."

10. Newcott, "Remembering the Night," para. 9.

11. Hansen, "Oops List," 66.

12. Nichols, "Were America's Nuclear Codes," para. 1.

13. *Week* Staff, "Cuban Missile Crisis," para. 5.

luck. This stark realization came to him when, as a high-level analyst, he was developing plans for nuclear war and saw a 1961 Joint Chiefs' memo that casually noted that the death toll from a full-scale US nuclear attack would likely reach 600 million casualties.

With such groups as ISIS attempting to acquire nuclear devices, the situation is becoming increasingly unstable, the staff of the *Week* writes.[14] The International Atomic Energy Agency has catalogued 2,200 attempts to steal or smuggle uranium. Since advanced nuclear weapons are becoming increasingly smaller in size, retired General James Cartwright proffers that this is making nuclear weapons "more thinkable." As if in acknowledgement, the US Air Force in 2015 tested its first remote precision-guided atomic bomb. Presently, there are 16,000 nuclear weapons in existence, 93 percent of them possessed by the US and Russia—each country with roughly 4,500 to 4,700 warheads in its stockpile. As if that is not menace enough, Russia, China, and the US are increasing their defense budgets, with President Obama in 2016 proposing a $1 trillion weapons modernization program to stretch over the next thirty years. The funds presently designated for nuclear updating are at $1.2 trillion. Provocations continue, with North Korea testing missile launches and the US and South Korea exercising month long invasion maneuvers off their coast.

Further threats attributed to human error are evidenced by the US Air Force's investigation of charges that there is extensive drug use by troops who are assigned to protect and manage our nuclear weapons.[15] Additionally, the documentary movie *Zero Days* introduced the deadly imagery of cyberwarfare, involving such weapons as the Stuxnet computer virus that apparently the US has already used against Iran.[16] Understandably, the Doomsday Clock, as the symbolic countdown to Armageddon as determined by experts at the Science and Security Board of the Bulletin of the Atomic Scientists, moved its hands at the end of 2015 from five minutes to three minutes before midnight. In 2017, it was set at two minutes; in 2021, it is set at one hundred seconds before a global catastrophe.[17]

How tragic, how pathetic, is the defining narrative that is emerging: of an earth having evolved over billions of years to give birth to the miracle of a self-conscious humankind who, in turn, through arrogance, greed, and fear is bringing itself to the edge of an obliteration that it is apparently incapable of halting. Wherever one turns today, there is being exposed a relentlessness

14. *Week* Staff, "Is Nuclear Armageddon More Likely," paras. 1–7.

15. Lamothe, "Air Force Launches Investigation."

16. Gibney, dir., *Zero Days*.

17. Mecklin, "Doomsday Clock."

toward ruin—whether through exponential population growth; nuclear war; and scarcity of potable water, food, and resources, impelled by an insatiable appetite to possess and a violent power to control. One recalls those times in Scripture when God in disgust threatened to wipe out the human race—yet always with the promise of starting over again with a remnant. And so, the diminishing church today must trust that this promise is again being made, that it will be as a remnant, that "the powers of death shall not prevail against it" (Matt 16:18). Yet, sadly, within the churches today, for many Christians, there is a shrinking of the global Christian narrative into a personal story. The tendency is no longer to understand the divine promise as entailing a covenant that gives meaning to the whole of history but as only a narrow plot promising ancillary meaning to the individual. Not long ago in Sunday School, we learned the stories of biblical heroes and heroines who gave history a narrative plot. Christian language became incorporated into our native tongue, providing a rich lexicon of words such as sin, grace, prayer, atonement, and salvation. We sang these narratives as liturgy; lived as rhythmic seasons the plots of confession, forgiveness, and fulfillment; and rehearsed its gestures into an effortless choreography. Yet, as a spiritual director, I am now discovering that for many retreatants this precious inheritance of Christian narrative has evaporated—or never was.

CHAPTER SIX

DETERIORATION OF RELIGIOUS MOTIVATION

We reach now what may be the heart cause of the church's demise in our time. The primary motivations that for centuries have grounded Christianity's appeal are now vaporizing. Almost all of those motivations for faith were instrumental in nature, in which Christian belief could be offered as a means for acquiring something that most persons deeply desired and acknowledged as needing. The deep crisis that renders ours a post-Christian society then is that Christian belief is no longer being perceived as providing a viable means for acquiring any desired ends. What the church has to offer is what our society is socializing us to no longer need or even want. Expressed candidly, for the modern sensibility, Christianity has lost any basic utility. Therefore, any usefulness that the church is finding to offer tends to be a co-opted one—as variations in providing a means for personal coping in living a way of life that is basically post-Christian.

Viewed through Christian eyes, the modern crisis centers not only in this loss of taste for meaning deeper than the corporeal, but even more in being increasingly oblivious to the loss. As a result, modern living is reminiscent of that described by Koheleth, author of Ecclesiastes, for whom "all things are wearisome; more than one can express . . . a striving after wind" (Eccl 1:8, 17 NRSV). So he surmises that there is nothing more for persons "than to eat, and drink, and enjoy themselves . . ." (Eccl 8:15 NRSV). In sum, "bread is made for laughter, and wine gladdens life, and money answers everything" (Eccl 10:19). But while Koheleth draws his conclusion after a life of earnest searching for meaning, the pathos today is that such a conclusion is becoming the operating assumption, robbing life of serious prior skirmishing with the fundamental questions of life and death. While Christian doctrines were offered as distilled rejoinders to issues regarded as universal, they are no longer acknowledged as being issues, let alone being unavoidable. Thus, much of Christianity's diminishment resides in having answers to questions no longer being asked, in providing healing for a sickness no longer being acknowledged, and in imparting solace for yearnings stifled by consumption.

JUDGMENT, FEAR, AND HELL

One of the most powerful incentives for faith during these many centuries has been fear of divine punishment, epitomized by the threat of hell. The beginning of the Wesleyan revival can be dated when, on one Thursday evening, several severely anxious persons knocked on John Wesley's door and fearfully pleaded for help "to flee from the wrath to come."[1] Such motivation goes back to the beginning, when Jesus himself declared that those without faith he "will throw into the furnace of fire: where will be weeping and gnashing of teeth" (Matt 13:42 NRSV). "Just as the weeds are collected and burned up with fire, so will it be at the end of the age," when the angels will "separate the evil from the righteous, and throw them into the furnace of fire . . ." (Matt 13:40, 50). "Keep awake, therefore, for you do not know on what day your Lord is coming" (Matt 24:42 NRSV). In fact, declares St. Ephrem, "Jesus keeps the hour of his coming unknown so that in every moment we will be threatened into watchfulness."[2]

This theme appears clearly as well in Paul's preaching, as in his first letter of which we have a copy (ca. 51 AD). He greets the Christians in Thessalonica as those who believe "in Jesus who delivers us from the wrath to come" (1Thess 1:10). He regards this threat as imminent, for "you yourselves know well that the day of the Lord will come like a thief in the night. When people say, 'There is peace and security,' then sudden destruction will come upon them as travail comes upon a woman with child, and there will be no escape" (1 Thess 5:2–3). So impending was this coming that Paul was forced in time to address the problem of delay (1 Thess 4:13ff). This has been a conundrum for the church, as, through its history, the threat has tended to be placated by delay. Yet, periodically, the alarm has been revived when societal crises recall Jesus's warning that "when you hear of wars and rumors of wars, do not be alarmed; this must take place, but the end is not yet . . . . There will be earthquakes in various places, there will be famine; this is but the beginning of the sufferings" (Mark 13:7–8).

---

1. McTyeire, *History of Methodism*, 177.
2. International Commission on English in the Liturgy, *Liturgy of the Hours*, 1:176.

A classic renewal of this motivation was the Great Awakening, a widespread evangelical revival in New England (1740–1743) of which Jonathan Edwards's sermon "Sinners in the Hands of an Angry God" was classic. In my youth, yearly revivals were the local church's instrument of evangelism and its own regeneration, complete with rotating red lights and a visiting revivalist who in a thundering voice described the shrieking of hell's tortured sinners. Churches were equipped with a kneeling rail and a wailing area, where trained parishioners waited to embrace those in whom fright had been revived. From time to time, charismatic leaders would arise in various locations, leaders who would predict a time and place for the coming and gathered the white-clothed faithful in anticipation, only to be forced to confess a miscalculation.

The Old Testament had its versions of this motivation, with the working assumption being that "the fear of the Lord is the beginning of wisdom" (Prov 9:10). The prophet Jeremiah records God as saying, "I will put the fear of me in their hearts, that they may not turn from me" (Jer 32:40). Likewise, the psalmist grounds moral behavior in the certainty that God repays "all according to their work" (Ps 62:12 NRSV). "Tremble before him, all the earth" (Ps 96:9). "Put them in fear of the Lord" (Ps 9:20). "My flesh trembles for fear of thee, and I am afraid of your judgment" (Ps 119:120). The one who sins does so because "deep in his heart there is no fear of God before his eyes" (Ps 36:1).

Expressions of this motivation have been deep in Roman Catholicism, as graphically expressed in the "Dies Irae," the "Day of Wrath,"[3] which is the fearful medieval hymn about judgment day (ca. 1250). After Vatican II, it was used as a sequence in Catholic funerals, in the Masses for the Dead, and on All Souls' Day. The "Dies Irae" describes when God "shall give portents in the heavens and on the earth, blood and fire and columns of smoke. The sun shall be turned to darkness, and the moon to blood, before the great and terrible day of the Lord comes" (Joel 2:30–32). "Guilty, now I pour my moaning: All my shame with anguish owning . . . rescue me from fires undying."[4] And in the *Liturgy of the Hours,* we read the dictum to "live in hourly expectation."

I was probably eight years old when, one evening, my parents and I drove up the hill to get an ice cream cone at the dairy. Suddenly, we were part of a line of traffic that had come to a complete standstill in the middle of the highway. Drivers and passengers were scrambling out of

---

3. International Commission on English in the Liturgy, *Liturgy of the Hours,* 4:2013–5.

4. Church Pension Fund, eds., "Dies Irae," 73.

their vehicles. People began kneeling, some crying, and the mumbling began: "Lord, save me!" St. Paul had insisted that "the Lord is at hand," and all it took was a rare and unexpected display of the Northern Lights to unearth the imbedded fear of Christ's second coming, resurrecting guilt to the edge of panic. But now, after two thousand years, "at hand" has lost its credibility. While today the Northern Lights are still an attraction, no longer are they so for biblical reasons.

I know of almost no mainline pastors, who in the last decade of their ministry, have been encountered by many, if any, searchers motivated to "flee from the wrath to come." If they had, they would have most likely regarded the encounter as more strange than deep, more misdirected than weighty, and more psychologically rooted than ignited by authentic searching. While vestiges might remain, they tend to be secularized, as when anxiety arose for some persons over the advent of the millennium or when the end of the Mayan calendar approached. Even though several of my friends did hoard supplies just in case, and even though they were practicing Christians, they attached no theological dimension to the threat or regarded divine judgment as operative. This is so even for the doomsday preppers, whose preparation is for a secular apocalypse. For example, developers in Texas have announced plans for a $300-million luxury resort community with underground condos connected by tunnels, guaranteeing survival.[5] "It is going to be a five-star preparation," they promise.

There are a few exceptions. A Colorado talk-radio minister recently declared that tragic flooding in Colorado was God's judgment upon the decadence of homosexuality, marijuana, and abortion.[6] Another evangelical commentator expressed elation that deaths caused by arson in a gay bar were God's judgment, declaring that it hardly mattered, since they would have burned in hell anyhow.[7] Although there is always an extreme element that might be inclined to concur, for the general populus such proclamations are no longer taken seriously, regarded instead as being bizarre.

Thus, since the fearful threat of judgment and hell has been such a significant evangelical motivator throughout the church's history, it follows that Christian diminishment occurs in significant part because such a threat is no longer effective. Yet the church has not abandoned this imagery of a coming judgment, in which there will be a separation of the sheep from the goats, with eternal rewards dispensed to believers and destruction forthcoming for sinners. For a number of aging Christians, this motivation likely

5. M. Robinson, "This Luxury Condo Development," para. 2.

6. Christopher, "Pastor Blames Colorado Floods," para. 1.

7. Broverman, "Nine Truly Terrible Reactions," para. 7.

remains for their faith and morals. Favorite Scriptures heard in Christian nursing homes are these: "Conduct yourselves with fear throughout the time of your exile . . ." (1 Pet 1:17); and therefore, "gird up your minds, be sober, set your hopes completely on the gifts to be conferred on you when Jesus Christ appears" (1 Pet 1:13). In devotional pamphlets, they still read a plea for Christians to live in this world so as to avoid harsh judgment in the next. I married as a virgin for precisely this reason. But this motivation largely remains as a vestige with the aged, soon to pass.

THIS-WORLDLY REWARD

The Old Testament had no significant concept of an afterlife. Instead, there was Sheol, the abode of the dead, vague and undefined, a place of woe as a vaguely dark and gloomy region beneath the earth. It was there that the departed persisted but were not punished in a dull and inactive existence. "There is no work or thought or knowledge or wisdom in Sheol, to which you are going" (Eccl 9:10). Therefore, the motivation for choosing a faithful existence had to be found in this life before death. The reward for obeying God was worldly advantage, while disobedience resulted in misfortune, with a clear correlation between morality and reward. Thus, the consistent warning by the prophets centers in this belief that Israel was facing destruction because of their misdeeds, for the way of God was that both nation and individual would reap what was sown, for better or for worse. Although this reward was sometimes delayed, there was a clear and direct connection between belief and the subsequent compensation of victory/prosperity/health or judgment/ disaster/exile. Graphic is the prophetic promise for the faithful—myriads of herds and overflowing harvests—while for the disobedient would come brutal hardship and tragedy. Divine justice guaranteed an equity of reward and punishment based on conduct. "The judgments of the Lord are true, and all of them just" (Ps 19:8). Thus, when Israel was taken into foreign captivity, the prophet Baruch is clear as to the cause: "We are brought low . . . because we sinned against the Lord, our God, not heeding his voice" (Bar 2:5 NAB). "Had you walked in the way of God, you would have dwelt in enduring peace" (Bar 3:13 NAB). This correlation was the motivation for individuals as well, for with the righteous there would be "riches and honor, enduring wealth and prosperity." This is the working premise of the psalmist, that "the wicked perish, the enemies of the Lord are like the glory of the pastures, they vanish—like smoke they vanish away" (Ps 37:20). But "no good thing does the Lord withhold from those who walk uprightly" (Ps 84:11). "The Lord rewarded me according to my righteousness" (Ps 18:20).

Yet there are crisis times of agony for the psalmists, when the dire situation seems to question this motivation as foundation for faith. "Behold, these are the wicked; always at ease, they increase in riches" (Ps 73:12). The prosperity of the rich evokes doubt, forcing the psalmist to utter pleas for God to stop being deaf, silent, absent, hiding, sleeping—for the righteous are being treated as sheep for the slaughter (Ps 44:22–26). "Why dost thou stand afar off, O Lord? Why dost thou hide thyself in times of trouble?" (Ps 10:1). "How long will you judge unjustly and show partiality to the wicked?" (Ps 82:2). Jeremiah echoes the cry: "Why does the way of the wicked prosper? Why do all who are treacherous thrive?" (Jer 12:1). Thus there is a frightening quivering of the foundations when the psalmist is forced to confess that "the way of the Most High has changed."[8] This apparent imbalance between righteousness and reward tempts him to cry out that "in vain I have kept my heart clean and washed my hands in innocence" (Ps 73:13). Yet he pulls back from the edge of this conclusion, doggedly believing that the balance will happen somehow, if for no better reason than that to doubt the divine correlation would be "untrue to the generation of thy children" (Ps 73:15). He realizes that Israel's faith is at stake at this point. Thus he is forced to believe without empirical evidence that, whatever may seem to be the case, "truly you [God] set them in slippery places; you make them fall to ruin . . . destroyed in a moment, swept away utterly by terrors!" (Ps 73:18–19 NRSV). The reason the wicked person acts as he does is that "there is no fear of God before his eyes" (Ps 36:1). His "thoughts are, 'There is no God.'" Or if he believes in one, he believes that "God has forgotten, he has hidden his face, he will never see it" (Ps 10:11). Thus, for both wicked and righteous alike, behavior is determined by whether or not a person is rooted in fear based on divine justice. Rewards and punishments must happen in this life, for there is no afterlife when the balance could be righted. Thus, the intense plea of the psalmist is this: "Give us joy to balance our affliction, for the years when we knew misfortune" (Ps 90:15).

In the midst of this Old Testament struggle to trust the reward-punishment motivation, there appears the book of Job as a classic eruption of misgiving. The author reworked an ancient tale featuring a man named Job who as a perfect God-fearing person had huge wealth and good fortune as proof of his religious belief. God and Satan decide to have a contest by testing the strength of Job's faith. So, since Job is "blameless and upright, fearing God, and turning away from evil," on him is heaped unjust

---

8. Gelineau, *Psalms*, 139.

misfortune. Yet with a steadfast mantra Job insists: "The Lord gives and the Lord takes away, blessed is the name of the Lord" (Job 1:21). He is appropriately rewarded when "the Lord gave Job twice as much as he had before" (Job 42:10). While this was the original story, a later author split it in two and inserted thirty-five chapters of terror and devastation plummeting the innocent Job, driving him to despair. Robbed of all instrumental motivation for belief, he becomes emblematic of our modern age. The writer finds resolution through an experience of awe by being confronted by the power, mystery, and beauty of creation. This is sufficient for him to remain with the psalmists, trusting that, in spite of all appearances to the contrary, such a God must know what he is doing. With this assumption, the author is able to retain the original ending in which Job is rewarded for his faithfulness—staggeringly so, with fourteen thousand sheep, six thousand camels, a thousand donkeys, seven sons, and three daughters more beautiful than any other women in the land (Job 42:12–15). But today, ours is no longer a time of happy endings. Ours is an era characterized by poverty and war and violence and the many tragedies we have been detailing. Never have the have-nots been so numerous or anger so evident in lashing out at whomever for whatever is the closest available villain for the way things are. Ours is a condition being sensed as out of control, defying any just calculus for rewarded virtue. Ours is a world instigated by evolutionary chance, casting us out into a competitive free-for-all.

Atheism is the consequent conclusion for unhappy endings. Thus, in a deep sense, the contemporary demise of Christianity resides in this perceived absence of any recognizable correlation between faith and this-worldly reward. On the contrary, almost axiomatic is the assumption that the greedy attain high places. In a Ziggy cartoon, Ziggy looks up at the sky and mumbles, "Sir, have you noticed that the meek are getting creamed?" In previous times, when God's existence was largely taken for granted, any perceived absence of a moral correlation would lead either to a confession of unrecognized sins or a trust that satisfaction was simply delayed. But today, the absent correction counts, instead, as heavy evidence of divine nonexistence. While through the ages the why concerning the lack of correlation would elicit deep ponderings, in our time, the why is fading into a simple statement of fact. The why question makes sense only when the prophets and psalmists could take God for granted, against which they could cast their laments. But without a God, there is no longer a quandary left to force deep pondering—only the cheerless axiom that this is simply the way things are. Today, the lament no longer evokes a question but a conclusion, for, in fact, the evil do prosper, and, indeed, the good do go empty away. Period. It was with intense tragedies that our postmodern era was ushered in—the

Holocaust, Hiroshima, and 9/11, with subsequent earthquakes, tornadoes, tsunamis, and epidemics, leaving little empirical evidence of any moral/reward correlation or even of an impotent God who could be cursed. The foolish turner of the other cheek is guaranteed a concussion.

Furthermore, the contemporary attitude toward pain and suffering has undergone a significant change. While the psalmist could confess that "there is no health in my bones because of my sin" (Ps 38:3), his parallel belief was that "the Lord is close to the broken-hearted and saves the crushed in spirit" (Ps 34:18). The church through the ages has celebrated multiple saints who were brought to holiness through experiencing pain and suffering. Reviewing the history of sainthood, one prelate joked, "Unless you contract tuberculosis, the odds of sainthood are against you." But no longer are there many persons left who regard suffering as a redemptive discipline kindly distributed by a loving God. In fact, pain and sickness today are no longer theological issues but conditions requiring medical and/or psychological attention. No matter how deep might be the faith of a couple practicing Christian Science, they are prosecuted if their child dies by being deprived of medical treatment. Almost totally gone is the formerly assumed correlation between sickness and the deserving. When it was discovered that I had an aortic aneurysm needing immediate surgery, it never occurred for me to ask, "Where have I sinned?" Former saints who used flagellation to intensify pain for spiritual reasons are examples today of masochism. Even questionable are any who might pray the historic prayer asking for suffering now so as to avoid greater suffering in the life to come.

Over two centuries ago, Immanuel Kant was still able to insist that morality depends on a correlation between good deeds and rewarded consequences. But he anticipated our modern era in realizing that, in this life, there is no such correlation. Therefore, he concluded that morality is impossible unless we postulate an afterlife in which the balance will be rectified.[9] But today, a rational hypothesis for those philosophically inclined is a far cry from a vital faith. Nor is a hypothesis hardly an apt adversary against which to rail. While Job's answer to undeserved suffering is an awe-filled encounter with the mystery of creation, in our time, the cosmos has been steadfastly defrocked of its mystery, into a lonely infinity of empty space, dotted by stars composed of dust and ice that are rarely apparent beyond the urban lights. Koheleth in Ecclesiastes takes a further step toward postmodernity. Even if there were some correlation between goodness and reward, the quality of life itself is still vanity. Riches contaminate the heart, and death is the common lot awaiting both the good and the bad,

---

9. Kant, *Critique of Practical Reason*, 128–36.

indiscriminately stripping both wise and foolish of everything. Nakedness is life's beginning, and nakedness is its end, rendering tragic the fact of one's birth. But since we are alive, during our short time, let us "eat, drink, and be merry," for aging comes quickly when "the pitcher is shattered at the spring, and the broken pulley falls into the well, and the dust returns to the earth as it once was . . ." (Eccl 12:6–7 NAB).

Efforts at restoring this-worldly rewards as a motivation for faith have been attempted mostly within megachurches based on a theology of prosperity. We have already described this intertwining of Christianity with the American Dream, in which the affluence promised by the free enterprise system is undergirded as being the reward that faith promises. Recompense for being a faithful Christian is upward financial mobility through hard work, vocational loyalty, frugality of resources, deferred pleasure, the wisdom of savings, and a faithful family life. In a successful upper-class environment, this angle might play, but as persons are increasingly experiencing things as not working out that way, sullied are those once-honored virtues that no longer have a payoff. With the betrayal of promised rewards comes a sense of the god who failed.

Given the individualism endemic to modern society, another consequence of insolvent promises is the instigation of guilt. Within a prosperity theology, failure to succeed is never the result of a skewed system but the consequence of an individual's failure, evoking shame rather than disillusionment. Good persons get what they deserve, while those who are left empty fully deserve their plight. This helps explain the present alliance between conservative politicians and conservative Christians, in which defense of an economic system with its harsh demarcation between haves and have-nots dovetails with a religious version that proclaims a moral calculus as divinely operative. Illustrative is a sign board outside my local Baptist church: "Believe to Receive." In this light, we can understand the diminishment of faith happening as the growing economic inequality of the 1 percent versus the 99 percent intensifies. The psalmist, as his society was beginning to lose its reward-punishment underpinnings, cries out, "If the foundations are destroyed, what can the righteous do?"—or any longer believe (Ps 11:3). Understandably, then, psychotherapist Bruce Rogers-Vaughn in his *Caring for Souls in a Neoliberal Age* describes the change in patients over his thirty-year practice as their becoming "more on edge," with an "amorphous dread." He faults the therapy, counseling, and pastoral care most often given today as being misdirected, for it encourages adaptation to modern society rather than resistance to it, providing coping so as to function better according to its values of production and consumption, relieving symptoms rather than dealing with contextual causes, and thereby pressing individuals to take total responsibility for their own plight.

OTHERWORLDLY REWARD
AS COMPENSATION

Since Christianity's appeal based on some form of this-worldly compensation is being drained of empirical credibility in our time, another motivation to which the church still appeals is in shifting reward from this life to an afterlife. During the period of Christianity's birth, life expectancy was short and the threat of death was always looming. Therefore, a ready point of contact was the proclamation of Christ's resurrection as the promise of an afterlife for the faithful. Eternal life was the promised exchange for suffering and deprivation endured during this life. Thus, even though the motivation of reward for faithfulness was often empirically lacking, the recompense could be stretched into an eternity where the account would be balanced. A hymn nearly two hundred years old celebrates this traditional promise: "Saints all longing for their heaven; prophets, psalmists, seers, and sages, all await the glory given. Life eternal!"[10] The gospel of Matthew in particular stresses this motivation for faith. We are to live so as to "store up for [ourselves] treasures in heaven . . ." (Matt 6:20). The ongoing motivational mantra is the promise that "great will be your reward in heaven," when "all these things shall be yours" (Matt 6:18, 33). The beatitudes rest on such a motivation, where in the kingdom to come compensation awaits those who are faithful despite what they lack now—the poor, mourning, hungry, persecuted, meek, merciful, pure, and the peacemakers—all of these shall receive a generous recompense. "Set all your hopes on the gift to be conferred on you when Jesus Christ appears" (1 Pet 1:13).

Early on, St. Pachomius speaks for the desert fathers and mothers in anchoring the motivation for entering the ascetic life as that of earning a future reward through disciplined deprivation now.[11] Augustine makes clear this motivation: "*Blessed are those who hunger and thirst for justice,* that is, here on earth. *They shall be satisfied*, that is, in heaven."[12] Theologians such as St. Gregory of Nyssa insist that Christians are to become

10. "Sing with All the Saints of Glory," in Hymnal Revision Committee, ed., *United Methodist Hymnal*, 702.

11. Orthodox Church in America, "Venerable Pachomius the Great," para. 17.

12. Augustine, as cited in International Commission on English in the Liturgy, *Liturgy of the Hours*, 4:393. Italics in original.

"blind to the life here below by . . . seeking the things that are above."[13] My mother attempted to steer my behavior by putting the fear of God in me, coupled with the promise that good acts would "put jewels in your crown." This approach to motivation expands to include the idea of investment. The saints lived an overabundance of faithfulness so as to create a heavenly storehouse of merit from which others could draw.

Here again, by appealing to a heavenly reward, the church was offering to potential believers a means related to a recognizable and desirable end as faith's consequence. St. Francis Xavier tirelessly toured France in an effort to recruit university students as missionaries by using this stratagem to counter their indifference: "What a tragedy; how many souls are being shut out of heaven and falling into hell, thanks to you!"[14]

Early on, this approach was intensified so as to absorb more than ethical behavior. Preached was a universal fall, with its consequential original sin. Because of Adam's disobedience, every human being was born with a deficit account, one so deep, in fact, that human efforts were incapable of bringing one's account back even to zero. Thus, the personal reward motivation focused more on one's belief than on one's doing—belief in a God-man whose innocent death could pay the deficit for believers. Almost every Protestant Sunday school classroom that I have entered has had John 3:16 somewhere on its wall, promising "that whoever believes in him may not perish but have eternal life." Here too the motivation is one of means-consequence. But the postmodern mindset is increasingly incredulous of any original garden of Eden in which an original couple through one disobedient act provoked a peevish God into punishing the whole human race and all its history with a debilitatingly sinful propensity, angrily casting them into a harsh exile by restructuring creation with suffering and agony as ongoing reprimands.

As for heaven and earth and hell, where in fact are they? Hell, once conceived as being in the hot center of the earth, has been scientifically evicted. As for heaven, the Mormons and Jehovah's Witnesses are about the only denominations of any size whose leaders any longer conceive of it as a physical place out there somewhere in the cosmos, populated by faithful persons living with the happy family they had on earth, at home with a God conceived as a physical being. Almost no mainline theologian any longer holds Christ's ascension to be literal, as an ascent into a physical heaven someplace. Remnants of this heavenly reward motivation sometimes remain in humorous cartoons of St. Peter with a huge record book at a podium, processing folks for entry

13. International Commission on English in the Liturgy, *Liturgy of the Hours*, 3:234–35.

14. International Commission on English in the Liturgy, *Liturgy of the Hours*, 1:1211.

through pearly gates. But the physical scaffolding for conceiving this other-worldly reward system is becoming increasingly shaky.

Even more telling, those who do believe in an afterlife as some kind of continued existence are increasingly divorcing this belief from any religious/moral behavior as a screening requirement for entrance. Here again, what we are encountering is the church's diminishment as rooted not in an increase of persons opting for atheism but as the consequence of our postmodern ethos, in which such matters as heaven, Eden, and talking snakes are no longer much in currency. Yet last week, the sign in front of my local Assembly of God church persisted: "Our only goal is getting to heaven."

FEAR OF DEATH

As far back as we can go in recorded history, death has been a mystery, usually accompanied with a composite of fright and awe, wavering on a threshold between entrance into something intriguingly more or exit into an ominous nothingness. Environmental contingencies and short life expectancy made the specter of death omnipresent, posing a chronic uncertainty in which the unavoidable unknown posed ultimate questions. Persons even in the Middle Ages could anticipate at best only half the life expectancy of today's adult, so that reaching what we consider middle age was an accomplishment. Medication for rampant diseases was minimal, and the medical treatment that was done was often counterhealing.

Advances in modern medicine have extended our average life span from forty five in 1900 to seventy-nine today, with science determined to make progress toward solving the symptoms endemic to the aging process itself. Most diseases are regarded as potentially curable or at least manageable, so that death at an age previously regarded as normative is presently viewed as an unfortunate exception. Living to a ripe old age is simply a working expectancy, so that, to the modern mind, death is experienced less as a definitive closure than as a medical failure, palliatively shrouded and cleanly cremated. In fact, a growing number of transhumanists are convinced that, through bioengineering, aging can be made curable, like any other malady. Meanwhile, an increasing number of frozen bodies await the day when death shall be solved. All of this is in heavy contrast to the psalmist's motivation for faith: "Make us know the shortness of our life that we may gain wisdom of heart" (Ps 90:12).

Part of the American Dream is earning enough to purchase sufficient health insurance and an adequate retirement plan to provide security from birth to death. Symbolic is the rapid increase of retirement communities, where one can slide gracefully from one stage of living to the next, having been promised increasing services and security as needed, being eased medically into a prepaid, gradual, nonthreatening conclusion. Thus, for a price, one can purchase a nonreligious version of the monk's evening prayer: "Grant us a restful night and a peaceful death." No longer is death imaged as an inevitable confrontation with a grimacing enemy but as a gradual process of wearing out, until passing way appears preferable to exerting one's waning energy to continue.

Caitlin Doughty, in her book *Smoke Gets in Your Eyes: And Other Lessons from the Crematory*, portrays honestly this modern approach to death. Indicatively, cremations now outnumber burials. Dying usually occurs within the environment of hospital sterility, as an inconvenience that the crematorium can expedite. All that is needed is a phone call, a credit card number, an unseen incineration, and the family is presented with an attractive urn of sanitized ashes—with an optional remembrance gathering conveniently arranged to accommodate the busy schedules of family and friends. At these observances, death is an unpermitted guest, displaced by words and tokens of filtered remembrances and appropriate humor that portray persons at their distilled best. More than what cosmetics formerly attempted through embalming, cremation now turns death into an inconvenient abstraction. What a contrast to death as encountered in Tolstoy's *Death of Ivan Ilych*, where death is an awakening to life lived as "falsehood and deception, hiding life and death . . ."[15]

Indicative of this changing modern attitude toward death is what is happening within the right-to-die movement. It began in the Netherlands as a compassionate but rare response to terminally ill patients who were unacceptably in extreme and unrelenting pain, done only after careful professional screening. Now in the United States, when asked if a doctor should be allowed by law to end the patient's life by some painless means if the patient and his or her family request it, when that patient has a disease that cannot be cured, 70 percent of the public surveyed by Gallup said yes.[16] This reflects the growing number of persons seeking this service if for any reason they conclude that a friendly ending is preferable to continued living. Clearly gone is any fear of death and any thought of divine judgment upon suicide. Death has become the choice of a preferred convenience, expendable when living becomes inconvenient, much as one might take medication to deal with any undesirable condition. This change in the modern mindset toward death has encouraged the Dutch Right to

15. Tolstoy, *Death of Ivan Ilych*, 152.
16. "Euthanasia," chart 1.

Die Society, globally the largest of its kind, to offer a network of travel-ing euthanasia doctors, determined to make a suicide pill available to any person aged seventy and older simply for the asking. Emblematic is the ar-rangement by which the ashes of well-known author Truman Capote were sold by relatives in a Los Angeles auction for $43,750.[17] A local mortician shared with me that, due to the increasing number of unclaimed ashes, "I have the best fertilized roses in the county."

Our secular society is expressing interest in near-death experiences, resulting in a further allay of death as threat or judgment. Appearing in print are multiple descriptions of dying, in which the person has undergone an enchanting adventure into light, a welcoming homecoming with friends and relatives, disengaged from any imagery of morality, judgment, reward, or eternal punishment. This experience is so positive that the person is sad in having to return from it. Not surprisingly, then, John Updike's final book of poems (*Endpoint*) characterizes clergy as "comical purveyors of what makes sense only to the terrified."[18] This terror over death that once pro-vided a motivation for Christian faith is what is quickly becoming inopera-tive, removing death as an event of religious encounter.

In our colonial period, there was a deep fascination with the last words a person would utter, for on them would hang one's eternal fate. Surrounded by family, the dying person was urged to make a deathbed confession as a guarantee of eternal life. Sometimes baptism would even be postponed until that ominous final hour so that one could enter heaven with forgiveness assured. When a priest is available, Catholicism still pro-vides last rites for the dying, involving confession and a eucharistic viati-cum as food for the journey. For medieval monks, the focus was not only on how one died one's death, but the specter of death was made a powerful daily determinate of how one lived one's life. A skull was placed on the monk's desk, often of a dear monastic brother, rendering finitude never far from one's thoughts. Into the mid-twentieth century, death was often a home event, emotionally engrossing the whole family in a vigil. Now 80 percent of Americans die in hospitals, nursing homes, or clinics,[19] carefully shielding the family from seeing the dying process, screened to show only sanitized snippets, professionally keeping death from proximity. In the hospital, death is institutionalized; the remains simply disappear, efficient-ly reappearing to music in flowered funeral parlors. The hospital world of ingenious technology has even eliminated natural death, substituting for

17. John, "Truman Capote's Ashes Sold," para. 1.

18. Updike, *Endpoint and Other Poems*, 24.

19. Stanford School of Medicine, "Where Do Americans Die," para. 2.

it a clinical stoppage. Family is in a separate room awaiting a nurse who will indicate when a medical technician has made a final determination by electronic graph, eliminating the possibility of a death ritual. Katherine Anne Butler, in her *Knocking on Heaven's Door: The Path to a Better Way of Death*, shows graphically how our medical facilities leave no room to think of death as a profound dimension of living. While cremation is presently the favored choice for disposal, even more indicative of our changing attitudes is the increasing popularity of flameless green cremations, where the remains are liquefied and poured down the drain.

A feature article in the *Week* magazine recently asserted that, for many families, "death has become a new bourgeois rite of passage that, much like weddings or births, must now be minutely planned and personalized."[20] Thus trained professionals are readily available for hire, orchestrating the event so as to create the desired effect. Cemeteries are no longer feared as haunted but are now opened to host moonlit tours, cocktail parties, dance performances, and even yoga classes. How foreign is this modern ethos to St. Damian's eleventh-century response to a person seeking consolation in facing death: "For God's chosen ones, there is great comfort; the torment lasts but a short time. Then God bends down, cradles the fallen figure, and whispers words of consolation. With hope in his heart, man picks himself up and walks again toward the glory of happiness in heaven."[21] But without this divine promise of a compensatory future life, Dostoevsky warns, everything is permitted.[22]

In the religion of ancient Greece, Charon the ferryman took souls to Hades across Acheron, the river of woe. How indicative that the river by this name has become so popular with tourists and rafters that photographers from *National Geographic* were unable to exclude colored lights from a nearby bar.

OMNIPRESENCE, OMNISCIENCE, SIN, AND FORGIVENESS

The god-question for the Christian is not about whether a god exists, for gods of all colors and misshapes are available for sale. What matters is the identity of that possible god. Therefore, for the Judeo-Christian tradition, God is not a deity-in-general but a particular one with a specific character.

20. *Week* Staff, "Planning an Artisanal Death," para. 2.

21. International Commission on English in the Liturgy, *Liturgy of the Hours*, 3:1384.

22. Dostoevsky, *Brothers Karamazov*, 721–22, 789.

Above all, this God is omniscient and omnipresent—present everywhere, every time, with everyone. From this, Judeo-Christian morality follows: "I the Lord test the mind and search the heart, to give to all according to their ways, according to the fruit of their doings" (Jer 17:10 NRSV). To be so fully known can be devastating, for as Jeremiah confesses, "The heart is devious above all things, and desperately corrupt; who can understand it" (Jer 17:9). Thus, the psalmist is convinced that persons who do evil do so because they deny this omniscient Presence, insisting: "Who can see us, who can search out our crimes?" (Ps 64:5–6). In heavy contrast, believers act ethically because they believe otherwise: "O Lord, thou hast searched me and known me. Thou knowest when I sit down and when I rise up; thou discernist my thoughts from afar . . . . Even before a word is on my tongue, lo, O Lord, thou knowest it altogether" (Ps 139:1–2, 4). For the Christian as well, such a God is a daunting motivator of behavior, with Jesus warning: "Nothing is covered up that will not be revealed, or hidden that will not be known. Whatever you have said in the dark shall be heard in the light, and what you have whispered in private rooms shall be proclaimed upon the housetops" (Luke 12:3). Every act done in secret, every temptation stalking one's soul—these are immediately known by the omniscient and omnipresent God. Baldwin of Canterbury insists that this is the working assumption of Christians, that "the Lord knows the thoughts and intentions of our hearts . . . better than we."[23] Central in my own United Methodist upbringing was this traditional prayer I memorized from the holy communion rite: "Almighty God, unto whom all hearts are open, all desires are known, and from whom no secrets are hid . . ." This was a central, and at times frightening, impetus for my youthful correct behavior.

How different it is to be immersed in our postmodern society! Of the diverse persons who ask me for spiritual direction, the dilemma they most commonly confess is the absence of God. For them, God has been eclipsed. Typical is this recent sharing by a retreatant: "I no longer sense God—my spirit life is dry. It is as simple as that." Vague, obscure, missing, concealed—emptiness. Experientially, God is dead. Even though I am a committed Christian, I confess that I have never had a self-authenticating experience of God's presence. Never. I have had numerous rich experiences from which I choose to infer the divine presence, but this is indirect, needing a transition by wager. Most of my theological colleagues would acknowledge the same.

Yet, ironically, there is in our modern awareness an omnipresent omniscience of a thoroughly secularized sort. As we have already explored, we live within an all-knowing and ever-present governmental/economic

23. International Commission on English in the Liturgy, *Liturgy of the Hours*, 3:312.

complex of surveillance, complete with its alternative system of rewards and punishments. Confidentiality and privacy are a thing of the past. What we speak, hear, taste, see, and smell, where we are and with whom we relate—all of this is known, but the scrutiny is no longer divine. An invisible secular presence probes our personal preferences, desires, temptations, and conversations, intent not on moral accountability but on manipulating us for the sake of control and exploitation.

I heard that Nobel Prize winner novelist William Faulkner, after a lecture at Princeton University, was asked about the seeming absence of God in the life of his characters. "I have always thought," he responded, "that God was in the wholesale and not the retail business." But for the Christian, God must be both—a cosmic Creator who knows as well each fallen sparrow by name. So even if one might give the name god to the power displayed in the formation of galaxies, without the retail dimensions, this is not the Christian God. At the heart of the Christian's faith is a wagering on the transformative power of an unconditional divine love so intimate that even the hairs of one's head are counted, not one of them falling to the ground without God's caring omniscient omnipresence.

Deeply related to such a God is the concept of sin. Throughout Christianity's long history, faith has been motivated through acknowledgement of the taintedness of our motivations and actions. "I do not understand my own actions," confesses Paul, "for I do not do what I want, but I do the very thing I hate. . . . So then it is no longer I that do it, but sin which dwells within me. . . . Wretched man that I am! Who will deliver me from this body of death?" (Rom 7:15, 17, 24). Without this aching recognition of circular ensnarement, the motivation for seizing upon the Christian proclamation is no longer operative. Today, there is indifference to the Christian offer of unconditional love, because without a sensitivity to one's sinfulness, there is no need for the gift of restorative forgiveness. Yet this was the message of the early church: "To give repentance . . . and forgiveness of sins" (Acts 5:31). "Through this man [Jesus] forgiveness of sins is proclaimed to you" (Acts 13:38). The heart of Paul's mission was to preach "everywhere" so that people "may receive forgiveness" (Acts 26:18). Christ is the one in whom "we have redemption through his blood, the forgiveness of our trespasses . . ." (Eph 1:7, Col 1:14).

But this is precisely a message that is losing its motivational point of contact for faith, for ours is a time in which the terminology of sin and its cognates is becoming archaic. No longer does an exposed scandal force a politician into a confession of guilt. Situations that once could convict one of sin are being woven into the fabric of acceptability. Selfishness is the virtue of ambition, aggression of an achiever; discrete affairs, premarital sex, not even the death penalty function any longer as a working deterrent. Being caught only forces an admission that a mistake might have been made, with the only intimidation being embarrassment. Even devastating acts of aggression perpetrated by one nation against another never involve the syntax of confession and forgiveness, but, at best, that of conceding and apologizing. Sin, guilt, repentance, confession, forgiveness, restoration—this is the redemptive process that is the core of what Christianity has to offer. But replacements are appearing as a wide array of therapies, with thousands of self-help books. As useful as these may be in behavior modification, what is missing is the central Christian declaration: "Your sins are forgiven . . . rise, take up your bed and go home" (Matt 9:5–6). An honored theme of classical writers, such as Goethe in his *Faust,* has been the fear of losing one's soul to the devil. But no longer viable is the imagery of a devil, and as for a soul, few persons would acknowledge that they even have one. The Christian gospel of forgiveness has centered from the beginning in Christ's sacrificial love as a healing for our sinful inclinations. Yet the popular New Testament scholar Marcus Borg discounts this belief as no longer providing any effective motivation whatsoever, for people today simply do not feel much guilt that is in need of expiation.[24] For the church to persist with its cross imagery is to perpetuate a negative portrait of God—as a father who demands the murder of his own son before being willing to forgive.

THE POWER OF PRAYER

Another motivation to which the church has traditionally appealed is the power of prayer. Scripture is permeated with the working assumption that prayer has to do with appeal, solicitation, and even pleading. The root meaning of the word prayer is to ask, entreat, beg. Abraham provides us with a classic story of prayer as bargaining with God. God is intent on destroying the cities of Sodom and Gomorrah for their egregious sin (Gen 18:16ff). Upon hearing this, Abraham begins his prayerful negotiating: "Suppose there are fifty righteous who are in it; wilt thou then destroy the place?" Forty-five? Forty? Thirty? Twenty? The negotiating continues vigorously until a final agreement: ten. Likewise, Moses pleads with God not to destroy Israel because of their golden calf idolatry, and, as a result, God changes his mind. David lies prostrate before the Lord in prayerful pleading for his dying son. The psalms are punctuated with prayers as cries for restoration, deliverance, victory, strength, forgiveness, vindication, rectification, prosperity, vengeance, even good weather. Jesus strongly continues

24. Borg, *Heart of Christianity,* 170–71.

this theme of changing God through prayer, using the analogy of a widow who constantly badgers a corrupt judge until he finally provides her vindication. Jesus also likens prayer to pestering one's neighbor until he gets out of bed and grants his request (Luke 11:5ff). So should our prayer life be, he insists, for "will not God vindicate his elect who cry to him day and night?" (Luke 18:1ff). In fact, the consequences of prayer are such that one need not take thought of the morrow, for what we are to eat or drink or wear (Luke 12:22). "Ask and it will be given you; seek, and you will find; knock, and it will be opened to you" (Luke 11:9). "Truly I say to you, whoever says to this mountain, 'Be taken up and cast into the sea,' and does not doubt in his heart, but believes that what he says will come to pass, it will be done for him. Therefore I tell you, whatever you ask in prayer, believe that you receive it and you will" (Mark 11:24–26). Jesus even insists that prayer possesses the power to cast out demons (Luke 10:17). "Nothing will be impossible to you" (Matt 17:21). Luther, Calvin, and Wesley all exemplified this belief in prayer, often spending hours daily in intercession, holding the plight of the world up before the face of God, persistently attempting to influence God's decisions by holding him to his own promises. Prayer effects specific consequences in daily life through asking.

Christians today might still be inclined to ask God for safe travels for a friend, and yet, when pushed, would likely be forced to admit that they were not petitioning a God who actually steers errant eighteen-wheelers or applies automobile brakes when requested. Spontaneously, we might be inclined to pray for a friend who is undergoing serious surgery, but, if pressed into theological self-awareness, would most likely realize that we were praying not so much for a miracle as for the surgeon's steady hands. If pressed hard on prayer, mainline Christians in the end would likely respond with a shrug, "It can't hurt."

This ambiguity concerning prayer reflects a theological conundrum. Even if the Christian God might be one who can and does intervene on rare occasions, what are we to do with the host of cases in which God does not? Our postmodern period was born under the shadow of Hiroshima, the Holocaust, and 9/11. If God can intervene, why did they happen? What is the believer to do with the tragic sweep of epidemics, physical catastrophes, and arbitrary tragedies? In fact, what happens to a loving Creator when we realize that this world is so designed that everything that lives must devour something else in order to survive? Even if one holds to a divine power that undergirds everything that exists, of what consequence is this if that God is not compassionately involved in taking sides, as Scripture insists, with the widow, the orphan, and the oppressed? At the monastery, we receive abundant calls and letters pleading for our prayers on behalf of every known disease and difficulty. We offer them faithfully, taking on ourselves some of the pathos. But as for what exactly we are praying, I confess ambiguity. I am clear that for a person in need of healing, helpful is a conscious awareness of being surrounded by prayer. In this, research on the phenomenon of placebos provides secular grounding to some of what used to be called faith healing. The data is clear that if a person believes a new pill will cause change for the better, it does, even though what has been consumed is a sugar pill. So too with prayer.

But most contemporary Protestant theologians no longer regard prayer as having the power formerly promised as motivation for Christian belief, especially not the ability to change God. Early in the twentieth century, P. T. Forsyth spoke for many theologians in declaring that "in prayer we do not ask God to do things contrary to Nature."[25] Later in the century, Paul Tillich insisted that the change effected by prayer is not in God but in us. C. S. Lewis likely declared that "prayer doesn't change God, it changes me."[26] Yet the defining nature of prayer as practiced by many Christian laity retains this syntax of request. So as one pastor sadly confesses, "Before long they will realize that God doesn't seem to make house calls anymore." What is operative here is the undercutting of one more motivation for becoming a Christian. Being pierced is belief in providence.

THE NEED FOR COMMUNITY

This modern undercutting of motivations for becoming Christian became graphic for me recently when, in meeting with some Christian spiritual directors, I asked this question: "Many of the retreatants with whom I work are no longer churchgoers; so what response would you give to them if they asked why they might want to become one?" There was an uncomfortable silence. Finally, indicatively, their attempts at answer were basically nontheological, and all of them variations on the theme of community: family activities, a good environment for their children, social interaction as vocational contacts, opportunities for personal friendships. Yet these are features available at any good community center, health club, or even yoga program. At best, they are simply supportive supplements to a life no longer determined by the gospel.

Chris Colin describes an interesting phenomenon emerging in Japan: rent-a-friend companies. One of them, Client Partners, begun in 2009 with multiple branches, offers to rent out a person by the hour, the only

25. Forsyth, *Soul of Prayer*, 23.
26. Attenborough, dir., *Shadowlands*.

rule being "no romance and no lending of money."[27] While a few of these pretend friendships turn out to be a bit strange, mostly they consist of only needing someone who is willing to listen and often no more than a companion with whom to watch TV. The CEO understands her company as meeting a significant vacuum in modern culture—the need for spiritual health craved by the many persons whom our society has rendered deeply lonely, forcing them to hide their feelings so as to go no deeper than appearances. Ours is a populace overworked and overextended, often consumed by carrying several jobs, leaving little time or energy for developing friendships—so, pitifully, they are willing to pay for pretense. One might think that at last we have discovered one remaining motivation into which the church might tap, but Christian community requires having time—for developing mutual commitments, for listening patiently to one another, for trusting others with one's stories—something far deeper than what rent-a-Christian can touch. Research in 2016 by Duke University scientists finds that men are more likely to believe in God after having sex.[28] Perhaps we might reinstate temple prostitutes.

ATTEMPTS AT REHABILITATION OF PAST MOTIVATION

Formerly, a Catholic family was regarded as extraordinarily blessed if there emerged a son who became a priest or a daughter who became a nun—for special divine merit was understood as accruing to the whole family. With Vatican II, however, there was a significant shift from selective callings to inclusive ones, in which Christians were encouraged to discover God's own particular life vocation for them from a widened variety of possibilities. Thus, a Christian garage mechanic could be just as holy in God's sight as the ascetic ordained Trappist monk who eschewed the pleasures and comforts of middle-class existence. Celibacy became regarded as no more spiritual than marriage, and singleness no holier a choice than family life. The cleavage between church and world was lessened, encouraging bridging and engagement rather disconnection and suspicion. The cloister was by nature no more meritorious than the marketplace. Papal infallibility was less stressed in favor of mutual discernment by the gathered people of God. The rigors of penance and mortification were deemphasized in favor of works of mercy and social justice. Understanding the meaning of faith was stressed more than obedience to ecclesiastical authority. The motivational

27. *Week* Staff, "Inside Japan's Booming Rent-a-Friend," para. 9.

28. A. Jones, "Oxytocin Enhances Spirituality," para. 1.

shift was from getting to giving, to we rather than me, to this life more than the next, and on eliminating suffering now rather than bearing it for the sake of eternal reward later. In a real sense, the former motivations for becoming a Christian were functionally inverted. No longer was the emphasis on obedience for the sake of clear and hefty consequences but on an invitation into a life of service for its own sake.

This opening of the windows begun by St. John XXIII was indeed a liberating freshness on behalf of a renewed church in the modern world. It was the reason why I became a Catholic and consequently a priest. Yet its impact on a number of cradle Catholics was undercutting or at least challenging, for being severely questioned were the motivations that bonded them in obedience to the church and its traditions. Thereby was intensified a splitting within the Catholic church that has increased ever since, between those reacting tenaciously against these changes and those motivated to implement Vatican II even further. Many lay persons experienced a severe erosion of their motives, resulting in the growing phenomenon of former Catholics. There was a mass exit from monasteries and religious orders, and, for many who remained, there was a deep confusion about motivations for remaining.

Perhaps the most damaging diminishment has been the catastrophic loss of priests and candidates for the priesthood. While various reasons have been suggested, it is largely because the traditional motives for these signature callings have been severely weakened. Key is Vatican II's de-emphasis on negative motivations for being Christian, focusing instead on the positive character of living the Christian life now and on earth. Above all, this entailed a minimizing of "fear" as a defining motive. Punishment was deemphasized; funerals stressed resurrection rather than the "Deus Irae" terrors of hell; instead of collecting merits for attaining heaven, the focus was on divine love as a gracious and unearned gift; good works were a response to grace rather than its cause; self-denial shifted toward authentic selfhood; purgatory as a post-death time of punishment faded in favor of a disciplined commitment in this life; and stress on reward, indulgences, and the storehouse of merit began disappearing. Instead of an emphasis on deprivations now for the sake of a full life later, the shift was toward a fullness of life now that extended into a life to come. Community was central rather than individual piety, and downplayed was the hierarchy of meritorious callings. Rather than being world-denying, the emphasis was on creation-affirming and society-critiquing, eliciting a passion for global justice. But above all, what was being removed was the fright of God's anger—"So terrible and awesome are you; who can stand before you and your great anger?" (Ps 76:8 NAB). "Will you be angry with us forever?" (Ps 85:6 NAB).

While our society certainly is living in fear, that fear has been drained of its former religious context and replaced, as we have seen, by secular causes with proposed secular remedies. Since 9/11, the ubiquitous fear is of terrorists, and the solution is no longer that of divine protection but of homeland security and military supremacy. Acknowledging that religious fear is no longer functioning as a motivation for Christian belief, attempts are being made to resurrect this need in order to reestablish a point for motivational contact. Indicative is Ralph Martin's *Will Many Be Saved*, which we previously mentioned. Martin fully concurs that, because of Vatican II, there is no longer any motivational basis left for evangelism in the modern world. Therefore, the only hope for the church is to restore the previous fear of hell. Without such alarm, Martin insists, the umbilical cord for faith is severed, leaving no reason for conversion. This approach as a new evangelism receives enthusiastic endorsement by sixteen archbishops and Catholic authorities whose acclaim appears in the opening pages of Martin's book. Their clear insistence is that Jesus's own command for us to evangelize is firmly rooted in Martin's belief "that the eternal destinies of human beings are really at stake, and for most people the preaching of the gospel can make a life-or-death, heaven-or-hell difference."[29] Therefore, it is vital that this threat of hell "be unashamedly stated," for the "salvation of unbelievers" is a "matter of life or death as regards one's eternal destiny," not a means to "a greater fullness of life." Their declaration is staunch: unless this motivation of fear is resurrected, Christianity no longer has any reason left to present to the world for faith. As in this morning's breviary, we read: "May we live in this world so as to avoid harsh judgment in the next."[30]

While this divisive mandate to reverse the counterproductive consequences of Vatican II makes a welcome contact with Catholic conservatives, there is a catch-22 involved. The Council was properly called by a pope, and its decisions were made by the worldwide leadership of the Catholic Church; therefore Vatican II cannot be rejected. Thus, the conservative approach has been to place the problem not on Vatican II itself but on progressives who have misunderstood and misused it. One must understand that its intent was to temper what may have previously been overemphasized but was never meant to replace. The error happened when progressives mistakenly adopted it as a substitute rather than a moderation. Thus, for conservatives, the primal reason for the sizable post-Vatican II exit from the church was the dilution of the product by progressives, diluting the answer

---

29. R. Martin, *Will Many Be Saved*, 204.

30. International Commission on English in the Liturgy, *Liturgy of the Hours*, 2:1508.

that had been successfully offered through the ages. They rest their case in early Christianity, as expressed in an anonymous second-century homily that continues to appear in the breviary: "The day of judgment like a flaming furnace is already approaching. Sun, moon and stars will be consumed and the whole earth will become like lead melting in the fire."[31] Indeed, other homilies over time have threatened the world into a severe choice of repentance or of "departing into everlasting fire which was prepared for the devils and his angels" (Matt 25:41 NRSV).

This conservative Catholic ethos is propagated by such reactionary groups as the *Fatima Crusader*. Here, the purported Marian appearances at Fatima are made a basis for steadfastly opposing ecumenism, permissive internal diversity, tolerance for other religions, and "protestantizing of the Mass"—symbolically expressed in their insistence upon restoring the Latin Mass. On the one hand, their doggedness is on pressuring the Vatican to release the Third Secret revealed at Fatima that supposedly discloses the frightening things to come. On the other hand, there is a harkening back to the fear characterizing the Cold War era, claiming that unless the Vatican is forced to respond to Mary's request that Russia be consecrated to her Immaculate Heart, Russia will enslave the world, raising up wars and persecutions against the church.[32]

George Weigel's *Evangelical Catholicism: Deep Reform in the Twenty-First Century* clearly draws the battlelines by identifying neo-conservativism's bedrock issues for which neither compromise nor accommodation will any longer to be tolerated—such matters as contraception, abortion, and gay marriage. It is therefore imperative, Weigel insists, that the Catholic Church exert intense pressure on all legislators and demand unabashed doctrinal obedience from the laity.[33] Catholics who no longer believe everything that the church teaches should leave, for the church dare no longer tolerate "baptized pagans" or "nominal believers."

In a speech delivered at the University of Notre Dame in 2016,[34] Archbishop Charles Chaput, a leader of this conservative wing within the US Catholic hierarchy, took a similar stand, even declaring that "we should never be afraid of a smaller, lighter church," purged of the "silent apostasy" of the many who no longer accept without exception the full orthodox teachings of the church. The only way to reverse the church's diminishment, he insists, is retrenchment, returning to the old church of our baptism rather

31. International Commission on English in the Liturgy, *Liturgy of the Hours*, 4:526.

32. Cardinale et al., "Fatima Crusade," paras. 1, 23.

33. Weigel, *Evangelical Catholicism*, 228–30.

34. Gibson, "Archbishop Chaput Welcomes 'Smaller Church,'" paras. 1, 3, 13, 32.

than "the new 'church' of our ambitions and appetites." Anything less is "not just lying but an act of betrayal."

While this neo-conservative reaction had support under the papacies of St. John Paul II and Benedict XVI, Pope Francis has emerged as a champion of the inclusive and expansive spirit of Vatican II, insisting on a church "which is poor and for the poor," choosing "to lend our voices to their causes" in "eliminating the structural causes of poverty," no longer "overemphasizing certain rules or a particular Catholic style of the past." Instead of confronting non-Catholics with fearful threats, Pope Francis in his 2018 Christmas message invited atheists to join him in the cause of peace.[35] At another time, he referred to persons without any religious tradition as being "precious allies."[36] Here and elsewhere he repeatedly echoes the *Dogmatic Constitution on the Church* from Vatican II, affirming that "God himself is not far from those others who seek the unknown God in darkness and shadow," who while not yet believing in God "strive to lead a good life."[37] Yet while this outreach is firm, what remains vague is what point of contact remains, if any, for why anyone might want to become a Christian, other than being willing to cooperate with Catholics on social justice projects.

The conservative analysis is correct in placing the cause for Christianity's demise in the waning societal motivational points of contact to which Christianity could formerly appeal. While Vatican II attempted to adapt the product so as to be commensurate with motivations that might stimulate today's secular clientele, the conservative approach attempts to reverse the secular ethos itself, restoring an otherworldly fear with which they then might gain traction. But, as we have been seeing, the dynamic of modernity is irreversibly different now than before Vatican II, in which restoration of otherworldly threats and rewards is not only a non-winnable effort, but the attempt sullies the progressive faith options as well. Roger Lundin, in his book *Believing Again*, traces the history of doubt and concludes that we cannot return to any previous age as a basis for believing again.[38]

While this new evangelism has focused primarily on fallen-away Catholics, a 2015 Pew study indicates that 77 percent of persons raised Catholic and who no longer identify themselves with the church cannot even envisage themselves as ever returning to the Catholic Church.[39] Thus,

35. Pope Francis, "*Urbi et Orbi*," paras. 11–18.
36. Reuters, "Pope Urges All Religions," para. 9.
37. Pope Paul VI, *Lumen gentium (Dogmatic Constitution on the Church)*, para. 16.
38. Lundin, *Believing Again*.
39. Ohlheiser, "Vast Majority," para. 2.

this conservative-progressive cleavage within Catholicism, centering in the issue of motive, has bequeathed to Pope Francis a deep dysfunctionality that is eating away at the veracity that once gave power to Catholic authority. Among retreatants with whom I work who identify themselves as having been born Catholic or who are non-practicing Catholics, without authority, there is not much left upon which to fall back. It is surprising how slight is their knowledge of Scripture and how superficially literal is their theological understanding of doctrine. Before Vatican II, personal Bible reading was not encouraged, homilies at Mass were infrequent, liturgy was in Latin, and variations on the theme of fear provided motivation for Mass attendance. Therefore, when fear diminished and ecclesiastical authority became questioned, what tended to remain were practices with little understanding for doing them.

A 2017 study by the Public Religion Research Institute[40] indirectly supports our thesis that the decline of Christianity in our society is not so much the result of conclusions drawn as it is the erosion of motives once operative. From fallen-away younger adults who were raised in Christian families, what one usually hears is not reasons but only that the religion of their childhood no longer speaks to them. As Dan Cox reports, while recent surveys have found that only about 10 percent of Americans report that they do not believe in God, and only about 3 percent identify as atheist, the true number of atheists could be as high as 26 percent, with those who no longer believe in a God uncomfortable accepting the label of atheist.[41] Their nonbelief, rather than being a thought-through conclusion, is a gradual erosion to a "not much left," caused by multiple factors on even believers without their awareness, threatening to erode them into living as functional atheists. All of us are creatures of habit, and when we break a habit for very long, it relinquishes its hold on us. Yet to be seen then is the effect on us habitual church goers after the pandemic has broken that habit for over a year—but it is likely to be another significant factor in the church's relentless diminishment.

SCANDAL, HYPOCRISY, AND MORAL AUTHORITY

As I write this particular section, the Roman Catholic Church is being shaken at foundation depth by the findings of an eighteen-month grand jury

---

40. D. Cox and Jones, "America's Changing Religious Identity," para. 1.
41. D. Cox, "Way More Americans," para. 3.

investigation in Pennsylvania.[42] I was raised in one of the six dioceses under investigation. Not only are more than three hundred priests involved in this lucid disclosure of horrifying abuses with youth but being disclosed as well is the intentional and systematic protection given perpetrators by church leaders at various levels. Discovered are not only individuals but rings of priests. Shocking accounts include multiple incidences of violence, sadism, assault, grooming, pornography, and rape. Secret archives created playbook strategies for maintaining secrecy with codes and euphemisms. Consequently, reporters have been forced to employ a lexicon of "rot," "horrifying," "shocking," and "atrocities." Bishops closet perpetrators, and millions of dollars have been spent by the Catholic Church to defeat bills that would extend the statute of limitations. When one multiplies these Pennsylvania statistics by the rest of the dioceses in the US, the tsunami is staggering. The clear and damning conclusion is that the Catholic Church is unable to govern herself, making necessary and inevitable these multiple investigations from without. In 2021, an independent commission investigating the Catholic Church in France found that 330,000 children were sexually abused mostly by priests and clerics over a 70 year period. Until the 2000s, the church showed "deep, total, and even cruel indifference" toward its victims, said the commission head.[43] As far back as the 1990s, a series of sexual harassment disclosures rocked Europe, Latin America, Chile, and Australia. Meanwhile, sexual harassment charges are emerging as well regarding Protestant clergy and agencies, and, in 2019, the Southern Baptist Church conducted a three-day Caring Well conference to review charges of sexual harassment.[44]

Catholic bishops are presently reacting in such a way that priests and bishops found guilty will likely be prosecuted ecclesiastically and legally. Yet while delayed justice may be served, this hardly touches what is really exacerbating church diminishment. Being exposed for all to see is the truth of Reinhold Niebuhr's dictum that the only Christian doctrine for which there is empirical evidence is that of original sin.[45] As one pundit puts it, being put under heavy judgment is the heart of the gospel—the veracity of its claim to offer healing, when the healers are those who are producing abuse on this scale. Furthermore, in overreacting by making punishment and exclusion its only response to abusers, the church is turning its back on the redemptive power that it claims to offer—the gospel promise of conversion and restoration. Conservative Christians put the blame on liberals for embracing

42. "Attorney General Shapiro Details Findings."

43. *Week*, "The world at a glance," 8.

44. Crary, "Southern Baptists Ready," para. 2.

45. Richardson, "Unoriginal Sin," para. 1.

the sexual revolution, while liberals fault conservatives for their exploitive clericalism. Others point to celibacy as the culprit, still others at homosexuality. But in spite of sexuality being at the heart of humanness, the church has largely failed to respond creatively, tending instead to do so restrictively, through the negativities of restraint and sublimation. Since even atheists can be positive about the ethical teachings of Jesus, what is left if, at its center, the church is no longer a practicing example of its redemptive product? "You will know them by their fruits" (Matt 7:16).

CHAPTER SEVEN

FORFEITURE OF OBJECTIVE
TRUTH AND PURE FAITH

Postmodern, a label used to characterize our present world, refers to a situation in which objectivity has been so severely undercut that subjectivity has become our major determinate. What one claims to know as true depends on one's arbitrary point of view. Thus, not only is Christianity regarded as no longer having a rational objective basis for affirming God, but there is no longer any objective base for establishing anything with certainty.

Nietzsche was adumbrative in offering the term nihilism to our situation, understood as a situation in which the highest values are losing their value, there is no uniting purpose, no Truth, no thing in itself. Truths cannot be known as being more than fictions, some of which are accepted as being more useful than others. Thus, all so-called facts are interpretations, and all interpretations depend on perspectives. Herein is a significant factor in the church's diminishment, for the traditional claim of Christianity to be the truth makes little sense in a world that denies any objective truth and in which the fictions that are being chosen are from perspectives that are post-Christian.

The internet was once regarded as a promising disseminator of democratized information on behalf of creating an informed public. Instead, it has become a vehicle of alarming misinformation, encapsulating us within closed information loops. Without any reliable filter for sorting this overflow, all input can appear equally true, providing evidence capable of documenting whatever truth one might wish to believe. Without any agreed-upon authority for differentiating fact from fiction, journalist Jonathan Mahler of the *New York Times* declares that we have entered "a post-truth era."[1] Thus, President

---

1. Mahler, "Problem with 'Self-Investigation,'" para. 2.

Trump's press secretary can speak easily of alternative facts,[2] and the president himself can declare as hoax whatever he does not like, accuse the major media of being distributors of fake news, and function so that nothing is true until I say so. "Truth? What is truth?" scoffed Pilate (John 18:38). In such an arena, Christianity is reduced to the status of opinion.

Further, throughout the history of Christianity, religious experience has been used as a reliable basis for faith, with mystics given special acclaim. But in our postmodern world where subjectivity reigns, experience itself is dismissed as being an agent of certainty about anything. Thus, neuroscientists are researching a physical predilection that could be called a god gene, which creates religious experience in certain persons.[3] Those who are intense mystics themselves tend to disregard their experiences as proof of faith, discounting their importance. Teresa of Avila, who in the latter part of her life received deep multiple consolations, insists that faith rooted in experience is built on sand. In Protestantism, the theological giant Karl Barth insists the same—that faith is not based on experience but on obedience and worship. He even declares that faith based on religious experience is pagan, for, in being subjective, it begins with the self, rendering everything that one claims to express God as being simply a projection of the self.[4] To the church who through the ages declares certainty for faith through unique experience, our post-Christian world dilutes all experience to the status of subjectivity, arbitrariness, and fictionality.

In spite of this muting, we will presently explore how postmodernism, rightly understood, is actually producing a level playing field for Christianity—rooting all of us in the humbling realization that, since nothing is known by anyone for certain, each person's meaning rests on faith alone. Research into the life of John Wesley has revealed a biographical foreshadowing of this modern religious situation. Throughout his life, Wesley's spiritual struggle for spiritual perfection kept foundering on the issue of certainty, with every assurance of his own salvation failing to last. While his conversion came as a heartwarming experience at Aldersgate, he found that it was unable to sustain him, as he was periodically plagued by intense periods of despair and angst. "I see more than I feel," he declared. In a letter written on June 27, 1766, to his brother Charles, John confesses: "In one of my last [letters] I was saying I do not feel the wrath of God abiding on me;

2. "Alternative facts" was a phrase used by U.S. Counselor to the President Kellyanne Conway during a Meet the Press interview on Jan. 22, 2017, in which she defended White House Press Secretary Sean Spicer's false statement about the attendance numbers of Donald Trump's inauguration as president of the United States.

3. Muller, "NeuroTheology."

4. Barth, *Dogmatics in Outline*, 15–16.

nor can I believe it does. And yet (this is the mystery) I do not love God. I never did . . . I am only an honest heathen . . . I have never had any other evidence of the eternal or invisible world than I have now; and that is none at all . . . . If I have any fear, it is not that of falling into hell but of falling into nothing."[5] Wesley's struggles for certainty were happening around the time when Kant was undercutting all rational certainty for religion, declaring that in so doing he was "making way for faith."[6] This is the reality to which our postmodern world is forcing Christianity. Being purged of all motives for faith outside itself, defrocked of all instrumental value with which to evangelize or even defend itself, Christianity is being distilled into pure faith or none at all. Faith is not knowledge and can never be more than a personal "assurance of things hoped for" (Heb 11:1). Wesley regarded his uncertainty as a personal failing, but St. Benedict in his *Rule* recognized that this condition is characteristic of all believers. While a novice on entering the monastery would exchange his secular clothes for the monastic habit, his secular clothes were to be kept as a constant reminder that he could leave at any moment,[7] never forgetting that staying is a moment-by-moment wager. So it is for the post-Christian believer—that faith, ironically, is made authentic by the proximity of freedom to walk away.

Thus, as we will be contending, what remains for the postmodern Christian is a way of life grounded in nothing more, nor less, than a radical ongoing decision, one that in the face of modern society is profoundly countercultural. More appropriate than ever before are these words of Jesus: "Blessed are those who have not seen and yet believe" (John 20:29). What we will be exploring is the anatomy of this "yet believe." Scripture is quite critical of the hireling whose motivation in caring for the sheep is his pay, for, when threats come, out of self-interest, he will flee for his own life. Analogously, the Christian who is motivated instrumentally by any pay/reward arrangement is not authentically Christian—for self-interest remains at the center of the person's orienting motivation, with the self functioning as god. The book of Job points toward this essential nature of faith, exploring what is left when all motivational rewards for faith are shredded. What remains is pure faith, faith as *sui generis*, self-authenticating—a faith that does not need nor seek any justification beyond itself. While St. Gregory admits that a Christian might begin the faith trek out of fear or desire for reward, s/he must undergo conversion so as to become a Christian who loves for its own sake. Speaking to the church as a whole, he warns: "If she still does good only

5. Heitzenrater, *Elusive Mr. Wesley*, 1:198–9.

6. Stern, *Faculty Theory of Knowledge*, 126.

7. Benedict of Nursia, *Rule of St. Benedict*, 271.

out of fear, then inwardly she has not withdrawn from evil; for she commits sin by desiring to sin, if only she could sin without punishment."[8] Leo the Great likewise points toward true faith as what remains in the absence of all traditional motivations: "For the one who loves God, it is sufficient to please the one he loves, and there is no greater recompense to be sought than the loving itself."[9] Thus, ironically, it is in this post-Christian era, in which all the motivations that once buttressed faith are being scrapped, that the true heart of Christianity is being exposed—pure faith, intrinsically rooted in nothing other than its own self, as an end in itself. Losing all instrumental motivation for becoming Christian, what is left is being possessed by a way of life that has integrity for its own sake, self-authenticating, rooted in a disciplined disposition. No longer is there a foundational *because* but a wagered *nevertheless*. Echoing William James, faith is "the will to believe"—to wager that a life grounded in the Christian faith is qualitatively superior to any nonreligious option. This is a matter of knowing within—as Pascal insists, "from the heart."[10] So at the heart of Bernard of Clairvaux's faith is the insistence that the only authentic reason for loving God is God. In his famed sermon on love,[11] he insists that love is "sufficient in itself." "It is its own reward." "I love because I love, I love in order that I may love." "Its profit lies in its practice." "When God loves, all he desires is to be loved in return; the sole purpose of his love being to be loved, knowing that those who love him are made happy by loving him." The only reward desired for loving God is God, just as is a lover's passion for the beloved. "I would not be seeking him unless God was not already seeking me out"—enabling my loving by my being loved. The case for Christianity is the quality of life gifted to the believer.

What this understanding reveals is that the church through the ages has actually been walking the edge of perfidy in offering faith as a means, as a bargaining chip with a redeemable reward, thereby obscuring faith as being an end. In fact, Christianity's emergence from Judaism was marked by this reversal of motivation. No longer was the heart of faith understood as obedience in order to receive, but as response to having been offered—as an end transforming the means, as being gifted rather than earning. The faith being offered was of an incarnate God who graciously loves the unlovable, embraces the unrepentant, and accepts the unacceptable—for those realizing themselves to be undeserving. Thus the question of questions: "Who

8. Walsh, *Witness of the Saints*, 485.

9. Walsh, *Witness of the Saints*, 183.

10. Pascal, *Pensées*, 127.

11. International Commission on English in the Liturgy, *Liturgy of the Hours*, 4:1333–34.

do you say that I am?" (Matt 16:15). Faith wagers that in the Christ event we behold the character of God as unconditional love.

This means that the heart of faith is not so much cognitional as volitional, of knowing the gospel to be true only through a willed commitment to live as if it were true. This approach has a sturdy tradition throughout Christian history, as in the work of such theologians as Irenaeus, Augustine, Anselm, Bonaventure, and Francis of Assisi. Their theme is not "I understand in order to believe," but "I believe in order to understand." Their theological task of faith seeking understanding is done by living it.

Language reflects living, and living, in turn, shapes language. For early Christianity, the linguistic mode of faith tended to be indicative: "It is so." During the autocratic medieval era, the mode became more declarative:"It IS so!" With the Enlightenment, the mode became interrogative: "Is it so?" Now in our post-Christian postmodern era, truth is no longer regarded as objective but subjective, depending on the orienting perspective that one brings to experience. Therefore, the mode of faith is now subjunctive, living "as if it is so." The subjunctive mode expresses the contingent and hypothetical. It is used to temper statements with qualifiers, as in moderating direct statements with dimensions of desire, hope, wish, need, uncertainty, or doubt. This is the mode needed to characterize the Christian today, one that expresses the unknown, uncertain, incomplete, vague, and indefinite; tempered by such modifiers as maybe, perhaps, nevertheless, if, and not yet; impulsed by feeling, desiring, needing, preferring, hoping, hunching, willing, risking, and wagering. The poet Rainer Rilke lived the subjunctive, insisting that we never give up our wishing, for, while there may be no such thing as fulfillment, there are wishes whose worth consists in our living them. This is a spirituality punctuated by even though, maybe so, and perhaps. Each subjunctive sentence is rooted in something unknown or uncontrollable. It is the language muttered by those who, in wandering behind the scenery, have discovered its composition to be cardboard. Each *now* is the creative edge between the *no longer* and the *not yet*.

It is impossible for any person to live without something on the basis of which s/he regards it preferable to live than to die. Thus faith is unavoidable, for no matter how shallow or deep, how narrow or expansive, whether chosen or imposed, one must trust something that makes life worth living; otherwise, one will die or shrivel from soul-starvation. Therefore, all of us have a god that justifies and flavors our weekday actions—even if it is only the reward of Sunday afternoon football with enough money to hoist a wet one. We only go around once, and the proof of one's something is the quality of life resulting from risking one's life and dying one's death upon it. The defining question for each human being, then, is not shall I be a person of faith, but what in fact is functioning now as my faith. Authenticity is determined by the depth, quality, and consistency of one's commitment. Inauthenticity is a matter of existing in unquestioning oblivion of what one's something is, resulting in a squandered life. In the absence of all certainty, one must nevertheless wager on something, living one's life based on an as if. So it is that Christians are grounded in an ongoing act of will, on which our wagering does not makes us strange—for every human being lives by faith.

My own gambling chip is the Christ event, chosen in full realization that I may be mistaken; and yet I prefer living by it and being wrong than in living any other as if and being right. If the cosmos is not informed by love, Camus insists, then I shall live love with all my might in protest.[12] Whether my faith is a wager on truth or a protest of its absence—this cannot be known, nor does it matter. As we will be proposing, Christian life for the remnant entails living as if God is lovingly incarnate within an evolving cosmos, living as if God is ongoingly being crucified in suffering love with us as companion, living as if God is resurrecting the created beauty of our living by ascending it into the divine memory and imagination, living as if the Spirit is prodding and luring all things toward consummation in a new heaven and new earth, in which God "shall wipe away every tear from our eyes and death shall be no more" (Rev 21:4). And the distilled gesture that embodies and feeds this wager is the participative communal drama called Eucharist.

We turn now to the question of why anyone might want to make such a gamble.

12. Camus, *Myth of Sisyphus*, 27, 39, 57.

CHAPTER EIGHT

THE BURNED OF GOD

W hy would anyone be inclined to take this wager into the Christian faith? Thomas Merton ends his *Seven Storey Mountain* (1999) by describing his call as that of being one of the burned ones—branded, marked, claimed.[1] The burned of God are those who in the midst of their immersion in our post-Christian condition still find themselves unable to let go of the god-question. As we noted, Albert Schweitzer in his *Quest of the Historical Jesus* (1910) researched the quests by the finest Christian scholars in their attempt to discover the objective Jesus. He was forced to conclude that Jesus is, remains, and will always be the "One unknown, without a name." Nevertheless, Schweitzer insists, Jesus persistently "speaks to us the same word: 'Follow thou me!'"[2] The world of the burned searcher is the one that Franz Kafka portrays in *The Castle* (1953)—addressed by a relentless call by one who hides or may not even exist—to do something that is far from clear. In his *Trial* (1954), this world is where one is tainted by a sense of guilt about something before someone who is apparently inaccessible—yet whom one is not free to disregard. T. S. Eliot identifies burnedness as an internal tearing up of what once seemed sufficient for meaning, which he wagers to be the work of "Christ the Tiger."[3] For others, it is more like heartburn edged by a void, a yearning for a shapeless more, a no answerable only to a yes, whether severe or mildly persistent.

Many are the pastors today whose task is to feed others yet find themselves being the ones unfed; still, they cannot send the resignation letter. Mother Teresa identifies the issue as infecting the wider population as well. During a speech in 1994 at the National Prayer Breakfast in

1. Merton, *Seven Storey Mountain*, 306.

2. Schweitzer, *Quest of Historical Jesus*, 403.

3. Eliot, "Gerontion," in *Complete Poems and Plays*, 21.

234

Washington DC, she said "spiritual poverty is much harder to overcome."[4] The burned ones are those who, in sensing this emptiness, are unable to feed, dull, or numb it. We cannot walk away. We cannot hang it up. We cannot find self-help that helps. We are the haunted ones, gnawed as if by an absentee God whose presence, at best, consists of hints—hints that the soul-depth hole is God-shaped. In the words of John Updike, God for us burned ones is no longer a verb but an "ominous hollow noun."[5] Camus experienced this world as absurd, for, in reply to our questions, comes an "absolute deafness"; yet we cannot stop asking.

Sometimes in the midnight hours, we priests and ministers let it all hang loose. We remember how in our seminary years we sensed what would happen if we preached to parishioners what we had been learning/thinking. No infallible Scripture left, no physical resurrection, no virgin birth, no physical miracles, no Jesus returning on pink clouds, no biblical foretelling of the future—being called to preach to a world where the good are not rewarded. A shroud of humanness tainted the whole. But we learned how to use qualifiers for dependent clauses within parentheses modifying brackets exegeted in footnotes explaining meaning in terms of mythopoetics. When does the sum of a 1,001 qualifications add up to a functional denial of the original? This is not something that atheists are throwing in the face of serious Christians. Our finest Christian theologians readily acknowledge this for themselves. The Christian and the atheist, said Kierkegaard, both look no different in being tax collectors, or shopkeepers, or postmen[6]—or when feeding the pigeons. But there is a difference: for the Christian, pigeon feeding does not placate the something. Martin Marty, in his *Cry of Absence: Reflections for the Winter of the Heart*, speaks of the "Siberias of the heart"—the experience of the desert space left when the divine is distant, the sacred is remote, and the One others call God is silent.[7] Isaiah confesses that "truly thou art a God who hidest thyself" (Isa 45:15). The Christian poet W. H. Auden speaks for the burned ones in acknowledging that "our dominant experience is of God's absence."[8] Yet it is an experience, and it does burn.

After depicting the inhabitants of our society as hollow people wandering in a waste land, T. S. Eliot cries out, "Shall I at least set my lands in order? London Bridge is falling down falling down falling down."[9] Not

---

4. Leigh, "Five of Mother Teresa's," para. 4.

5. Updike, *Poorhouse Fair*, 91.

6. Kierkegaard, *Fear and Trembling*, 53–54.

7. Marty, *Cry of Absence*, 5–8.

8. S. Smith, *Cambridge Companion to W. H. Auden*, 47.

9. Eliot, "Waste Land," in *Complete Poems and Plays*, 73.

only society, but the church is moving relentlessly toward diminishment, "not with a bang but a whimper." Yet for the burned ones, this whimper is more like the rumbling for a nevertheless. The death-of-God theologians describe it as being not "the absence of the experience of God, but the experience of the absence of God."[10] But that is an experience, and it is of something. Christianity from the beginning has appealed to losers, to misfits, to the marginal—those whom James Fowler in his *Stages of Faith* (1995) identifies as having known the "sacrament of defeat."[11] Dorothy Day in her *Long Loneliness* (1996) insists that Israel's honeymoon with God be understood not as a frolicking in a land filled with milk and honey but an existence in desert harshness under discipline—with the requisites for this spiritual journey being ache, solitude, emptiness, yearning, and craving. "For you I long, for you my soul is thirsting. My body pines for you, like a dry weary land without water" (Ps 62:2).[12] These are the burned ones, for whom the only God worth seeking, worth struggling for and with, is the unknowable One—the unexperienceable, the unnamable, and the unimaginable. The case for faith is the shadow implied darkly by what we do know—eclipse, longing, ache, and yearning. Even the mystics identify their experiences as immersion in transcendent darkness. Thus a post-Christian Christian spirituality must be born within the burned ones who are fully aware, as Bonhoeffer insists, of living in a world without God.

As Steven Weinberg contends in his *First Three Minutes* (1993), it is the effort to understand the meaning of our universe that is one of the few things that lifts human life a little above the level of farce, giving it "some of the grace of tragedy."[13] Theologian Julian Hartt takes the next step: "What does it mean to be rooted and grounded in finiteness and yet to have the sense and taste of the infinite ineradicably present?"[14] Thus, Barth calls God "the author of our universal homesickness."[15] What these thinkers are describing is the gambling arena in which the burned ones are forced to toil, in which risk is the anatomy of its perimeters. They sense that living lacks authenticity unless by a free and mindful choice, by which one gives it away in order to find it. Kierkegaard calls this a leap of faith into faith—a gambling that begins less as a *towards* than as an *out of*. The Christian adventure involves wagering on the objective

10. Altizer and Hamilton, *Radical Theology*, 27–28.

11. Fowler, *Stages of Faith*, 198.

12. Gelineau, *Psalms*, 113.

13. Weinberg, *First Three Minutes*, 155.

14. Woodyard, *Living without God*, 31.

15. Barth, *Dogmatics in Outline*, 35.

uncertainty of the Christ event with an intensity of subjectivity[16]—done not once and for all but repetitively, as a discipline of rehearsed willing, as if treading water over a bottomless sea.

Although in our postmodern world there no longer remain any uniquely religious experiences, T. S. Eliot wisely counsels that what we do have are "hints followed by guesses."[17] Probably all of us have experienced inklings of grace-gifted moments, undeserved, unattended, unexpected—a bird at sunset, one of Beethoven's final string quartets, the touch of a friend, a crocus in the snow, the unexpected salt of an ocean wave, a promise kept. Likewise, we have all had times of dereliction, disappointment, and betrayal. Therefore, a primal question is which experiences one shall choose as the aperture through which to view and thus experience all else. Nikos Kazantzakis in his *Saviors of God* (1966) portrays all of us as standing before a veil on which to paint our fondest hints. But then he states, "We sing even though we know that no ear exists to hear us; we toil though there is no employer to pay us our wages when night falls."[18] He claims to know too much, for he uses the indicative rather than subjunctive, with its modifiers such as maybe and perhaps. Nevertheless, Kazantzakis wisely speaks of each person needing to tame the "dread mystery," for which it does not take much—"just cultivating a field, kissing another human, studying a stone, an animal, an idea."[19] Annie Dillard in her *Pilgrim at Tinker Creek* (1974) astutely observes that although Moses lived a lifetime of varied experiences, the meaning of his life consisted of living with two of them serving as his life's embracing parentheses. One was the hint of God perceived for a moment through the cleft in a rock; the other was the final half hour of his life as he viewed the promised land he would never enter. One's life depends on a few experiences that frame all the rest.

While such evocations issue into a wagered assumption, they remain transient without discipline. After the hints and guesses, Eliot insists that what needs to follow is "prayer, observance, discipline."[20] In a deep sense, faith depends not only on where one stands but with whom one does the standing. Theologian Walter Lowe, drawing from his own Anglo-Catholic tradition, maintains that the subjective Christian wager is given its objective foundation through the disciplined communal rehearsal of spiritual

16. R. Ellsberg, *All Saints*, 491.

17. Eliot, "Dry Salvages," in *Complete Poems and Plays*, 130.

18. Kazantzakis, *Saviors of God*, 56.

19. Kazantzakis, *Saviors of God*, 79–80.

20. Eliot, "Dry Salvages" in *Complete Poems* and Plays, 136.

practice.[21] Christian faith by its very nature is church faith, in which a person is baptized into an alternative world of proclamation, poetry, music, incense, and sacrament, thereby honing the mind, eye, ear, taste, smell, and touch to discern the sacred in, with, and under all things. Faith establishes one's orienting disposition, shaped by and rendered steady within community, lived out as a mindful commitment to a rule that the person explicates for appropriation, as the anatomy of living as if the heart of the Christian belief is true. Christians are those who wager a disciplined life upon a vision that is radically uncertain but who need to do so, because they are infected by the cabin fever of an inveterate gambler—until, in spite of experiences to the contrary, they hunch that the ability to take such an absurd risk is itself the gift.

In anticipating the healing power that Alcoholics Anonymous has tapped, John Wesley made a significant contribution to Christian spirituality by insisting on the need for each Christian to participate in a disciplined support/accountability group.[22] Change required practicing "the forms of holiness" through communal commitment to a personal rule to which one was held accountable, involving worship, prayer, Bible reading, the Eucharist, intercessions, and social works of love. Just as runners must undergo daily the discipline of their sport, and musicians must practice with regularity the art of their proficiency, so it is for the person of faith. What needs to be rehearsed, until it becomes second nature is an inward disposition, a sensibility, a habitual way of functioning that is an appropriation of the mind of Christ through participation in the body of Christ. No one has the option of not living a rule, for we are all creatures who live by habit. What matters is if it is consciously chosen, the identity of the community in which it is rehearsed and the resultant quality of life so lived. After Wesley returned to England, in failure and in complete discouragement, doubting whether or not he even believed in Christ, he asked his friend Peter Böhler if he should stop preaching. Böhler replied, "By no means. Preach faith till you have it; and then, because you have it you will preach faith."[23]

In the months before his martyrdom, Dietrich Bonhoeffer came to this same understanding, practicing "religionless Christianity"[24] by "living without God before God."[25] Living in the hostile environment of Nazi rule, experiencing the severity of Gestapo imprisonment, it became clear

21. Lowe, "Against Experience," 3.
22. Weems, *John Wesley's Message Today*, 47–52.
23. V. Green, *John Wesley*, 56.
24. Bonhoeffer, *Letters and Papers*, 52.
25. Bonhoeffer, *Letters and Papers*, 218.

to him that no countervailing religious experience could be sufficient for undergirding an ongoing wager of nevertheless. What he needed for faithful perseverance as a Christian needed to be objective—which he found in the daily disciplines of the church, in such practices as the sign of the cross, memorized psalms, daily Bible reading, and the Eucharist. In this, he anticipated a Christian spirituality for our time, grounded in commitment to a God not experienced, living under promise through discipline, nurtured by the agencies of communal rehearsal, sufficient for an ongoing wagering upon one's yearning.

Some Christians claim to have undergone a transforming conversion experience. Even so, what really matters is how one lives it out in the days and months and years that follow. A marriage is doomed from the start if the commitment is for as long as one remains in love. It might not last beyond the first honeymoon argument. Without a covenantal vow for richer or poorer, in sickness or in health, it will not last, drained of its vitality by inevitable aridity. Thus the church's diminishment relates in part to the growing inability of our younger generation to make and keep promises. It takes serious discipline to live as a Christian in today's society that no longer provides support. It entails living a life *as if* so as to live *as if not*—of having without having, of succeeding without being seduced, of attending without belonging, and of never being other than a little kid at heart. It entails so living that it makes no sense for God not to exist. In involves risking where to stand in order to detect God's incognito—mostly with the humiliated guises of the oppressed, outside the wall. What shall I do, asks the prophet Habakkuk, as "I await the day of distress," as his own society too was on the edge of collapse, as God's judgment "shook the earth," making "the nations tremble" (Hab 3:16, 36). Prescient of the spirituality needed today by the Christian remnant, his was a subjunctive faith, based not on any because but willed as a nevertheless, as an in spite of, an although, and a yet.

> *Though* the fig tree does not blossom and no fruit
> is on the vines;
>
> *Though* the produce of the olive fails and the fields
> yield no food;
>
> *Though* the flock is cut off from the fold and there
> is no herd in the stalls,
>
> *Yet* I will rejoice in the Lord"
> (Hab 3:17–18 NRSV; italics added).

We turn now to unpacking this *though* and *yet* so as to discern a spirituality for the burned ones, sufficient to ground them as the remnant for the long haul. Annie Dillard likens such a spirituality to that of a "monk on the road who knows precisely how vulnerable he is, who takes no comfort among death-forgetting men, and who carries his vision of vastness and might around in his tunic, like a live coal which neither burns nor warms him, but with which he will not part."[26] Unpacking this "vision of vastness and might" we will do later, but first we need to sketch out how Christianity's diminishment is actually forging a postmodern Christian spirituality sufficient for outliving the diminishment. It has to do with not being "conformed to this world but . . . transformed by the renewal of your mind . . ." (Rom 12:2).

26. Dillard, *Pilgrim at Tinker Creek*, 278.

CHAPTER NINE

TOWARD A POSTMODERN
CHRISTIAN SPIRITUALITY

O ver sixty years ago, H. R. Niebuhr wrote his famed *Christ and Culture*,
proposing a typology of five ways in which Christians through the
centuries have related to society—Christ against, of, above, in paradox, and
transforming culture. He concludes by choosing the transforming posture as
the most faithful response. While I agree that this should be the goal, how
this transforming is to be done strategically depends on the particular historical period in which Christians find themselves, with the five types providing
particular strategies from which to choose. As we have been exploring, the
church's crisis consists especially of a decrease in numbers and finances, the
aging of its declining congregations, and the waning of ecclesiastical vocations, pushing the churches toward a survival mode in which the strategic
temptation has been to assume a Christ *of* culture posture, in which pastors
functioning as CEOs generate marketing plans for reversing the decline by
appealing to current tastes. But our analysis has disclosed the betrayal involved in this approach, for our present crisis resembles the one confronting
the Hebrew prophets, living in the midst of a society upon which the divine
judgment is falling, with hope residing in God's promise of birthing a faithful remnant. Thus while a vision of Christ transforming culture remains the
ultimate goal, the posture presently needed is one of Christ *against* culture,
understood not as opposition to culture as such but as Christ against *this*
culture. In his *Exiles: Living Missionally in a Post-Christian Culture*, Michael
Frost declares that, whether acknowledged or not, the metanarrative of
Christianity has shifted from Christendom to exile. Thus it is as appropriate
now as when the author of First Peter first wrote, to address Christians as
"aliens and exiles" (1 Pet 2:11). During our present period of growing eviction, the church must become rooted in a postmodern spirituality that is

capable of undergirding her for outlasting this society's approaching demise. This does not mean for the churches to forfeit the mercy and justice dimensions of their ministries, for without caring for those in need, no matter how minimal the results may be, the church would betray herself. Nor does this mean for the churches to forfeit evangelism and outreach, for without these, the church would lose her contagious enthusiasm for the Way. Rather, the churches must be brought to a firm realism, so that they will not to be undone by the inevitable failure that will accompany all their attempts at reversing their diminishment. Jesus insists that we must read the signs of the time, and, in so doing, it is clear that we can no longer measure faithfulness in terms of the former criteria of success.

Establishing a post-Christian spirituality may well begin by drawing on insights emerging from recent disclosures[1] regarding Mother Teresa's dark struggle with faith. During a retreat on September 19, 1946, she experienced God's call to enter the Calcutta slums, seeking out "the poorest of the poor." With only the clothes she was wearing and five rupees, she began to establish Christian communities in the slums of India, and within forty years, her Missionaries of Charity were in seventy-seven countries around the globe, with over 350 communities in poverty-stricken areas, involving thousands of sisters. In 1979, her worldwide acclaim was solidified in being awarded a Nobel Peace Prize; and after her death in 1997 at age eighty-seven, a groundswell of support led to her beatification in 2003.

More than a social justice saint to be admired, however, she functions well as a Christian who with exposed clay feet can escort us toward a post-Christian spirituality. While Mother Teresa's ministry is widely known, only recently, in violation of her intent, was her innermost spiritual pilgrimage made public, as gleaned from private letters, journalings, and conversations. The controversy subsequent to the publication of *Mother Teresa: Come Be My Light*, edited by Brian Kolodiejchuk, indicates how radical a post-Christian spirituality might appear to others. The atheist Christopher Hitchens, in his *Newsweek* article "The Dogmatic Doubter," called Mother Teresa's writings "desperate documents" showing that she had "all but lost her own faith"— reduced by the church's dogmatism to becoming "a confused old lady" who "for all practical purposes ceased to believe."[2] In denouncing her, Hitchens freely used such words as hysterical, insecure, fanatical, and even self-hating, leaving us with what he saw as a tattered portrait of a "troubled and miserable

---

1. Kolodiejchuk, ed., *Mother Teresa.*
2. Hitchens, "Dogmatic Doubter."

lady," exploited by the church after her death "to recruit the credulous to a blind faith in which she herself had long ceased to believe."[3]

The heart of Mother Teresa's spiritual struggle began shortly after she began her work with the poor, when she experienced a "terrible sense of loss," a "deep inner darkness."[4] This emptiness increased, not so much in intensity as in a spiritual exhaustion effected by its unrelenting persistence. A barrage of words and phrases depict her agony: "untold darkness," "terrible loneliness," "utter forsakenness," "torturous pain," "icy cold emptiness," "inexplicable brokenness," "repulsion," "abandonment," and "faithlessness." These were the extreme marks of burnedness. They left her soul "a blank in which there is no God," "walled off by an abyss of pain," "consumed with a deep sense of being unwanted, unloved, and uncared for," for "God has destroyed everything in me." The *bas relief* for this pain was an inability to shake her intense "longing for God," no matter how unfulfilled it seemed to be. Hers was not a craving for what she had never experienced, for before entering the slums she had experienced "a deep union with God." Thus, what she was feeling was like a lover abandoned, forced to endure "the tortures of loneliness"[5] as her only traveling companion. As the psalmist experienced it, "My one companion is darkness" (Ps 88:18). That to which she was clinging was a double negative—that one would not be searching for God unless one had not already been found.

In originally entering a religious order, Mother Teresa had been renamed for Thérèse of Lisieux. This turned out to be very appropriate, for the deep spiritual turmoil lived during Thérèse's final eighteen months of her young life was much like what Mother Teresa was to endure for a goodly portion of her life. Both were brought to a point where only silence kept them from possible heresy, for to speak further would possibly be blasphemous. Both spoke of their feelings being treacherous, kept from atheism only by the intensity of their burnedness—longing for a God who might well be nonexistent. Ironically, it was this inner agony that gave shape to Mother Teresa's order. To the traditional vows of poverty, chastity, and obedience, she added a fourth one to serve as focus for the other three. Novices were to "devote themselves with abnegation to the care of the poor and needy who, crushed by want and destitution, live in conditions unworthy of human dignity." This committed members of her order to a deep dying to the things of this world, a self-emptying so deep that her nuns could be spiritually able

3. Hitchens, "Dogmatic Doubter."
4. Kolodiejchuk, ed., *Mother Teresa*, 1.
5. Kolodiejchuk, ed., *Mother Teresa*, 222.

to take on as their own the darkness, loneliness, and god-forsakenness to which society condemns the poor.

Part of Mother Teresa's spiritual agony resulted in having her introvert personality reinforced by the contemplative formation that she received. Consequently, this spirituality based on inner experience was unable to sustain her radical plunge into an intensely extrovert apostolate. Painful confusion was inevitable, not only for her but for her whole order. A spirituality of being was called upon to function strenuously as an undergirding spirituality for doing. Yet she continued to have her novices formed by requiring two years of radical disengagement from the world for the sake of being grounded in an intensely contemplative life. This bifurcation of prayer and work contributed to the wedge she experienced between her own external faithfulness and her internal emptiness. Indicatively, she found that her only prayer time was in a third-class compartment on a crowded train,[6] meaning that contemplation was nearly impossible for her to maintain.

At first, Teresa's spiritual director attempted to interpret her spiritual struggle as a recognizable step in the spirituality delineated by St. John of the Cross.[7] For him, the first spiritual stage was the "dark night of the senses," in which the soul was to rid itself of sensate attachments that hindered contemplation. The second stage was the "dark night of the soul," in which intense experiences of rejection and abandonment purged the soul of remaining imperfections that inhibited union with God. While other Christian saints have undergone such darkness, Mother Teresa's uniqueness was that it was not a stage but a condition lasting for nearly fifty years, halted only by death. Consequently, her spiritual director was forced to conclude that hers was a darkness "for which there is no remedy."[8] Thus, it was itself the very spirituality into which she was being called.

This abandonment she was experiencing appeared to her as being from God the Father. And it was this agony that began drawing her into an identification with Jesus, coming to recognize that he himself had experienced this same abandonment by God the Father, climaxing in the agony of his passion. Since she and Jesus shared the same intense thirst for union with the Father, the experience of separation from him that they shared was like "the tortures of hell," crescendoing in Jesus's final derelict scream against the apparent cosmic emptiness. Consequently, the Eucharist became a drinking with Jesus "the chalice of his agony," with an identification taking on even physical overtones. Although desiring deeply to share her darkness

---

6. Kolodiejchuk, ed., *Mother Teresa*, 276.

7. Dubay, *Fire within*, 161–71.

8. Kolodiejchuk, ed., *Mother Teresa*, 214.

with her director, she often found herself physically incapable of uttering a word—as did the One who "was oppressed, and he was afflicted, yet he opened not his mouth" (Isa 53:7). She could only address the darkness with the words of Jesus: "My God, why . . ."

How a person dies one's death often discloses how one has lived one's life. Close to death, Mother Teresa whispered, "I want Jesus," meaning holy communion. She stared at a picture of Jesus and gasped the words, "I have never refused you anything." Although the darkness of her relationship with God the Father never ebbed, this merging with Jesus grew into constancy. This is the key for how she was able to minister among the poorest of the poor—that she was no longer doing it for Jesus but with him. No matter how hidden remained the face of God the Father, it was in the composite faces of the poor that she began to see the face of Jesus in "distressing disguise." "As you did it to the least of these" was becoming, in a literal sense, a spiritual union with Jesus. Thus by 1961, fifteen years after her call to ministry with the poor, she was able to affirm that she was no longer alone in her loneliness, for now "I have his [Jesus] darkness, his pain, his terrible longing for God—to love and not to be loved . . . I know I have Jesus in that unbroken union, for my mind is fixed on him and in him alone, in my will."[9] By 1977, she acclaimed that it was Jesus's very hunger for intimacy that rendered him the hungry One, the thirsty One, the naked One, the homeless One. His was the universal cry of all loneliness, all hunger, all nakedness, all homelessness, and all aloneness. As her bonding with Jesus intensified, Mother Teresa found herself no longer lamenting her agony but offering it up, gladly willing to spend eternity in her pain of being "a miserable nothingness" if only she could do so with Jesus.

But there would be several further steps to her emerging spirituality. Her deep identification began and intensified with the human Jesus, and thus instead of alleviating her separation from God the Father, it was intensified. By 1981, she had pushed her understanding of Jesus's dereliction all the way, declaring that Jesus did more than becoming "like us in all things but sin." In his passion, "he *became* sin." Taking on himself the sin of the whole world meant undergoing the horrible experience of total rejection and abandonment by God the Father. What Jesus dreaded most at Gethsemane was knowing that, on the cross, his own Father would disclaim him as his Son. From this imaging of Jesus's dereliction, Teresa drew the radical conclusion for herself and her sisters: "Do you realize that when you accept the vows you accept the same fate as Jesus?"[10] Since Jesus had no place

9. Kolodiejchuk, ed., *Mother Teresa*, 223.
10. Kolodiejchuk, ed., *Mother Teresa*, 251.

where he could lay his head, so "we too must share with him the dark holes of the destitute." They with Jesus were to share the agony and sinfulness of the world's rejected and unwanted, those who in their condition were unable to know any intimacy with a loving fatherly God who cared.

What Teresa was discovering, for herself and for us, was that this experience of abandonment was not the absence of spirituality but was a central element in a Christian spirituality appropriate for life in a post-Christian world. Above all, it meant taking on the depth of alienation implicit in a modern world intent on living so far from God. Secondly, it meant perceiving the craving for the love endemic in both poor and affluent as an unrecognized hunger for the unanswering God. Third, it meant the awareness that experience can no longer be a basis for an index of faith. Stripped of any direct experience of God and absented from any self-authenticating consolations as bolsters for faith, it was by walking in a companionship of the divine absence that she could trust Jesus. Now the lonely doubting that had plagued her for so long was becoming a mutual doubting, in which she and Jesus cried out together: "My God, my God, why hast thou forsaken me?" As a result, she began to speak of loving the darkness, for it had become a shared darkness, a shared cross, a shared passion, and a shared calling. This consolation that transpired was deep and transformative, because now she could confess "I would not like at any price to give up my sufferings," for they had become the common chalice which she and Jesus drank together, to the dregs. No longer able to contemplate, she now spoke freely of talking for hours with Jesus on the streets.

While this expansive humanness of Jesus filled some of the spiritual abyss shaped by the absence of God the Father, it did not remain sufficient. Since union with God seemed inaccessible for Teresa, the only step that remained was to trust that Jesus had somehow found a way to the other side of the darkness as veil. This would require the hardest post-Christian faith-step of all—the wager that would bridge the chasm between Jesus's penultimate cry of abandonment and his final whisper of faith. Teresa's abandonment had bonded her with Jesus's scream. This is the moment when the world stands unknowingly on tiptoe. Is this cosmic scream the bitter fate awaiting us all—that our finale is a forsakenness by the One who doesn't exist? But then, inexplicably, as if from the other side of the impending darkness, comes the whisper: "Father, into your hands I commit my spirit." This is the still point of history's turning wheel, when Mother Teresa and we stand before the final paradox, to decide on which side of the paradox to wager, as "Jesus uttered a loud cry, and breathed his last" (Mark 15:37). For the Christian, everything depends on Jesus's leap of faith—and thus on our response to his. Dare we trust Jesus, who at the deepest moment of his dereliction was so able to trust the Father that the curtain of his darkness was "torn in two, from top to bottom"? Christian faith is sheer wager, trusting the One who was able to trust his very being into the hands of the God who was experientially absent. A breviary prayer says this well: "Lord Jesus, you were rejected by your people, betrayed by the kiss of a friend, and deserted by your disciples. Give us the confidence that you had in the Father and our salvation will be assured."[11] Unable to base faith on any direct experience of a loving God, Christians are driven to trust the Jesus who could trust the Father, thus functioning as our mediator.

The classical Reproaches from the Good Friday liturgy[12] could well serve as Mother Teresa's litany: "O my people, what have I done to you? How have I offended you?" This is the pleading of a God who, after leading his people from slavery to freedom, from starvation to manna, and from desert to a promised land, received in return a sponge of vinegar and a spear in his side, crying out "Why?" Teresa could identify with Jesus in regard to the vinegar and spear part of their mutual experience; but as for trusting that their mutual cry was as well the cry of God the Father, for this she had to wager on the wager of Jesus.

Teresa calls this radical trust "pure faith," a willingness to "drink the cup." Deprived of consolations in our post-Christian world, Jesus's words to the doubting Thomas are for us: "Blessed are those who have not seen and yet believe" (John 20:29). Bereft of all experience of certitude, facing strong odds to the contrary, pure faith entails the heroic courage to make the Christological wager—a wager that feels so unreasonable that, in finding oneself able to make it, it paradoxically takes on the quality of gift. The Greek and Latin roots for the word *believe* are "to give away one's heart."

This postmodern Christian spirituality is truly paradoxical, for it means living a life rooted in love without feeling love, living by faith without sight, wagering without knowing. We are reminded of Martin Luther, for whom faith meant being under law yet living by grace, of being a sinner yet declared righteous, of believing but without certainty—all the while walking on the knife-edge of doubt. This is courage. Ironically, it was this deprivation of consolations that purified Teresa's motivations. While in the past, as we have seen, persons have largely been attracted to Christianity through self-interest, attracted into coveting consolations of an assured heaven, or of worldly success, or of strength for personal coping. The popular interest today in spirituality without religion is largely of this kind, searching for

---

11. International Commission on English in the Liturgy, *Liturgy of the Hours*, 3:1233.

12. International Commission on English in the Liturgy, *Roman Missal*, 321.

emotional supplementation for a stifled life suffocated by society's individualistic materialism. And when consolations are not forthcoming, the temptation is to trade one spirituality for another, one denomination for another, one congregation for another, or one nonreligious experience for another. But being removed from all such consolations, tautly caught between emptiness and longing, this was where Teresa came to the realization that emotions are deceptive and unreliable. Never give way to your feelings, she warned her sisters, and never rely on them either for your strength or your conviction.[13] Thus, having lost what she called "the sweetness of presence," the alternative was love through intention—an act of sheer will to love in the face of what emotionally feels impossible. This is the beginning of a post-Christian spirituality, faith based not on a *because* but on an *in spite of*, living heroically one's wagering of an *as if*. Thérèse of Lisieux says it well: "I sing what I want to believe."[14]

Mother Teresa masterfully hid her inner darkness from others, radiating outwardly her hallmark smile, testifying especially to Christians that "all is well." She wondered if this made her a hypocrite, portraying as if true what she herself could not experience with certainty as being true. Her answer came in recognizing that Jesus's final hours were not atypical but were expressive of the dark inner struggle characterizing his whole life, closeted from even his closest disciples. This heroic spirituality that she shared with Jesus was the inner stigmata of pure faith that was externally able to sustain others who were unable to face such a nakedness of leap for themselves. By internally taking on this cross of disbelief, her outward smile was a bridge for others. This was not a matter of pretending the untrue to be true but of providing encouragement for others to trust the burnedness of their restlessness.

If I ever become a saint, Mother Teresa once said, "I will surely be 'the saint of darkness.'[15] I will continually be absent from Heaven—to light the light of those in darkness on earth."[16] Pope Francis confirmed her as the "saint of darkness" when she was canonized September 4, 2016. Unlike much of the maudlin spirituality being peddled today, hers was a post-Christian spirituality rooted not in what one can gain but in what the absent God takes away. For the burned of God, it involves offering love to the unlovable as a way of feeding the hidden God. Moses, on his last afternoon on a lonely mountain

13. Kolodiejchuk, ed., *Mother Teresa*, 245.

14. Thérèse of Lisieux, as cited in Archives du Carmel de Lisieux, "Biography of Sr. Marie."

15. Kolodiejchuk, ed., *Mother Teresa*, 230.

16. Kolodiejchuk, ed., *Mother Teresa*, 1.

top, able to see the promised land only as a horizon, surely knew such spirituality—of seeing from afar without being allowed to enter.

From Mother Teresa's pilgrimage, we can draw these morsels for shaping a post-Christian spirituality: 1) to acknowledge fully the impact of God's seeming absence in today's densely secular society; 2) to face honestly the odds against the existence of a God in our postmodern universe—where in cold cosmic emptiness, our tiny earth seems to resemble an afterthought, lost in the backwaters of countless galaxies; 3) to reject vigorously the societal and cultural distractions designed to suppress the deep rumblings of being one of the burned ones—the ache, the yearning, that modernity threatens to squeeze dry; 4) to recognize that a viable spirituality can no longer be grounded in nor sustained by any special feelings or emotions—for the atheist and the remnant Christian both agree that there is no direct and indisputable experience of God, and even the saints who experienced consolations regarded them as fluff, nonessential to faith; 5) to concede that any God worth the name exists only for those for whom his absence is intolerable. Thus what remains for the serious Christian is pure faith—living in wagered identification with Jesus, preferring to live the way of life that follows than to be faithful to any other option.

For better or worse, Christians are in it with Jesus, all the way, being intensely and centrally Christological, trusting him who was able to trust the One who by ourselves we are unable to trust. For Meister Eckhart, the burned ones ask for nothing but God and thus are able to live the wager without a why.[17] While Bernard of Clairvaux exclaims "I love because I love,"[18] Teresa's version would be, "I believe because I believe." Thus, serious Christians, as doubt paints its wild streak across their faces, defrocked of all reasons outside of faith for faith, nevertheless finds this spirituality strangely self-justifying, as if we would not be searching if the unknown One were not searching for us, with an interior burning evidencing a Presence.

There is something heroic about giving away one's life to a vision that might be illusory, as a way of resisting capitulation to the flaccid littleness of today's self-serving living. To be burned is to live with a gnawing emptiness that births a desire, a longing, an ache, a hungering for more. St. Columban speaks of it as being wounded by the God who produces a soul-thirst that exacerbates that thirst that "grows ever greater as one drinks."[19] Thomas Merton calls this burning of the heart an indirect experience of

17. Schürmann, "Meister Eckhart," para. 7.

18. "Treatise 'On Loving God,'" in Bernard of Clairvaux, *Bernard of Clairvaux*, 173.

19. St. Columban, as cited in Consecrated Hearts, "Prayer by St. Columban."

God, a grounding that lures us into a struggle to make it habitual.[20] Given the human capacity for pettiness and distraction, burning often needs to erupt as a harsh emptying, of feeling turned inside out and upside down, preparing us for the strange taste of humility. Alcoholics Anonymous and its many creative variations provide arenas for grooming such burnedness. "Unless a grain of wheat falls into the earth and dies, it remains alone; but if it dies it bears much fruit" (John 12:24). It has to do with trusting the one who claims to have come in order that we "might have life, and have it more abundantly" (John 10:10 NAB).

What does it feel like to live out the abundance of this Christian wager? We might call it a state of beingness. Honed through contemplation and rehearsed by liturgy, what is birthed is a deep-rooted interiority of soul that enables one to live *as if* accepted, belonging, undergirded, centered, tranquil, mellow, non-defensive, non-comparing, authentic, mindful, open—above all, tefloned against exterior hurts. This is the peace that the world cannot give. To be otherwise is to feel insecure, comparative, competitive, aggressive, egoistic, selfish, possessive, unloved, lonely, insufficient, unstable, unfocused, superficial, needy, driven, fragile, unduly sensitive, easily hurt, with a mushy center. The sound of this grounding peace is that of an alto flute or of an "Adagio" by Albinoni, Pachelbel, or Mahler. This postmodern Christian spirituality entails the art of longing for God. For the burned, it is meaningless to argue about whether or not there is a God, for this is unknowable; but what is worth arguing is whether failure to struggle with the god-question renders one less than human.

Ironically, this ache within the burned soul is for what in the Narnia stories is called joy. Asland the lion stands for the object of this yearning for the unconditioned. When the good mare Hwin confronts the lion for the first time, she says, "Please, you are so beautiful. You may eat me if you like. I would sooner be eaten by you than fed by anyone else."[21] So the old hymn sings of a Christian vision that "satisfies my longings as nothing else can do."[22] What we have in Mother Teresa is an extreme version of a postmodern Christian spirituality, rendering naked its anatomy, hinting at the fuller Christian vision to which we now turn.

---

20. Merton, *New Seeds of Contemplation*, 218.

21. C. S. Lewis, *Horse and His Boy*, 193.

22. "I Love to Tell the Story," in Hymnal Revision Committee, ed., *United Methodist Hymnal*, 156.

CHAPTER TEN

TOWARD A MINIMALIST
CHRISTIAN VISION AS WAGER

Since the nature of our human mode of knowing is that of subject relating to an object, it follows that God is simply unknowable, for the
Christian God is not an object. In this sense, faith is not a relationship but
a participation. St. Paul was seized by a promising image with which the
imagination could work. The Christian God is the One in whom "we live
and move and have our being" (Acts 17:28). To live in God and God in us
involves this triune participation. St. Paul describes it this way: "For it is the
God who said, 'Let light shine out of darkness,'" [God as Creator] who has
shone in our hearts [God as Inspirer] to give the light of the knowledge of
the glory of God in the face of Jesus Christ" [God as Redeemer] (2 Cor 4:6).
The Christian wager has to do with this Trinitarian fullness. Thus, what we
are inclined to call God's hiddenness or absence is not by divine choice but
is the inevitable consequence of our existing within the God in whom we
live and move and have our being.

The focus of Christian revelation is not upon the unknowable Jesus
of history, as if Jesus as model or teacher could touch deeply our burnedness. The focus is upon the Christ event—that is, upon the biblical drama
in which Jesus is the central actor, disclosing in miniature the plot defining
the cadence of history. In whole and in part, this inherent dynamic on which
the Christian gambles is the rhythm of creation, fall, incarnation, crucifixion,
resurrection, ascension, and Pentecost. The Creator God is incarnate within
an incomplete creation, suffering in ongoing crucifixion as the God who takes
into his own becoming the works of humanity in response to the evocation of
the Pentecostal Spirit. This narrative of the Creator/Redeemer/Inspirer God is
practiced as liturgy within the church as the body of Christ, twice in seasons
of rehearsed intensity as Advent/Christmas/Epiphany and as Lent/Easter/

Pentecost, distilled ongoingly in eucharistic participation. This is the liturgy that gives content to Barth's insistence that, after the Christological wager, all else is worship lived out in obedience. The psalmist understands this as being "bound by the vows I have made you" (Ps 55:13).[1]

Postmodern Christian faith, then, is rooted in wagering on the wager of Jesus, thereby trusting him as the aperture for beholding the biblical narrative as the defining plot of history. It entails living as if the heart of this Christian narrative is so, in order to make it so—even if, in the eyes of the nonbeliever, it may sound like risking upon little more than gossip about rumors. Yet in being betrayed by the American Dream, feeling exiled by the dry rot of our culture, one is piqued by a burning search for an alternative vision. Burnedness is the discomfort of those unfed by half-living—in which by living anemically the blandness of lukewarmness, one is readied to put everything on the line as a wager. Plato[2] insists that in dealing with the hem of the divine, the thinker must give way to the poet. So it is that the task of the Christian theologian is primarily that of a poet, imaging the fuller dimensions involved in the *as if* as a *why not*, followed by a *may it be so*.

A barrier to this wagering is that the heart-content of the Christian faith has often been clouded over by centuries of conceptualizations, elaborations, and accoutrements, attempting to provide proof more than trusting the passion of focused witness. This obsession with how has often obscured the what—especially in matters of Christology and Eucharist. Since, in our era, it is no longer regarded possible to prove anything, the theological task of the church is no longer basically epistemological but phenomenological. That is, what is needed is not proof but clear and evocative description—distilling the Christian drama so as to make clear the essence of the Christian wager. Catholics have a catechism of 803 pages; *The Catholic Source Book*[3] contains 540 pages; and Alban Butler's *Lives of the Saints* extends to thirteen volumes—all excellent materials, but these, along with numerous additional resources, can be overwhelming. An equivalent is the Protestant offering of the entire Bible to be wagered upon as literally true. Too much can result in having too little to make as a genuine offer. Thus, in order to encounter the burned ones, there needs to be clarity about the *sine qua non* of the Christian faith, a distillation that provides a Christian minimalism to be offered. The reasons that persons often give for discounting or leaving the Christian faith has to do with rejecting nonessentials, peripherals, optionals, and discountables. What is needed is shedding these incidentals,

---

1. Gelineau, *Psalms*, 104.

2. Plato, *Plato's Cosmology*, 27, 30.

3. P. Klein, *Catholic Source Book*.

removing the cultural encrustations, relinquishing attempts at an objective reconstruction of the past, minimizing the how so as to be grasped by the what—and thus be opened to wager on the orthodox heart-meaning of the faith. Using Immanuel Kant's language, this Christian phenomenology acknowledges that, in regard to content, we are dealing with appearance; and as for the noumenon, the way things truly are, this is unknown and unknowable on this side of existence. What is possible and thereby necessary is to clarify the essence of what the Church truly does have to offer, in regard to which Christians can also test the seriousness of their wager.

THE PERSONAL VISION OF RECONCILIATION

A minimalist distillation of Christian belief has two overlying dimensions: the deeply personal and the expansively cosmic. The crucifixion provides the icon-focus for the personal dimension, and the resurrection provides the icon-focus for the cosmic. The deeply personal theme is built upon this thesis: that each person is created for love, and only in being claimed by unconditional love is there a humbling change of heart and mind, evoking healing into a new way of being, thinking, and doing. Expressed in minimal words, at soul depth is a craving in every person to be loved. Here, two Christian doctrines converge: the *imago dei* (being created in the likeness of the loving God) and metanoia (being in need of conversion). Our wayward behavior basically emerges from an unfulfilledness of this desperate yearning to be loved unconditionally. This is the only kind of love that can satisfy our longing, coming as a pure gift—gracious, unearned, undeserved, and without conditional strings, received as a *nevertheless* and an *in spite of*. In contrast, one way or another, most things we do are efforts to earn love or to compensate for not receiving it. Yet love acquired by our works (or admiration and popularity, as their surrogates) does not change us, for it remains self-centered and is anxiously unreliable and unstable. Only unconditional love, received as a humbling change of heart and mind, can evoke and enable a new way of being, thinking, and doing.

Through years of offering spiritual direction, I have become convinced that we are all wounded, scarred by the past—by our own deeds and by those perpetrated on us by others. This woundedness of unloving misdeeds is passed on unto the third and fourth generation. Deprived of love at our core, we are thwarted into believing ourselves to be unlovable and obsessed in efforts to hide it. Thus the struggle for wholeness needs to begin in acknowledging the negativities one has done and identifying with clarity those that have been hurtfully done to us. Then by wagering upon the divine forgiveness offered in the Christ event, this restorative exchange bequeaths the capacity to forgive, as one has been forgiven.

One of the most imaginative and forceful portraits of this personal dimension of the Christian faith occurs in the figure of Marmeladov in Fyodor Dostoevsky's *Crime and Punishment*. Marmeladov is a dissipated drunk whose hopeless addiction forced his own daughter into prostitution. The scene is a bar room, where Marmeladov suddenly finds himself gifted with the courage to respond to those who are tormenting him.

> I ought to be crucified, crucified on a cross, not pitied! Crucify me but pity me! Then I will go of myself to be crucified, for it is not merry-making I seek but tears and tribulation! But He will pity us Who has had pity on all, Who has understood all and all things, He is the One, He too is the judge. He will come in that day and He will ask: 'Where is the daughter who gave herself for her cross and consumptive step-mother and for the little children of another? Where is the daughter who had pity upon the filthy drunkard, her earthly father, undismayed by his beastliness?' And He will say, 'Come to me! Thy sins which are many are forgiven thee for thou hast loved much.' He will judge and will forgive all, the good and the evil, the wise and the meek. And when He has done with all of them, then He will summon us. "You too come forth,' He will say, 'Come forth ye drunkards, come forth, ye weak ones, come forth, ye children of shame!' And we shall all come forth, without shame and shall stand before Him. And He will say unto us, 'Ye are swine, made in the Image of the Beast and with his mark; but come ye also!' And the wise ones and those of understanding will say, 'Oh Lord, why dost Thou receive these men?' And He will say, 'This is why I receive them, oh ye wise—that not one of them believed himself to be worthy of this.' And He will hold out His hands to us and we shall fall down before Him . . . and we shall weep . . . and we shall understand all things . . . Lord, Thy Kingdom come![4]

This is the Christian vision of an ontological tenderness in which the stained past is not only forgiven but bleached white as snow, so that even our most scarlet of sins are taken into God as his own (Isa 1:18). Both the sheep and the goat struggle inside each of us, capable of being tamed only by a love that devours guilt, leaving only whatever griminess we ourselves persist on clutching. Crucified forgiveness is the highest, the most beautiful form of love, portraying a vision of reconciliation so deep that it can plunder

---

4. Dostoevsky, *Crime and Punishment*, 44–45. Abbreviated with some words changed for clarity.

hell into functioning as a redemptive purgatory. How else can Hitler come to embrace the Jews as his sisters and brothers? The crucified Jesus is the offer of God's unconditional forgiveness. In fact, the breviary reading for Holy Saturday from an ancient homily⁵ goes as far as to identify this day as when Jesus enters hell itself, seeking out Adam and Eve as his lost sheep. Showing them the spittle on his face, the scourges on his back, his punctured hands and feet, he declares this was done for them too and for "all those who have slept ever since the world began." A throne awaits, the bridal chamber is adorned, and "the treasure houses of all good things lie open." And he leads them out, harrowing hell of its inhabitants and robbing death of its power.

When a blind student graduated from our seminary, she gave me, her professor, a lovely walnut cross in thankfulness. For unknown reasons, I could not figure out what to do with it, so I kept it in its box through my various movings. Years later, in building the interior of the new Rustic Hermitage at our Hermitage Spiritual Retreat Center, I felt strangely drawn to resurrect that cross. I went outside looking for something, quickly returning, and with glue fastened to the polished cross a corpus of bent twigs and an acorn head. The empty cross had professed to say too much and thus too little. But the crucifix, now hanging over the altar, needs only one's pointed finger: "Behold your God."

To become even more confessional, in the process of my being birthed, a nurse informed my waiting father that the labor was such that he would likely lose his wife. Half an hour later, the report was reversed: the loss would likely involve me, his son. Mother and me—a life-and-death struggle even from the womb. Years later, I came to a burnout—and through a painful struggle came to recognize that the cause of my insatiable doing was to fill the burning emptiness so that I would be worth keeping. In a deep sense, for over forty years, what I really wanted was to hear my mother say, maybe just once, "Paul, I love you." She couldn't, because she was using me to be her perfect only child as a poker chip for purchasing from her father those same words—but he couldn't either, because his mother . . . On and on, sins as lovelessness unto the third and fourth generation.

The climax in my long pilgrimage into burnedness came when I was brought to wager upon the promise offered in Paul's letter to the Romans. "For I am sure that neither death, nor life, nor angels, nor principalities, nor things present, nor things to come, nor powers, nor height, nor depth, nor anything else in all creation, will be able to separate us from the love of God in Christ Jesus our Lord" (Rom 8:38–39). My wager needed to entail an ongoing rehearsal. For this, I extracted a mantra from that promise: "Paul, God

5. International Commission on English in the Liturgy, *Liturgy of the Hours*, 2:498.

loves you!" This I posted on my front door, bathroom mirror, computer, and dashboard, as reminders for repetition. The wagered *as if* was reinforced into an *it is so*, embraced by a eucharistic community who knew how to practice love. In time, I was able to bury a note of forgiveness in my mother's grave: "It was in wanting to be loved that we kept stumbling over each other. But we understand each other now, and I forgive. Forgive me."

So central is this dynamic of loving forgiveness at the heart of Christian faith that there appears in Scripture, according to my counting, forty-nine words or analogies for it. To be forgiven out of love is to have the taint and bruisedness of our past "discarded," "brushed aside," "forgotten," "erased," "pardoned," "buried," "healed," "hidden," "cancelled," "consumed," "removed," "overlooked," "blotted out," "covered over," "broken off," "washed away," "stripped off," "trodden under foot," "blown away as if a cloud or mist," "thrown behind God's back," "drowned in the depths of the sea," "remembered no more," and "cast away" "as far as the east is from the west." The wounds, the shame, the guilt, the blemishes, the hurts—forgiveness diminishes them to the status of never having happened, disempowered through memory displacement. Consequently, not to then forgive one's own self is an act of unconscionable ungratefulness.

Even for persons who may have been blessed with abundant parental love, that is still insufficient. All human love is conditional love, needing to be maintained by deserving it through an ongoing earning. The syntax of conditional love is: if you, then I. It is a because. Unconditional love is: even though, still I. It is a nevertheless, an in spite of, deplete of all conditions. Only the God disclosed in the Christ event can shower this latter kind of love, the kind we crave. This is the theme of *The Beauty and the Beast*[6]—that something must be loved for it to become lovable. So it is in *How the Grinch Stole Christmas!*[7] And so it is that Christian leaders from St. John Cassian[8] to Pope Francis liken faith to a process of healing, with the church functioning as a field hospital, in which, through being embraced by a community of love, persons can be changed. The result is living the single-mindedness of an undivided heart, so gambling one's transformation that nothing makes sense if God does not exist.

Living as if one is unconditionally loved begins the process of being purged of the drive to justify one's life through doing. Neutralized is the coveting of recognition by others, opened instead to live a life of generous hospitality—of loving as one is being loved. The power of such wagering is

---

6. Originally a French folktale.

7. Dr. Seuss, *How the Grinch Stole Christmas!*

8. Hilarion of Volokolamsk, "Teaching of St. John Cassian," paras. 12ff.

evidenced in the courage to face down one's basement and attic demons, of which likely candidates are the fear of abandonment (being of no consequence), of rejection (never measuring up), and of suffocation (unable to find one's own voice). As one becomes more content with being a nobody as measured by society's images of success, so to that degree does one lose a taste for whatever involves a first and a last, winners and losers, mine and not yours, or winner take all.

In contrast to such healing, not to be able to forgive is self-poisoning, like letting a rusty knife remain in one's heart, so that it can continue to be twisted in an obsessive rehearsing of an injured past, making unavailable immersion in the freshness of each new now, postponing mindful living until some vague future. But in being forgiven, one is enabled to forgive, thereby being opened to the singularity of each new moment. Therein is one called to be a custodian of life—everywhere, in everything, and for everyone—confronting as foe whoever and whatever prohibits, contorts, exploits, or destroys the sacredness of life. William of St. Thierry, in his *On the Contemplation of God*, distills well in a prayer this personal dimension that is central to the Christian faith: God, "what else is your salvation but receiving from you the gift of loving you by being loved by you . . . . You first loved us so that we might love you . . . because we could not be what you created us to be except by loving you . . . and we could not have loved you except by your gift."[9] To be loved is to become loving—always, everywhere, with everyone, viewing the world as an expanding community in the making.

Alfred North Whitehead developed his philosophy in which creativity was the primary nature of God. When his beloved son died in military combat, in his sorrow, Whitehead was brought to wager as well on a consequent nature of God, as involving the ontological tenderness of a divine fellow sufferer who forgives, embraces, and takes all that is good into his eternal memory.[10] This image serves well as a transition to the cosmic dimension of the Christian faith.

THE COSMIC VISION OF CONSUMMATION

The expansively cosmic dimension of the Christian faith is built upon this thesis: that deep within each of us is not only the insatiable desire for unconditional love, but also an Edenic yearning for a new heaven and earth, proleptically present in each moment in foretaste of the Spirit's calling for us to be co-creators of the kingdom of God. Expressed in minimal words, at

9. International Commission on English in the Liturgy, *Liturgy of the Hours*, 1:271.
10. Whitehead, *Process and Reality*, 323.

soul depth is the innate hope that life will not have been lived in vain. The vision of personal redemption is incomplete unless consummated cosmically, as internal relates to external and doing relates to being. John Denver sings of yearning for a place "I've never been before."[11] Dorothy with Toto sings of there being a "somewhere over the rainbow . . . heard of once in a lullaby."[12] Don Quixote fights windmills for the sake of the "impossible dream."[13] Many of the musicals offered on Broadway have been shaped by this yearning for the more that is yet to be. So it is that the personal dimension of faith is not sufficiently purified if its focus remains only the healing of one's own self, even if it issues in intercessions for the healing of others. The serious Christian must gamble that history and thus the cosmic venture will not be futile, useless, abortive. Expressed personally, deep in us is the gnawing hope that, in spite of the fragility of everything around us, somehow the world will be better for us having been here. It is this burning that the second dimension of Christian belief touches with vision, promising a new heaven and new earth for which in the Lord's Prayer we continually pray "Thy kingdom come." Here is a sweeping vision of cosmic resurrection, for which Jesus uses such imagery as a wildly inclusive banquet with invitations hand-delivered out into "the streets and alleys," gathering all "the poor and the crippled, the blind, and the lame" (Luke 14:21). This sweeping promise embraces not only human history but the universe itself, which is "groaning in travail"—for it too "will be set free from its bondage to decay" (Rom 8: 21–22). Wagering on such a vision in the face of the tragic dilemma of our present post-Christian condition might seem borderline naïveté—yet for Christians the real impossibility is not to make this gamble. If God is Creator, then, for faith, an ultimately failed creation is an oxymoron. Hope that is seen is not hope, the writer of Hebrews reminds us, and life without hope defies the living of it (Heb 11:1).

Nicolas Berdyaev, the brilliant Russian Orthodox thinker, addresses directly this cosmic vision, discerning not only the inner yearning for healing in the soul of the burned ones, but likewise recognizing deep within us this dream of paradise that will not die in the human soul—"a dream of joy and freedom, of beauty, of soaring creative power, a dream of love."[14] This yearning is touched by the divine promise of a cosmos transformed in beauty, including not only humanity but also animals and plants,

11. Denver and Taylor, "Rocky Mountain High."

12. E. Y. Harburg, "Over the Rainbow," in Fleming, dir., Wizard of Oz.

13. Joe Darion, "The Impossible Dream (The Quest)," in Hiller, dir., Man of La Mancha.

14. Berdyaev, Destiny of Man, 284.

mountains and fields, rivers and seas, stars and sky, even the blades of grass. This is theological poetry at its finest, of which the psalmists sing in prelude, when at God's word "the heavens were made," and "by the breath of his mouth" all the stars danced into being, and God formed the oceans by gathering "the waters of the sea as in a bottle" (Ps 33:6–7). The universe is God's priestly vestment, the palms of his hands cupped as a chalice. Such imagery of creation identifies history as the theater for history's thrashing in passionate birthing, in which the divine midwifery is drawing forth the kingdom of God as means, meaning, and meaningful goal for the whole. The cosmos is becoming the banquet of Christ's body and blood, with the purpose of history being our fashioning of gifts for the divine-human "wedding feast of the Lamb." Isaiah suggests that the gifts most likely to delight the Prince of Peace would be tanks beaten into tractors and bombers fashioned into swing sets for the childlike who refuse to "learn war any more" (Isa 2:4; Matt 18:1–4).

The *Pastoral Constitution on the Church in the Modern World*, adopted at Vatican II, makes an official pronouncement on this vision:

> We do not know the time when earth and humanity will reach their completion nor do we know the way in which the universe will be transformed. In this new earth, righteousness is to make its home, and happiness will satisfy, and more than satisfy, all the yearnings for peace that arise in human hearts . . . . Love and the fruits of love will remain, and the whole of creation, made by God for [us], will be set free from the frustrations that enslaves it . . . . Our hope in a new earth should not weaken, but rather stimulate our concern for developing this earth, for on it there is growing up the body of a new human family, a body even now able to provide some foreshadowing of the new age . . . . The better ordering of human society is of great importance to the kingdom of God. The blessings of human dignity, brotherly communion and freedom—all the good fruits on earth of [our] cooperation with nature in the Spirit of the Lord and according to his command—will be found again in the world to come, but purified of all stain, resplendent and transfigured . . . . On this earth the kingdom is already present in sign; when the Lord comes it will reach its completion.[15]

Yet while imaginatively grasped by this proleptic vision, Berdyaev speaks for many of us in being troubled that the outward appearance of history seems to contradict this vision, appearing as a succession of

---

15. Abbott, *Documents of Vatican II*, 237.

failures. And so, he is forced to ask the key question: will our creativity really have an eternal part in the shaping of this kingdom-shaped crescendo? That is, will our creative acts have an honorable place in eternal life, in the becoming of God? If not, then history is sound and fury signifying nothing—for the whole and for every speck within it. In his *Beginning and the End,* he makes answer by wagering an imaginative yes—that "the products of great creative minds prepare the way for the Kingdom of God, and enter into it. Greek tragedy, the pictures of Leonardo, Rembrandt, Botticelli; Michelangelo's sculpture and Shakespeare's dramas; the symphonies of Beethoven and the novels of Tolstoy; the philosophical thought of Plato, Kant and Hegel; the creative suffering of Pascal, Dostoyevsky, and Nietzsche; the quest for freedom and for what is true and right in the life of society—all enter into the Kingdom of God."[16] Jesus's version appears in a parable where persons are given varied talents to use in creating increase for God, regarding it as an unthankful betrayal to return home without souvenirs from the far country. Ernest Becker was a burned philosopher. In his *Denial of Death,* he proposes in the face of death a Christian-like wager. Reacting strongly against our modern culture that insists on shopping and "drinking and drugging ourselves out of awareness," he calls for the wager of a "new heroism." "In our anguished searching," may we at least "fashion something—an object or ourselves—and drop it into the confusion, make an offering of it, so to speak, to the life force."[17] To this burnedness, the Christian responds by offering each act, each thought, each feeling as gifts to be eucharistically offered into God as transubstantiation, as time is taken into the kingdom as eternity.

The doctrine of the ascension is helpful here. The incarnation insists that God is immersed in God's creation, and the ascension wagers that God does not shed what God assumes but takes humanity with him into the godhead—spit, nail holes, and bleeding brow, as it were. Kazantzakis in his *Saviors of God* identifies the meaning of history as being the transubstantiating of matter into spirit, with the goal being God's ecstasy, as an "ascension of flesh into God."[18] Pierre Teilhard de Chardin in his *Hymn of the Universe* perceives the world as a vast divine incarnation, with everything in it being a sacrament through which God gathers up our incompleteness into his struggle with nothingness.[19] Bernard of Clairvaux in his *On Loving God* employs the imagery of a cosmic wedding feast. There "we shall eat and drink at table as Christ

16. Berdyaev, *Beginning and End,* 250.

17. Becker, *Denial of Death,* 285.

18. Kazantzakis, *Saviors of God,* 28, 95, 111.

19. Teilhard de Chardin, *Hymn of the Universe,* 109, 120, 147.

takes to himself the Church in all Her glory, without blemish or wrinkle or any defect." We shall experience "fullness without disgust, insatiable curiosity which is not restless, an eternal and endless desire which knows no lack, and lastly, that sober intoxication which does not come from drinking too much, which is no reeking of wine, but a burning for God."[20]

Theologians through the ages have tried to discern from the Genesis narrative what the *imago dei* is, the image of God in which we are all created. In this narrative, God is the Creator who has just woven the Milky Way into a celestial tapestry and has finished teaching the dolphins to swim. This is the God who in delight shouts, "This is good; very, very good!" And immediately God imagines creating creatures who like himself would be capable of experiencing this same joy of creating. Therefore, in being created in God's image, we are made creators, to be stewards who, as artisans, are to help bring into completion God's beloved earth as an Eden—the name meaning *delight*. There, in the "cool of the evening," God and humanity are to walk together, enjoying and sharing their artistry. Therefore, no matter what, there remains deep within us this yearning, since we have never lost our anatomy as co-creators. Mary is paradigmatic in hearing and accepting the annunciation call to participate in the divine-human birthing. Meister Eckhart insists "that from all eternity God lies on a maternity bed giving birth, for the very essence of God is birthing."[21] Our call is thus best understood not as obedience to God's will but as being midwives for God's yearnings. Thus, instead of the future being divinely predesigned, the Spirit is luring and probing and throbbing within creation, calling each today from tomorrow in struggling toward the feast of transfiguration.

Christian living as a foretaste of this vision is what renders history a pilgrimage. Wagering entails seeing Christologically, reframing everything in terms of the Christ event—in the pattern of incarnation, crucifixion, resurrection, ascension, and Pentecost. In this sense, Christ is the One "in whom the whole structure is joined together and grows into a holy temple in the Lord; in whom you also are built into it for a dwelling place of God in the Spirit" (Eph 2:20–22) as the divine incarnation through whom all things are made. God is the crushed and bloody One undergoing crucifixion throughout history, in so doing birthing resurrection in an ascension-craving that lures all things in a Pentecostal calling to participate in the earth's kingdom-completion though which God is becoming All in all. The fragments of our struggle are nailed to the cross, lifted redemptively into the kingdom as God's eternal resurrection. Light over darkness, freedom

---

20. Bernard of Clairvaux, *Bernard of Clairvaux*, 199.
21. Harrington and Hall, *Three Mystics Walk into Tavern*, 60.

over necessity, beauty over ugliness—these are the ingredients being incorporated into creation's eighth day, undergirded by the hope that is greeted at each sunrise and saluted at each sunset. The traditional sacraments are introductory wagers into this sacramental universe.

Not only is this vision capable of being tasted in the poetry of words, but we are gifted with hints in viewing El Greco's *View of Toledo*, in singing the final movement of Beethoven's *Symphony No. 9*, and in dancing to Mahler's *Resurrection Symphony*. But again, it is the Eucharist that is the empowering vision-center—the microcosm of the macrocosm. Theologian Georgia Harkness identifies religion as "distilled gesture," and, for the Christian, the Eucharist is the primal gesture. Eating together as the kingdom is the kingdom, realizable now as foretaste of what is not yet but as the edging for every horizon. Jesus maintains that it is to "sit at table" in the kingdom of God that lures people to "come from east and west, and from north and south," at which "some are last who will be first, and some are first who will be last" (Luke 13:29–30).

But how can the Christian gamble upon the beauty of such a sacramental vision, when our postmodern era is so rooted in the pathos of twisted emptiness? It is because experience is not the basis for faith but the consequence. Thus wagering on the burnedness of this deepest yearning is the first step. This is followed by formation within the Church's worship as an anticipatory liturgy, bringing shape and promise to the chaos. Each Sunday is a little Easter, commemorating the resurrection as aperitif for the week. This is why the early church forbade Christians to kneel on this day, for dancing is far more appropriate. Cyril of Jerusalem proposes that when communion is received, "while your lips are still wet, take your finger and hallow all the senses."[22] Here he is echoing God's counsel to "buy from me . . . salve to anoint your eyes, that you may see" (Rev 3:18). Early Christians were likewise encouraged to keep a host in their homes on which to nibble daily—thereby continuing to taste "the sweetness of the Lord" (1 Pet 2:3).

There is even more. One of the most deadly of sins is to take things for granted. If you have seen one snowfall, you've seen them all. If you have already visited the ocean, there is no reason to do it again. Thus many persons today are bored—been there, done that, and "there is nothing new under the sun." Yet if a person is struck by a terminal sickness, things can become quite different, forcing one into the stark realization that, from now on, everything may well be for the last time. Never again to kiss one's spouse, or feel the embrace of one's children, or watch the spring birth dogwoods with daffodil trimmings. Realizing that everything may be for the last time can enable

22. Clément, *Roots of Christian Mysticism*, 124.

one to experience all as if for the first time—a bird awakening the dawn, the fond eyes of a friend, golden leaves fluttering their swan song, the playful romp of a puppy, the sheer greenness of nature. Everything can again take on the fresh aroma of a curious child at play. Desire is intensified, feelings deepened, senses reignited, so that deeply spiritual can become a cello well played, a motorcycle aimed at the sunset, saluting a brash field of wildflowers, a contagious laugh, a playful kite at the end of her string—all become gift wrapped. Immersion in each unique now can be mindfully embraced by realizing each morning that "this night your soul is required of you" (Luke 12:20). To be authentically alive is to be touched by the sheer mystery that anything and thus everything exists. It is through departing tears that the ordinary bears forth the grandeur of the extraordinary, but often too late. Jesus asks the blind man, "What do you want?" (Mark 10:51). With him, we burned folks respond: "I want to see." Isaiah was so gifted, for "morning after morning God opens my ear that I may hear" (Isa 50:4 NAB). It takes so little to mean so much—waving at another driver, lifting with humor the spirits of a harassed checkout clerk, inviting to lunch a lonely friend, or telephoning a death row prisoner on the day of his execution. At this point, the Christian could well be charged with sentimentality. But the only excuse is that of being in love, because, as Catherine of Siena keeps repeating as if a mantra, "God is madly in love, even drunk with love, for creation."[23]

Only those who have tasted such hints of life's gifted beauty, declares Barth, can be grasped by the longing for resurrection, as a promise completed.[24] Moses was awakened by a bush aflame with burning color, and, from then on, everything was different. We all have had Moses moments— but only some persons wager upon them. When the poet Elizabeth Barrett Browning did, she exclaimed: "Earth's crammed with heaven, / And every common bush afire with God."[25] When a friend recently made this wager, he sent me this note: "Blessed are we who have had moments when trees bathing in mist seem to be praying with upraised arms, with the bird accompaniment sounding like an angelic chorus, as soaring hawks give praise by surfing the mystery. It is then that we are drawn to kneel and kiss the earth, unable to look up at the face of the sky because assuredly it is only a thin veil covering the face of God." So it was for Jesus, who lived the wager that the kingdom of God is in our midst. A crescendo is practiced when, in the fourth eucharistic prayer, the priest prays that you, God, "the Source of life," may so "fill your creatures with blessings that we might glorify you without

23. Tagliaferri, "Lyrical Mysticism," 78.

24. Barth, Dogmatics in Outline, 153.

25. Browning, "Aurora Leigh," in Complete Poetical Works, 134.

ceasing . . . giving voice to every creature under heaven"[26]—apparently inviting the rabbits and frogs to join in the hallelujah chorus. The last verse of the final 150th psalm concurs: "Let everything that breathes praise the Lord!" Robert Bellah provides, once again, the Christian conclusion, that "it is in the Eucharist that it all comes together with all the company of heaven, the communion of the saints, and of all souls, all enfolded in one time. Time out of time, all equally present—past, present, and to come. Nunc stans, the eternal now."[27] Many are the persons who in our time will regard as maudlin madness our toasting such a vision with uplifted chalice; but our wager is that there will always remain a remnant who believe that it is madness not to do so. In the light of this vision, atheism can seem to be, to use Annie Dillard's phrase, "a massive failure of imagination."[28]

With clarity about these two dimensions essential to a minimalist Christian wager, we are ready now to take a further step in tackling with a Christian-informed imagination the major obstacle that many of the burned of God face.

26. International Commission on English in the Liturgy, *Roman Missal*, 656.

27. Tipton, "Logic of the Holy," para. 16.

28. Dillard, *Pilgrim at Tinker Creek*, 147.

CHAPTER ELEVEN

TOWARD A POSTMODERN
CHRISTIAN THEOLOGY

Evil and the Becoming of God

S t. Vincent of Lerins (fifth c.) in his "First Instruction"[1] asks if there should be any large-scale development in Christian theology through the centuries. His answer is a vigorous yes—but not as alteration, in changing one thing into another. The Spirit calls for doctrinal "expanding in order to be itself." Thus, what was originally given "in a seminal form" needs to undergo "more ample development in the course of time." More recently, sainted John Henry Newman likewise encourages such doctrinal development. That is what we will now attempt.

From the beginning, Christian thinkers have exercised theological development by wrestling with the best thinking that emerges in each epoch. As early as the preface of the Gospel of John, we find the influence of Greek philosophical thought. While apologetics was one of the motives for this interaction, it was more impulsed as faith seeking understanding. "These things I have spoken to you, while I am still with you. But the Counselor, the Holy Spirit, whom the Father will send in my name, he will teach you all things, and bring to your remembrance all that I have said to you" (John 14:25–26). Consequently, Christian tradition is never finished but is expansive, as believers keep repondering it in light of the signs of the time. While the why questions addressed by Christianity and the how questions explored by the sciences are different issues with different methods, the how has implications for better conceptualizing the answers to why.

We have referred to the recurrence of the Jesus of history movement as some New Testament scholars have again attempted to extract an historic

---

1. International Commission on English in the Liturgy, *Liturgy of the Hours*, 4:363.

Jesus from the husks of tradition that have turned him into the Christ of faith. But the Bible is not history, nor does it purport to be, as if its writers were intent on creating objective accounts that were free of interpretation, offering it for readers to provide their own interpretation. Instead, the gospels and epistles were intended to be interpretations—dramatic portrayals of life as seen from particular vantage points as believers, with the composite whole functioning much like a great novel in which Jesus is portrayed as the central actor. When interpreting a significant piece of literature such as *Moby Dick*, its meaning is beyond the authority of Herman Melville to determine; even as its author he cannot provide a definitive interpretation of its meaning. A literary creation, once placed in the public domain, takes on a life of its own, continuing over time to gain richness through the interpretations of those participating in the discernment process. Thus, while it may be interesting, it is misguided to attempt to determine its meaning through efforts at reconstructing the original context in which Melville was writing, as in gleaning from external sources what Melville may have said, did, read, or ate on the day when he wrote a particular section. Thus correlatively misguided are efforts at identifying objectively what Jesus originally said, really meant, and actually intended. Instead, what we have, and all we can ever have, are interpretations, behind which there is no real Jesus incipient to the sources and editing. In fact, each of the persons who was present at the various biblical scenes actually saw and heard things differently, dependent on a host of variables. Thus for us in our postmodern world, where there is nothing but interpretation, there is no objective Jesus of history—not even for Jesus himself. None of us knows who we are objectively, and neither can others so know us. Therefore, what we have, and all that we need, is a dramatic narrative entitled the Christ of faith. Thus the focus for the Christian is not on the objectivity of an empty tomb but on what life looks like as seen by those who have wagered their lives as if, upon the so what. The Christological drama is by its very nature an interpretation, and efforts to extract an objective history from it is to destroy the narrative creation that it is. To do so is to write an alternative story based on the perspective of the interpreter, who chooses a vantage point different from that of the various biblical writers. The meaning of the Christ drama can be known only through participation in the narrative—as wrapped in the words, imagery, sacraments, and liturgy that through the centuries have expanded its meaning-context. In this sense, scriptural meaning is deeper now than when originally written, because, since then, Augustine has written his exegesis, Handel has composed his *Messiah*, and Shakespeare has created *King Lear*. Nor is faith about extracting certain insights from the life or teachings of Jesus. It is about wagering upon the primal plot that emerged as Jesus walked it forth, not from a preknown memorized script but step by step as he endeavored to live "not my will but thine" (Luke 22:42)—wherever that might lead him. John the Baptist asked of Jesus if he was the One (Matt 11:3). This was Jesus's own ongoing question; and so his response was to name for John some of the results of his pilgrimage, in effect soliciting John's interpretation. What we have is an ongoing narrative, the meaning of which continues to evolve through discernment of those who are living it as if from within. The biblical hermeneutic is participative—an action-reflection from within the believing community.

With this understanding, we are ready to struggle with the central conundrum that through the centuries has blocked countless persons from entry into the Christian wager. It is one that in our time especially is haunting the burned of God. In the end, life's primary enigma is not sin, even though it infects all of history. The Genesis saga of Adam and Eve is sufficiently illuminating of the roots of sin. Kierkegaard wisely confesses that while he does not understand why Adam and Eve did what they did, through their narrative he understands only too well why he does what he does.[2] Arrogance—desiring to be as god; and concupiscence—living as less than human. These are the reasons that tradition has wisely extracted for understanding the motives of our misdoings. Instead, the issue of issues is evil—that destructiveness evident throughout all of nature, for which humans are not the cause.

Theodicy is the traditional name for efforts to justify a supposedly loving God with the existence of evil. It comes from two Greek words: *theos*, meaning God, and *dikai*, meaning justice. The philosopher Leibniz used the term first, concluding that even with all of life's negativities, ours is still the "best of all possible worlds." But Archibald MacLeish in his drama about Job (*J. B.*) speaks for our time in thinking otherwise, posing the dilemma as a jingle: "If God is God, He is not good, if God is good, He is not God."[3] How can one praise God as a world Designer when everything rots, rusts, cracks, or dies; where disease of every ingenious kind wreaks indiscriminate havoc on all that lives; where earthquakes desecrate both the good and the bad; and where floods rival droughts as to which will claim the most victims. Humans are enmeshed in a carnivorous earth so structured that its growling stomach devours the life out of every living being, featuring death as the final broken promise.

This spectrum of evil appears in the large sweep of nature, from black holes to the tornado that wiped out a town of two hundred last night in

2. Kierkegaard, *Sickness unto Death*.

3. MacLeish, *J. B.*, 11.

Illinois. But it is abundantly evident as well in the infinitely small. A recent edition of *National Geographic* had an illustrated article focusing on the mighty mites.[4] Although they are no larger than a period at the end of this sentence, they are "the terror of the microscopic world." They appear almost everywhere, entering even our hair follicles, mating with their sisters before they've fully emerged, and, during hatching, killing off their mothers. They live several weeks until they fill themselves with feces and die, decomposing on almost every surface. Predatory to the core, they come in amazing varieties—some armed with sharklike teeth, others equipped to jab, others to stab, but all of them to stalk.

We live daily the retail versions of such destruction, simply in cutting a finger. Germs flock for an invasion, as white blood cells rush for a defensive battle. Everything that lives is engaged in this ongoing conflict of life with death, inside and without. Even as a child, I remember being haunted by how much in my small world seemed counter to a world that I was taught to believe was designed by a loving Creator. The hawk beautifully surfing the breeze is actually in pursuit of a rabbit to ravish. Thus, whether colossal or minute, there is a red line of terror running through all of creation, forcing this logic: either God is loving but not all-powerful or all-powerful but not loving. Thus the conundrum: are we as believers dealing here with indifference, impotence, or demonry?

Few in our postmodern world can any longer conclude with Leibniz that this is the "best of all possible worlds," or with the poet John Keats that our world is intentionally designed to create character, with the pains and difficulties of our physical order ordained for our good and for our happiness.[5] At the wake for my father who had been eaten out by cancer until his painful death, believer after believer attempted to comfort me with language about a loving God who called my father home. Deep in my soul was nothing but rage: "Torture is a hell of a way to call a faithful Christian home!"

Job's resolution came as an ecstatic encounter with the beauty of the universe, soliciting trust that behind such mystery must be wisdom, that such a Creator must know what he is doing, even if we do not. Actually this attempted resolution exposes the conundrum as two-sided, for while evil is the enigma for believers, beauty is the enigma for the unbeliever. While death defies the Christian, a mockingbird defies the atheist—while both expose the agnostic as lacking in courage to struggle with life at its deepest level. The gnawing god-question is this: "Ultimately, are we alone?" And we betray our humanness if we do not strain all our imaginative powers before wagering

4. Engelhaupt, "Meet Your Face's Tiny Tenants," 17.
5. George Ford, ed., *Selected Poems*.

either upon the unknown as God or giving emptiness the finger. The dual task for the Christian is to name the absence so as to account for the presence and the presence so as to account for the absence.

Christian thinking about theodicy has traditionally operated within the parameters set by the first three chapters of Genesis. The working assumption was that since sin and evil cannot be conceived as the work of a loving God, they must somehow be the fault of humans. Therefore, sin happens because God gifts us with freedom, and, in our arrogance, we choose to be as god, so that Adam as the first person became less than human. But how can this account for evil—for disease, earthquakes, floods, famines, and death—those things for which humans seemingly have no initiating responsibility? The Genesis narrative attempts to hold humans responsible for physical evil as well by claiming that God must have restructured creation negatively as punishment for Adam and Eve's disobedience. This includes such negativities as the pain of childbirth, the destructive behavior of animals, and the earth that defies our efforts at tilling. Because of God's righteous judgment upon the disobedient first couple, the earth groans in travail, and creation's beauty is tragically flawed. Admittedly, the earth does fall in important ways when humans exploit it rather than serving as its stewards, as in climate change. Yet while this Genesis explanation might somewhat absolve God of responsibility for evil, it does so in a way that renders God ungodly. Why would a loving God deprive the free first couple from knowing the difference between good and evil in advance? Why would a loving God deliberately tempt the couple not only by creating a forbidden tree but by placing it at the very center of the garden? Where did Satan as tempter come from in the first place—unless God created him as a tormentor? Why would a loving God ever condemn the whole human race because of one sin by the very first couple? Wouldn't an all-knowing God have known in advance that Adam and Eve would do what they did and thus would not have permitted it to happen? Why would a loving God place on the shoulders of the first couple such overwhelming odds—in which one wrong step would condemn the whole of humanity to ongoing sinning throughout all of its history within a hostile earth? Wouldn't it make far more sense to give each person at birth the same freedom as the original couple, thereby making responsibility personal, granting the judgmental consequences that each deserved? If God wanted to undo the original damage, what took him so long to do it? In the interim, why did God permit the terrible suffering that Israel and all of humanity endured as preparation? Thus, in the end, what we have is a narrative that reeks of an uncaring, jealous, and vindictive God who can hardly qualify as divine. Teresa of Avila puts it charitably: "I do not wonder, God, that you have so few friends from the way you treat them."[6]

While this is the way Christian tradition uses the story, Jewish theologians have not, suggesting that there is more than one possible approach. So, is there a different way to defend an all-wise, all-knowing, and all-loving moral Creator in the face of evil's abundant facticity? It was my own personal descent to the bottom of the Grand Canyon that forced my rethinking. Hiking the first half-mile was a welcomed contrast to the resort atmosphere on the rim. But after three hours, thirst became my first clue that I did not belong. Toads, lizards, vultures, a coiled rattlesnake—they were all at home, they belonged, while in contrast a sign warned that my life was as thin as my canteen strap. Mile after panting mile, I became a living participant in the electronic display viewed at the rim museum, in which a beeper sounded every second for three minutes as a way of dramatizing the age of this canyon. Only with the last beep did the entire history of humanity appear. I recalled how one scientist had graphically imaged the duration of cosmic history in terms of thirty books, each with 450 pages, and every page representing a million years. Humans did not appear on the scene until the final page of the last volume. It appeared that humans were an afterthought in this panorama stretching out below me—miniscule in this enormous layering of nonhuman time which for billions of years was utterly mindless of our absence, and then blatantly hostile to our appearance. Clearly, we were not created in an instant by God's loving word, as the biblical narrative states, for the recent skeletal remains on display were six million years old,[7] confirming indisputably our long and harsh evolutionary struggle to make an appearance. Each mile marker down the trail brought an accumulating sense of alienation. No longer could I entertain this desolate environment to be a home lovingly fashioned for humans by a caring Creator. It felt as if I were descending backwards into an uncongenial abyss, in which I was on display as a humorless postscript to a mindless whole.

Sleepless that night at the vast canyon bottom, listening as the Colorado River relentlessly ate away at the canyon walls, there died for me the possibility of wagering that at the beginning of all this there was an all-powerful, loving God who designed this creation, in which the routine activity of every organism is to devour something else in order to survive. And what on earth was such a God doing for over thirteen billion years before we humans arrived? Could it be, could it just be, that in some strange way this God as loving is better imaged as likewise a later arriver? To be

6. Teresa of Avila, as cited in R. Ellsberg, *All Saints*, 450.
7. White et al., "*Ardipithecus ramidus*," 84.

a Christian necessitated for me another option than the two unacceptable ones toward which tradition was driving me—that of a sadomasochistic Designer or an impotent Watcher.

As temperatures fell below freezing and with my water half gone, it became clear that what made us freaks in this cosmos was that we became self-conscious. Self-consciousness rendered me capable of being mesmerized now as I stared mindfully up and beyond the rim, out into the vast beauty of a solar system with a diameter of seven-billion miles, hinting of an infinitely expanding cosmos out beyond which are one hundred million observable galaxies—yet here am I, a mere dot, awesomely asking why. This yearning, this longing, this burnedness as an instinct to ponder, this is what renders us humans as misfits within this mindless whole of which we are no longer really a part. Everything around me was oblivious to this star-spangled grandeur of dancing eyes. Yet it almost seemed as if this pregnancy of night stillness was waiting for mutual recognition. There is no way ever to have predicted that in this vastly inhospitable universe self-consciousness would ever have happened, that there could ever have emerged creatures capable of perceiving such beauty and of being able to love. Yet since this is so of us, how could it be any less true of God? Could it be that a fully self-conscious loving Deity has likewise been emerging through this incredible ongoing adventure? Since I was unable any longer to wager on a self-consciously loving, all-powerful, and all-wise God who designed this problematic cosmos, what if the lovingly compassionate Deity of the Christian wager was not the beginning but the goal—through a cosmic dynamism by which God is becoming All in all? Could the ongoing yearning for fullness that burns within me, and which is surging in and through all things that exist, can this be the Holy Spirit struggling incarnately toward consummation, rendering history a writhing evolution internal to God's own unfolding?

By dawn, the Grand Canyon was taking on the imagery of a cauldron of life struggling against death, of being confronting nonbeing, likening the earth to a bloody chalice. Its restless sides teemed with life propelled in insatiable reaching for more. Ceaseless wind, rushing rivulets, clutching root-fingers of trees—I began feeling these to be sister-brothers in kinship with my own restlessness. This interior deepness of straining, yearning, craving—surely this first emerged in an anciently remote moment in some unknown where, when the threshold was passed into self-consciousness. It was when a human creature looked up and actually saw the Milky Way for the first time, with an awe-tinged smile. Not that she was seeing any thing, but that she was seeing, truly, and feeling something new. Or it may have happened deep in a cave, by flickering torchlight, when embraced by the silence of maternal darkness, she wondered and then wondered about wondering. Yet this novelty of feeling must soon have gained a negative edging; perhaps it was the sobbing of someone who then fell still, very still. It was over, he was there but no longer here—and it was not possible any longer just to walk away. To have become lost in something or someone and then threatened by its loss . . . The once is now, was, to be no more. Yet here is an I realizing that there is a me for which this too will happen: I shall die! Why? Terror, abandonment, finitude—holding the hand of a similar creature, for no known reason. Or perhaps this moment related to an equally strange feeling during the emptying out of the sex drive— something about an other, about this one, about a feeling of affection. Such are the initial moments that were to swell and expand into a communal framing. Understandably, anthropologists today are recognizing evidence of worship as marking our human emergence, where standing stones acknowledged rhythmic skies as patterned, graves marked remembrances with hope, and altars pleaded for forgiveness. Is it possible, then, to wager upon the Christ event as a mutual intersection of divine-human recognition, participating in the calling to a co-creative covenant, in a mutuality of self-conscious emergence, God with humankind. Life for eons has been thrashing about, gasping and grasping, expanding and trying, groping and hoping, reaching out in tentative directions for seemingly inchoate reasons, yet in a common direction—as the pulsating work of God as Holy Spirit, dancing and luring and probing and sweeping in the evolving of earth and cosmos toward Fullness through fullness.

Images, ideas, and implications rumbled in my mind during the Grand Canyon ascent. Self-consciousness as the capacity to make an object out of oneself is what bequeathed creativity (by imagining possibilities), birthed freedom (by entertaining consequences in advance), and tendered morality (by seeing from the perspective of others). Could this provide a clue as well for understanding God's own process of becoming? The Genesis narrative became suggestive of what I would come to call the Reverse Trinity. In the origination of God's creating, there was a "formless void and darkness" as "the Spirit of God swept over the face of the waters," restlessly shaping being from nonbeing (Gen 1:1–2). God as the Holy Spirit surged forth within all things, in what Paul came to describe as the "eager longing" of creation, "groaning in travail" as birthing, in a manner echoing our own "inward groaning" for fullness (Rom 8:19ff). As Christians, could we wager upon our own wrenching and agonizing at soul depth as being a participation in the churning of the enfleshing God, exploding outwardly in myriads of creative longings toward the fullness of a supraconscious loving God? Incarnation, as the old monastic hymn puts it, is God's "torrent of desire,"[8] with Calvary the signature act of God as participant/sufferer/combatant within the whole. The defining pattern of history then would be as a dramatic co-creative adventure of incarnation through crucifixion into resurrection. God would be omnipresent wherever anything is, in all things as immanence, and with all things in emerging transcendence. God would be omnipotent in having the ability to do whatever is increasingly possible. God would be omniscient in knowing whatever is knowable through participation. The where of the cosmos would be in God, and the where of God would be the cosmos. As Barth insists, God "is in himself historical," whose "goal is history."[9]

Ascent from the canyon floor was physically grueling, and yet I experienced a strange sense of peace. I reached the top, ready to celebrate. Inside the restaurant, at the table to my right, sat an elegantly dressed woman who sent back her goblet for being water stained. A man in a dinner jacket to my left refused his steak for being slightly on the done side of medium. Feeling an exile of a different type, I ordered a special bread and a vintage wine. Taking them outside, I toasted the sunset on the canyon rim. Tomorrow was Easter Day.

Since that day, I have been pondering the implications of this event. It seems that the inability of Christian theologians to create a viable theodicy has been due in part to the influence of Greek philosophy. Central, for example, has been the impact of Aristotle, with his insistence that since God by definition must be perfect, and perfect means totally complete, incapable of addition or change, the world must then be complete, as intended.[10] Thus God has to be an unmoved Mover. When some Greek thinkers acknowledged that this harshly unstable world does not reflect a perfect design, they could only conclude that it or some part must have been created by an evil power. Thus humans must search for a mystic release from this fleshly prisonhouse of the soul. But for Greek thinkers who were most influential in shaping Christian theology, being and not becoming was the ultimate reality, so that God as Being itself must be understood as eternally complete, incapable of change—so much so that, instead of being directly related to and being affected by the world, the unmoved Mover can know creation only indirectly. By knowing himself, God knows the world and its history as timelessly complete.

This imagery forced Christian thinkers to great lengths to explain how God's incarnation could entail true involvement within history. Furthermore,

---

8. "Easter Mid-Morning Hymn."
9. Barth, *Dogmatics in Outline,* 28.
10. Aristotle, *Basic Works,* 878.

it undercut the scriptural god-language that used human characteristics such as anger, hope, yearning, agony, and even repentance. Biblical prayer was firmly built upon the premise that God could be changed by human appeal. Abraham was acclaimed for successfully bargaining with God concerning the number of good persons needing to be found in order to save Sodom. Throughout Scripture, history is portrayed as significantly horizontal, moving toward the promised kingdom of God. *When* is a favorite scriptural adverb. This biblical imagery was instrumental in helping to birth the modern use of change and becoming as defining categories.

Further clarity came through conversations with Jacques Maritain when we both taught at Princeton University. As a neo-Thomist in following Aristotle, he affirmed that Christian hope centered in trusting that the end of history would be a restoration of Eden. My insistence was that this would render history a meaningless circle, in which humanity's agonies and struggles and creativity would add nothing to the whole, returning history without increase to whence it began. His philosophic base forced him to declare that God has no need of us, and thus history can add nothing to God as unmoved Mover. But for me, such a God would be ungodly. Drawing from the philosopher Charles Hartshorne,[11] I used the analogy of how cruel a human father would be if he were unmoved by the pleadings of his suffering children. So would it be with God. Thus the heart of the Christian wager must be on an incarnationally suffering God who is the most moved of Movers. The German-Jewish philosopher Hans Jonas in his "Concept of God after Auschwitz" concludes that, in creating humans, God withdrew in order to give space for human freedom. By taking this risk, God becomes a suffering God, as our sufferings become God's as well.[12]

St. Maximus of Turin (fifth c.) insists that Christian theology affirms "an upward movement in the whole of creation, every element raising itself to something higher."[13] In our time, Teilhard de Chardin identifies this surging as a divine immanence functioning as the thread of continuity within evolution, breaking through into self-consciousness within a humanity that yearns to see the face of God, as history sweeps toward a transcendent omega point of divine supraconsciousness. The poet Rilke suggests that God is grasped best as a "direction."[14] This direction for the Christian is the Spirit's relentless forward surging as God is becoming All

---

11. Hartshorne, *Divine Relativity*, 45.

12. Jonas, "Concept of God," 630.

13. International Commission on English in the Liturgy, *Liturgy of the Hours*, 2:815–16.

14. Rilke, *Selected Poems*, 29, 39, 121, 171, 199.

in all. The Christ event could be understood as God self-consciously gazing back upon his own struggling, greeting humanity in mutual recognition, expressed in an ontological yearning of tenderness that acknowledges
burnedness as the homesick woundedness of love. If humans are created in
God's own image, then the human pilgrimage from birthing to maturation
must somehow be analogous to the divine pilgrimage. One's personality is
not a given but forged by growth through struggle. So might it be with God,
who through strife, yearning, and hope is in ongoing conflict of light over
darkness. Berdyaev goes as far as to suggest parallels between the epochs of
human history and those of God's becoming, posing the Renaissance, for
example, as God's adolescence.[15]

The imagery of a Reverse Trinity previously mentioned seems most
imaginative for providing a plausible Christian theodicy. Traditionally,
the triune God has been understood as beginning with God the Father
as an all-powerful, all-knowing, fully self-conscious loving Creator who
designed in advance a perfect earth, consequently restructuring it negatively into its present fallen condition as punishment for disobedience by
the original couple. The Father then sends his Son the Redeemer as incarnation into this world, bridging through suffering the alienated distance
existing between humans and the Father by enabling forgiveness and defeating death. Then God as Spirit proceeding from the Father through the
Son comes as gift to those who believe in the Christ event. In contrast, the
analogy of a Reverse Trinity images the creative beginning as with God
the Holy Spirit moving over the darkness of nonbeing, and through the
long process of incarnation, supremely disclosed through the Christ event,
moving co-creatively with humanity toward the fullness of a loving Father
through becoming All in all. The new heaven and earth begins as hunger,
buds as promise, and consummates in mutual hope. Using the traditional
imagery of God as eternally begetting the Son within himself, the movement of Christ as the divine immanence in all things could be conceived as
the begetting of the universe—for "He was in the world and the world was
made through him . . ." (John 1:10). "In him all things were created . . . in
him all things hold together" (Col 1:16–17). This immanence of all things
in God and God incarnate in all things could be viewed as the begetting of
God in transcending emergence. God's introduction of himself to Moses is
best translated "I will be who I will be" (Exod 3:14).

Consequently, our interaction with God, as we mentioned before, is
best understood not in terms of obedience to the will of God understood as
a divine pre-creation blueprint. Instead, faithfulness is a co-creative calling

15. Berdyaev, *Meaning of History*, 121, 176.

to discern into being through the inspiration of the Holy Spirit the yearnings of God seeking birth everywhere. The psalmist suggests this in terms
of "the plans [or thoughts] of God's heart" (Ps 33:11). The Christian is to
live playfully as co-creator with God, reveling in translating the yearnings
of God's imagination into fleshly incarnations of beauty. A depth indicator
of one's conversion then would not be in terms of disciplinary obedience
but in terms of childlike creativity. Faith, says Barth, involves the transition
from "you must" to the freedom of "you may."[16] Play is the wrestling sport of
love. It is through our senses that God delights in the creation he loves. Thus
providence is not to be understood in terms of a divine predetermination or
a manipulation of natural law, but, as Whitehead suggests, through "mag-
netized feelings" operative within us as the promptings of God's longings,
prodding us to live creatively at the beckoning edge of the Spirit's lure. God's
imagination is at the cusp of everything, as the verging ache for fullness.
God's beyond is the horizon of all becoming. Key is the cross at history's
center, revealing death as not being God's creation nor evil God's doing—but
both being God's enemies. The crucifixion is the emblematic affirmation that
God is no watcher but a full combatant with us in the battle of being against
nonbeing, of existence against nothingness, of life against death.

The greatest of miracles is that anything exists, anything at all. Thus
we are radically contingent, sustained instant by instant as sheer gift over
an abyss of nonbeing that functions like a magnet—in each moment and
at every intersection attempting to draw everything back into nothingness,
countervailing the creative intent of God. This proclivity is active within each
of us, akin to Freud's death wish conflicting with the life wish, requiring courage to persevere against being drawn back into nothingness. Death is not a
something that God created, nor is it an instrument of divinely conceived
punishment. It is the inevitable backside of the creative process itself, so that
if anything exists, nonbeing cannot not be. Consequently, death is the final
evil, contradictory to the core of God's creative intent, and sin is doing whatever serves nonbeing—as in destroying rather than creating, exerting one's
own being rather than enabling the being of others, or existing minimally
rather than living life to its fullness. Violence and killing are treasonous acts,
for they do the work of the enemy, with suicide the ultimate (though often
understandable) capitulation, as when persons become so worn down by life
that they no longer have the willpower to resist the relentless pull of nothingness. Creativity as the *imago dei* is the defiance of death.

Once again, we are brought to the Eucharist as the center of Christian
living. In this defining act, the faithful gather around what Augustine calls

16. Barth, *Dogmatics in Outline*, 19.

the great table,[17] participating as microcosm in what God is doing macro-cosmically in and through all of history. Here, we reenact the plot of the Christ event, becoming rebonded in the vision of a new heaven and earth promised through the divine-human co-creativity that is making all things new. Our hands are shaped like a manger to receive but also contoured like a container to lift up from the paten our offerings of crucified brokenness, sufferings, conflicts, sins, anxieties, doubts, incompleteness, yearnings, hopes, dreams, as well as the creative works of our hands. These are raised along with Christ's own crucified brokenness and faithfulness into God, where they are never to be forgotten but through God's redemptive memory woven into the tapestry of God's promised kingdom. Then, with the chalice, we toast this vision as pledge of our own wager, in return nurtured by the empowered elements to discern life's creative possibilities as they become initiated in our living through God's imagination. Transubstantiation into God is an apt term for the status of these expressions of the work of our hands and the struggles of our living. The high point of this eucharistic drama occurs when the elements are raised with these words: "Through him, and with him, and in him, in the unity of the Holy Spirit, all glory and honor is yours, Almighty Father, forever and ever." Here the goal of history is envisaged as foretaste in what Barth calls "the theatre of God's glory."[18] The cross-purposes of our existence are redeemed by being taken up into the end-purposes of God's becoming. The psalmist cries out this hope as a question: "You have kept count of my tossings; put my tears in your bottle. Are they not in your record?" (Ps 56:8 NRSV). The Christian wagers that indeed they are, so that, in our intercessions, the particulars of our unre-deemed world are lifted up before the face of God, soliciting their consum-mation with the steadfastness of the persistent widow. It is the Eucharist that celebrates the church as the body of Christ, drawing her perimeters so that no one is permitted to stand outside the circle as a potential enemy. Christian theologizing is a Eucharist of the mind, from which flows this vision on which a Christian theodicy can rest.

For persons philosophically inclined, the writings by Friedrich Wilhelm Joseph Schelling (1775–1854) are helpful. In his second period, Schelling images the Spirit as creative energy moving relentlessly through everything that is, impulsed by a craving for self-conscious fullness.[19] Na-ture is the visibility of this Spirit, evident in the dialectical process of

---

17. International Commission on English in the Liturgy, *Liturgy of the Hours*, 1:1407.

18. Barth, *Dogmatics in Outline*, 58.

19. Copleston, *History of Philosophy*, 7:126ff.

expansion and contraction, going out and returning enriched, compelling all things from within toward fullness. Self-awareness of the Whole emerges in the advent of the human soul. Schelling finds in our personal becoming a promising analogy for conceiving God. Just as our personhood is forged through expansive growth from conception to adulthood, so is the expansive development in God toward supraconsciousness. God is being ongoingly birthed through struggle with nothingness. All things are immanent in God, with the universe being a living evolving system. Art is the highest human calling, with the poet especially able to grasp the whole in its parts. In and through our creating, we touch the creativity of God, rendering the universe a supreme work of art, through which God is realizing the purpose of the Whole—much like the thinking out of thought, the feeling forth of desire, the yearning expansion of becoming. Likewise helpful is the *as if* philosophy of Hans Vaihinger (1852–1933). While insisting that there is no absolute truth, that only feelings and sensations are true, he affirms that certain fictions are nevertheless useful postulates for living.[20] Thus religion, even though a fiction, can have utility in being lived as if true. Here, Vaihinger's thinking is not yet postmodern, for in claiming to know religion to be fictitious, he claims to know too much. For the postmodern mind, this cannot be known.

This chapter is intended for those for whom the conundrum of evil is a major block in making a wager of pure faith. In fact, after proposing the best that our theological imagination can offer, it is wise to be humbled by the declaration I heard was made by a medieval council, that all statements about God are likely to be as false as they are true.

20. Vaihinger, *Philosophy of 'As If,'* xlv, 84, 99.

CHAPTER TWELVE

THE REMNANT AS A FUTURE
FOR THE CHURCH

An Eight-Step Plan

S t. John of the Cross maintains that the beginning, the entire climb, the summit, all is faith—so get used to the darkness.[1] It is in this darkness that the serious Christian wagers, functioning in large part as a poet. Our knowing is through analogies, hunching that the more has a name, that the depth is becoming loving, and that the yet is beckoning us to participate. The Christ event is wagered on as being the definitive analogy that discloses the essential pattern structuring history with meaning—of incarnation through crucifixion for resurrection to ascension into God, with a Pentecostal call summoning humanity as co-creators, through which God is becoming All in all.

So understood, we turn now to explore the future of the church in terms of a remnant to which the burned ones in particular are being called in our time. Candidates can be found in most churches, much like Israel's remnant, who, by sensing spiritual starvation in an alien land, came to their senses. Burned by the meaning question, they feel like alien residents in no longer being able to find centering in a society profoundly sick, in which the inauthentic self becomes a burden to itself. Augustine describes this condition for prefacing a faith wager in terms of holy desire.[2] For some, this desire entails reaching toward the Eucharist as if toward a viaticum, a banquet in a brown paper bag for shared munching along the path. For others, it feels like an Abraham-like pilgrimaging without a map to a place to which they have

---

1. Cross, *Ascent of Mount Carmel.*

2. International Commission on English in the Liturgy, *Liturgy of the Hours,* 3:219–20.

never before been. For still others, it means seeking a life that would be tragic if God did not exist and a betrayal if one did not bring back something from the far country. St. Bernard expresses this pregnant condition in terms of a double irony, of seeking "him whom your soul loves, because you cannot seek unless you are sought, and when you are sought you cannot but seek."[3] These are varied expressions of the burned ones, who, whether realizing it yet or not, are being called as leaven for birthing a remnant church.

Remnant imagery occurs throughout biblical history. The remnant appeared as the righteous few whom God sought in order to save Sodom. They were the ones who survived Noah's great flood to begin humanity again. They were the chosen ones wooed in the Sinai desert. They were the faithful poor who were salvaged during the Babylonian exile. They were the monastic survivors providing leaven during the Dark Ages. They are now the burned ones within today's churches and elsewhere, whom Christ is calling to be a mini-soul for the world by forming remnant communities as laboratories of resurrection—while claiming for themselves only the status of rewashed harlots. They are called to establish supportive accountability within house churches eucharistically bound, no longer motivated by futile efforts at institutional growth, accepting the role of being the first to give up their life jackets. Early Christianity lived out of such house churches of practiced we-ness, with remnant sparks continuing in our time in varied expressions of tent ministries, fraternities of clergy, United Methodist covenant groups, and Catholic Worker houses. They function in the tension between being a leaven for society and an ulcer in the stomach of the monster—expressing compassionate love in short-term mercy ministries and long-term tough love in justice ministries. Subversive characteristics of pure faith are a sense of inner peace, an easy humor, a spontaneous love, a dogged persistence, and a seditious hope, drawing the distinction everywhere between needs and wants. They endeavor to live each moment deliciously, cherish beauty everywhere, share lavishly, pray extravagantly, create playfully, ponder deeply, tender compassion, intercede for the world, act nonviolently, and question society at every infected joint—always honoring the *why* haunting the mind's edges.

In his *Treatise on the Lord's Prayer*, St. Cyprian provides his own version of the remnant, as we who practice

> humility in our daily lives, [have] an unwavering faith, a moral sense of modesty in conversation, justice in acts, mercy in deed, discipline, refusal to harm others, a readiness to suffer,

3. "Sermon Eighty-Four on the Song of Songs," in Bernard of Clairvaux, *Bernard of Clairvaux*, 276.

peaceableness with [others], a wholehearted love of the Lord, loving in him what is of the Father, having awe of him because he is God, preferring nothing to him who preferred nothing to us, clinging tenaciously to his love, standing by his cross with loyalty and courage, whenever there is any conflict involving his honor and his name, manifesting in our speech the constancy of our profession and under torture confidence for the fight, and in dying the endurance for which we will be crowned—this is what it means to wish to be a coheir with Christ . . .[4]

The burned ones are touched by the radicalness of Basil the Great when he declares that "the bread in your cupboard belongs to the hungry, and the coat hanging unused in your closet belongs to the [person] who needs it, the shoes rotting in your closet belong to the [person] who has no shoes; the money which you put in the bank belongs to the poor. You do wrong to everyone you could help but fail to help."[5] It means living John Chrysostom's dictum: "Not to share one's wealth with the poor is to steal from them and to take away their livelihood. It is not our own goods which we hold, but theirs."[6]

As we have been saying, the Christian faith which the burned ones are to model resonates with Jesus's response to Thomas: "Blessed are those who have not seen and yet believe" (John 20:29). This is the wager of pure faith, removed today from cultural support, rational certainty, emotional uniqueness, and any advantage regarding worldly success or otherworldly reward. Its test is the quality of life knowable through the living of it. For remnant Christians, this means forging a habitual disposition through discipline, priming the flavor of an acquired taste by which to see, feel, and imagine in a unique way, establishing internally an alternative world in which to live and from which one's outward actions flow. This temperament necessitates ongoing personal and communal rehearsing through spiritual practices that discipline one's will to act with the kingdom of God as hope. One lives *as if* in order to believe that vision, and believes it in order to make it so, purified by a determination to live it; for, even if untrue, one would not wish to live otherwise. This wagering of as if entails living in our society as if not. As St. Paul expresses it, Christians are "those who mourn as though they were not mourning, and those who rejoice as though they were not rejoicing, and those who buy as though they had no goods, and those who

4. International Commission on English in the Liturgy, *Liturgy of the Hours*, 3:368.
5. R. Ellsberg, *All Saints*, 258–89.
6. Pope John Paul II, *Catechism of Catholic Church*, 2446.

deal with the world as though they had no dealings with it. For the form of the world is passing away" (1 Cor 7:30–31).

We can describe the burned ones by paraphrasing the anonymous "Letter to Diognetus":

> Christians are outwardly indistinguishable from others, either by nationality, language, or customs. They do not inhabit separate cities, speak a strange dialect, or follow some outlandish way of life. With regard to dress, food and manner of life they follow the customs of whatever city they happen to be living in. Yet there is something extraordinary about their lives. They live in their own countries as though they were only passing through. They play their full role as citizens, but labor under all the disabilities of aliens. Their homeland is a foreign country. They live in the flesh but are not governed by the flesh. They are obedient to the laws, yet they live on a level that transcends the law. Christians love all persons, but all persons persecute them. Condemned because they are not understood, they are put to death, but raised to life again. They live in poverty but enrich many; they are totally destitute but possess an abundance of everything. They suffer dishonor but that is their glory. They are defamed, but vindicated. A blessing is their answer to abuse, deterrence their response to insult. For the good they do they receive the punishment of malefactors, but even then they rejoice, as though receiving the gift of life. We may say that the Christian is to the world what the soul is to the body. As the soul is present in every part of the body, while remaining distinct from it, so Christians are found in all the cities of the world but cannot be identified with the world.[7]

Gerard Manley Hopkins, in his translation of Saint Francis Xavier's prayer "O Deus ego amo te," expresses the theological foundation of the remnant in this manner: "Why should not I love thee, Jesu, so much in love with me? Not for heaven's sake; not to be out of hell by loving thee; not for any gains I see; but just the way that thou didst me I do love and I will love thee."[8] This is *sola fides*, the pure faith that entails dying with a crucifix in one's hand and an empty cross in one's pocket.

There are five basic options possible for today's diminishing churches, caught as they are within the demise of modern society:

---

7. International Commission on English in the Liturgy, *Liturgy of the Hours*, 2:840.

8. Francis Xavier, translated by G. M. Hopkins, in W. H. Gardner and MacKenzie, eds., *Poems of Gerard Manley Hopkins*, 270.

1. Support—seek validation by providing a religious justification for present society.

2. Supplement—provide services to fill gaps in society's present disfunctioning.

3. Cope—provide spiritual support to enable individuals to live in the midst of society as it is.

4. Compensate—promise rewards in a future life as motivation for individuals who are no longer able to find sufficient meaning in what present society provides.

5. Alternative—create countercultural remnant communities determined to outlast the demise of our society.

Whichever option is chosen, there will continue to be church closings, mergers of congregations, selling of church buildings, diminishing of denominational translocal agencies, minimization of ecumenical ventures, online clergy training, part-time local pastors, and an increasing reliance on lay leadership. This irreversible diminishment of the churches will be demoralizing unless a remnant alternative plan is put into place now. Not long ago, the *Christian Century* dedicated a whole edition to the theme of "When a Congregation Dies."[9] In case study after case study, it became clear that, while the decision to close these churches was based on membership loss and the cost of building maintenance, above all, its demise was due to a lack of vision. When the church doors closed, the congregation simply dispersed. Yet, in almost all of these closings, there was a residue of anywhere from twenty to fifty persons, enough to become a remnant. But because they had no prepared plan, dissipation resulted. A few persons joined other churches, but many simply faded away in depressed resignation. Most closings happened not even with a minor bang but simply with a cowed whimper. What this phenomenon needs to make clear to denominational leaders, clergy, and seminaries is that instead of permitting such dispersals to happen, what is needed is the training of a nucleus within each diminishing congregation that can create renewal for as long as is possible, at the same time readying a remnant capable of continuing if the church doors need to be locked. By understanding church as the people of God, edifice closure should be no reason for disbanding, and the number of parishioners left when there is a closing is usually large enough for a new beginning. In fact, selling off the church building can be liberating—but only if there has been groomed in advance a remnant with a lay leadership that has a vision.

9. Mabry-Nauta, "The Last Sunday."

EIGHT-STEP PLAN

In the alternative that we are proposing, the diminishment of numbers and finances are no longer defining determinants. Central in this plan (option 5) is the creation of small remnant communities. Stanley Hauerwas and William Willimon use the name resident aliens for these candidates who could become a remnant church, those who realize that the task of transforming the world is no longer a feasible mission, while refusing any longer to function as chaplains of the empire. Instead, the Christian task is to preserve Christianity as a peculiar vision by creating formative communities of the cross who will practice love of enemies, suffering for righteousness, and worshipping Christ in all things. John Howard Yoder agrees, calling for churches to be intentionally distinctive minorities in our post-Constantinian time, intent on nothing more nor less than being the church.[10] Such intentional communities already exist in various forms, and from their experimental efforts we can draw wisdom—such as from Reba Place Fellowship, the Ecumenical Institute, the Community of Jesus, Church of the Savior, covenant discipleship groups,[11] and expressions of the new monasticism. What we are proposing is an eight-step plan for creating the remnant church. The steps are: 1) recruitment; 2) instruction; 3) renewal core group(s); 4) creating a rule; 5) theological visioning; 6) liturgical/sacramental deepening; 7) practical planning; 8) implementation.

Recruitment

As a beginning, the pastor of a diminishing congregation needs to identify persons in the congregation who evidence some elements of burnedness. As we have indicated, these are ones who seem to be yearning for more, for depth, for integrity, with at least a hint of being an exile in today's society. Risking sentimentality, helpful are characteristics that Trappist Matthew Kelty identifies as making for a monastic call: "To ask for healthy persons from a culture as sick as ours is to ask a great deal . . . . There will have to be a love for life and a desire to truly live . . . a sense of wonder . . . musing, pondering, mulling . . . those who love the night, know the moon . . . watch the wind in the grass on the hill . . . can take discipline, and can accept the responsibility of being who they are and what they are . . . who like music . . . notice the rain, feel the wind, hear the birds, and smell the soup."[12]

10. Yoder, *Original Revolution.*

11. Watson, *Covenant Discipleship.*

12. Kelty, *Aspects of Monastic Calling,* 37.

Overstated, but such characteristics point toward the kind of persons the pastor needs to identify.

After concluding that there is a potential nucleus, the pastor brings the remnant idea to the local church leadership for approval. If granted, the idea is shared with the congregation. Extensive details need not be given at this point, but focus should be on the idea of creating a renewal core group that would enable participants to deepen their faith by growing spiritually.

The purpose would be dual. 1) After a period of training, this nucleus group would serve as leaven in providing spiritual renewal for the larger congregation, so that it could continue to function meaningfully within the present church building as long as this seems feasible. 2) If closing the church doors does become necessary, this group would be ready to serve as a continuity team in providing transition into a new congregational form.

This initial proposal of a renewal core group could be presented through a sermon(s) or, preferably, a congregational meeting, where discussion is possible. This idea should be introduced positively as a creative hope rather than appearing to be a veiled notice of the congregation's imminent demise. The theme of the plan as presented is spiritual renewal, inviting everyone to participate but requiring a one-year commitment to the group, which would meet probably twice a month. It is crucial that this renewal core group not be seen as elite or permitted to so become. Several decades ago, when the Ecumenical Institute fostered renewal groups in local churches, the strategy was to gain leadership for the purpose of bringing the whole congregation into their preconceived perspective. This process often provoked competitive resistance. Instead, the remnant plan must be transparent at every point, inviting everyone to participate in the renewal core group and making periodic reports to the congregation as it progresses. It is important that this group reflect the congregation's diversity as much as possible, with no attempt at forcing uniformity. The societal analysis presented in this book need not be shared at this point. The concern is only that the congregation acknowledge the tenuous nature of their future and sense something of the societal reasons for their remnant status.

Instruction

The renewal core group is then recruited from the congregation, with individual invitations made as appropriate. The size of this initial group is not overly important at this point. The first sessions will introduce and experiment with some of the most important traditional Christian spiritual practices. The intent is to enrich each person's faith through intentional discipline. Some of these seventeen practices can be presented as a series by the pastor, informed lay persons, and/or, as was successfully done by the Ecumenical Institute, through short handouts for group discussion. The order of presentation depends on the group, but the disciplines worth considering are these.

1. Journaling. Each group member needs to have a notebook or other resource for note-taking as an aid in appropriating each discipline. In addition, one needs to be taught how to journal regarding the happenings of one's day and week—not as a diary of activities but an instrument for discerning insights gained through these happenings. The intent is to encourage one to live life as an action-reflection pilgrimage, making regular entries.

2. Daily offices. Christians need to develop devotional practices for structuring one's day/week, possibly using short liturgies and biblical passages. The Catholic breviary provides seven extensive rituals to divide the day, and most denominations have similar resources. Minimal would be three times daily: in the morning, giving thanks for the new day; at noon, praying for strength to continue one's day to the glory of God; and at evening, prayers in which to offer up, positively and negatively, the day's happenings, surrendering one's life into God. We live only one day at a time, with each morning a new gift.

3. Prayer as conversation. Employing Br. Lawrence's idea of practicing the Presence, prayer involves turning the normal ongoing internal babbling of I with me into an I with God (or Jesus) dialogue, thereby fostering praying without ceasing. Prayer is the very breathing of the Christian, becoming as natural as one's heartbeat. Results of this companion presence are disciplined faithfulness and mutual decision-making, rendering loneliness obsolete.

4. Meditation (*lectio divina* as sacred reading). Here, either individually or corporately, one slowly reads, rereads, and re-rereads a short passage of Scripture until grasped by a word or phrase worth chewing, perhaps providing a focus for the day. A section from a spiritual book can likewise be used.

5. Contemplation. While meditation focuses the mind on reflection, contemplation is intent on emptying the mind. Society's constant noise is draining, like being trapped in a room with the TV stuck at highest volume. By pulling the plug, one can savor the silence as sacred. In contemplation, one accomplishes this stillness by using a word or phrase as a mantra, such as "Give me peace." This is repeated as rapidly

as needed in order to prevent the mind from having time or space to wander, keeping it busy so that it stays out of the way. With practice, in time, this mantra will simply stop. One is being emptied of thinking, feeling, and sensing. When wandering does happen, gently return oneself to the focused peace by reusing or speeding up the mantra, putting the mind to sleep. A visual focus is sometimes helpful, such as a candle, alternating with closed eyes, or using the beat of one's heart or the rhythm of one's breathing as a physical mantra. Contemplation is incredibly renewing as one relinquishes oneself into God, rests in God's sustaining arms, and abandons doing into pure being. Only God can satisfy and quiet our restlessness.

6. The body as companion. Here, focus is on one's body as intended to be a temple of the Holy Spirit, thus needing to be nurtured as a worthy residence. This involves attention to such matters as weight, nutrition, exercise, fasting, and appearance.

7. Hospitality. Here is developed a generous, receptive, welcoming, open liberality of kindness toward everyone. The Christian must realize that in feeding the hungry, clothing the naked, and being concerned for the imprisoned, "you do it to me" (Matt 25:40). Mercy ministry deals with the symptoms of society's dysfunction, and justice ministry addresses the structural causes. Both are essential. Christians must be stewards of their lives, their time, and their possessions, using an inventory for intentional accountability.

8. Being informed. Christians need to expand their arena of living by being currently informed through diverse sources about happenings in the world, minimally, perhaps by listening daily to one of National Public Radio's short summaries on the hour. One then needs to express in intercessions the world's hurts, fears, sufferings, and bitterness, helping them within one's own self to die of malnutrition but always evoking God's power and pledging one's help in rectification. We are responsible before God for all living things. In addition, one needs to keep a fluid prayer list of individuals needing special attention.

9. Confession and forgiveness. Growth entails walking intentionally into one's less developed shadow side. Through this openness, we become increasingly able to acknowledge the sins that we have done and those that have been done to us. Special attention needs to be paid as well to the impact of the three p's with which society tempts us: possessions, power, and prestige. By making periodic assessments, one is able to make confession and receive the newness of forgiveness,

using whatever resources one's denomination may make available. The Twelve Steps used by Alcoholics Anonymous are an evocative vehicle for this process. At the end of one's day, it is helpful to do an examen of consciousness (one's accomplishments and failings) and a weekly examen of conscience in preparation for confession.

10. Living in the now. By receiving forgiveness, one is freed from the past in order to participate so mindfully in each unique present that one is not distracted by the future. "Take no thought of the morrow" (Matt 6:34), advises Jesus, but live mindfully in each today so that "my cup overflows" (Ps 25:5). This is an attitude that takes time to make habitual.

11. Eucharist. To be explored here is holy communion as the central distilled gesture that is at the heart of Christian faith and worship, functioning as the Christian's metadrama. Here one needs to identify its rich meaning and varied practices, recognizing it as emblem of the communion of saints through the centuries. The Eucharist needs to be done frequently, so much so that John Wesley recommends that it be done daily.[13]

12. Creativity. We are undergirded by the imagination of God, so that by becoming attentive to the Spirit's yearnings in each unique situation, we are better able to render each place better for having been there. The Spirit lures, pulls, sweeps, and evolves everything, calling us to participate. This involves even small things such as a needed hug, washing another's dishes, helping a child with homework, giving another driver the right of way, helping a neighbor with a repair, participating in a food pantry, writing a legislator, and planting tomatoes.

13. Sacramentals. Through these various spiritual practices, one becomes aware of how living spaces reflect and in turn nurture who we are as Christians—not only one's home, but also one's car and place of employment. By becoming intentional about these locations, the locations can become increasingly sacred as meaning-environments. One might use flowers and plants to recall God's creativity, Christian symbols (e.g., cross, icon, and water as reminder of one's baptism), an altar, special music, pictures, and decentralizing one's TV.

14. Vision. It is important for each person to identify and rehearse regularly the larger picture provided by one's faith wager, perhaps by engaging the dual minimalist Christian dimensions we have delineated—that of healing through Christ's unconditional love and history as deriving its

13. Wesley, *John Wesley*, 334–44.

meaning in terms of the kingdom of God. Clarity of vision can often be enabled through small group discussion and/or a spiritual director.

15. Spiritual direction. Real change requires regular support and account-ability, which the remnant core group can provide, and a one-to-one relationship with a spiritual director. A spiritual director needs to be an excellent listener, able to discern patterns, and detect issues resident beneath the surface.

16. Pondering. A mark of spiritual depth is when persons find themselves taking time, more than occasionally, to reflect on life's conundrums as they intersect with faith's beliefs, e.g., death, mystery, evil, hope, love. To evoke this practice, one might need group interaction. It entails asking such questions as why, so what, and what if.

17. Retreat. It is important that a person take time apart, away from one's regular activities, expectations, environment, and noise, disengaged from all technology. Silence is imperative, being unavailable for inter-ruption and being open to the leadings of the Holy Spirit. One might wisely examine the entries in one's journal in order to detect patterns needing attention and review one's faithfulness to one's rule. But it is important that one not fill the time with input. The ideal location for a retreat is one that encourages simplicity, involves at least one over-night, and is in the context of nature.

Renewal Core Group(s)

After the renewal core group spends time in understanding and experiment-ing with some of these spiritual practices, if the group is large, it is time to divide it into smaller renewal core groups. The ideal would be eight to twelve persons in each, attempting to reflect the diversity of the congregation. Each group should choose a facilitator and adopt an expressive name by which to be identified. While each will meet separately, unity of the total group might better be maintained by beginning corporately for a hymn, joint prayer, and/or Eucharist, before dispersing into separate spaces. At this, point each group needs to deepen its trust level through bonding by sharing autobiographi-cally. This can be enabled by providing questions in advance, such as, "Share several key things that we need to know about you in order for us to become closer friends." Confidentiality must be promised and strictly practiced. Sev-eral rounds of such sharing might be useful.

Creation of Rule

When each renewal core group has completed this deeper sharing, persons are invited to write out in advance for sharing with their group how they actually live out a typical day and week, including such elements as activities, relationships, church involvements, diet, finances, and spiritual practices, recording the average time spent for each. In sharing these, persons then propose changes that they regard as needed in order to render their report into a concrete personal rule by which they are willing to be held accountable. After receiving group feedback, each person privately writes out his/her rule, making it concrete in terms of a schedule. After presenting it to the group, each person signs his/her rule as a promise to live by it for six months, countersigned by the group as a promise to provide supportive accountability. A token marking this promise is powerful, such as a common cross or medallion. In following sessions, time is spent hearing from each person about the successes and failures in keeping one's rule, receiving group feedback as appropriate. These sessions might begin or end with a short Eucharist or, in the absence of an ordained person, a love feast. Throughout, a facilitator is needed to keep the group focused on the particular task.

Theological Visioning

As these sessions providing supportive accountability become more regularized so as to require minimal time, these groups should be ready to help each other deepen the theological context in which each person is actually living. Honest sharing can be encouraged by making clear from the start that a diversity of faith perspectives will inevitably emerge from the group. This theological envisaging will not be easy and is not likely to be very deep at first, often expressed with clichés. It can begin in various ways, such as inviting each person to share a few of the important events in one's spiritual journey; reflect theologically upon them, indicating any unresolved theological issues that might remain; then listening, as others in the group reflect theologically on what they hear. A goal here is to help persons learn to theologize—not simply indicating doctrines that they believe, as, for example, the incarnation, but to look at life incarnationally or, in believing the resurrection, to reflect on the so what—what difference does that make for the person.

Another method for beginning such envisaging appears in my book *Theological Worlds: Understanding the Alternative Rhythms of Christian Belief.* There is described a typology of five contrasting theological orientations that have characterized Christians through the centuries. Each world is shaped by a person's particular basic need/yearning (*obsessio*), correlated with the specific healing (*epiphania*) that the Christian faith offers. A self-scoring Theological Worlds Inventory appears in my *Worlds within a Congregation: Dealing with Theological Diversity*,[14] and an abbreviated version is in my *Art of Spiritual Direction: Giving and Receiving Spiritual Guidance*.[15] This is a brief summary of the five theological worlds that can help persons find themselves theologically.

1. World One—Separation and Reunion. One's obsessio here is a sense of feeling alienated from things, weary of life as lived on the surface, somehow rendering one an alien. The epiphania comes through an experience of reunion, sometimes mystic-like, enabling one to participate meaningfully in the mystery of things, through Christ as the Revealer, whose love tears open the veil shrouding life.

2. World Two—Conflict and Vindication. One's obsessio is a sense of life as struggle, characterizing not only oneself but society and history, making one feel like a warrior. The epiphania comes in wagering upon Christ as the Messiah who takes our part in the struggle, promising redemption as victory.

3. World Three—Emptiness and Fulfillment. One's obsessio is a sense of personal inadequacy, of hollowness, of not belonging, of being orphaned. The epiphania is Christ as Enabler, the one who so overflows with love for us that we belong, becoming whole in relating with others, in spite of feeling unworthy.

4. World Four—Condemnation and Forgiveness. One's obsessio is a sense of sinfulness and guilt, making one feel like a fugitive. The epiphania is forgiveness as reprieve, as adoption, which is not something that we can earn but is what the sacrificial Christ as Savior can provide—forgiving love for the undeserving, acceptance for the unacceptable.

5. World Five—Suffering and Endurance. One's obsessio is a sense of being stressed out by life, for life at times seems too much, making one feel like a victim or refugee. The epiphania is Christ as a suffering partner, his companionship providing strength for the long haul with a love that outlasts with long-suffering.

14. W. Jones, *Worlds within a Congregation*, 45–65.
15. W. Jones, *Art of Spiritual Direction*, 258–64.

Liturgical/Sacramental Deepening

Hopefully by this time, members of the renewal core group(s) will have experienced personal growth through spiritual disciplines, been deepened by supportive accountability, and become better able to articulate the theological content of their faith wagers. The next step is to explore how they can better enter into a fuller understanding of the life of the congregation as the body of Christ. In my *Worlds within a Congregation,* there are charts indicating how each of the theological worlds favors a particular type of congregational worship, along with favorite hymnology for expressing it. Also provided is a typology of how various preaching styles appeal best to each world and descriptions of how each world tends in particular to understand baptism, the Eucharist, and funerals. An alternative approach into this liturgical/sacramental deepening would be to have persons share what they find most meaningful in worship and how this meaning could be enhanced. They then can do the same in regard to how they understand baptism, the Eucharist, and funerals, with how these might be emphasized and/or modified in order for them to be made more meaningful. The purpose here is to understand better how the structure of liturgy and sacraments reflects and supplements theological meaning.

Practical Planning

Having reached this point, the renewal core group(s) can celebrate in having actually become a remnant church. Thus it is likely time to make a crucial decision regarding the likelihood of edifice survival. If continuation appears possible, the next step is to plan how the growth that the group(s) has experienced can now become a leaven for renewal within the larger congregation. One method that has worked well is for those persons who have emerged during the core experiences as leaders to be encouraged now to recruit their own small group from the congregation, in order to duplicate some version of what they have personally experienced.

On the other hand, if the renewal core group(s) discerns that edifice survival is no longer feasible, it is time for them to do concrete planning regarding the transition. The total group(s) should determine how best to divide the congregation into remnant communities (i.e., house churches), each being an *ecclesiola in ecclesia*—small churches within the larger one. In doing this, attention should be paid to such matters as residential location, age, gender, family size, record of attendance, etc. While these communities might reflect the diversity of the congregation, other factors might suggest selectivity in terms of one or more of the above factors, such as singleness, aging, or those with young children. These remnant communities will normally meet weekly, as a continuation of what the whole church had been doing. Likely, each community will prefer to choose its own time and create a schedule of homes in which to meet. Leaders who have emerged from within the previous core meetings should be distributed among the new remnant communities so as to provide experienced lay leadership. Activities within these communities might involve some of the practices in spiritual growth that the original core group experienced and providing supportive accountability for the growth of each member. These groups are to reflect intentionally the original house churches as described biblically in Acts, where there were reflections on the gospel, a "sharing of joys and sorrows," "speaking the truth in love," and "caring for the needs of others" (Acts 5:32–35.)

These groups should gather as well at least monthly for common worship at a celebration center, perhaps with a potluck supper, encouraging new persons to participate. Ideally, this gathering space would be in another church where some exclusive space is available or in a rented space in a school or community center. This space would be used not only for monthly worship but also for corporate meetings, fellowship suppers, educational offerings, and social service, as well as offered for public use, if feasible. This space needs to be of efficient size so as not to needlessly drain resources. Efforts should be made to make it an environment of uncommon beauty, reflecting how beauty requires imagination far more than elaborate expenditures. Planned liturgies could well reflect the congregation's varied theological perspectives (worlds) and diverse personality types, hopefully with a Eucharist. Task forces would be encouraged to emerge as the vigor of individuals percolates into both mercy and justice ministries.

In developing these multiple remnant communities, a pastor/coordinator will be needed for providing oversight and enthusiasm. This could be the present pastor, who would appreciate having the position redefined as a part-time vocation. Or the transition might be enabled by hiring a retired pastor, a part-time seminarian, or a trained lay person. Whichever of those are chosen, responsibility is best assured by providing a stipend, with a signed contract clearly naming the expectations. At least one representative from each remnant community needs to be chosen to form a coordination team that with the pastor/coordinator can make decisions affecting the whole, such as creating a budget and dispersing funds originally involved in sale of the church building and property.

Implementation

While this concrete plan is being created by the renewal core group(s), consultation needs to be made with the denominational leadership as specified by the respective polity. When ready, a congregational meeting is held where the remnant plan can be adopted and a decision made to sell the church building. Parts of the plan may need to be adjusted as indicated by that meeting. If the congregational vote is positive, the concrete proposal is then shared as to how the total congregation might be divided into remnant communities, giving time for swapping members between these groups, if for good reason. The congregation will need to set a date for the transitioning event (not a closing), with at least one member from each of the proposed communities serving as a committee to create a transitional liturgy of thanksgiving and promise. This event should include a thankful remembrance of the key happenings during the church's pilgrimage, a blessing of the objects to be transitioned, and a celebrative blessing of the next phase in the congregation's life. A date for the transitioning event is set, with an understanding that regular weekly congregational worship in the church building will end with that event. It is crucial that on the following Sunday the congregation worship at a new celebration center, if at all possible, with the remnant communities meeting the following week. There should be no interval time between the end of worship in the church building and the new beginning, for continuity is crucial to success.

A thesis undergirding this remnant plan is that the likelihood of success is greatly intensified by not beginning with step 7, the Practical Planning. Experience has indicated that efforts at keeping a diminishing congregation afloat is both demoralizing and sapping of energy, until, in fatigue, the desire is simply to have an end to it. But by establishing a spiritual deepening within a core nucleus, what is created is a faith sufficiently deep to energize an excited and committed determination.

A lake community outside Kansas City is providing something of a variant model for the remnant church. Twenty-five to thirty members now meet weekly in a community clubhouse, at no charge. They choose a lay leader every two years. At regular intervals, sign-up sheets are circulated: to volunteer as liturgists, to set up and take down items for worship, to supply flowers for the altar, and to provide coffee/treats at worship. One member is in charge of recording congregational funds, which are run through the local United Methodist Church district office. Two or three times each year, members have a short meeting to disburse surplus offering funds to select charities. Expenses are mostly for hiring two part-time retired clergypersons who alternate at worship, a pianist, and a monthly fee to the UMC district office for writing checks. Members have made a rolling cabinet for holding the hymnals and song notebooks, a movable lectern and altar, paraments, and a stained glass cross for the altar. One member is in charge of recruiting volunteers for soup kitchen duties, especially in providing holiday meals for the lonely. Another member has taken responsibility for purchasing coats for the city mission store and recruiting working shifts there as needed. A carload of volunteers takes a yearly mission trip with another church. One of the clergypersons in charge indicated that this is only a minimal model for congregational continuity, because it lacked the deepening of personal and communal spiritual growth that transition into a remnant community would have provided.

This remnant approach to ecclesiastical decline has implications as well for present-day seminaries. In the 1960s to 1980s at Saint Paul School of Theology in Kansas City where I taught, we developed a creative curriculum based on the premise that the radical cultural upheavals of the time needed to provide the impetus for and context in which to train full-time leaders to prepare the church for renewal through social justice engagement. But, as we have been exploring, today's societal context must be understood as being far different, thereby necessitating the training of leaders capable of preparing our churches for a countercultural survival mode, in which spiritual formation is foundational. This entails recognition that the presently available clientele for training tends to have limited financial resources, needs to maintain their present employment during training, cannot handle the large debt that traditional seminary education would involve, and, upon graduation, will have diminishing opportunities for full-time pastoral employment. Thus, with fewer persons able to participate in a traditional residential seminary education, there will need to be considerable online training, unfortunately with minimal opportunities for formation through covenant community and action-reflection experiences. Therefore, the educational focus needs to be on preparing each student to appropriate his/her own spiritual/theological credo version, shaped by engagement with the diverse contexts of the church's historical traditions. For this, there needs to be interactive online instruction in biblical theology and church/doctrinal history. Using tools rooted in personality diversity, such as the Myers-Briggs Personality Inventory and the Enneagram, can help in this personal appropriation. There needs to be some weeklong (or at least intensive weekends) team-taught units by a theologian and a practical specialist, having such themes as "Liturgy, Homiletics, and Religious Education"; "Spiritual Direction and Pastoral Care"; and "Mercy and Justice Ministries," as well as a unit in "Modern Society, Ecclesiastical Diminishment, and the Remnant Church." Each student would be expected to find a qualified spiritual director and be involved in local exposures to marginality and social need. There may also be need for a practicum in "Economic Preparation for Part-Time and Tent Ministry." Degree requirements leading to ordination should continue to be offered in spite of diminishing candidates, but requirements also need to be developed for certification in part-time ministry.

For the sake of final clarity, let us return to the book *The Underground Church* that, in spite of its promising title, I found disappointing. Robin Meyers does well in his repetitive insistence that "the American church is joined at the hip to a declining Empire."[16] But his answer is a humanistic Jesus who, as a teacher of nonviolent love, fosters compassion and justice for all, functioning as the basis for an alternative community. The book's dust jacket attempts to convince the reader that this proposal is daring, dangerous, explosive, and subversive, one that "could turn the world upside down." Yet, in the end, what we really have is a reechoing of optimistic social gospel liberalism. Instead of being subversive, it is actually supplemental, pinning together the frayed safety net of modern society. Not only is his model not seriously countercultural, but it has no interest in finding a way to perpetuate the theological heart of the gospel. Any success achieved by following Meyers's model would actually result in supporting modern society and, rather than reaching the unchurched, would most likely drain off frustrated liberals from existing congregations.

From a contrasting conservative perspective, we recently have Rod Dreher's *Benedict Option: A Strategy for Christians in a Post-Christian Nation*. Dreher calls upon conservative Christians to make a strategic withdrawal from public life, contending that progressives have unfortunately won the culture wars. Consequently, for the Christian right to continue fighting as a sub-culture is to waste its energies and resources over unwinnable battles. Instead, he proposes building communities, institutions, and networks of alternative resistance "that can outwit, outlast, and eventually overcome the occupation."[17] For this, he identifies monasteries as models— even though those of us who have been living monastically for many years know how precarious today's monasteries are, undergoing the same demise as the churches themselves. Furthermore, while monastic communities foster intensity of personal spirituality, few monks today regard themselves as significantly countercultural, witnessed in recent elections in how easily a one-issue perspective co-opted them. While there are some similarities between Dreher's proposal and the remnant plan, there is a fundamental difference. Dreher identifies the crisis situation as cultural, focusing on its

16. Robin Meyers, *Underground Church*, 8.

17. Dreher, *Benedict Option*, 12.

deteriorating impact on personal morality. The analysis with which we are basically concerned is structurally socioeconomic. Many of the cultural changes that I see as advancement, he deplores. Thus, his conservative version of Christianity insists that strenuous opposition to such matters as same-sex marriage must be a bedrock for faith—being "a core teaching of the Christian faith, . . . none more important to obey."[18] I do agree with Dreher on the internal thinness of many present-day churches, sharing with him a concern about how individual desire has become the basis for modern ethics and lamenting with him the loosening of communal ties. We agree as well that church and culture are colliding as both undergo steady decline and that Christians need to be faithful Christian disciples before being patriotic Americans. But his model does not honor theological diversity, and if retrenchment against some aspects of political correctness did occur, Dreher would seem quite content with the socioeconomic dynamics of our present society.

Another present expression of committed community that might suggest possible collaboration is new monasticism. Yet such experiments as described by Rory McEntee and Adam Bucko in their book *The New Monasticism* feel thin, tending to reflect the popular favoring of spirituality over against religion, existing outside the context of any particular religious tradition or faith context. Rather than presupposing any socioeconomic critique, the focus is on personal contemplative living and supportive community service.

CONCLUSION

The concerns addressed in this book have been sixfold:

1. To explore the contemporary diminishment of Christianity and the plight of the churches in light of the self-destructive dynamic threatening the future of our post-Christian society.

2. To understand what is left on which faith can rest, when the traditional motivations for Christian belief are being shredded.

3. To identify the burned of God as those who in our time are being called to birth a Christian remnant.

4. To establish viable postmodern minimalist beliefs on which to ground a faithful continuation of Christianity within the church.

18. Dreher, *Benedict Option*, 196.

5. To explore the Christian traditions for illumination regarding the problem of physical evil, which is a major modern conundrum inhibiting the faith wager.

6. To develop a model for developing a remnant church, whereby precarious congregations can begin now to prepare for continuity in a new form.

Jesus was critical of us, we who know "how to interpret the appearance of the sky but cannot interpret the signs of the times" (Matt 16:3). Yet with eyes and mind honed by wagering on the Christ event, we can interpret the signs. In so doing, there can emerge a remnant church able to trust the promise that "the powers of death shall not prevail against it" (Matt 16:18). Each evening, I begin the Eucharist with my own prayer that distills the heart of my Christian wager in attempting to preserve faithfully the heart of the Christian faith:

> Eternal God, with the saints and all your people on earth, we kneel here in unity with the whole of your beautiful but suffering creation and every speck within it—the creation which you hold in being, the creation into which you incarnate yourself, and the creation through which your Spirit yearns and lures and thrusts and urges all things toward completion as you become All in all. Accept these tokens of our work, the ponderings of our minds, and the yearnings of our souls, that united with Christ's sacrifice we raise to you this bread of life and this cup of forgiveness, praising you, blessing you, thanking you, making reparation to you, and interceding for all—especially those most in need of your healing in body, mind, spirit, and relationships. Then with your body and blood, nourish us into faithfulness to your promise of a new heaven and a new earth, that in all things your dream might be fulfilled. Amen.

BIBLIOGRAPHY

Abbott, Walter M. *The Documents of Vatican II.* New York: Guild Press, 1966.

Ackerman, Spencer. "DEA Sued over Secret Bulk Collection of Americans' Phone Records." *Guardian*, Apr. 8, 2015.

————. "West Point Professor Calls on US Military to Target Legal Critics of War on Terror." *Guardian*, Aug. 29, 2015.

Adamczyk, Alicia. "These Are the Odds You'll Win Tonight's $350 Million Powerball Jackpot." CNBC, June 1, 2019. https://www.cnbc.com/2019/05/31/these-are-the-odds-youll-win-the-350-million-powerball-jackpot.html.

Adams, John. "From John Adams to John Taylor, 17 December 1814." https://founders.archives.gov/documents/Adams/99-02-02-6371.

"Addressing the Youth Employment Crisis Needs Urgent Global Action." World Bank, Oct. 13, 2015. https://www.worldbank.org/en/news/press-release/2015/10/13/addressing-the-youth-employment-crisis-needs-urgent-global-action.

"The Age Gap in Religion around the World." Pew Research Center, June 13, 2018. https://www.pewforum.org/2018/06/13/the-age-gap-in-religion-around-the-world/.

Agence France-Presse. "Taiwan Hopes to Entice Brides with This Giant 'Shoe Church.'" Raw Story, Jan. 14, 2016. https://www.rawstory.com/2016/01/taiwan-hopes-to-entice-brides-with-this-giant-shoe-church/.

Agerholm, Harriet. "Donald Trump Wins: French Ambassador to the US Reacts by Posting Tweet Declaring the End of the World." *Independent*, Nov. 10, 2016.

Ahn, Christine. "Open Fire and Open Markets: The Asia-Pacific Pivot and Trans-Pacific Partnership." Truthout, Jan. 17, 2014. https://truthout.org/articles/open-fire-and-open-markets-the-asia-pacific-pivot-and-trans-pacific-partnership/.

Albright, Dann. "Average American Household Debt in 2020: Facts and Figures." Ascent, Nov. 18, 2020. https://www.fool.com/the-ascent/research/average-american-household-debt/.

Allen-Ebrahimian, Bethany. "Sixty-Four Years Later, CIA Finally Releases Details of Iranian Coup." FP, June 20, 2017. https://foreignpolicy.com/2017/06/20/64-years-later-cia-finally-releases-details-of-iranian-coup-iran-tehran-oil/.

Almond, Rosamund, et al., eds. "Living Planet Report 2020: Bending the Curve of Biodiversity Loss." https://www.zsl.org/sites/default/files/LPR%202020%20Full%20report.pdf.

Almukhtar, Sarah, and Rod Nordland. "What Did the U.S. Get for $2 Trillion in Afghanistan?" *New York Times*, Dec. 9, 2019.

Alston, Philip. "Extreme Poverty in America: Read the UN Special Monitor's Report." *Guardian*, Dec. 15, 2017.

Altizer, Thomas J. J., and William Hamilton. *Radical Theology and the Death of God.* New York: Bobbs-Merrill, 1966.

Amadeo, Kimberly. "US Military Budget, Its Components, Challenges, and Growth." Balance, Sept. 3, 2020. https://www.thebalance.com/u-s-military-budget-components-challenges-growth-3306320.

"American Redoubt." Wikipedia. https://en.wikipedia.org/wiki/American_Redoubt.

American Society of Plastic Surgeons. "Plastic Surgery Statistics Report." https://www.plasticsurgery.org/documents/News/Statistics/2019/plastic-surgery-statistics-report-2019.pdf.

"Americans' Views of Government: Low Trust, but Some Positive Performance Ratings." Pew Research Center, Sept. 14, 2020. https://www.pewresearch.org/politics/2020/09/14/americans-views-of-government-low-trust-but-some-positive-performance-ratings/.

"America's Changing Religious Landscape." Pew Research Center, May 12, 2015. https://www.pewforum.org/2015/05/12/americas-changing-religious-landscape/.

Amoros, Raul. "This Chart Shows the U.S. Border Security Spending by Year." Howmuch.net, July 16, 2019. https://howmuch.net/articles/the-cost-of-border-security-and-immigration-enforcement-in-the-us.

Anderson, Mark. "Trans-Pacific Partnership: Common Good or Corporate Good?" Seven Pillars Institute, July 28, 2015. https://sevenpillarsinstitute.org/trans-pacific-partnership-common-good-or-corporate-good/.

Anderson, Monica. "Fast Facts on Americans' Views about Social Media as Facebook Faces Legal Challenge." Pew Research Center, Dec. 10, 2020. https://www.pewresearch.org/fact-tank/2020/12/10/fast-facts-on-americans-views-about-social-media-as-facebook-faces-legal-challenge/.

———, and Jingjing Jiang. Pew Research Center, May 31, 2018. "Teens, Social Media and Technology 2018." https://www.pewresearch.org/internet/2018/05/31/teens-social-media-technology-2018/.

Anderson, Sarah, and Sam Pizzigati. "Executive Excess 2016: The Wall Street CEO Bonus Loophole." Institute for Policy Studies, Aug. 31, 2016. https://ips-dc.org/executive-excess-2016-wall-street-ceo-bonus-loophole/.

Anderson, Sherwood. *Winesburg, Ohio.* New York: Modern Library, 1919.

Angwin, Julia. *Dragnet Nation: A Quest for Privacy, Security, and Freedom in a World of Relentless Surveillance.* New York: St. Martin's Griffin, 2015.

Archives du Carmel de Lisieux. "Biography of Sr. Marie of the Trinity." https://www.archives-carmel-lisieux.fr/english/carmel/index.php/les-novices/marie-de-la-trinité/biography-of-sr-marie-of-the-trinity.

Arenge, Andrew, et al. "Poll: Majority of Millennials Are in Debt, Hitting Pause on Major Life Events." NBC News, Apr. 4, 2018. https://www.nbcnews.com/news/us-news/poll-majority-millennials-are-debt-hitting-pause-major-life-events-n862376.

Argenti, Paul. "The Biggest Culprit in VW's Emissions Scandal." Fortune, Oct. 13, 2015. https://fortune.com/2015/10/13/biggest-culprit-in-volkswagen-emissions-scandal/.

Aristotle. *The Basic Works of Aristotle*. Edited by Richard McKeon. New York: Random House, 1941.

Armiak, David, and Mary Bottari. "Kochs' 'Grassroots Leadership Academy' Is Training an Astroturf Army." Truthout, May 17, 2016. https://truthout.org/articles/kochs-grassroots-leadership-academy-training-astroturf-army/.

Armstrong, Karen. *Fields of Blood: Religion and the History of Violence*. New York: Anchor, 2015.

Armstrong, Robert, et al., eds. "Bio-Inspired Innovation and National Security." https://www.files.ethz.ch/isn/135637/Bio_Innovation_and_Nat_Sec.pdf.

Ash, Marc. "TPP: The Case for Treason." Reader Supported News, May 31, 2015. https://readersupportednews.org/opinion2/277-75/30480-tpp-the-case-for-treason.

Aspegren, Elinor. "Alabama Governor Quietly Signs Law Allowing Mega-Church a Private Police Force." *USA Today*, June 21, 2019.

Associated Press. "Before Venezuela, US Had Long Involvement in Latin America." AP News, Jan. 25, 2019. https://apnews.com/article/north-america-caribbean-ap-top-news-venezuela-honduras-2ded14659982426c9b2552827734be83.

———. "Curious Cops Snoop through Confidential Databases All the Time." *New York Post*, Sept. 28, 2016.

———. "Missouri Approves Concealed Guns at Schools and Open Carry in Public." *Guardian*, Sept. 11, 2014.

———. "New Year Brings New Lows as Bitter Cold Hits Much of US." *Washington Post*, Jan. 2, 2018.

"'Astoundingly Disturbing:' Obama Administration Claims Power to Wage Endless War Across the Globe." Democracy Now!, May 17, 2013. https://www.democracynow.org/2013/5/17/astoundingly_disturbing_obama_administration_claims_power.

Astor, Maggie. "Hottest April Day Ever Was Probably Monday in Pakistan: A Record 122.4°F." *New York Times*, May 4, 2018.

Aswell, Sarah. "Thirty-Four Grant Statistics for 2020." Submittable Blog, Oct. 20, 2020. https://blog.submittable.com/grant-statistics/.

Atkinson, Craig, dir. *Do Not Resist*. Brooklyn, NY: Vanish Films, 2016.

Attenborough, Richard, dir. *Shadowlands*. London: Carnival, 1993.

"Attorney General Shapiro Details Findings of Two-Year Grand Jury Investigation into Child Sex Abuse by Catholic Priests in Six Pennsylvania Dioceses." Office of Attorney General Josh Shapiro, Aug. 14, 2018. https://www.attorneygeneral.gov/taking-action/press-releases/attorney-general-shapiro-details-findings-of-2-year-grand-jury-investigation-into-child-sex-abuse-by-catholic-priests-in-six-pennsylvania-dioceses/.

Aubrey, Allison. "With Heavy Drinking on the Rise, How Much Is Too Much?" WBUR, Aug. 16, 2007. https://www.wbur.org/npr/543965637/women-who-love-wine-are-you-binge-drinking-without-realizing-it.

Auden, W. H. *Selected Poetry of W. H. Auden*. New York: Modern Library, 1959.

Auxier, Brooke, and Lee Rainie. "Key Takeaways on Americans' Views about Privacy, Surveillance and Data-Sharing." Pew Research Center, Nov. 15, 2019. https://www.pewresearch.org/fact-tank/2019/11/15/key-takeaways-on-americans-views-about-privacy-surveillance-and-data-sharing/.

Bacevich, Andrew. "'Under God': Same-Sex Marriage and Foreign Policy." Commonweal, July 6, 2015. https://www.commonwealmagazine.org/under-god.

Badham, Van. "It Hurts, but I'm Going to Defend Ashley Madison and 33 Million Adulterers." *Guardian*, July 21, 2015.

Bailey, Sarah Pulliam. "Books & Culture Survives Financial Crisis." Christian Century, Sept. 9, 2013. https://www.christiancentury.org/article/2013-09/christianity-today-s-books-culture-survives-chopping-block.

———. "Megachurch Pastor Steven Furtick's 'Spontaneous Baptisms' Not So Spontaneous." Reliigion News Service, Feb. 24, 2014. https://religionnews.com/2014/02/24/megachurch-pastor-steven-furticks-spontaneous-baptisms-spontaneous/.

Ball, James. "NSA Monitored Calls of Thirty-Five World Leaders after US Official Handed Over Contacts." *Guardian*, Oct. 25, 2013.

Ballard, Jamie. "In 2020, Do People See the American Dream as Attainable?" YouGovAmerica, July 18, 2020. https://today.yougov.com/topics/politics/articles-reports/2020/07/18/american-dream-attainable-poll-survey-data.

Balmer, Randall. "Doing Something for Self: The Evangelical Critique of Capitalism." Sojourners, Mar. 9, 2020. https://sojo.net/articles/how-did-we-get-here/doing-something-self-evangelical-critique-capitalism.

Bamford, James. "The Agency That Could Be Big Brother." *New York Times*, Dec. 25, 2005.

Barnhart, C. L., and Jess Stein, eds. *The American College Dictionary*. New York: Random House, 1967.

Bartels, Larry. "Your Genes Influence Your Political Views. So What?" *Washington Post*, Nov. 12, 2013.

Barth, Karl. *Dogmatics in Outline*. Translated by G. T. Thomson. London: SCM, 1949.

Barton, Bill. "Cops Killed Nearly Thirteen Times More People than Mass Shooters." Criminal Legal News, Mar. 18, 2020. https://www.criminallegalnews.org/news/2020/mar/18/cops-killed-nearly-13-times-more-people-mass-shooters/.

Bauman, Tristia, et al. "Housing Not Handcuffs: Ending the Criminalization of Homelessness in U.S. Cities." http://nlchp.org/wp-content/uploads/2018/10/Housing-Not-Handcuffs.pdf.

Bauman, Valerie. "Incarceration vs Education: America Spends More on Its Prison System than It Does on Public Schools—and California Is the Worst." *Daily Mail*, Oct. 25, 2018.

Beans, Laura. "Despite $93 Billion in Profits, Big Oil Demands Continued Tax Breaks." EcoWatch, Feb. 10, 2014. https://www.ecowatch.com/despite-93-billion-in-profits-big-oil-demands-continued-tax-breaks-1881859506.html.

Becker, Ernest. *The Denial of Death*. New York: Free, 1973.

Beckett, Samuel. *Waiting for Godot*. New York: Grove, 2011.

Beilke, Dustin. "Obama Administration Enables Billionaire Takeover of US Public Schools." Truthout, Jan. 24, 2016. https://truthout.org/articles/obama-administration-enables-billionaire-takeover-of-us-public-schools/.

Bell, Daniel M., Jr. *The Economy of Desire: Christianity and Capitalism in a Postmodern World*. Church and Postmodern Culture. Ada, MI: Baker Academic, 2012.

Bendavid, Naftali. "Europe's Empty Churches Go on Sale." *Wall Street Journal*, Jan. 2, 2015.

Benedict of Nursia. *The Rule of St. Benedict*. Collegeville, MN: Liturgical, 1981.

Benedict XVI, Pope. *Caritas in Veritate*. San Francisco: Ignatius, 2009.

Benjamin, Medea, et al. "Military Spending Has Many Points of Contention: Closing Overseas Bases Isn't One of Them." Hill, July 17, 2019. https://thehill.com/opinion/national-security/453486-military-spending-has-many-points-of-contention-closing-overseas.

Bennett, Jeannette N. "Fast Cash and Payday Loans." Federal Reserve Bank of St. Louis, Apr. 2019. https://research.stlouisfed.org/publications/page1-econ/2019/04/10/fast-cash-and-payday-loans.

Bennett, Kanya. "Three Hundred Sixty-Five Days and 605 Armored Military Vehicles Later: Police Militarization a Year After Ferguson." ACLU, Aug. 7, 2015. https://www.aclu.org/blog/criminal-law-reform/reforming-police/365-days-and-605-armored-military-vehicles-later-police.

Bennett-Smith, Meredith. "Womp! This Country Was Named the Greatest Threat to World Peace." HuffPost, Jan. 2, 2014. https://www.huffpost.com/entry/greatest-threat-world-peace-country_n_4531824.

Berardelli, Jeff. "Atlantic Ocean Circulation Is the Weakest in at Least 1,600 Years, Study Finds—Here's What That Means for the Climate." CBS News, Feb. 26, 2021. https://www.cbsnews.com/news/climate-change-atlantic-ocean-gulf-stream-system-amoc-weakest-1600-years/.

Berdyaev, Nicolas. The Beginning and the End. New York: Harper, 1952.

———. The Destiny of Man. London: Geoffrey Bles, 1949.

———. The Meaning of History. London: Geoffrey Bles, 1949.

Bergland, Christopher. "The Mystery of How Memories Form Just Got Less Mysterious." Psychology Today, Oct. 5, 2020. https://www.psychologytoday.com/us/blog/the-athletes-way/202010/the-mystery-how-memories-form-just-got-less-mysterious.

Bernard of Clairvaux. Bernard of Clairvaux: Selected Works. Translated by G. R. Evans. Classics of Western Spirituality. Mahwah, NJ: Paulist, 1987.

Best, Richard. "Lockheed Martin's Top Competitors (LMT)." Investopedia, updated Jan. 9, 2020. https://www.investopedia.com/articles/stock-analysis/081916/lockheed-martins-top-competitors-lmt.asp.

Beynon, Steve. "After Years of Failure to End the Crisis, Veteran Suicide Takes Center Stage on Capitol Hill." Stripes, Mar. 5, 2020. https://www.stripes.com/veterans/after-years-of-failure-to-end-the-crisis-veteran-suicide-takes-center-stage-on-capitol-hill-1.621428.

Bignell, Paul. "Secret Memos Expose Link between Oil Firms and Invasion of Iraq." Independent, May 10, 2016.

"Billion-Dollar Dynasties: These Are the Richest Families in America." Forbes, Dec. 17, 2020. https://www.forbes.com/sites/kerryadolan/2020/12/17/billion-dollar-dynasties-these-are-the-richest-families-in-america/?sh=450e56f2772c.

Bird, Warren. "How Many Megachurches? 1,750 in the United States." Leadership Network, May 22, 2012. https://leadnet.org/how_many_megachurches/.

———, and Scott Thumma. "Megachurch 2020: The Changing Reality in America's Largest Churches. Faith Communities Today." https://faithcommunitiestoday.org/wp-content/uploads/2020/10/Megachurch-Survey-Report_HIRR_FACT-2020.pdf.

Bivens, Josh, and Lawrence Mishel. "Understanding the Historic Divergence Between Productivity and a Typical Worker's Pay: Why It Matters and Why It's Real." Economic Policy Institute, Sept. 2, 2015. https://www.epi.org/publication/understanding-the-historic-divergence-between-productivity-and-a-typical-workers-pay-why-it-matters-and-why-its-real/.

Blessing, Elizabeth. "Trilateral Commission." Investopedia, updated Mar. 1, 2021. https://www.investopedia.com/terms/t/trilateralcommission.asp.

Board of Governors of the Federal Reserve System. "Report on the Economic Well-Being of U.S. Households in 2018." https://www.federalreserve.gov/publications/files/2018-report-economic-well-being-us-households-201905.pdf.

Boehlert, Eric. "What Shrinking Newsrooms Mean in the Age of the Koch Brothers and Billionaire Donors." HuffPost, Apr. 4, 2014; updated June 10, 2014. https://www.huffpost.com/entry/what-shrinking-newsrooms_b_5125760.

Bolen, Ed, et al. "More than 500,000 Adults Will Lose SNAP Benefits in 2016 as Waivers Expire." Center on Budget and Policy Priorities, updated Mar. 18, 2016. https://www.cbpp.org/research/food-assistance/more-than-500000-adults-will-lose-snap-benefits-in-2016-as-waivers-expire.

Bonhoeffer, Dietrich. Letters and Papers from Prison. Edited and translated by Eberhard Bethge. New York: Macmillan, 1965.

Bonifaz, John, and Ben Cohen. "There's Never Been a Better Time to Be a Corporation." Truthout, Feb. 1, 2015. https://truthout.org/articles/there-s-never-been-a-better-time-to-be-a-corporation/.

Bonnefoy, Pascale. "Documenting U.S. Role in Democracy's Fall and Dictator's Rise in Chile." New York Times, Oct. 14, 2017.

Bonnot, Bob. "Merging, Megasizing and Marriage: Regarding Parishes and Priests." Focus on Future Church 17, no. 1 (Summer 2015) 5.

Borden, Taylor, and Dominic-Madori Davis. "How Much Money You Need to Make to Live Comfortably in Every State in America." MooreNews.Net, Mar. 10, 2021. https://www.moorenews.net/articles/5/5/7060/How-Much-Money-You-Need-To-Make-To-Live-Comfortably-In-Every-State-In-America.html.

Borg, Marcus. The Heart of Christianity: Rediscovering a Life of Faith. New York: HarperOne, 2003.

———. Meeting Jesus Again for the First Time. San Francisco: Harper, 1995.

Bottum, Joseph. An Anxious Age: The Post-Protestant Ethic and the Spirit of America. New York: Image, 2014.

Bourie, Steve. "Casinos by State." https://www.americancasinoguidebook.com/casinos-by-state.html.

Bowler, Kate. Blessed: A History of the American Prosperity Gospel. Oxford, UK: Oxford University Press, 2013.

Bregman, Rutger. "The Solution to Just about Everything: Working Less." Correspondent, Apr. 22, 2016. https://thecorrespondent.com/4373/the-solution-to-just-about-everything-working-less/168119985-db3d3c10.

Briffault, Richard. "Election 2020 Sees Record $11 Billion in Campaign Spending—Mostly from a Handful of the Super-Rich." Salon, Oct. 16, 2020. https://www.salon.com/2020/10/16/election-2020-sees-record-11-billion-in-campaign-spending--mostly-from-a-handful-of-the-super-rich_partner/.

Broverman, Neal. "Nine Truly Terrible Reactions to the Orlando Shooting." Advocate, June 21, 2016. https://www.advocate.com/crime/2016/6/21/9-truly-terrible-reactions-orlando-shooting.

Browning, Elizabeth Barrett. The Complete Poetical Works of Elizabeth Barrett Browning. New York: Thomas Y. Crowell, n.d.

Brownstein, Ronald. "Trump Settles on His Reelection Message." Atlantic, Mar. 7, 2019.

Brueggemann, Walter. Finally Comes the Poet. Minneapolis: Fortress, 1989.

Buchanan, John M. "The History Channel's Violent God." Christian Century, Apr. 2, 2013. https://www.christiancentury.org/article/2013-03/bible-s-violent-god.
———. "Sustaining a Resource." Christian Century, June 28, 2013. https://www.christiancentury.org/article/2013-06/sustaining-resource.
Bullivant, Stephen. "Contemporary Catholicism in England and Wales: A Statistical Report Based on Recent British Social Attitudes Survey Data." https://www.stmarys.ac.uk/research/centres/benedict-xvi/docs/2018-feb-contemporary-catholicism-report-may16.pdf.
Bultmann, Rudolf. Jesus Christ and Mythology. New York: Charles Scribner's Son, 1958.
———. Kerygma and Myth. New York: Macmillan, 1957.
Bump, Philip. "Eighty-Six Percent of Trump Counties Make Less in a Year than Twenty-Seven Trump Staffers Are Worth." Washington Post, Apr. 1, 2017.
———. "The Twenty-Five Top Hedge Fund Managers Earn More than All Kindergarten Teachers Combined." Washington Post, May 10, 2016.
Burt, Chris. "Biometric Systems Market to Grow by Over $30B in Next Five Years, Report Says." BiometricUpdate.com, Dec. 10, 2020. https://www.biometricupdate.com/202012/biometric-systems-market-to-grow-by-over-30b-in-next-five-years-report-says.
Butler, Alban. Butler's Lives of the Saints. 13 vols. Collegeville, MN: Liturgical, 2010.
Butler, Katherine Anne. Knocking on Heaven's Door: The Path to a Better Way of Death. New York: Scribner, 2013.
Butler, Smedley. "Smedley Butler on Interventionism." https://fas.org/man/smedley.htm.
Buttrick, George A. The Interpreter's One-Volume Commentary on the Bible. Edited by Charles M. Laymon. Nashville: Abingdon, 1971.
Cachero, Paulina. "US Taxpayers Have Reportedly Paid an Average of $8,000 Each and Over $2 Trillion Total for the Iraq War Alone." Business Insider, Feb. 6, 2020. https://www.businessinsider.com/us-taxpayers-spent-8000-each-2-trillion-iraq-war-study-2020-2.
Camia, Catalina. "Mark Sanford Wins Special Election for Congress." USA Today, May 7, 2013.
Camp, Lee. "The Pentagon Failed Its Audit amid a $21 Trillion Scandal (Yes, Trillion)." Truthdig, Dec. 18, 2018. https://www.truthdig.com/articles/the-pentagon-failed-its-audit-amid-a-21-trillion-scandal-yes-trillion/.
Campbell, Andy. "Ocean Fish Populations Cut in Half Since the 1970s: Report." HuffPost, Sept. 16, 2015. https://www.huffpost.com/entry/crucial-marine-populations-cut-in-half-since-the-1970s-report_n_55f9ecd2e4b00310edf5b1b2.
Camus, Albert. The Myth of Sisyphus. Translated by Justin O'Brien. New York: Vintage, 1959.
———. The Plague. Translated by Stuart Gilbert. New York: Alfred A. Knopf, 1957.
"Canada's Changing Religious Landscape." Pew Research Center, June 27, 2013. https://www.pewforum.org/2013/06/27/canadas-changing-religious-landscape/.
Caplan, Bryan. The Case Against Education: Why the Education System Is a Waste of Time and Money. Princeton, NJ: Princeton University Press, 2018.
"Carbon Emissions of Richest 1 Percent More than Double the Emissions of the Poorest Half of Humanity." Oxfam International, Sept. 21, 2020. https://www.oxfam.org/en/press-releases/carbon-emissions-richest-1-percent-more-double-emissions-poorest-half-humanity.

Cardinale, Anthony, et al. "Fatima Crusade of Ft. Erie Priest Raises Church Ire Broadcasts Take in Millions, But Campaign Shows Deficit." *Buffalo News*, Jan. 6, 1991.

Carrington, Damian. "The Anthropocene Epoch: Scientists Declare Dawn of Human-Influenced Age." *Guardian*, Aug. 29, 2016.

———. "Plummeting Insect Numbers 'Threaten Collapse of Nature.'" *Guardian*, Feb. 10, 2019.

Carroll, Rory. "Welcome to Utah, the NSA's Desert Home for Eavesdropping on America." *Guardian*, June 14, 2013.

Carter, Stephen L. *The Culture of Disbelief: How American Law and Politics Trivialize Religious Devotion.* New York: Anchor, 1994.

Casper, Jayson. "The Top Fifty Countries Where It's Hardest to Be a Christian (2020)." Christianity Today, Jan. 13, 2021. https://www.christianitytoday.com/news/2021/january/christian-persecution-2021-countries-open-doors-watch-list.html.

Catholic News Agency Staff. "Survey Finds Correlation between Catholic Mass Attendance, Political Views." Catholic News Agency, Sept. 21, 2020. https://www.catholicnewsagency.com/news/45913/survey-finds-correlation-between-catholic-mass-attendance-political-views%C2%A0.

Ceniza-Levine, Caroline. "Ninety-Four Percent of New Jobs Created Share This One Trait—Are You Prepared?" Forbes, July 23, 2017. https://www.forbes.com/sites/carolinecenizalevine/2017/07/23/94-of-new-jobs-created-share-this-one-trait-are-you-prepared/?sh=6e92ebb8123c.

Center for Applied Research in the Apostolate. "Catholic Beliefs and Attitudes." https://cara.georgetown.edu/beliefattitude.pdf.

———. "Frequently Requested Church Statistics." http://cara.georgetown.edu/frequently-requested-church-statistics/.

———. "Sacraments Today: Belief and Practice among U.S. Catholics." https://cara.georgetown.edu/sacraments/.

Centers for Disease Control and Prevention. "About CDC's Opioid Prescribing Guideline." https://www.cdc.gov/drugoverdose/prescribing/guideline.html.

———. "All Injuries: Mortality." https://www.cdc.gov/nchs/fastats/injury.htm.

———. "Over Half of U.S. Teens Have Had Sexual Intercourse by Age 18, New Report Shows." https://www.cdc.gov/nchs/pressroom/nchs_press_releases/2017/201706_NSFG.htm.

———. "Prescription Opiods." https://www.cdc.gov/drugoverdose/opioids/prescribed.html.

———. "Suicide among Adults Aged 35–64 Years: United States, 1999–2010." https://www.cdc.gov/mmwr/preview/mmwrhtml/mm6217a1.htm.

Cha, Ariana Eunjung. "'Big Data' from Social Media, Elsewhere Online Take Trend-Watching to New Level." *Washington Post*, June 6, 2012.

Chan, Casey. "FBI Can Secretly Turn On Laptop Cameras without the Indicator Light." Gizmodo, Dec. 8, 2013. https://www.gizmodo.com.au/2013/12/fbi-can-secretly-activate-laptop-cameras-without-the-indicator-light/.

Chang, Alvin. "Sinclair's Takeover of Local News, in One Striking Map." Vox, Apr. 6, 2018. https://www.vox.com/2018/4/6/17202824/sinclair-tribune-map.

"The Changing Global Religious Landscape." Pew Research Center, Apr. 5, 2017. https://www.pewforum.org/2017/04/05/the-changing-global-religious-landscape/.

Charen, Mona. "Why Are Americans So Sad?" National Review, Nov. 30, 2018. https://www.nationalreview.com/2018/11/americans-suffer-diseases-of-despair-drug-addiction-suicide/.

Chaucer, Geoffrey. *The Canterbury Tales*. Translated by Neville Coghill. London: Penguin Classics, 2003.

Chetty, Raj, et al. "The Association between Income and Life Expectancy in the United States, 2001–2014." Jama Network, Apr. 26, 2016. https://jamanetwork.com/journals/jama/article-abstract/2513561.

Childress, Kyle. "Guns in the Pulpit." Christian Century, Mar. 7, 2016. https://www.christiancentury.org/article/2016-02/guns-pulpit.

"Choices Made Now Are Critical for the Future of Our Ocean and Cryosphere." Intergovernmental Panel on Climate Change, Sept. 25, 2019. https://www.ipcc.ch/2019/09/25/srocc-press-release/.

Chivers, C. J. "How Many Guns Did the U.S. Lose Track of in Iraq and Afghanistan? Hundreds of Thousands." *New York Times Magazine*, Aug. 24, 2016.

Christopher, Tommy. "Pastor Blames Colorado Floods on Gays, Marijuana, Abortions Offending 'Whoever Wrote the Bible.'" Mediaite, Sept. 21, 2013. https://www.mediaite.com/online/pastor-blames-colorado-floods-on-gays-marijuana-abortions-offending-whoever-wrote-the-bible/.

Church Pension Fund, eds. "Dies Irae." In *The Hymnal*, 76–77 (#65). Norwood, MA: Plimpton, 1933.

Citizens against Government Waste. "Critical Waste Issues for the 117th Congress." https://www.cagw.org/reporting/critical-waste-117.

Clark, Stuart. "Artificial Intelligence Could Spell End of Human Race—Stephen Hawking." *Guardian*, Dec. 2, 2014.

Clément, Olivier. *The Roots of Christian Mysticism: Texts from the Patristic Era with Commentary*. New York: New City, 1993.

Cohan, William D. "Jamie Dimon's $13 Billion Secret—Revealed." Vanity Fair, Sept. 6, 2017. https://www.vanityfair.com/news/2017/09/jamie-dimon-billion-dollar-secret-jp-morgan.

Cohen, Michael. "James Clapper Might as Well Be Called Director of US Fearmongering." *Guardian*, Feb. 6, 2014.

Cohen, Noam. *Know-It-Alls: The Rise of Silicon Valley as a Political Powerhouse and Social Wrecking Ball*. New York: New, 2017.

Cohen, Patricia. "Paychecks Lag as Profits Soar, and Prices Erode Wage Gains." *New York Times,* July 13, 2018.

Collins, Alan, and Adam Cox. "Bad Economic News Increases Suicide Rates—New Research." Conversation, May 29, 2019. https://theconversation.com/bad-economic-news-increases-suicide-rates-new-research-117228.

Collins, Chuck, et al. "Dreams Deferred: How Enriching the 1 Percent Widens the Racial Wealth Divide." https://ips-dc.org/racial-wealth-divide-2019/.

Conan, Neil. "Who Is Hezbollah?" NPR: Talk of the Nation, July 19, 2006. https://www.npr.org/transcripts/5568093.

Confessore, Nicholas. "Koch Brothers' Budget of $889 Million for 2016 Is on Par with Both Parties' Spending." *New York Times,* Jan. 26, 2015.

Congressional Budget Office. "Federal Net Interest Costs: A Primer." https://www.cbo.gov/publication/56780.

Congressional Research Service. "The U.S. Income Distribution: Trends and Issues." https://fas.org/sgp/crs/misc/R44705.pdf.

Consecrated Hearts. "A Prayer by St. Columban." https://consecratedhearts.com/prayers/a-prayer-by-saint-columban/.

"Correctional Facilities Industry in the US: Market Research Report." IBISWorld, updated July 28, 2021. https://www.ibisworld.com/united-states/market-research-reports/correctional-facilities-industry/.

Cooper, Helene. "Obama Nominates Gayle Smith to Lead U.S.A.I.D." *New York Times*, Apr. 30, 2015.

Copleston, Frederick. *A History of Philosophy*. 9 vols. Garden City, NJ: Doubleday, 1963.

"COVID-19 to Add as Many as 150 Million Extreme Poor by 2021." World Bank, Oct. 7, 2020. https://www.worldbank.org/en/news/press-release/2020/10/07/covid-19-to-add-as-many-as-150-million-extreme-poor-by-2021.

Cowell, Alan. "After 350 Years, Vatican Says Galileo Was Right: It Moves." *New York Times*, Oct. 31, 1992.

Cox, Daniel. "Way More Americans May Be Atheists than We Thought." FiveThirtyEight, May 18, 2017. https://fivethirtyeight.com/features/way-more-americans-may-be-atheists-than-we-thought/.

————, and Robert P. Jones. "America's Changing Religious Identity." PRRI, Sept. 6, 2017. https://www.prri.org/research/american-religious-landscape-christian-religiously-unaffiliated/.

Cox, Harvey. *The Market as God*. Cambridge, MA: Harvard University Press, 2016.

Cox, Jeff. "Deficit Projected at $2.3 Trillion for 2021, Not Counting Additional Stimulus, CBO Says." CNBC, Feb. 11, 2021. https://www.cnbc.com/2021/02/11/deficit-projected-at-2point3-trillion-for-2021-not-counting-additional-stimulus-cbo-says.html.

Crary, David. "Southern Baptists Ready to Put Spotlight on Sex-Abuse Crisis." National Catholic Reporter, Oct. 1, 2019. https://www.ncronline.org/news/accountability/southern-baptists-ready-put-spotlight-sex-abuse-crisis.

Creighton, Jolene. "Harvard Scientists Hold Secret Meeting Aimed at Creating a Synthetic Human Genome." Futurism, May 15, 2016. https://futurism.com/harvard-scientists-hold-secret-meeting-aimed-creating-synthetic-human-genome.

"Criminal Justice Facts." Sentencing Project. https://www.sentencingproject.org/criminal-justice-facts/.

Crocker, Richard R. Review of *An Anxious Age* by Joseph Bottum. Christian Century, Aug. 18, 2015. https://www.christiancentury.org/reviews/2015-08/anxious-age-joseph-bottum.

Cronan, Brenda. "Some 95 Percent of 2009–2012 Income Gains Went to Wealthiest 1 Percent." *Wall Street Journal*, Sept. 10, 2013.

Cross, Saint John of the. *Ascent of Mount Carmel*. Phoenix: Aquinas, 2017.

Crossan, John Dominic. *The Historical Jesus: The Life of a Mediterranean Jewish Peasant*. New York: HarperOne, 1993.

Curran, Ian. "Headed toward Christ: The Grand Narrative of Evolution." Christian Century, Mar. 17, 2016. https://www.christiancentury.org/article/2016-03/headed-toward-christ.

Curry, Andrew. "World's Oldest Temple to Be Restored." National Geographic, Jan. 20, 2016. https://www.nationalgeographic.com/travel/article/150120-gobekli-tepe-oldest-monument-turkey-archaeology.

Curtin, Joseph. "Let's Bag Plastic Bags." *New York Times*, Mar. 3, 2018.

Curtin, Sally, et al. "Increase in Suicide in the United States, 1999–2014." https://pubmed.ncbi.nlm.nih.gov/27111185/.

Cutten, George Barton. *The Threat of Leisure*. Whitefish, MT: Literary Licensing, 2011.

Daley, David. "'America as the No. One Warmonger": President Jimmy Carter Talks to *Salon* about Race, Cable News, 'Slut-Shaming' and More." Salon, Apr. 10, 2014. https://www.salon.com/2014/04/10/america_as_the_no_1_warmonger_president_jimmy_carter_talks_to_salon_about_race_cable_news_slut_shaming_and_more/.

Dart, John. "Church-Closing Rate Only 1 Percent: More Churning among Evangelicals." Christian Century, May 6, 2008. https://www.christiancentury.org/article/2008-05/church-closing-rate-only-one-percent.

———. "Seminaries Expand Online Options." Christian Century, Sept. 12, 2013. https://www.christiancentury.org/article/2013-09/seminaries-expand-online-options.

———. "UCC Has Been Progressive Pacesetter." Christian Century, July 18, 2013. https://www.christiancentury.org/article/2013-07/ucc-has-been-progressive-pacesetter.

Daugherty, Owen. "Sanders Asks Why Once-Free Drug Now Costs $375,000 a Year." Hill, Feb. 4, 2019. https://thehill.com/policy/healthcare/428318-sanders-questions-why-once-free-drug-now-costs-375000.

Davidson, Jordan. "Water Stress Could Affect Half the World's Population in Just Five Years." Nation of Change, Aug. 28, 2019. https://www.nationofchange.org/2019/08/28/water-stress-could-affect-half-the-worlds-population-in-just-5-years/.

Davies, Rob. "US Corporations Have $1.4tn Hidden in Tax Havens, Claims Oxfam Report." *Guardian*, Apr. 14, 2016.

Day, Dorothy. *The Long Loneliness: The Autobiography of Dorothy Day*. New York: HarperOne, 1996.

Dayen, David, and Rachel Cohen. "Amazon HQ2 Will Cost Taxpayers at Least $4.6 Billion, More than Twice What the Company Claimed, New Study Shows." Intercept, Nov. 15, 2018. https://theintercept.com/2018/11/15/amazon-hq2-long-island-city-virginia-subsidies/.

Dear, John. "The School of Prophets." National Catholic Reporter, Nov. 17, 2009. https://www.ncronline.org/blogs/road-peace/school-prophets.

Dearie, James. "Survey: Majority of Britons, Record High, Report Having No Religion." National Catholic Reporter, Sept. 7, 2017. https://www.ncronline.org/news/people/survey-majority-britons-record-high-report-having-no-religion.

DeBrabander, Firmin. *Do Guns Make Us Free?: Democracy and the Armed Society*. New Haven, CT: Yale University Press, 2015.

Decker, Steven. "Cold Weather Training: Embrace the Cold." US Army, Oct. 2, 2017. https://www.army.mil/article/194712/cold_weather_training_embrace_the_cold.

Deike, John. "Duke Energy Announces Coal Ash Spill Cleanup Will Take Two-Plus Years; Emails Show Collusion Between Regulators and NC Utility." EcoWatch, Mar. 14, 2014. https://www.ecowatch.com/duke-energy-announces-coal-ash-spill-cleanup-will-take-2-years-emails--1881877790.html.

Delbanco, Andrew. "Getting Real." *New York Times,* Jan. 29, 1995.

Delehanty, Casey, and Erin Kearns. "Wait, There's Torture in Zootopia?: Examining the Prevalence of Torture in Popular Movies." https://papers.ssrn.com/sol3/papers.cfm?abstract_id=3342908.

DenHoed, Andrea. "Josh Duggar's Ashley Madison Problem." *New Yorker,* Aug. 21, 2015.

Denver, John, and Mike Taylor. "Rocky Mountain High." New York: RCA Victor, 1972.

"Deputy Attorney General Sally Quillian Yates and FBI Director James B. Comey Deliver Statement before the Senate Judiciary Committee." United States Department of Justice, July 8, 2015. https://www.justice.gov/opa/speech/deputy-attorney-general-sally-quillian-yates-and-fbi-director-james-b-comey-deliver.

DeRoos, Dan. "ATF Releases the Number of Registered Machine Guns and Explosive Devices in Ohio." Nineteen News, updated Sept. 20, 2019. https://www.cleveland19.com/2019/09/20/atf-releases-number-registered-machine-guns-explosive-devices-ohio/.

Desjardins, Jeff. "U.S. Military Personnel Deployments by Country." Visual Capitalist, Mar. 18, 2017. https://www.visualcapitalist.com/u-s-military-personnel-deployments-country/.

De Witt, Bob. "Pittsburgh Diocese Plans to Close 60 Percent of Parishes by 2023." America: Jesuit Review, May 1, 2018. https://www.americamagazine.org/faith/2018/05/01/pittsburgh-diocese-plans-close-60-percent-parishes-2023.

Diamant, Jeff. "How Catholics around the World See Same-Sex Marriage, Homosexuality." Pew Research Center, Nov. 2, 2020. https://www.pewresearch.org/fact-tank/2020/11/02/how-catholics-around-the-world-see-same-sex-marriage-homosexuality/.

DiBenedetto, Bill. "NGO: Forty-Five Percent of Corporations Obstruct Climate Change Policy." Triple Pundit, Sept. 23, 2015. https://www.triplepundit.com/story/2015/ngo-45-percent-corporations-obstruct-climate-change-policy/31751.

Digangi, Christine. "Americans Are Dying with an Average of $62K of Debt." ABC News, Mar. 25, 2017. https://abcnews.go.com/Business/americans-dying-average-62k-debt/story?id=46323519.

Dillard, Annie. *Pilgrim at Tinker Creek.* New York: Bantam, 1974.

Disilver, Drew. "Global Inequality: How the U.S. Compares." Pew Research Center, Dec. 19, 2013. https://www.pewresearch.org/fact-tank/2013/12/19/global-inequality-how-the-u-s-compares/.

Dixon, Amanda. "Adding It Up: Here's How Much Americans Spend on Financial Vices." Bankrate, Sept. 12, 2018. https://www.bankrate.com/personal-finance/smart-money/financial-vices-september-2018/.

Dixon, Jennifer. "Michigan Spends $1B on Charter Schools but Fails to Hold Them Accountable." *Detroit Free Press,* June 22, 2014; updated Jan. 16, 2017. https://www.freep.com/story/news/local/michigan/2014/06/22/michigan-spends-1b-on-charter-schools-but-fails-to-hold/77155074/.

Dochuk, Darren. *From Bible Belt to Sunbelt: Plain-Folk Religion, Grassroots Politics, and the Rise of Evangelical Conservatism.* New York: W. W. Norton, 2012.

Dostoevsky, Fydor. *The Brothers Karamazov.* Translated by Constance Garnett. New York: Random, 1950.

———. *Crime and Punishment.* Translated by Constance Garnett. New York: Dell, 1959.

Doughty, Caitlin. *Smoke Gets in Your Eyes: And Other Lessons from the Crematory*. New York: W. W. Norton, 2015.

Drake, Bruce. "Six New Findings about Millennials." Pew Research Center, Mar. 7, 2014. https://www.pewresearch.org/fact-tank/2014/03/07/6-new-findings-about-millennials/.

Draper, Robert. "They are Watching You—and Everything Else on the Planet." *National Geographic*, Feb. 2018. https://www.nationalgeographic.com/magazine/article/surveillance-watching-you.

Drawbaugh, Kevin. "Seven Big U.S. Companies Paid CEOs More than Uncle Sam in 2013: Study." https://www.reuters.com/article/us-usa-tax-ceopay/seven-big-u-s-companies-paid-ceos-more-than-uncle-sam-in-2013-study-idUSKCN0J20CJ20141118.

Dreher, Rod. "Christianity in Collapse." American Conservative, May 12, 2015. https://www.theamericanconservative.com/dreher/christianity-in-collapse-benedict-option/.

———. *The Benedict Option: A Strategy for Christians in a Post-Christian Nation*. New York: Penguin Random House, 2017.

Drutman, Lee. "The Political 1 Percent of the 1 Percent in 2012." Sunlight Foundation, June 24, 2013. https://sunlightfoundation.com/2013/06/24/1pct_of_the_1pct/.

———. "What We Get Wrong about Lobbying and Corruption." *Washington Post*, Apr. 16, 2015.

Dubay, Thomas. *The Fire within: St. Teresa of Avila, St. John of the Cross, and the Gospel on Prayer*. San Francisco: Ignatius, 1989.

Dunham, Will. "Methane-Spewing Microbe Blamed in Earth's Worst Mass Extinction." Scientific American, Mar. 31, 2014. https://www.scientificamerican.com/article/methane-spewing-microbe-blamed-in-earths-worst-mass-extinction/.

———. "Most Distant Star Ever Detected Sits Halfway across the Universe." Reuters, Apr. 2, 2018. https://www.reuters.com/article/us-space-icarus/most-distant-star-ever-detected-sits-halfway-across-the-universe-idUSKCN1H921F.

Dutton, Kevin. *The Wisdom of Psychopaths: What Saints, Spies, and Serial Killers Can Teach Us about Success*. New York: FSG Adult, 2013.

Eagle, David. "More People, Looser Ties: Social Life in the Megachurch." Christian Century, Apr. 8, 2016. https://www.christiancentury.org/article/2016-03/more-people-looser-ties.

"Easter Mid-Morning Hymn." In *Prayer for Mid-Morning and Mid-Afternoon*, 19. Internal booklet of Assumption Abbey, Ava, MO, 2014.

Edwards, Jonathan. *Sinners in the Hands of an Angry God*. Alachua, FL: Bridge-Logos, 2003.

Egan, Matt. "Thirty Percent of Bank Jobs Are under Threat." CNN, Apr. 4, 2016. https://money.cnn.com/2016/04/04/investing/bank-jobs-dying-automation-citigroup/.

Eliot, T. S. *Complete Poems and Plays*. New York: Harcourt Brace, 1952.

Elliott, Debbie. "David Vitter, Running For Governor, Accused of Being 'Wrong on Fornication.'" NPR, Oct. 15, 2015. https://www.npr.org/sections/itsallpolitics/2015/10/15/448967752/david-vitter-running-for-governor-accused-of-being-wrong-on-fornication.

Ellsberg, Daniel. *The Doomsday Machine: Confessions of a Nuclear War Planner*. New York: Bloomsbury, 2017.

Ellsberg, Robert. *All Saints: Daily Reflections on Saints, Prophets, and Witnesses for Our Time*. New York: Crossroad, 1997.

Ellsmoor, James. "United States Spend Ten Times More On Fossil Fuel Subsidies than Education." Forbes, June 15, 2019. https://www.forbes.com/sites/jamesellsmoor/2019/06/15/united-states-spend-ten-times-more-on-fossil-fuel-subsidies-than-education/?sh=b7c07d644735.

Engelhaupt, Erika. "Meet Your Face's Tiny Tenants." *National Geographic*, May 2020. https://www.nationalgeographic.com/magazine/article/face-mites-the-tiny-tenants-that-likely-live-in-your-pores.

Environmental Working Group. "The Pollution in People: Cancer-Causing Chemicals in Americans' Bodies." https://www.ewg.org/research/pollution-people.

Esteves, Junno Arocho. "Vatican Statistics Show Decline in Number of Consecrated Men and Women between 2013–2018." Crux, Mar. 26, 2020. https://cruxnow.com/vatican/2020/03/vatican-statistics-show-decline-in-number-of-consecrated-men-women-between-2013-2018/.

"Euthanasia." Britannica ProCon.Org. https://euthanasia.procon.org/opinion-polls-surveys/#rasmussen.

Evers-Hillstrom, Karl. "Majority of Lawmakers in 116th Congress Are Millionaires." Open Secrets, Apr. 23, 2020. https://www.opensecrets.org/news/2020/04/majority-of-lawmakers-millionaires/.

———. "State of Money in Politics: The Price of Victory Is Steep." Open Secrets, Feb. 19, 2019. https://www.opensecrets.org/news/2019/02/state-of-money-in-politics-the-price-of-victory-is-steep/.

Everstine, Brian. "U.S. Approved More than $175 Billion in Weapons Sales in 2020." Airforce Magazine, Dec. 4, 2020. https://www.airforcemag.com/u-s-approved-more-than-175-billion-in-weapons-sales-in-2020/.

"Facts about the Priest Shortage, Optional Celibacy, and Women's Roles." https://www.futurechurch.org/future-of-priestly-ministry/optional-celibacy/facts-about-priest-shortage-optional-celibacy-and.

"The Facts of Life Sentences." Sentencing Project, Dec. 2018. https://www.sentencingproject.org/wp-content/uploads/2018/12/Facts-of-Life.pdf.

Fahmy, Dalia. "Eight Key Findings about Catholics and Abortion." Pew Research Center, Oct. 20, 2020. https://www.pewresearch.org/fact-tank/2020/10/20/8-key-findings-about-catholics-and-abortion/.

Fang, Lee. "CIA'S Venture Capital Arm Is Funding Skin Care Products That Collect DNA." Reader Supported News, Apr. 9, 2016. https://readersupportednews.org/news-section2/318-66/36231-cias-venture-capital-arm-is-funding-skin-care-products-that-collect-dna.

———. "Lobbyists for Spies Appointed to Oversee Spying." Intercept, Apr. 9, 2015. https://theintercept.com/2015/04/09/lobbyists-for-spies-appointed-to-oversee-spying/.

———. "TV Pundits Praising Suleimani Assassination Neglect to Disclose Ties to Arms Industry." Intercept, Jan. 6, 2020. https://theintercept.com/2020/01/06/iran-suleimani-tv-pundits-weapons-industry/.

Farand, Chloe. "US Has Regressed to Developing Nation Status, MIT Economist Warns." *Independent*, Apr. 21, 2017.

Farhi, Paul. "National Geographic Gives Fox Control of Media Assets in $725 Million Deal." *Washington Post*, Sept. 9, 2015.

Fass, Sarah, et al. "Child Poverty and Intergenerational Mobility." National Center for Children in Poverty, Dec. 2009. https://www.nccp.org/publication/child-poverty-and-intergenerational-mobility/.

"Fatal Drug Overdoses Hit a Record High Last Year. COVID-19 Is Making the Problem Worse." Advisory Board, July 17, 2020. https://www.advisory.com/daily-briefing/2020/07/17/overdose.

Feeding America. "Facts about Poverty and Hunger in America." https://www.feedingamerica.org/hunger-in-america/facts.

Fenster, Andrea. "New Data: Solitary Confinement Increases Risk of Premature Death after Release." Prison Policy Initiative, Oct. 13, 2020. https://www.prisonpolicy.org/blog/2020/10/13/solitary_mortality_risk/.

Ferdman, Roberto. "The Most American Thing There Is: Eating Alone." *Washington Post*, Aug. 18, 2015.

Ferner, Matt. "Former Military Chief: Iraq War Was a 'Failure' That Helped Create ISIS." HuffPost, Nov. 30, 2015. https://www.huffpost.com/entry/iraq-war-isis-michael-flynn_n_565c83a9e4b079b2818af89c.

Fessenden, Marissa. "Asteroid Impacts Once Made the Earth's Oceans Boil for a Whole Year." Smithsonian Magazine, May 18, 2015. https://www.smithsonianmag.com/smart-news/asteroid-impacts-once-made-earths-oceans-boil-whole-year-180955332/.

"Few Catholics See Contraceptive Use as Morally Wrong." Pew Research Center, Feb. 27, 2012. https://www.pewresearch.org/fact-tank/2012/02/27/few-catholics-see-contraceptive-use-as-morally-wrong/.

Fifield, Anna. "Contractors Reap $138bn from Iraq War." Financial Times, Mar. 18, 2013. https://www.ft.com/content/7f435f04-8c05-11e2-b001-00144feabdc0.

"The Fight over Obama's Trade Deal." Scrbd, May 22, 2015. https://www.scribd.com/document/383835336/The-Week-May-22-2015.

Fitzpatrick, John, and Peter Marra. "The Crisis for Birds Is a Crisis for Us All." *New York Times*, Sept. 19, 2019.

Flanders, Laura. "Peter Buffett: Big Philanthropy and Philanthro-Feudalism." Truthout, Dec. 1, 2013. https://truthout.org/video/peter-buffett-big-philanthropy-and-philanthro-feudalism/.

Fleming, Victor, dir. *The Wizard of Oz*. New York: Loew's, 1939.

Fletcher, Joseph F. *Situation Ethics: The New Morality*. Philadelphia: Westminster, 1966.

Folkenflik, David. "Disgraced Governor Eliot Spitzer to Co-Host CNN Show with Kathleen Parker." NPR, June 23, 2010. https://www.npr.org/sections/thetwo-way/2010/06/23/128030622/disgraced-governor-eliot-spitzer-to-co-host-cnn-show-with-kathleen-parker.

Folley, Aris. "Top Oil Firms Have Spent $1B on Branding, Lobbying Since Paris Agreement: Study." Hill, Mar. 27, 2019. https://thehill.com/policy/energy-environment/436117-top-oil-firms-spend-millions-on-lobbying-to-block-climate-change.

Ford, George H., ed. *Selected Poems of John Keats*. New York: Appleton-Century-Croft, 1950.

Ford, Glen. "US Funds 'Terror Studies' to Dissect and Neutralize Social Movements." Truthout, June 22, 2014. https://truthout.org/articles/us-funds-terror-studies-to-dissect-and-neutralize-social-movements/.

Ford, Lucy. "L'Oscar Hotel Review: A Former Church in London's Theatreland That's Become a Saucily Decadent Place to Stay." Country Life, Dec. 3, 2019. https://www.countrylife.co.uk/travel/weekends-away/loscar-hotel-review-former-church-londons-theatreland-thats-become-saucily-decadent-place-stay-208674.

Forde, Kaelyn. "The Other Student Debt: US Kids Struggle to Pay for School Meals." Aljazeera, Sept. 27, 2019. https://www.aljazeera.com/economy/2019/9/27/the-other-student-debt-us-kids-struggle-to-pay-for-school-meals.

Forsyth, P. T. The Soul of Prayer. Vancouver, BC: Regent College Publishing, 2002.

Fottrell, Quentin. "Fortune 500 CEOs Are Paid from Double to 5,000 Times More than Their Employees." MarketWatch, May 19, 2018. https://www.marketwatch.com/story/fortune-500-ceos-are-paid-from-double-to-5000-times-more-than-their-employees-2018-05-16.

Fowler, James W. Stages of Faith: The Psychology of Human Development and the Quest for Meaning. San Francisco: HarperCollins, 1995.

Fox, Matthew. "On the Fiftieth Anniversary of Thomas Merton's Death." Matthew Fox, Dec. 9, 2018. https://www.matthewfox.org/blog/on-the-50th-anniversary-of-thomas-mertons-death.

Francis, David. "How the U.S. Lost Billions over Nine Years in Iraq." CNBC, June 19, 2014. https://www.cnbc.com/2014/06/19/how-the-us-lost-billions-over-nine-years-in-iraq.html.

Francis, Pope. The Joy of the Gospel. Washington, DC: United States Conference of Catholic Bishops, 2013.

———. Laudato sì (On Care for our Common Home). Washington, DC: United States Conference of Catholic Bishops, 2015.

———. "Transcript: Pope Francis's Speech to Congress." Washington Post, Sept. 24, 2015.

———. "'Urbi et Orbi' Message of His Holiness Pope Francis." Vatican, Dec. 25, 2018. https://www.vatican.va/content/francesco/en/messages/urbi/documents/papa-francesco_20181225_urbi-et-orbi-natale.html.

Fraser, Steve. The Age of Acquiescence: The Life and Death of American Resistance to Organized Wealth. New York: Basic Books, 2016.

Frazee, Gretchen. "Did Trump's Tax Cuts Boost Hiring? Most Companies Say No." PBS, Jan. 28, 2019. https://www.pbs.org/newshour/economy/making-sense/did-trumps-tax-cuts-boost-hiring-most-companies-say-no.

Frei, Hans W. The Eclipse of Biblical Narrative: A Study in Eighteenth- and Nineteenth-Century Hermeneutics. New Haven, CT: Yale University Press, 1974.

French, David. "Make America Live Again." National Review, Nov. 29, 2018. https://www.nationalreview.com/2018/11/declining-life-expectancy-in-america/,

Frenkel, Sheera. "Iranian Authorities Block Access to Social Media Tools." New York Times, Jan. 2, 2018.

Friedersdorf, Conor. "What Do Donald Trump Voters Actually Want?" Atlantic, Aug. 17, 2015. https://www.theatlantic.com/politics/archive/2015/08/donald-trump-voters/401408/.

Friedman, Milton. "A Friedman Doctrine—the Social Responsibility of Business Is to Increase Its Profits." New York Times, Sept. 13, 1970.

Friedman, Thomas L. "A Manifesto for the Fast World." New York Times Magazine, Mar. 28, 1999.

Friedman, Zack. "Fifty Percent of Millennials Are Moving Back Home with Their Parents after College." Forbes, June 6, 2019. https://www.forbes.com/sites/zackfriedman/2019/06/06/millennials-move-back-home-college/?sh=60868311638a/.

———. "Seventy-Eight Percent of Workers Live Paycheck to Paycheck." Forbes, Jan. 11, 2019. https://www.forbes.com/sites/zackfriedman/2019/01/11/live-paycheck-to-paycheck-government-shutdown/?sh=1a073c164f10.

———. "Student Loan Debt Statistics In 2021: A Record $1.7 Trillion." Forbes, Feb. 20, 2021. https://www.forbes.com/sites/zackfriedman/2021/02/20/student-loan-debt-statistics-in-2021-a-record-17-trillion/?sh=4c8457714310.

Frost, Michael. *Exiles: Living Missionally in a Post-Christian Culture.* Grand Rapids: Baker Books, 2006.

"Fully Staffed, New U.S. Cyber Command Teams Look to Deploy Artificial Intelligence." MeriTalk, Dec. 1, 2017. https://www.meritalk.com/articles/fully-staffed-new-us-cyber-command-teams-look-to-deploy-artificial-intelligence/.

Fuchs, Erin. "ACLU Sues Government Over 'Dragnet' Surveillance of Americans." Business Insider Australia, June 12, 2013. https://www.businessinsider.com.au/aclu-sues-over-prism-2013-6.

Fukuyama, Francis. *The End of History and the Last Man.* New York: Free, 1992.

Fung, Brian. "Cellphone Users Nationwide Just received a 'Presidential Alert.' Here's What to Know." *Washington Post,* Oct. 4, 2018.

Funk, Robert W. *The Five Gospels: What Did Jesus Really Say?* New York: HarperOne, 1996.

Gabbatiss, Josh. "US Military Wants to Use Sea Creatures as Underwater Spies to Monitor Enemy Activity." *Independent,* Apr. 1, 2019.

Galant, Michael. "Honduran Labor Fight Reveals Exploitation behind the Migrant Crisis." Truthout, May 23, 2019. https://truthout.org/articles/honduran-labor-fight-reveals-exploitation-behind-the-migrant-crisis/.

Galbraith, John Kenneth. *American Capitalism: The Concept of Countervailing Power.* Oxfordshire, UK: Routledge, 2017.

Gallagher, Ryan, and Glenn Greenwald. "How the NSA Plans to Infect 'Millions' of Computers with Malware." Intercept, Mar. 12, 2014. https://theintercept.com/2014/03/12/nsa-plans-infect-millions-computers-malware/.

Garcia, Feliks. "US Government Spent over $500m on Fake Al-Qaeda Propaganda Videos That Tracked Location of Viewers." *Independent,* Oct. 6, 2016.

Gardner, Marilyn. "The Elusive Search for 'Golden Age of Leisure.'" *Christian Science Monitor,* Mar. 20, 1997.

Gardner, Matthew, et al. "Corporate Tax Avoidance Remains Rampant under New Tax Law." https://itep.sfo2.digitaloceanspaces.com/04119-Corporate-Tax-Avoidance-Remains-Rampant-Under-New-Tax-Law_ITEP.pdf.

Gardner, W. H., and N. H. Mackenzie, eds. *The Poems of Gerard Manley Hopkins.* New York: Oxford University Press, 1967.

Gelineau, Joseph. *Psalms: A New Translation; Singing Version.* New York: Paulist, 1963.

Gelles, David. "The Mind Business." Financial Times, Aug. 12, 2014. https://www.ft.com/content/d9cb7940-ebea-11e1-985a-00144feab49a.

George, Susan. *Shadow Sovereigns: How Global Corporations Are Seizing Power.* Cambridge, UK: Polity, 2015.

Gerard, Leo. "Who Is Killing American Manufacturing?" IndustryWeek, Feb. 23, 2016. https://www.industryweek.com/talent/article/21982448/who-is-killing-american -manufacturing.

Gerson, Joseph. *Empire and the Bomb: How the U.S. Uses Nuclear Bombs to Dominate the World*. Ann Arbor, MI: Pluto, 2007.

Gibney, Alex, dir. *Zero Days*. New York: Magnolia, 2016.

Gibson, David. "Archbishop Chaput Welcomes 'Smaller Church' of Holier Catholics." National Catholic Reporter, Oct. 21, 2016. https://www.ncronline.org/news/ people/philadelphia-archbishop-chaput-welcomes-smaller-church-holier- catholics.

————. "U.S. Nuns Haunted by Dead Jesuit: The Ghost of Pierre Teilhard de Chardin." *Washington Post*, May 22, 2014.

Gilens, Martin, and Benjamin Page. "Critics Argued with Our Analysis of U.S. Political Inequality. Here Are Five Ways They're Wrong." *Washington Post*, May 23, 2016.

Gillam, Carey. "Weedkiller 'Raises Risk of Non-Hodgkin Lymphoma by 41 Percent.'" *Guardian*, Feb. 14, 2019.

Gillum, Jack. "FBI behind Mysterious Surveillance Aircraft over US Cities." AP News, June 2, 2015. https://apnews.com/article/4b3f220e33b64123a3909c60845da045.

Giroux, Henry. *America's Addiction to Terrorism*. New York: Monthly Review, 2015.

Giving USA. *Giving USA 2020: The Annual Report on Philanthropy for the Year 2019*. https://givingusa.org/giving-usa-2020-charitable-giving-showed-solid-growth- climbing-to-449-64-billion-in-2019-one-of-the-highest-years-for-giving-on- record/.

Glendinning, Victoria. "Talk with Rebecca West." *New York Times*, Oct. 2, 1977.

Glenn, Heidi. "As Social Issues Drive Young From Church, Leaders Try To Keep Them." STLPR, Jan. 18, 2013. https://news.stlpublicradio.org/2013-01-18/as-social- issues-drive-young-from-church-leaders-try-to-keep-them.

"Global Antibiotics 'Revolution' Needed." BBC News, May 19, 2016. https://www.bbc. com/news/health-36321394.

"The Global Religious Landscape." Pew Research Center, Dec. 18, 2012. https://www. pewforum.org/2012/12/18/global-religious-landscape-exec/.

Goethe, Johann Wolfgang von. *Goethe's Faust*. Translated by Walter Kaufmann. New York: Anchor, 1962.

Goitein, Elizabeth. "How the FBI Violated the Privacy Rights of Tens of Thousands of Americans." Brennan Center for Justic, Oct. 22, 2019. https://www.brennancenter. org/our-work/analysis-opinion/how-fbi-violated-privacy-rights-tens-thousands- americans.

Gokhale, Ketake. "The Same Pill That Costs $1,000 in the U.S. Sells for $4 in India." *Chicago Tribune*, Jan. 4, 2016.

Goldenberg, Suzanne. "Half of All US Food Produce Is Thrown Away, New Research Suggests." *Guardian*, July 13, 2016.

Gombrich, E. F. *The Story of Art*. New York: Phaidon, 1950.

Gonzalez, Juan, and Amy Goodman. "Snowden Documents: NSA Technology Lets the Government Generate Transcripts of Private Phone Calls." Truthout, May 7, 2015. https://truthout.org/video/snowden-documents-nsa-technology-lets-the- government-generate-transcripts-of-private-phone-calls/.

Goodman, Amy, with Denis Moynihan. "Corporate Lobbyists Flood Warsaw Climate Talks." Democracy Now!, Nov. 21, 2013. https://www.democracynow.org/2013/11/21/corporate_lobbyists_flood_warsaw_climate_talks.

Goodstein, Laurie. "Poll Shows Major Shift in Identity of U.S. Jews." New York Times, Oct. 1, 2013.

Gore, Al. "Four Hundred PPM." HuffPost, May 10, 2013; updated July 10, 2013. https://www.huffpost.com/entry/carbon-dioxide-400-parts-per-million_b_3253361.

Gotsch, Kara. "Families and Mass Incarceration." Sentencing Project, Apr. 24, 2018. https://www.sentencingproject.org/publications/6148/.

Gottschalk, Marie. Caught: The Prison State and the Lockdown of American Politics. Princeton, NJ: Princeton University Press, 2016.

Gould, Elise. "Job Openings Surged in March as the Economy Continues to Recover from the Pandemic." Economic Policy Institute: Working Economics Blog, May 11, 2021. https://www.epi.org/blog/job-openings-surged-in-march-as-the-economy-continues-to-recover-from-the-pandemic/.

Gould, Stephen Jay. Wonderful Life: The Burgess Shale and the Nature of History. New York: W. W. Norton, 1990.

Graeber, David. Bullshit Jobs: A Theory. New York: Simon & Schuster, 2018.

Granquist, Mark. "Ways to Be Lutheran: New Churches Experiment with Polity." Christian Century, Apr. 4, 2014. https://www.christiancentury.org/article/2014-03/ways-be-lutheran/.

Grant, Tobin. "Analysis: Seven Point Five Million Americans Lost Their Religion Since 2012." https://religionnews.com/2015/03/12/analysis-7-5-million-americans-lost-religion-since-2012/.

Grazier, Dan. "The Littoral Combat Ship and the Folly of Concurrency." POGO, July 17, 2020. https://www.pogo.org/analysis/2020/07/the-littoral-combat-ship-and-the-folly-of-concurrency/.

———. "Smaller Budgets Will Result in a More Effective Military." POGO, Apr. 10, 2019. https://www.pogo.org/testimony/2019/04/smaller-budgets-will-result-in-a-more-effective-military/.

"Great Barrier Reef Has Lost Half of Its Corals Since 1995." BBC News, Oct. 14, 2020. https://www.bbc.com/news/world-australia-54533971.

Green, Erica, and Stephanie Saul. "What Charles Koch and Other Donors to George Mason University Got for Their Money." New York Times, May 5, 2018.

Green, Vivian Hubert Howard. John Wesley. Lanham, MD: University Press of America, 1987.

Greenberg, Andy. Sandworm: A New Era of Cyberwar and the Hunt for the Kremlin's Most Dangerous Hackers. New York: Doubleday, 2019.

Greenberg, Jon. "Kristof: U.S. Imprisons Blacks at Rates Higher than South Africa during Apartheid." Politifact, Dec. 11, 2014. https://www.politifact.com/factchecks/2014/dec/11/nicholas-kristof/kristof-us-imprisons-blacks-rates-higher-south-afr/.

Greenblatt, Alan. "Median CEO Pay Tops $10 Million For The First Time." WESA, May 27, 2014. https://www.wesa.fm/national-international-news/2014-05-27/median-ceo-pay-tops-10-million-for-the-first-time.

Greene, Amanda. "What Would Jesus Brew? Lots, Beer Makers Say." Washington Post, Mar. 23, 2012.

Greene, Leonard. "Critics See 'Gay Bullying' at Seminaries." New York Post, Mar. 24, 2002.

Greenfieldboyce, Nell. "Light Pollution Hides Milky Way from 80 Percent of North Americans, Atlas Shows." NPR, June 10, 2016. https://www.npr.org/sections/thetwo-way/2016/06/10/481545778/light-pollution-hides-milky-way-from-80-percent-of-north-americans-atlas-shows.

Greenwald, Glenn. "Facebook Is Collaborating with the Israeli Government to Determine What Should Be Censored." Intercept, Sept. 12, 2016. https://theintercept.com/2016/09/12/facebook-is-collaborating-with-the-israeli-government-to-determine-what-should-be-censored/.

———. "NSA Collecting Phone Records of Millions of Verizon Customers Daily." *Guardian*, June 6, 2013.

Gregg, Aaron. "Navy to Pay $22 Billion for Nine Nuclear-Powered Submarines." *Washington Post*, Dec. 2, 2019.

Gross, Andrew. "Nearly 80 Percent of Drivers Express Significant Anger, Aggression or Road Rage." AAA, July 14, 2016. https://newsroom.aaa.com/2016/07/nearly-80-percent-of-drivers-express-significant-anger-aggression-or-road-rage/.

Grossman, Cathy Lynn. "After Long Slump, Number of Catholic Seminarians on the Rise." Christian Century, Oct. 10, 2013. https://www.christiancentury.org/article/2013-10/after-long-slump-number-catholic-seminarians-rise.

———. "Christians in Decline, Nones on the Rise." Christian Century, May 13, 2015. https://www.christiancentury.org/article/2015-05/christians-lose-ground-nones-soar-new-portrait-us-religion.

———. "Christians Lose Ground, 'Nones' Soar in New Portrait of US Religion." *Washington Post*, May 12, 2015.

———. "Obama: Defeating Poverty Takes Money and 'Transformative Power' of Faith Groups." *Washington Post*, May 12, 2015.

———. "Tracking the 'Nominals.'" Christian Century, Oct. 10, 2013. https://www.christiancentury.org/article/2013-10/tracking-nominals.

Grundy, Trevor. "Methodists in England Like an Iceberg . . . Crumbling into the Sea." Religion News Service, Sept. 2, 2014. https://religionnews.com/2014/09/02/methodists-england-like-iceberg-crumbling-sea/.

Gryboski, Michael. "Disciples of Christ on Track to Lose Half of Its Membership in Ten Years." Christian Post, Aug. 25, 2019. https://www.christianpost.com/news/disciples-of-christ-on-track-to-lose-half-of-its-membership-in-10-years.html.

Hahn, Heather. "US Dips below Majority of Membership." UM News, Nov. 25, 2019. https://www.umnews.org/en/news/us-dips-below-majority-of-membership.

Haider, Areeba. "The Basic Facts about Children in Poverty." Center for American Progress, Jan. 12, 2021. https://www.americanprogress.org/issues/poverty/reports/2021/01/12/494506/basic-facts-children-poverty/.

Haisley, Emily, et al. "Subjective Relative Income and Lottery Ticket Purchases." *Journal of Behavioral Decision Making* 21 (2008) 283–95.

Hall, Shannon. "Exxon Knew about Climate Change Almost Forty Years Ago." Scientific American, Oct. 26, 2015. https://www.scientificamerican.com/article/exxon-knew-about-climate-change-almost-40-years-ago/.

———. "NASA: Earth's Poles Are Tipping Thanks to Climate Change." PBS, Apr. 8, 2016. https://www.pbs.org/newshour/science/nasa-earths-poles-are-tipping-thanks-to-climate-change.

Halsey, Ashley, III. "House Republicans Move Ahead with Plan to Shift 38,000 FAA Workers." *Washington Post*, Feb. 11, 2016.

Hamilton, Isobel Asher. "Bulletproof Panels, Private Jets, and Rumored Secret Passages: What It Costs to Protect the World's Richest Tech Moguls." Business Insider Africa, May 25, 2019. https://africa.businessinsider.com/tech/bulletproof-panels-private-jets-and-rumored-secret-passages-heres-what-it-costs-to/n9enhsy.

Hanauer, Nick, and David Rolf. "The Top 1 Percent of Americans Have Taken $50 Trillion From the Bottom 90 Percent—and That's Made the U.S. Less Secure." Time, Sept. 14, 2020. https://time.com/5888024/50-trillion-income-inequality-america/.

Handwerk, Brian. "Hundreds of Galaxies Were Found Hiding behind Our Milky Way." *Smithsonian Magazine,* Feb. 9, 2016. https://www.smithsonianmag.com/science-nature/hundreds-galaxies-were-found-hiding-behind-our-milky-way-180958078/.

Hansen, Chuck. "The Oops List: Why Won't the Government Come Clean about Its Nuclear Weapons Accidents?" *Bulletin of the Atomic Scientists* 56, no. 6 (Nov.–Dec. 2000) 64–67.

Hansler, Jennifer. "Pompeo: Melting Sea Ice Presents 'New Opportunities for Trade.'" CNN, May 7, 2019. https://www.cnn.com/2019/05/06/politics/pompeo-sea-ice-arctic-council/index.html.

Harari, Yuval Noah. *Homo Deus.* New York: Harper, 2017.

Hare, Kristen. "More than Eighty-Five Local Newsrooms Closed during the Coronavirus Pandemic." Poynter, Aug. 31, 2021. https://www.poynter.org/locally/2021/the-coronavirus-has-closed-more-than-60-local-newsrooms-across-america-and-counting/.

Harkness, Georgia Elma. *Georgia Harkness: The Remaking of a Liberal Theologian.* Edited by Rebekah Miles. Louisville, KY: Westminster John Knox Press, 2010.

Harnack, Adolf von. *What Is Christianity?* Translated by Thomas Bailey Saunders. New York: Harper and Brothers, 1957.

"Harper's Index." *Harper's Magazine,* Apr. 2013. https://harpers.org/archive/2013/04/harpers-index-349/.

———. *Harper's Magazine,* Nov. 2018. https://harpers.org/harpers-index/?issue_month=11&issue_year=2018.

Harrington, Brooke. "Panama Papers: The Real Scandal Is What's Legal." Atlantic, Apr. 6, 2016. https://www.theatlantic.com/business/archive/2016/04/panama-papers-crimes/477156/.

Harrington, James C, and Sidney G. Hall III. *Three Mystics Walk into a Tavern: A Once and Future Meeting of Rumi, Meister Eckhart, and Moses de León in Medieval Venice.* Lanham, MD: Hamilton, 2015.

Harris, Katelynn. "Forty Years of Falling Manufacturing Employment." *Beyond the Numbers* 9, no. 16 (Nov. 2020). https://www.bls.gov/opub/btn/volume-9/forty-years-of-falling-manufacturing-employment.htm.

Harrison, David. "American Consumers Shun Plastic but Borrow More for Homes and Cars, Fed Report Shows." *Wall Street Journal,* Nov. 17, 2020.

Harter, Jim. "Employee Engagement on the Rise in the U.S." Gallup, Aug. 26, 2018. https://news.gallup.com/poll/241649/employee-engagement-rise.aspx.

Hart-Landsberg, Martin. "Security Guards Outnumber High School Teachers in the United States." Pacific Standard, Mar. 27, 2014; updated May 3, 2017. https://psmag.com/education/security-guards-outnumber-high-school-teachers-united-states-77475.

Hart Research and Echelon Insights. *The Shriver Report Snapshot: Catholics in America.* http://www.shrivermedia.com/wp-content/uploads/2015/09/Key-Findings-from-Poll-of-Catholics.pdf.

Hartshorne, Charles. *The Divine Relativity: A Social Conception of God.* New Haven, CT: Yale University Press, 1948.

Hartt, Julian. *Christian Critique of American Culture: An Essay in Practial Theology.* New York: Harper and Row, 1967.

Hartung, William D. "The Obama Administration Has Brokered More Weapons Sales than Any Other Administration Since World War II." Nation, July 26, 2016. https://www.thenation.com/article/archive/the-obama-administration-has-sold-more-weapons-than-any-other-administration-since-world-war-ii/.

———. "The Pentagon's War on Accountability." Le Monde Diplomatique, May 25, 2016. https://mondediplo.com/openpage/the-pentagon-s-war-on-accountability.

Harwell, Drew, and Craig Timberg. "How America's Surveillance Networks Helped the FBI Catch the Capitol Mob." *Washington Post,* Apr. 2, 2021.

Hauerwas, Stanley. *The Peaceable Kingdom: A Primer in Christian Ethics.* Notre Dame, IN: University of Notre Dame Press, 1983.

———, and William Willimon. *Resident Aliens: Life in the Christian Colony.* Nashville: Abingdon, 2014.

Heath, Brad. "New Police Radars Can 'See' inside Homes." *USA Today,* Jan. 19, 2015.

Hedges, Chris. "An Interview with Julian Assange." Nation, May 8, 2013. https://www.thenation.com/article/archive/interview-julian-assange/.

———. "The Last Gasp of American Democracy." Truthdig, Jan. 6, 2014. https://www.truthdig.com/articles/the-last-gasp-of-american-democracy/.

Heeb, Gina. "National Debt Set to Become Larger than the Entire U.S. Economy, CBO Says." Forbes, Feb. 11, 2021. https://www.forbes.com/sites/ginaheeb/2021/02/11/national-debt-set-to-become-larger-than-the-entire-us-economy-cbo-says/?sh=115ac2bb1e8e.

Hegel, Georg W. F. *The Philosophy of Right.* Mineola, NY: Dover, 2005.

Heitzenrater, Richard P. *The Elusive Mr. Wesley.* 2 vols. Nashville: Abingdon, 1984.

Helgeland, Brian, dir. *Forty-Two.* Burbank, CA: Legendary, 2013.

Henderson, Peter. "Kochs Help Republicans Catch Up on Technology." Reuters, May 17, 2012. https://www.reuters.com/article/us-usa-politics-kochs/kochs-help-republicans-catch-up-on-technology-idUKBRE84G0E820120517.

Hendricks, Mike. "New Plan Emerges for St. Paul School of Theology Campus." *Kansas City Star,* Oct. 9, 2013.

Henney, Megan. "Amazon Earned $5.6B in 2017, but Paid No Federal Taxes." FOX Business, Feb. 27, 2018. https://www.foxbusiness.com/markets/amazon-earned-5-6b-in-2017-but-paid-no-federal-taxes.

Herbst, Jeffrey. "The Algorithm Is an Editor." *Wall Street Journal,* Apr. 13, 2016.

Hess, Abigail Johnson. "U.S. Student Debt Has Increased by More than 100 Percent over the Past Ten Years." CNBC Make It, Dec. 22, 2020. https://www.cnbc.com/2020/12/22/us-student-debt-has-increased-by-more-than-100percent-over-past-10-years.html.

Hicap, Jonah. "Churches in Sweden Offering 'Drop-In Weddings' Struggle to Keep Up with Demand." Christian Today, June 20, 2016. https://www.christiantoday.com/article/churches-in-sweden-offering-drop-in-weddings-struggle-to-meet-demand/88815.htm.

Higgins, Lori. "Can School Vouchers Give Kids a Shot at a Better Education?" *Detroit Free Press,* Jan. 14, 2017.

"Highly Sensitive Tactile E-Whiskers for Robotics, Other Applications." Homeland Security News Wire, Jan. 22, 2014. http://www.homelandsecuritynewswire.com/dr20140122-highly-sensitive-tactile-ewhiskers-for-robotics-other-applications.

Hilarion of Volokolamsk. "The Teaching of St. John Cassian on the Eucharist and the Communion." https://mospat.ru/en/news/49981/.

Hiller, Arthur, dir. *Man of La Mancha.* Beverly Hills, CA: United Artists, 1972.

"History." https://churchbrew.com/history/.

Hitchens, Christopher. "The Dogmatic Doubter." Newsweek, Sept. 9, 2007. https://www.newsweek.com/dogmatic-doubter-100329.

Hobson, Theo. *Reinventing Liberal Christianity.* Grand Rapids: Eerdmans, 2013.

Hogan, Mack. "What We Know about the 'Mother of All Bombs' That Was Dropped on Afghanistan." CNBC, Apr. 13, 2017. https://www.cnbc.com/2017/04/13/what-we-know-about-the-mother-all-bombs-that-was-dropped-on-afghanistan.html.

Hornsby, Travis. "Student Loan Debt Statistics in 2021: A Look at the Numbers." Student Loan Planner, updated Jan. 19, 2021. https://www.studentloanplanner.com/student-loan-debt-statistics-average-student-loan-debt/.

Horowitz, Juliana, et al. "Most Americans Say There Is Too Much Economic Inequality in the U.S., but Fewer than Half Call It a Top Priority." Pew Research Center, Jan. 9, 2020. https://www.pewresearch.org/social-trends/2020/01/09/most-americans-say-there-is-too-much-economic-inequality-in-the-u-s-but-fewer-than-half-call-it-a-top-priority/.

Horton, Alex, and Aaron Gregg. "Use of Military Contractors Shrouds True Costs of War. Washington Wants It That Way, Study Says." *Washington Post,* June 30, 2020.

Hout, Michael. "Social Mobility." https://inequality.stanford.edu/sites/default/files/Pathways_SOTU_2019_SocialMobility.pdf.

"How Many Millionaires Are There in America?" DQYDJ, July 10, 2021. https://dqydj.com/how-many-millionaires-decamillionaires-america/.

Howell, James C. "In Defense of Church." Christian Century, Feb. 25, 2013. https://www.christiancentury.org/reviews/2013-02/defense-church.

Howell, Kellan. "Pentagon Admits Operating Military Drone Flights over U.S." *Washington Times,* Mar. 9, 2016.

Human Rights Watch. "USA and Torture: A History of Hypocrisy." Human Rights Watch, Dec. 9, 2014. https://www.hrw.org/news/2014/12/09/usa-and-torture-history-hypocrisy.

Hunnicutt, Benjamin Kline. *Kellogg's Six-Hour Day.* Labor and Social Change. Philadelphia: Temple University Press, 1996.

Hurlbut, Jesse Lyman. *Hurlbut's Story of the Bible.* Ithaca, NY: Yesterday's Classics, 2007.

Hutchinson, Peter, et al., dirs. *Requiem for the American Dream.* New York: Naked City, 2015.

Hyman, Louis. "Opinion: What Does Labor Day Mean in a Gig Economy?" *Los Angeles Times,* Sept. 2, 2019. https://www.latimes.com/opinion/story/2019-08-30/labor-day-gig-economy-unions-history.

Hymnal Revision Committee, ed. *United Methodist Hymnal.* Nashville: United Methodist, 1989.

Igielnik, Ruth, and Kim Parker. "Majorities of U.S. Veterans, Public Say the Wars in Iraq and Afghanistan Were Not Worth Fighting." Pew Research Center, July 10, 2019. https://www.pewresearch.org/fact-tank/2019/07/10/majorities-of-u-s-veterans-public-say-the-wars-in-iraq-and-afghanistan-were-not-worth-fighting/.

"In U.S., Decline of Christianity Continues at a Rapid Pace." Pew Research Center, Oct. 17, 2019. https://www.pewforum.org/2019/10/17/in-u-s-decline-of-christianity-continues-at-rapid-pace/.

"Income, Poverty and Health Insurance Coverage in the United States: 2019." United States Census Bureau, Sept. 15, 2020. https://www.census.gov/newsroom/press-releases/2020/income-poverty.html.

Ingraham, Christopher. "Amazon Paid No Federal Taxes on $11.2 Billion in Profits Last year." *Washington Post,* Feb. 16, 2019.

———. "For the First Time in History, U.S. Billionaires Paid a Lower Tax Rate than the Working Class Last Year." *Washington Post,* Oct. 8, 2019.

———. "Just 3 Percent of Adults Own Half of America's Guns." *Washington Post,* Sept. 19, 2016.

———. "One in Eight American Adults Is an Alcoholic, Study Says." *Washington Post,* Aug. 11, 2017.

———. "The Richest 1 Percent Now Owns More of the Country's Wealth than at Any Time in the Past Fifty Years." *Washington Post,* Dec. 6, 2017.

———. "Somebody Just Put a Price Tag on the 2016 Election. It's a Doozy." *Washington Post,* Apr. 14, 2017.

———. "There Are More Guns than People in the United States, According to a New Study of Global Firearm Ownership." *Washington Post,* June 19, 2018.

———. "There Are Now More Guns than People in the United States." *Washington Post,* Oct. 5, 2105.

Institute on Taxation and Economic Policy. "Corporate Tax Avoidance Remains Rampant under New Tax Law." ITEP, Apr. 11, 2019. https://itep.org/notadime/.

Insurance Information Institute. "Facts Plus Statistics: Aggressive Driving." https://www.iii.org/fact-statistic/facts-statistics-aggressive-driving.

International Commission on English in the Liturgy. *Liturgy of the Hours.* 4 vols. New York: Catholic Book, 1976.

———. *The Roman Missal.* Washington, DC: U.S. Conference of Catholic Bishops, 2008.

International Physicians for the Prevention of Nuclear War. "Body Count: Casualty Figures after Ten Years of the 'War on Terror': Iraq, Afghanistan, Pakistan." Translated by Ali Fathollah-Nejad. https://www.psr.org/wp-content/uploads/2018/05/body-count.pdf.

Irion, Robert. "It All Began in Chaos." *National Geographic,* July 2013. https://www.nationalgeographic.com/magazine/article/125-solar-system.

"Israel's Religiously Divided Society." Pew Research Center, Mar. 8, 2016. https://www.pewforum.org/2016/03/08/israels-religiously-divided-society/.

Jackson, Griffin Paul. "The Seven People Christians Trust More than Their Pastors." *Christianity Today,* Jan. 4, 2019. https://www.christianitytoday.com/news/2019/january/gallup-pastor-clergy-trust-professions-poll.html.

Jacobs, Ken, et al. "Producing Poverty: the Public Cost of Low Wage Production Jobs in Manufacturing." https://laborcenter.berkeley.edu/pdf/2016/Producing-Poverty.pdf.

Jacoby, Jeff. "How the Religious Right Embraced Trump and Lost Its Moral Authority." *Boston Globe,* Oct. 14, 2016.

Jaimungal, Candice. "Most Young Americans Are Afraid of Losing Their Jobs." YouGovAmerica, July 9, 2020. https://today.yougov.com/topics/economy/articles-reports/2020/07/09/most-young-americans-are-afraid-losing-their-jobs.

James, William. *The Varieties of Religious Experience*. New York: Random House, 1902.

———. *The Will to Believe*. Harlow, UK: Longmans, Green, 1896.

Jamison, Leslie, and Charles McGrath. "In the Age of Memoir, What's the Legacy of the Confessional Mode?" *New York Times Book Review*, Sept. 29, 2015.

Jan, Tracy. "Thirteen Million People in Poverty Are Disconnected from the Social Safety Net. Most of Them Are White." *Washington Post*, Feb. 4, 2019.

"January 2020 Was Earth's Hottest January on Record." National Oceanic and Atmospheric Administration, Feb. 13, 2020. https://www.noaa.gov/news/january-2020-was-earth-s-hottest-january-on-record.

Jaschik, Scott. "The Shrinking Humanities Major." Inside Higher Ed, Mar. 14, 2016. https://www.insidehighered.com/news/2016/03/14/study-shows-87-decline-humanities-bachelors-degrees-2-years.

Jefferson, Thomas. "To James Madison from Thomas Jefferson, 28 October 1785." https://founders.archives.gov/documents/Madison/01-08-02-0202.

Jenkins, Philip. "Decline and Revival in the Church of England." Christian Century, May 31, 2019. https://www.christiancentury.org/article/notes-global-church/decline-and-revival-church-england.

———. "Empty Buddhist Temples in Japan." Christian Century, May 5, 2016. https://www.christiancentury.org/article/2016-04/empty-temples-japan.

———. "The Irish Nones." Christian Century, July 5, 2013. https://www.christiancentury.org/article/2013-06/irish-nones.

———. "Secular South Africa?" Christian Century, Jan. 23, 2014. https://www.christiancentury.org/article/2014-01/secular-south-africa.

Jerman, Jenna, et al. "Characteristics of U.S. Abortion Patients in 2014 and Changes Since 2008." Guttmacher Institute, May 2016. https://www.guttmacher.org/report/characteristics-us-abortion-patients-2014.

"Jesus Christ's Return to Earth." Pew Research Center, July 14, 2010. https://www.pewresearch.org/fact-tank/2010/07/14/jesus-christs-return-to-earth/.

John, Tara. "Truman Capote's Ashes Sold at Auction for $43,750." Time, Sept. 26, 2016. https://time.com/4507458/truman-capotes-ashes-auction/.

John of the Cross. *The Collected Works of St. John of the Cross*. Translated by Kieran Kavanaugh and Otilio Rodriguez. Rev. ed. Washington, DC: ICS Publications, 2010.

John Paul II, Pope. *Catechism of the Catholic Church*. 2nd ed. Washington, DC: U.S. Catholic Conference, 2007.

Johnston, Ian. "How Plastic Is Damaging Planet Earth." *Independent*, Sept. 28, 2017.

Jonas, Hans. "The Concept of God after Auschwitz." In *Wrestling with God: Jewish Theological Responses during and after the Holocaust*, edited by Steven T. Katz et al., 628–36. New York: Oxford University Press, 2007.

Jones, Alison. "Oxytocin Enhances Spirituality, New Study Says." Duke Today, Sept. 20, 2016. https://today.duke.edu/2016/09/oxytocin-enhances-spirituality-new-study-says.

Jones, Beth Felker. "Jane Austen in California." Christian Century, May 20, 2013. https://www.christiancentury.org/reviews/2013-05/jane-austen-california.

———. "What Girls Want." Christian Century, Feb. 7, 2014. https://www.christian century.org/article/2014-01/what-girls-want.

Jones, Jeffrey M. "Is Marriage Becoming Irrelevant?" Gallup, Dec. 28, 2020. https:// news.gallup.com/poll/316223/fewer-say-important-parents-married.aspx.

———. "U.S. Church Membership Down Sharply in Past Two Decades." Gallup, Apr. 18, 2019. https://news.gallup.com/poll/248837/church-membership-down-sharply-past-two-decades.aspx.

Jones, Rick. "PC(USA) Statistics Show a Leveling Off in Membership Decline." Presbyterian Church (USA), May 28, 2020. https://www.pcusa.org/news/2020/5/28/pcusa-statistics-show-leveling-membership-decline/.

Jones, Robert P. "Do You Believe? Americans Less Likely to Believe in Historical Accuracy of Christmas Story than a Decade Ago." Religion News Service, Dec. 17, 2013. https://religionnews.com/2013/12/17/believe-americans-less-likely-believe-historical-accuracy-christmas-story-decade-ago/.

Jones, W. Paul. The Art of Spiritual Direction: Giving and Receiving Spiritual Guidance. Nashville: Upper Room, 2002.

———. Theological Worlds: Understanding the Alternative Rhythms of Christian Belief. Nashville: Abingdon, 1989.

———. Worlds within a Congregation: Dealing with Theological Diversity. Nashville: Abingdon, 2000.

Joustra, Robert, and Alissa M. Wilkinson. How to Survive the Apocalypse: Zombies, Cylons, Faith, and Politics at the End of the World. Grand Rapids: Eerdmans, 2016.

Jouvenal, Justin. "The New Way Police Are Surveilling You: Calculating Your Threat 'Score.'" Washington Post, Jan. 10, 2016.

Joyce, James. Ulysses. New York: Modern Library, 1946.

Kaeble, Danielle, and Mariel Alper. "Probation and Parole in the United States, 2017–2018." Bureau of Justic Statistics, Aug. 2020. https://bjs.ojp.gov/library/publications/probation-and-parole-united-states-2017-2018.

Kafka, Franz. The Castle. Translated by Willa and Edwin Muir. New York: Alfred A. Knopf, 1953.

———. The Trial. Translated by Willa and Edwin Muir. New York: Alfred A. Knopf, 1954.

Kaldveer, Zack. "U.S. and Monsanto Dominate Global Market for GM Seeds." Organic Consumers Association, Aug. 7, 2013. https://www.organicconsumers.org/essays/us-and-monsanto-dominate-global-market-gm-seeds.

Kant, Immanuel. Critique of Practical Reason. Translated by Lewis White Beck. New York: Liberal Arts, 1956.

———. Critique of Pure Reason. Translated by John Meiklejohn. New York: E. P. Dutton, 1946.

Kantor, Jodi, and David Streitfeld. "Inside Amazon: Wrestling Big Ideas in a Bruising Workplace." New York Times, Aug. 15, 2015.

Kaplan, Sarah, and Ben Guarino. "Scientists Detect Gravitational Waves from a New Kind of Nova, Sparking a New Era in Astronomy." Washington Post, Oct. 16, 2017.

Karlin, Mark. "It's Time to Call the 'American Dream' What It Is: A Commodified Myth." BuzzFlash, May 5, 2016. http://legacy.buzzflash.com/commentary/it-s-time-to-re-evaluate-the-american-dream-as-another-commoditized-goal.

Kasperkevic, Jana. "Value of Gun Manufacturers' Stocks Almost Doubled in 2015." Guardian, Dec. 31, 2015.

Kay, Grace. "Walmart CEO Says the Retail Giant Isn't Raising Its Minimum Wage to $15 per Hour to Keep 'Ladder of Opportunity.'" https://www.businessinsider.com/walmart-pay-minimum-wage-ceo-why-not-15-per-hour-2021-2.

Kazantzakis, Nikos. *The Odyssey: A Modern Sequel.* Translated by Kimon Friar. New York: Simon and Schuster, 1950.

———. *The Saviors of God: Spiritual Exercises.* Translated by Kimon Friar. New York: Simon and Schuster, 1966.

Kecmanovic, Jelena. "Could Our Efforts to Avoid Anxiety Only Be Making It Worse?" *Washington Post,* July 10, 2019.

"Keeping It on the Company Campus." Economist, May 16, 2015. https://www.economist.com/business/2015/05/16/keeping-it-on-the-company-campus.

Kelly, Jack. "U.S. Lost Over 60 Million Jobs—Now Robots, Tech And Artificial Intelligence Will Take Millions More." Forbes, Oct. 27, 2020. https://www.forbes.com/sites/jackkelly/2020/10/27/us-lost-over-60-million-jobs-now-robots-tech-and-artificial-intelligence-will-take-millions-more/?sh=11ae19841a52.

Kelly, Sharon. "Teflon's Toxic Legacy: DuPont Knew for Decades It Was Contaminating Water Supplies." EcoWatch, Jan. 4, 2016. https://www.ecowatch.com/teflons-toxic-legacy-dupont-knew-for-decades-it-was-contaminating-wate-1882142514.html.

Kelty, Matthew. *Aspects of the Monastic Calling.* Trappist, KY: Abbey of Gethsemani, 1968.

Kennedy, Sean. "The F-35 May Be Unsalvageable." Hill, Mar. 26, 2021. https://thehill.com/blogs/congress-blog/economy-budget/545040-the-f-35-may-be-unsalvageable.

Kennel-Shank, Celeste. "Forming Priests among the People." Christian Century, Feb. 2, 2017. https://www.christiancentury.org/article/forming-priests-among-people.

Kertzer, David. *The Pope and Mussolini: The Secret History of Pius XI and the Rise of Fascism in Europe.* London: Random House, 2014.

Keshner, Andrew. "CEOs Are Paid 278 Times More than the Average U.S. Worker." MarketWatch, Aug. 31, 2019. https://www.marketwatch.com/story/ceos-are-paid-278-times-more-than-the-average-us-worker-2019-08-15.

Kessler, Glenn. "Trump Made 30,573 False or Misleading Claims as President. Nearly Half Came in His Final Year." *Washington Post,* Jan. 23, 2021.

Ketwig, John. "Fiftieth Anniversary Commemoration vs. Truth." *Veteran* 45, no. 1 (Spring 2015) 1–2.

Kierkegaard, Soren. *Fear and Trembling.* Translated by Walter Lowrie. Princeton, NJ: Princeton University Press, 1941.

———. *The Sickness unto Death.* Translated by Walter Lowrie. Princeton, NJ: Princeton University Press, 1946.

King, Neil, Jr. "Evangelical Leader Preaches Pullback From Politics, Culture Wars." *Wall Street Journal,* Oct. 21, 2013.

Kingsbury, Katie. "Big Data: Not-So-Wealthy Republicans." *Boston Globe,* June 29, 2018.

Kinzer, Stephen. "Frustrating the War Lobby." *Boston Globe,* Sept. 14, 2016.

Kite, Allison. "James Takes On Predatory Payday Lending." *Kansas City Business Journal,* June 11, 2015.

Klein, Naomi. *The Shock Doctrine: The Rise of Disaster Capitalism.* London: Picador, 2008.

Klein, Peter. *The Catholic Source Book*. Orlando: Harcourt Religion, 2006.

Kline, Daniel B. "How Much Are Americans Spending on Financial Vices?" Nasdaq, Sept. 13, 2018. https://www.nasdaq.com/articles/how-much-are-americans-spending-financial-vices-2018-09-13.

Knight, Victoria. "In Ten Years, Half of Middle-Income Elders Won't Be Able to Afford Housing, Medical Care." KHN, Apr. 24, 2019. https://khn.org/news/in-10-years-half-of-middle-income-elders-wont-be-able-to-afford-housing-medical-care/.

Knutson, Jacob. "Gun Background Checks Hit Single-Month High in March." Axios, Apr. 3, 2021. https://www.axios.com/gun-background-checks-record-march-65357c72-6f9a-43ce-9fad-b6670ec7f543.html.

Kolbert, Elizabeth. *The Sixth Extinction: An Unnatural History*. New York: Picador, 2015.

Kolodiejchuk, Brian, ed. *Mother Teresa: Come Be My Light*. New York: Doubleday, 2007.

Kotch, Alex. "Documents Reveal a Powerful, Secretive Foundation's Blueprint for Spreading Right-Wing Ideology, State by State." Salon, May 17, 2017. https://www.salon.com/2017/05/17/documents-reveal-a-powerful-secretive-foundations-blueprint-for-spreading-right-wing-ideology-state-by-state_partner/.

———. "The Koch Brothers Are Using This State as Their Right-Wing Laboratory." https://truthout.org/articles/the-koch-brothers-are-using-this-state-as-their-right-wing-laboratory/.

Krantz, Matt. "Tax Free? Forty-One Big and Profitable U.S. Companies Paid No Tax." Investor's Business Daily, July 21, 2020. https://www.investors.com/etfs-and-funds/sectors/sp500-tax-free-big-profitable-u-s-companies-paid-no-tax/.

Kronman, Anthony T. *Education's End: Why Our Colleges and Universities Have Given Up on the Meaning of Life*. New Haven, CT: Yale University Press, 2008.

Kruse, Kevin M. *One Nation Under God: How Corporate America Invented Christian America*. Grand Haven, MI: Brilliance Audio, 2016.

Kupferschmidt, Kai. "Crop-Protecting Insects Could Be Turned into Bioweapons, Critics Warn." Science, Oct. 4, 2018. https://www.sciencemag.org/news/2018/10/crop-protecting-insects-could-be-turned-bioweapons-critics-warn.

Kuruvilla, Carol. "Fifty Years Later, Many U.S. Catholic Women Still Ignore Vatican's Contraception Ban." HuffPost, July 25, 2018. https://www.huffpost.com/entry/50-years-later-many-us-catholic-women-continue-to-ignore-vaticans-contraceptives-ban_n_5b588361e4b0de86f4925ad8.

Lakhani, Nina. "America Has an Infant Mortality Crisis. Meet the Black Doulas Trying to Change That." *Guardian*, Nov. 25, 2019.

Lafer, Gordon. *The One Percent Solution: How Corporations Are Remaking America One State at a Time*. Ithaca, NY: ILR, 2017.

Lamothe, Dan. "Air Force Launches Investigation into Drug Use among Troops Protecting Nuclear Weapons." *Washington Post,* Mar. 18, 2016.

Landau, Joel. "Ashley Madison Leak May Be Linked to Three Suicides, $500,000 Reward Being Offered to Identify the Hackers." *New York Daily News*, Aug. 24, 2015.

Langlois, Shawn. "Kanye West, with Debt Piling Up, Thanks God for $68 Million Tax Refund." MarketWatch, Nov. 2, 2019. https://www.marketwatch.com/story/kanye-west-with-his-debt-piling-up-thanks-god-for-his-68-million-tax-return-2019-10-29.

Lasch, Christopher. *The Culture of Narcissism: American Life in an Age of Diminishing Expectations*. New York: W. W. Norton, 1991.

———. *The Minimal Self: Psychic Survival in Troubled Times*. New York: W. W. Norton, 1985.

Lawrence of the Resurrection. *Brother Lawrence: The Practice of the Presence of God the Best Rule of a Holy Life, Being Conversations and Letters of Nicholas Herman of Lorraine (Brother Lawrence)*. Translated from the French. New York: Fleming H. Revell, 1895.

Lawson, Sean. "Did Intelligence Officials Lie to Congress about NSA Domestic Spying?" Forbes, June 6, 2013. https://www.forbes.com/sites/seanlawson/2013/06/06/did-intelligence-officials-lie-to-congress-about-nsa-domestic-spying/?sh=4b85d9ec5816.

Leahy, Stephen. "One Million Species at Risk of Extinction, UN Report Warns." National Geographic, May 6, 2019. https://www.nationalgeographic.com/environment/article/ipbes-un-biodiversity-report-warns-one-million-species-at-risk.

Lee, Nathaniel. "How Police Militarization Became an Over $5 Billion Business Coveted by the Defense Industry." CNBC, July 9, 2020; updated July 10, 2020. https://www.cnbc.com/2020/07/09/why-police-pay-nothing-for-military-equipment.html.

Lee-Ashley, Matt, and Jenny Rowland. "The Koch Brothers Are Now Funding The Bundy Land Seizure Agenda." ThinkProgress, Feb. 11, 2016. https://archive.thinkprogress.org/the-koch-brothers-are-now-funding-the-bundy-land-seizure-agenda-901B90b3e1c6/.

Leibniz, G.W. *Theodicy*. Middlesex, UK: Echo Library, 2008.

Leigh, Emme. "Five of Mother Teresa's Most Inspiring Quotes Regarding Poverty." https://borgenproject.org/mother-teresas-greatest-quotes-regarding-poverty/.

Leonard, Andrew. "The NSA Doesn't Like Having Its Privacy Invaded." Salon, Mar. 4, 2013. https://www.salon.com/2013/03/04/the_nsa_doesnt_like_having_its_privacy_invaded/.

Leonhardt, David. "The Fleecing of Millennials." *New York Times*, Jan. 27, 2019.

Levin, Dov. "Partisan Electoral Interventions by the Great Powers: Introducing the PEIG Dataset." *Conflict Management and Peace Science* 36 (2019) 88–106.

Lewis, C. S. *The Discarded Image: An Introduction to Medieval and Renaissance Literature*. Cambridge, UK: Cambridge University Press, 1964.

———. *The Horse and His Boy*. New York: Collier Books, 1976.

Lewis, Paul, and Adam Federman. "Revealed: FBI Violated Its Own Rules While Spying on Keystone XL Opponents." *Guardian*, May 12, 2015.

Lewis, Randolph. *Under Surveillance: Being Watched in Modern America*. Austin: University of Texas Press, 2017.

Lilla, Mark. "Europe and the Legend of Secularization." *New York Times*, Mar. 31, 2006.

Lin, Liza, and Newley Purnell. "A World with a Billion Cameras Watching You Is Just around the Corner." *Wall Street Journal*, Dec. 6, 2019.

Lindbeck, George. *The Nature of Doctrine: Religion and Theology in a Postliberal Age*. Louisville, KY: Westminster John Knox, 1984.

Lindner, Eileen, ed. *Yearbook of American and Canadian Churches 2010*. Nashville: Abingdon, 2010.

———. *Yearbook of American and Canadian Churches 2012*. Nashville: Abingdon, 2012.

Lipka, Michael. "Is Religion's Declining Influence Good or Bad? Those without Religious Affiliation Are Divided." Pew Research Center, Sept. 23, 2014. https://www.pewresearch.org/fact-tank/2014/09/23/is-religions-declining-influence-good-or-bad-those-without-religious-affiliation-are-divided/.

————. "Majority of U.S. Catholics' Opinions Run Counter to Church on Contraception, Homosexuality." Pew Research Center, Sept. 19, 2013. https://www.pewresearch. org/fact-tank/2013/09/19/majority-of-u-s-catholics-opinions-run-counter-to-church-on-contraception-homosexuality/.

————. "Vatican Synod on Family Highlights Discord between Church Teachings and U.S. Catholics' Views." Pew Research Center, Oct. 3, 2014. https://www. pewresearch.org/fact-tank/2014/10/03/vatican-synod-on-family-highlights-discord-between-church-teachings-and-u-s-catholics-views-2/.

Liptak, Adam. "One in One Hundred U.S. Adults Behind Bars, New Study Says." New York Times, Feb. 28, 2008.

Lipp, Kenneth. "AT&T Is Spying on Americans for Profit." Daily Beast, Oct. 25, 2016; updated Apr. 13, 2017. https://www.thedailybeast.com/atandt-is-spying-on-americans-for-profit.

"List of Wars Involving the United States." Wikipedia. https://en.wikipedia.org/wiki/List_of_wars_involving_the_United_States.

Liu, Joseph. "Public's Views on Human Evolution." Pew Research Center, Dec. 30, 2013. https://www.pewforum.org/2013/12/30/publics-views-on-human-evolution/.

Locke, John. An Essay Concerning Human Understanding. Edited by Roger Woolhouse. Reprint, London: Penguin Classics, 1998.

Long, Heather. "U.S. Inequality Keeps Getting Uglier." CNN Business, Dec. 22, 2016. https://money.cnn.com/2016/12/22/news/economy/us-inequality-worse/index. html.

Louise, Nickie. "These Six Corporations Control 90 Percent of the Media Outlets in America. The Illusion of Choice and Objectivity." Tech Startups, Sept. 18, 2020. https://techstartups.com/2020/09/18/6-corporations-control-90-media-america-illusion-choice-objectivity-2020/.

Lowe, Walter. "Against Experience." Unpublished manuscript.

Luhby, Tami. "The Rich Are Eight Times Likelier to Graduate College than the Poor." CNN Business, Feb. 4, 2015. https://money.cnn.com/2015/02/04/news/economy/college-graduate-rich-poor/index.html.

Lundin, Roger. Believing Again: Doubt and Faith in a Secular Age. Grand Rapids: Eerdmans, 2009.

Luthi, Ben. "Credit Card Debt Continues Its Pandemic Plunge." Investopedia, Jan. 12, 2021. https://www.investopedia.com/credit-card-debt-continues-its-plunge-during-the-pandemic-5095237.

Lynch, Conor. "America's Libertarian Freakshow: Inside the Free-Market Fetish of Rand Paul and Ted Cruz." Salon, Apr. 14, 2015. https://www.salon.com/2015/04/14/americas_libertarian_freakshow_inside_the_free_market_fetish_of_rand_paul_ted_cruz/.

Lyons, Gene. "Gene Lyons: 'We're Doomed,' He Said Cheerfully." Press Herald, May 23, 2019; updated Nov. 8, 2019. https://www.pressherald.com/2019/05/23/gene-lyons-were-doomed-he-said-cheerfully/.

Mabry-Nauta, Angie. "The Last Sunday: When It's Time for a Church to Close." Christian Century, Dec. 29, 2014. https://www.christiancentury.org/article/2014-12/last-sunday.

MacDonald, G. Jeffrey. "Andover Newton to Move, Partner with Yale." Christian Century, May 3, 2016. https://www.christiancentury.org/article/2016-05/andover-newton-partner-yale-shutter-campus.

———. "Housing Venture Roils Union Seminary." Christian Century, Feb. 3, 2016. https://www.christiancentury.org/article/2016-02/union-seminary-debates-condos-campus.

———. "Two Lutheran Seminaries to Close, Reopen as One." Christian Century, Jan. 19, 2016. https://www.christiancentury.org/article/2016-01/two-lutheran-seminaries-close-and-reopen-new-school.

Machiavelli, Niccolo. *The Prince.* Translated by Coralie Bickford-Smith. London: Penguin Classics, 2015.

Macias, Amanda. "American Firms Rule the $398 Billion Global Arms Industry: Here's a Roundup of the World's Top Ten Defense Contractors, by Sales." CNBC, Jan. 10, 2019. https://www.cnbc.com/2019/01/10/top-10-defense-contractors-in-the-world.html.

MacInnis, Cara, and Gordon Hodson. "Do American States with More Religious or Conservative Populations Search More for Sexual Content on Google?" *Archives of Sexual Behavior* 44 (2015) 137–47.

Mackenzie, James. "Donald Trump Eyes Afghanistan's $1 Trillion Mineral Reserves to Pay for Reconstruction after Sixteen Years of War." *Independent,* Aug. 21, 2017.

MacLeish, Archibald. *J. B.: A Play in Verse.* Boston, MA: Houghton Mifflin, 1956.

Manchester, Julia. "Transparency Advocate Says Government Agencies Face 'Use It or Lose It' Spending." Hill, Mar. 21, 2019. https://thehill.com/hilltv/rising/435121-government-transparency-advocate-says-theres-a-use-or-lose-it-phenomenon-in.

Madison, James. "Federalist Papers No. 51 (1788)." https://billofrightsinstitute.org/primary-sources/federalist-no-51.

Mahler, Jonathan. "The Problem with 'Self-Investigation' in a Post-Truth Era." *New York Times Magazine,* Dec. 27, 2016.

Malinowski, Bronislaw. *Magic, Science and Religion and Other Essays.* Garden City, NY: Doubleday Anchor, 1954.

Margaritoff, Marco. "More U.S. Veterans Have Committed Suicide in the Last Decade than Died in the Vietnam War." ATI, Nov. 11, 2019; updated May 19, 2021, https://allthatsinteresting.com/veteran-suicide.

Maritain, Jacques. "The Positions of St. Thomas on the Ordination of the Person to Its Ultimate End." https://maritain.nd.edu/jmc/etext/CG02.HTM.

Marr, Chuck, et al. "Substantial Income of Wealthy Households Escapes Annual Taxation Or Enjoys Special Tax Breaks." Center on Budget and Policy Priorities, Nov. 13, 2019. https://www.cbpp.org/research/federal-tax/substantial-income-of-wealthy-households-escapes-annual-taxation-or-enjoys.

Marshall, Alfred. "The Social Possibilities of Economic Chivalry." *Economic Journal* 17 (Mar. 1907) 7–29.

———. "Some Aspects of Competition." In *Memorials of Alfred Marshall,* edited by A. C. Pigou, 256–92. London, MacMillan, 1925.

Marte, Jonnelle. "U.S. Household Debt Tops $14 Trillion and Reaches New Record." Reuters, Feb. 11, 2020. https://www.reuters.com/article/us-usa-fed-household-debt/u-s-household-debt-tops-14-trillion-and-reaches-new-record-idUSKBN20521Z.

Martin, James. "A New Vision for the Church." https://www.americamagazine.org/content/all-things/new-vision-church.

Martin, Ralph. *Will Many Be Saved?: What Vatican II Actually Teaches and Its Implications for the New Evangelization.* Grand Rapids: Eerdmans, 2012.

Marty, Martin E. *A Cry of Absence: Reflections for the Winter of the Heart.* Eugene, OR: Wipf and Stock, 1983.

Masci, David, and Gregory Smith. "Seven Facts about American Catholics." Pew Research Center, Oct. 10, 2018. https://www.pewresearch.org/fact-tank/2018/10/10/7-facts-about-american-catholics/.

Mayer, Jane. *Dark Money: The Hidden History of Billionaires behind the Rise of the Radical Right.* New York: Doubleday, 2016.

———. "The Making of the Fox News White House." *New Yorker Magazine.* Mar. 4, 2019.

Mazzetti, Mark. *The Way of the Knife: The CIA, a Secret Army, and a War at the Ends of the Earth.* New York: Penguin, 2014.

McCarthy, Ellen. "Breaking Up with Your Smartphone Is Really, Really Hard. Just Ask These People." *Washington Post,* Feb. 8, 2018.

McCarthy, Michael. "US Jails Hold Ten Times More Mentally Ill People than State Hospitals, Report Finds." BMJ, Apr. 10, 2014. https://www.bmj.com/content/348/bmj.g2705.

McCarthy, Niall. "Private Security Outnumbers the Police in Most Countries Worldwide." Forbes, Aug. 31, 2017. https://www.forbes.com/sites/niallmccarthy/2017/08/31/private-security-outnumbers-the-police-in-most-countries-worldwide-infographic/?sh=2227e8f121of.

———. "Trump Plans to Slash U.S. Troop Numbers in Germany." Forbes, June 8, 2020. https://www.forbes.com/sites/niallmccarthy/2020/06/08/trump-plans-to-slash-us-troop-numbers-in-germany-infographic/?sh=65905e96dbef.

McCarthy, Tom, dir. *Spotlight.* Los Angeles: Open Roads, 2015.

McDonnell, Thomas, ed. *A Thomas Merton Reader.* New York: Doubleday, 1974.

McEntee, Rory, and Adam Bucko. *The New Monasticism: An Interspiritual Manifesto for Contemplative Living.* Maryknoll, NY: Orbis, 2015.

McGlothlin, David. "Arizona Tops in Guaranteeing Private Prisons New Customers." Pinal Central, Mar. 2, 2016. https://www.pinalcentral.com/san_tan_valley_sentinel/around_arizona/arizona-tops-in-guaranteeing-private-prisons-new-customers/article_6c99488e-e0a1-11e5-9b10-b38d3a2f62b1.html.

McGregor, Jena. "What Walmart's Patent for Audio Surveillance Could Mean for Its Workers." *Washington Post,* July 12, 2018.

McIntosh, Lia M., et al. *Blank Slate: Write Your Own Rules for a Twenty-Second-Century Church Movement.* Nashville: Abingdon, 2019.

McKenna, Josephine. "Vatican Seeks to Bury the Hatchet with American Nuns." *Washington Post,* Dec. 16, 2014.

McKie, Robin. "Biologists Think 50 Percent of Species Will Be Facing Extinction by the End of the Century." *Guardian,* Feb. 25, 2017.

McMillan, Tracie. "The New Face of Hunger." National Geographic, July 16, 2014. https://www.nationalgeographic.com/foodfeatures/hunger/.

McNeil, Donald G. "C.I.A. Vaccine Ruse May Have Harmed the War on Polio." *New York Times,* July 9, 2012.

McTyeire, Holland Nimmons. *A History of Methodism.* Nashville: Methodist Episcopal Church, South, 1892.

McVeigh, Karen. "Sea Level Rise Could Be Worse than Feared, Warn Researchers." *Guardian,* Feb. 2, 2021.

Mecklin, John, ed. "This Is Your COVID Wake-Up Call: It Is One Hundred Seconds to Midnight; 2021 Doomsday Clock Statement." Bulletin of the Atomic Scientists, Jan. 27, 2021. https://thebulletin.org/wp-content/uploads/2021/01/2021-doomsday-clock-statement-1.pdf.

Medsger, Betty. "Our Government Is Always Hiding Something: Column." *USA Today,* Mar. 29, 2014.

"Meet the Human Faces of Climate Migration." World Bank, Mar. 19, 2018. https://www.worldbank.org/en/news/feature/2018/03/19/meet-the-human-faces-of-climate-migration.

Menard, Martha Brown. "Almost Half of Middle-Class Americans Face Downward Mobility in Retirement." Benefits Pro, Sept. 5, 2018. https://www.benefitspro.com/2018/09/05/even-middle-class-americans-face-downward-mobility/?slretu rn=20210718110332.

Merle, Renae. "Giving Up Its U.S. Citizenship Could Save Pfizer $35 Billion in Taxes." *Washington Post,* Feb. 25, 2016.

Merritt, Carol Howard. "The Body in Motion." Christian Century, Apr. 17, 2015. https://www.christiancentury.org/article/2015-04/body-motion.

Merton, Thomas. *New Seeds of Contemplation.* New York: New Directions, 1961.

———. *The Seven Storey Mountain.* New York: Harcourt, Brace, 1948.

Mervosh, Sarah. "How Much Wealthier Are White School Districts than Nonwhite Ones? $23 Billion, Report Says." *New York Times,* Feb. 27, 2019.

Metaxas, Eric. "Jackie Robinson's Faith Missing from *Forty-Two* Movie." *Washington Post,* Apr. 12, 2013.

Meyer, Robinson. "Human Extinction Isn't That Unlikely." Atlantic, Apr. 29, 2016. https://www.theatlantic.com/technology/archive/2016/04/a-human-extinction-isnt-that-unlikely/480444/.

———. "Parts of the Arctic Spiked to Forty-Five Degrees above Normal." Atlantic, Apr. 27, 2018. https://www.theatlantic.com/science/archive/2018/02/its-54-degrees-warmer-than-normal-in-the-arctic/554303/.

Meyers, Robin. *The Underground Church: Reclaiming the Subversive Way of Jesus.* San Francisco: Jossey-Bass, 2012.

Midgette, Gregory, et al. "What America's Users Spend on Illegal Drugs, 2006–2016." https://www.rand.org/pubs/research_reports/RR3140.html.

"Military Personnel." https://www.globalsecurity.org/military/agency/end-strength. htm.

Millard, Egan. "Two Thousand Nineteen Parochial Reports Show Continued Decline and a 'Dire' Future for the Episcopal Church." Episcopal News Service, Oct. 16, 2020. https://www.episcopalnewsservice.org/2020/10/16/2019-parochial-reports-show-continued-decline-and-a-dire-future-for-the-episcopal-church/.

Miller, Emily MacFarlan, and Christian Century Staff. "Survey Reveals Public's Skepticism about Pastors." Christian Century, Feb. 13, 2017. https://www.christiancentury.org/article/survey-reveals-public's-skepticism-about-pastors.

Miller, Ryan. "Millennials Are Less Healthy and More Depressed than Gen X, Report Finds." *USA Today,* Apr. 24, 2019.

Miller, Todd. "More than a Wall: Corporate Profiteering and the Militarization of US Borders." TNI, Sept. 16, 2019. https://www.tni.org/en/morethanawall.

Miranda, Leticia, et al. "Here Are the Most Outrageous Incentives Cities Offered Amazon in Their HQ2 Bids." BuzzFeed News, Nov. 14, 2018. https://www.buzzfeednews.com/article/leticiamiranda/amazon-hq2-finalist-cities-incentives-airport-lounge.

Mis, Magdalena. "World Bank Invests in Firms Using Tax Havens, Says Oxfam." Reuters, Apr. 11, 2016. https://www.reuters.com/article/us-world-bank-africa-investment/world-bank-invests-in-firms-using-tax-havens-says-oxfam-idUSKCN0X8242?edition-redirect=in.

Mishel, Lawrence, and Jori Kandra. "CEO Compensation Surged 14 Percent in 2019 to $21.3 Million." Economic Policy Institute, Aug. 18, 2020. https://www.epi.org/publication/ceo-compensation-surged-14-in-2019-to-21-3-million-ceos-now-earn-320-times-as-much-as-a-typical-worker/.

Mishel, Lawrence, and Julia Wolfe. "CEO Compensation Has Grown 940 Percent Since 1978." Economic Policy Institute, Aug. 14, 2019. https://www.epi.org/publication/ceo-compensation-2018/.

Missouri Conference of the United Methodist Church. *Conference Journal 2020.* Columbia, MO: MCUMC, 2021.

Mohamed, Besheer, and Elizabeth Podrebarac Sciupac. "The Share of Americans Who Leave Islam Is Offset by Those Who Become Muslim." Pew Research Center, Jan. 26, 2018. https://www.pewresearch.org/fact-tank/2018/01/26/the-share-of-americans-who-leave-islam-is-offset-by-those-who-become-muslim/.

Moltmann, Jürgen. *The Crucified God.* New York: Harper and Row, 1973.

Monbiot, George. *How Did We Get into This Mess?: Politics, Equality, Nature.* New York: Verso, 2017.

Montanez, Rachel. "Burnout Is Sabotaging Employee Retention: Three Things You Must Know to Help." Forbes, June 5, 2019. https://www.forbes.com/sites/rachelmontanez/2019/06/05/burnout-is-sabotaging-employee-retention-three-things-you-must-know-to-help/?sh=b3ddc4b5foed.

Mooney, Chris, and Brady Dennis. "Global Greenhouse Gas Emissions Will Hit Yet Another Record High This Year, Experts Project." *Washington Post,* Dec. 3, 2019.

————. "The World Is About to Install 700 Million Air Conditioners. Here's What That Means for the Climate." *Washington Post,* May 31, 2016.

Mooney, Chris, and Andrew Freedman. "Earth Is Now Losing 1.2 Trillion Tons of Ice Each Year. And It's Going to Get Worse." *Washington Post,* Jan. 25, 2021.

Moore, Angela. "This Is Why Baby Boomers Are Divorcing at a Stunning Rate." MarketWatch, Oct. 20, 2018. https://www.marketwatch.com/story/your-failing-marriage-is-about-to-make-the-retirement-crisis-worse-2017-03-13.

"More People Are Gaming in the U.S., and They're Doing So across More Platforms." NPD, July 20, 2020. https://www.npd.com/news/press-releases/2020/more-people-are-gaming-in-the-us/.

Moreton, Bethany. *To Serve God and Wal-Mart: The Making of Christian Free Enterprise.* Cambridge, MA: Harvard University Press, 2010.

Morello, Carol, and Ruth Eglash. "U.S. and Israel Reach Agreement on Unprecedented Amount of Military Aid." *Washington Post,* Sept. 13, 2016.

Morgan, Steve. "Cybercrime to Cost the World $10.5 Trillion Annually by 2025." Cybercrime Magazine, Nov. 13, 2020. https://cybersecurityventures.com/cybercrime-damage-costs-10-trillion-by-2025/.

Morris, Chris. "Ten Iconic US Companies That Have Left America." CNBC, Apr. 21, 2016. https://www.cnbc.com/2016/04/21/10-iconic-us-companies-that-have-moved-headquarters-abroad.html.

Moskalenko, Sophia. "Why Social Media Makes Us Angrier—and More Extreme." Psychology Today, July 6, 2018. https://www.psychologytoday.com/us/blog/friction/201807/why-social-media-makes-us-angrier-and-more-extreme.

Moskowitz, Dan. "The Ten Richest People in the World." Investopedia, updated Sept. 1, 2021. https://www.investopedia.com/articles/investing/012715/5-richest-people-world.asp.

Moss, Otis, III. "Dance in the Dark: Preaching the Blues without Despair." Christian Century, Nov. 12, 2015. https://www.christiancentury.org/article/2015-11/dance-dark.

Moyers, Bill. "Henry Giroux: Zombie Politics and Casino Capitalism." Truthout, Nov. 22, 2013. https://truthout.org/video/bill-moyers-henry-giroux-zombie-politics-and-casino-capitalism/.

Mueller, John, and Mark G. Stewart. "Public Opinion and Counterterrorism Policy." Cato Institute, Feb. 20. 2018. https://www.cato.org/white-paper/public-opinion-counterterrorism-policy.

Mui, Ylan. "Conservative Koch Brothers' Network to Spend Up to $400 Million for the Midterm Election Cycle—Including $20 Million to Sell the GOP Tax Law." CNBC, Jan. 27, 2018; updated Jan. 28, 2018. https://www.cnbc.com/2018/01/27/koch-brothers-network-to-spend-400-million-in-midterm-election-cycle.html.

Mullen, Caitlin. "Four in Ten Workers Living Paycheck to Paycheck." Bizwomen, Feb. 25, 2020. https://www.bizjournals.com/bizwomen/news/latest-news/2020/02/four-in-10-workers-living-paycheck-to-paycheck.html?page=all.

Muller, René J. "NeuroTheology: Are We Hardwired for God?" Psychiatric Times 25 (May 2008) 6.

Mundy, Alicia. "The VA Isn't Broken, Yet." Washington Monthly, Mar./Apr./May 2016. https://washingtonmonthly.com/magazine/maraprmay-2016/the-va-isnt-broken-yet/.

Musarra, Annalisa. "Churches Lost $1.2 Billion in Recession." Washington Post, Mar. 22, 2012.

Nader, Ralph. "Food Science: What's the Harm." Center for Study of Responsive Law, Sept. 15, 2014. https://csrl.org/2014/09/15/food-science-whats-the-harm/.

"Nearly Half of U.S. Families Have No Retirement Savings." Economic Policy Institute, Dec. 10, 2019. https://www.epi.org/press/nearly-half-of-u-s-families-have-no-retirement-savings-policymakers-should-expand-social-security-to-meet-21st-century-retirement-needs/.

Negin, Elliot. "Corporations Should Stop Funding Climate Science Deniers in Congress." Hill, Feb. 8, 2021. https://thehill.com/opinion/energy-environment/537804-corporations-should-stop-funding-climate-science-deniers-in.

Nesbit, Jeff. "The Secret Origins of the Tea Party." Time Magazine, Apr. 5, 2016.

Newcott, Bill. "Remembering the Night Two Atomic Bombs Fell—on North Carolina." National Geographic, Jan. 22, 2021. https://www.nationalgeographic.com/history/article/remembering-night-two-atomic-bombs-dropped-on-north-carolina.

Newdick, Thomas. "The U.S. Navy's Submarine-Launched Aerial Drone Capacity Is Set to Greatly Expand." The Drive, Mar. 10, 2021. https://www.thedrive.com/the-war-zone/39700/the-u-s-navys-submarine-launched-aerial-drone-capacity-is-set-to-greatly-expand.

Neuhauser, Alan. "Seventy-Five Percent of Animal Species to be Wiped Out in 'Sixth Mass Extinction.'" US News, June 19, 2015. https://www.usnews.com/news/blogs/data-mine/2015/06/19/75-percent-of-animal-species-to-be-wiped-out-in-sixth-mass-extinction.

Newman, John Henry. *An Essay on the Development of Christian Doctrine.* Notre Dame, IN: University of Notre Dame Press, 1994.

Newport, Frank. "Percentage of Christians in U.S. Drifting Down, but Still High." Gallup, Dec. 24, 2015. https://news.gallup.com/poll/187955/percentage-christians-drifting-down-high.aspx.

———. "Understanding the Increase in Moral Acceptability of Polygamy." Gallup, June 26, 2020. https://news.gallup.com/opinion/polling-matters/313112/understanding-increase-moral-acceptability-polygamy.aspx.

Nichols, Tom. "Were America's Nuclear Codes Set to Zero? Looks Like It, and Worse." Insider, Jan. 27, 2014. https://www.businessinsider.com/nuclear-codes-zero-2014-1.

Niebuhr, H. Richard. *Christ and Culture.* New York: Harper and Row, 1975.

———. *The Kingdom of God in America.* New York: Harper and Row, 1937.

———. *The Meaning of Revelation.* New York: Macmillan, 1946.

Niebuhr, Reinhold. *The Children of Light and the Children of Darkness: A Vindication of Democracy and a Critique of Its Traditional Defense.* New York: Charles Scribner's Sons, 1944.

———. *The Nature and Destiny of Man.* New York: Charles Scribner's Sons, 1951.

Nietzsche, Friedrich. *The Will to Power.* Edited and translated by R. Kevin Hill. Translated by Michael A. Scarpitti. London: Penguin Classics, 2017.

"Nine out of Ten People Worldwide Breathe Polluted Air, but More Countries Are Taking Action." World Health Organization, May 2, 2018. https://www.who.int/news/item/02-05-2018-9-out-of-10-people-worldwide-breathe-polluted-air-but-more-countries-are-taking-action.

Nixey, Catherine. *The Darkening Age: The Christian Destruction of the Classical World.* Boston: Houghton Mifflin Harcourt, 2018.

Nixon, Ron. "Facial Scans at U.S. Airports Violate Americans' Privacy, Report Says." *New York Times,* Dec. 21, 2017.

Nordgren, Tyler. *Night Sky.* Ft. Lauderdale, FL: Quick Reference, 2015.

Nortey, Justin, and Claire Gecewicz. "Three-Quarters of U.S. Catholics View Pope Francis Favorably, Though Partisan Differences Persist." Pew Research Center, Apr. 3, 2020. https://www.pewresearch.org/fact-tank/2020/04/03/three-quarters-of-u-s-catholics-view-pope-francis-favorably-though-partisan-differences-persist/.

Noss, John B. *Man's Religions.* New York: Macmillan, 1949.

"Not Long Ago, the Center of the Milky Way Exploded." Science Daily, Oct. 6, 2019. https://www.sciencedaily.com/releases/2019/10/191006120913.htm.

Novak, Matt. "One in Three Americans Are on File in the FBI's Criminal Database." Gizmodo, Oct. 22, 2014. https://gizmodo.com/1-in-3-americans-are-on-file-in-the-fbis-criminal-datab-1649101073.

"NSF-Funded Researchers Say Antarctic Telescope May Have Provided the First Direct Evidence of Cosmic Inflation and the Origins of the Universe." National Science Foundation, Mar. 17, 2014. https://www.nsf.gov/news/news_summ.jsp?cntn_id=130760.

"Number One Walton Family." Forbes, Dec. 16, 2020. https://www.forbes.com/profile/walton-1/?sh=3fceb4946f3f.

O'Dell, Rob, and Nick Penzenstadler. "You Elected Them to Write New Laws. They're Letting Corporations Do It Instead." Center for Public Integrity, Apr. 4, 2019. https://publicintegrity.org/politics/state-politics/copy-paste-legislate/you-elected-them-to-write-new-laws-theyre-letting-corporations-do-it-instead/.

O'Flaherty, Kate. "Facebook Confirms Two Billion Users Will Now Need to Opt In to Facial Recognition." Forbes, Sept. 4, 2019. https://www.forbes.com/sites/kateoflahertyuk/2019/09/04/facebook-facial-recognition/?sh=ab49a6b989e1.

O'Harrow, Robert, et al. "The Rise in Domestic Extremism in America." *Washington Post*, Apr. 12, 2021.

Ohlheiser, Abby. "Vast Majority of U.S. Catholics Who Left Church Can't Imagine Returning, Study Says." *Washington Post*, Sept. 2, 2015.

"Oldest Ever Human Genetic Evidence Clarifies Dispute over Our Ancestors." Science Daily, Apr. 1, 2020. https://www.sciencedaily.com/releases/2020/04/200401111657.htm.

O'Neil, Jim. "Antimicrobial Resistance: Tackling a Crisis for the Health and Wealth of Nations." https://www.jpiamr.eu/wp-content/uploads/2014/12/AMR-Review-Paper-Tackling-a-crisis-for-the-health-and-wealth-of-nations_1-2.pdf.

OpenSecrets.org. "Super PACs." https://www.opensecrets.org/political-action-committees-pacs/super-pacs/2020.

———. "Twenty-Twenty Election to Cost $14 Billion, Blowing Away Spending Records." Oct. 28, 2020. https://www.opensecrets.org/news/2020/10/cost-of-2020-election-14billion-update/.

———. "Twenty-Twenty Outside Spending, by Super PAC." https://www.opensecrets.org/outsidespending/summ.php?chrt=V&type=S.

Orthodox Church in America. "Venerable Pachomius the Great, Founder of Coenobitic Monasticism." https://www.oca.org/saints/lives/2021/05/15/101384-venerable-pachomius-the-great-founder-of-coenobitic-monasticism.

Orwell, George. *Nineteen Eighty-Four*. New York: New American, 1962.

Osbourne, Michael, and Carl Frey. "Automation and the Future of Work: Understanding the Numbers." Oxford Martin School, Apr. 13, 2018. https://www.oxfordmartin.ox.ac.uk/blog/automation-and-the-future-of-work-understanding-the-numbers/.

Overberg, Paul, and Janet Adamy. "Elderly in U.S. Are Projected to Outnumber Children for First Time." *Wall Street Journal*, Mar. 13, 2018.

Owens, L. Roger, and Anthony B. Robinson. "Dark Night of the Church: Relearning the Essentials." Christian Century, Dec. 14, 2012. https://www.christiancentury.org/article/2012-12/dark-night-church.

Paley, Dawn. *Drug War Capitalism*. Chico, CA: AK, 2014.

Paltrow, Scot J. "Special Report: The Pentagon's Doctored Ledgers Conceal Epic Waste." Reuters, Nov. 18, 2013. https://www.reuters.com/article/us-usa-pentagon-waste-specialreport/special-report-the-pentagons-doctored-ledgers-conceal-epic-waste-idUSBRE9AH0LQ20131118.

———. "U.S. Army Fudged Its Accounts by Trillions of Dollars, Auditor Finds." Reuters, Aug. 19, 2016. https://www.reuters.com/article/us-usa-audit-army/u-s-army-fudged-its-accounts-by-trillions-of-dollars-auditor-finds-idUSKCN10U1IG.

Pappas, Stephanie. "Social Media Cyber Bullying Linked to Teen Depression." Scientific American, June 23, 2015. https://www.scientificamerican.com/article/social-media-cyber-bullying-linked-to-teen-depression/

Parker, Laura. "One Hundred Forty-Three Million People May Soon Become Climate Migrants." National Geographic, Mar. 19, 2018. https://www.nationalgeographic.com/science/article/climate-migrants-report-world-bank-spd.

Parra, Aritz, and Frank Jordans. "UN Chief Warns of 'Point of No Return' on Climate Change." AP News, Dec. 1, 2019. https://apnews.com/article/united-nations-madrid-antonio-guterres-ap-top-news-international-news-7d85d6d7b05c4436b6f4d162f6c06566.

Parsons, Jeff. "Ban 'Disturbing' Sex Robots in Britain: 'Sex Tech' Trend Could Make Human Relationships Seem Primitive, Warns Expert." Mirror, Sept. 15, 2015.

Pascal, Blaise. Pensées. Translated by A. J. Krailsheimer. London: Penguin Classics, 1995.

Passy, Jacob. "The Rent Is Too Damn High—Even for Middle-Income Americans." MarketWatch, Feb. 5, 2020. https://www.marketwatch.com/story/the-rent-is-too-damn-high-even-for-middle-income-americans-2020-02-04.

Patnaik, Utsa, and Prabhat Patnaik. A Theory of Imperialism. New York: Columbia University Press, 2016.

Paul VI, Pope. Lumen gentium. Vatican, Nov. 21, 1964. https://www.vatican.va/archive/hist_councils/ii_vatican_council/documents/vat-ii_const_19641121_lumen-gentium_en.html.

———. The Pastoral Constitution on the Church in the Modern World. Boston: Pauline Books and Media, 1965.

Payne, Emily. "Top Health Insurers' Revenues Soared to Almost $1 Trillion in 2019." Benefits Pro, Feb. 24, 2020. https://www.benefitspro.com/2020/02/24/top-health-insurers-revenues-soared-to-almost-1-trillion-in-2019/.

Peckman, R. William, and Brad Berhorst. "Author Acknowledges Dismal Trends, Lays Out Hopeful Future for Church in U.S." Catholic Missourian (July 11, 2014) 15, 19.

Peltier, Heidi. "The Growth of 'Camo Economy' and the Commercialization of the Post-9/11 Wars." https://watson.brown.edu/costsofwar/papers/2020/growth-camo-economy-and-commercialization-post-911-wars-0.

Pengelly, Martin. "NSA Listed Merkel among Leaders Subject to Surveillance: Report." Guardian, Mar. 29, 2014.

Penney, Jonathon. "Chilling Effects: Online Surveillance and Wikipedia Use." Berkeley Technology Law Journal 31 (2016) 117.

Perez, Evan. "Secret Court's Oversight Gets Scrutiny." Wall Street Journal, June 9, 2013.

Perkins, John, The New Confessions of an Economic Hit Man. San Francisco: Berrett-Koehler, 2016.

Perkins, Tom. "Progressive Kristallnacht Coming?" Wall Street Journal, Jan. 24, 2014.

Pesce, Nicole Lyn. "The Walton Family Gets $100 Million Richer Every Single Day." MarketWatch, Aug. 17, 2019. https://www.marketwatch.com/story/the-walton-family-gets-100-million-richer-every-single-day-2019-08-12.

Peterson, Kristina. "How the New Farm Bill Cuts $8 Billion from Food Stamps." Wall Street Journal, Jan. 28, 2014.

Pfeffer, Fabian, et al. "Wealth Levels, Wealth Inequality and the Great Recession." Stanford Center on Poverty and Inequality, May 2014. https://inequality.stanford.edu/publications/media/details/wealth-levels-wealth-inequality-and-great-recession.

Pham, Peter. "Christian Group Hopes to Lure Hungry Souls to Jesus by Building McDonald's Inside Church." Foodbeast, Dec. 2, 2014. https://www.foodbeast. com/news/mcdonalds-church/.

Philadelphia Inquirer. "John XXXIII Opened Windows for the Church." *Philadelphia Inquirer*, Apr. 26, 2014.

Physicians for Social Responsibility. "Climate Change and Famine." https://www.psr. org/wp-content/uploads/2018/05/climate-change-and-famine.pdf.

Pierre-Louis, Kendra. "Ocean Warming Is Accelerating Faster than Thought, New Research Finds." *New York Times*, Jan. 10, 2019.

Piketty, Thomas. *Capital in the Twenty-First Century.* Boston, MA: Belknap, 2017.

Plato. *Plato's Cosmology: The Timaeus of Plato.* Translated by Francis M. Cornford. Indianapolis, IN: Hackett, 1997.

Polack, Ellie. "New Cigna Study Reveals Loneliness at Epidemic Levels in America." Bloomberg, May 1, 2018. https://www.bloomberg.com/press-releases/2018-05-01/ new-cigna-study-reveals-loneliness-at-epidemic-levels-in-america.

Polychroniou, C. J. "Interview with Helena Norberg-Hodge: Globalized Monoculture is Consuming the Planet." Truthout, Mar. 31, 2016. https://truthout.org/articles/ globalized-monoculture-is-consuming-the-planet-an-interview-with-helena-norberg-hodge/.

Pomerantsev, Peter. *Nothing Is True and Everything Is Possible: The Surreal Heart of the New Russia.* New York: Public Affairs, 2015.

"A Portrait of Jewish Americans." Pew Research Center, Oct. 1, 2013. https://www. pewforum.org/2013/10/01/jewish-american-beliefs-attitudes-culture-survey/.

Pound, Jesse. "These Ninety-One Companies Paid No Federal Taxes in 2018." CNBC, Dec. 16, 2019; updated Dec. 17, 2019. https://www.cnbc.com/2019/12/16/these-91-fortune-500-companies-didnt-pay-federal-taxes-in-2018.html.

Pudelski, Sasha, and Carl Davis. "Public Loss Private Gain: How School Voucher Tax Shelters Undermine Public Education." https://files.eric.ed.gov/fulltext/ ED601973.pdf.

Putnam, Robert. *Our Kids: The American Dream in Crisis.* New York: Simon and Schuster, 2016.

"Priest Shortage at a Glance." FutureChurch. https://www.futurechurch.org/future-of-priestly-ministry/optional-celibacy/priest-shortage-at-glance.

Quackenbush, Casey. "A Third of the Himalayan Glaciers Will Melt by the End of the Century, a New Report Finds." Time, Feb. 5, 2019. https://time.com/5521000/ climate-change-himalayan-glaciers-melt-2100/.

Quart, Alissa. *Squeezed: Why Our Families Can't Afford America.* New York: Ecco, 2018.

Quigley, Caroll. *Tragedy and Hope: A History of the World in Our Time.* New York: Macmillan, 1966.

Rainie, Lee, et al. "Trust and Distrust in America." Pew Research Center, July 22, 2019. https://www.pewresearch.org/politics/2019/07/22/trust-and-distrust-in-america/.

Rall, Ted. "America Is in Decline. Get Used to It." Ted Rall, May 9, 2014. https://rall. com/2014/05/09/syndicated-column-america-is-in-decline-get-used-to-it.

———. "If We Learn Geography, the Terrorists have Won." Ted Rall, Apr. 23, 2013. https://rall.com/2013/04/23/syndicated-column-if-we-learn-geography-the-terrorists-have-won.

Rampell, Ed. "Do Not Resist: The Post-9/11 Iron Heel of the State." Hollywood Progressive, Feb. 10, 2017. https://hollywoodprogressive.com/do-not-resist/.

Rauber, Paul. "All the Environmental News in Case You Missed It." Sierra, Feb. 27, 2019. https://www.sierraclub.org/sierra/2019-2-march-april/speed/all-environmental-news-case-you-missed-it.

Rauschenbusch, Walter. *A Theology for the Social Gospel*. Nashville: Abingdon, 1917.

Ravitch, Diane. *The Death and Life of the Great American School System: How Testing and Choice Are Undermining Education*. New York: Basic, 2010.

Rawnsley, Adam. "Follow Your Heart: Darpa's Quest to Find You by Your Heartbeat." Wired, Nov. 10, 2011. https://www.wired.com/2011/11/follow-your-heart-darpas-quest-to-find-you-by-your-heartbeat/.

Ray, Julie. "Americans' Stress, Worry and Anger Intensified in 2018." Gallup, Apr. 25, 2019. https://news.gallup.com/poll/249098/americans-stress-worry-anger-intensified-2018.aspx.

Reedy, Christianna. "Kurzweil Claims That the Singularity Will Happen by 2045." Futurism, Oct. 5, 2017. https://futurism.com/kurzweil-claims-that-the-singularity-will-happen-by-2045.

Reich, Robert B. *The Common Good*. New York: Knopf, 2018.

———. "Global Capital and the Nation State." Robert Reich, May 19, 2013. https://robertreich.org/post/50890974932.

———. "The Jaw-Dropping Realities of our Widening Economic Divide." Reader Supported News, May 3, 2016. https://readersupportednews.org/opinion2/277-75/36673-the-jaw-dropping-realities-of-our-widening-economic-divide.

———. "Labor Day and the Election of 2012: It's Inequality, Stupid." Truthout, Sept. 3, 2012. https://truthout.org/articles/labor-day-and-the-election-of-2012-its-inequality-stupid/.

———. *The System: Who Rigged It, How We Fix It*. New York: Knopf, 2020.

Reid, Kathryn. "Five World Hunger Facts You Need to Know." World Vision, updated Oct. 29, 2020. https://www.worldvision.org/hunger-news-stories/world-hunger-facts.

"Religion." Gallup. https://news.gallup.com/poll/1690/religion.aspx.

Reuters. "Pope Urges All Religions to Unite for Peace, Justice." Voice of America, Mar. 20, 2013. https://www.voanews.com/a/pope-justice/1625457.html.

Reynolds, Matt. "Even a Mask Won't Hide You from the Latest Facial Recognition Rech." NewScientist, Sept. 7, 2017. https://www.newscientist.com/article/2146703-even-a-mask-wont-hide-you-from-the-latest-face-recognition-tech/.

Ribiat, Ron. "Quote of the Day: Canadian Photographer Mark Schacter." Religion News Service, Dec. 11, 2013. https://religionnews.com/2013/12/11/quote-day-canadian-photographer-mark-schacter/.

Ribitzky, Romy. "Active Monitoring of Employees Rises to 78 Percent." ABC News, Jan. 6, 2006. https://abcnews.go.com/Business/story?id=88319&page=1.

Rice, Doyle. "Baked Alaska: USA's Northernmost State Has Been Unusually Warm." USA Today, Jan. 2, 2018. https://www.usatoday.com/story/weather/2018/01/02/baked-alaska-usas-northernmost-state-has-been-unusually-warm/996303001/.

Richardson, Daniel. "Unoriginal Sin." Christian Century, June 11, 2014. https://www.christiancentury.org/article/2014-06/unoriginal-sin.

Ridlington, Elizabeth, et al. "Fracking by the Numbers: The Damage to Our Water, Land and Climate from a Decade of Dirty Drilling." https://environmentamerica.org/sites/environment/files/reports/Fracking%20by%20the%20Numbers%20vUS.pdf.

Rilke, Rainer Maria. *Selected Poems of Rainer Maria Rilke*. Translated by Robert Bly. New York: Harper and Row, 1981.

"Rise of Carbon Dioxide Unabated." National Oceanic and Atmospheric Aadministration Research News, June 4, 2020. https://research.noaa.gov/article/ArtMID/587/ArticleID/2636/Rise-of-carbon-dioxide-unabated.

Risen, James. "American Psychological Association Bolstered C.I.A. Torture Program, Report Says." *New York Times*, Apr. 30, 2015.

Ritchie, Hanna, and Max Roser. "Access to Energy." Our World in Data. https://ourworldindata.org/energy-access.

Ritschl, Albrecht. *The Christian Doctrine of Justification and Reconciliation*. Edited by H. R. Mackintosh and A. B. Macaulay. Whitefish, MT: Kessinger, 2006.

Robinson, John A. T. *Honest to God*. Philadelphia: Westminster, 1963.

Robinson, Melia. "This Luxury Condo Development Featuring 'DEFCON 1 Preparedness' Is Built for the Apocalypse." Business Insider Australia, Jan. 10, 2017. https://www.businessinsider.com.au/trident-lakes-texas-doomsday-shelter-2017-1.

Rogers-Vaughn, Bruce. *Caring for Souls in a Neoliberal Age*. London: Palgrave MacMillan, 2016.

Rolheiser, Ronald. *Secularity and the Gospel: Being Missionaries to Our Children*. New York: Crossroad, 2006.

Romm, Tony. "Appeals Court Ruling Upholds FCC's Canceling of Net Neutrality Rules." *Washington Post*, Oct. 1, 2019.

Roozen, David. "Negative Numbers: The Decline Narrative Reaches Evangelicals." Christian Century, Dec. 3, 2013. https://www.christiancentury.org/article/2013-11/negative-numbers.

Rosenbaum, Eric. "Millions of Americans Are Only $400 Away from Financial Hardship. Here's Why." CNBC, May 23, 2019. https://www.cnbc.com/2019/05/23/millions-of-americans-are-only-400-away-from-financial-hardship.html.

Ross, Brian, and Rehab El-Buri. "Obama's Pastor: God Damn America, U.S. to Blame for 9/11." ABC News, May 7, 2008. https://abcnews.go.com/Blotter/DemocraticDebate/story?id=4443788&page=1.

Roth, Zachary. *The Great Suppression: Voting Rights, Corporate Cash, and the Conservative Assault on Democracy*. New York: Crown, 2016.

Routley, Nick. "Mapped: The 1.2 Billion People without Access to Electricity." Visual Capitalist, Nov. 27, 2019. https://www.visualcapitalist.com/mapped-billion-people-without-access-to-electricity/.

Rovelli, Carlo. *Seven Brief Lessons on Physics*. New York: Riverhead, 2016.

Rudden, Jennifer. "Value of M&A Transactions Globally 1985–2020." Statista, Jan. 15, 2021. https://www.statista.com/statistics/267369/volume-of-mergers-and-acquisitions-worldwide/.

Rushkoff, Douglas. *Present Shock: When Everything Happens Now*. London: Current, 2014.

Salama, Vivan, et al. "President Trump Eyes a New Real-Estate Purchase: Greenland." *Wall Street Journal*, Aug. 16, 2019.

Sammon, Alexander. "One Hundred CEOs Have the Retirement Savings of 116 Million Americans." Mother Jones, Dec. 16, 2016. https://www.motherjones.com/politics/2016/12/ceo-executives-retirement-income-inequality/.

Sample, Ian. "Shocking but True: Students Prefer Jolt of Pain to Being Made to Sit and Think." *Guardian*, July 3, 2014.

Samuelson, Robert. "Is the American Dream Killing Us?" *Washington Post*, Apr. 2, 2017.

Sanchez, Sandra. "Terminating Border-Wall Contracts Would Cost 'Billions,' Says CBP Head, but US Has Options." Border Report, Dec. 15, 2020. https://www.borderreport.com/hot-topics/the-border-wall/terminating-border-wall-contracts-would-cost-billions-says-cbp-head-but-us-has-options/.

Sanchez, Yvonne Wingett, and Rob O'Dell. "What Is ALEC? 'The Most Effective Organization' for Conservatives, Says Newt Gingrich." USA Today, Apr. 5, 2019. https://amp.usatoday.com/amp/3162357002.

Sandler, Rachel. "Billionaire Leon Cooperman to Elizabeth Warren: 'Your Vilification of the Rich Is Misguided.'" Forbes, Oct. 31, 2019. https://www.forbes.com/sites/rachelsandler/2019/10/31/billionaire-leon-cooperman-to-elizabeth-warren-your-vilification-of-the-rich-is-misguided/?sh=33a73ac98812.

Sanger, David, and Matt Apuzzo. "James Comey, F.B.I. Director, Hints at Action as Cellphone Data Is Locked." *New York Times*, Oct. 16, 2014.

Sartre, Jean Paul. "Existentialism Is a Humanism." In *Existentialism from Dostoevsky to Sartre*, edited by Walter Kaufmann, 222–311. New York: Meridian, 1956.

Savage, Charlie. "C.I.A. Is Said to Pay AT&T for Call Data." *New York Times,* Nov. 7, 2013.

———. "N.S.A. Triples Collection of Data from U.S. Phone Companies." *New York Times*, May 4, 2018. https://www.nytimes.com/2018/05/04/us/politics/nsa-surveillance-2017-annual-report.html.

Savransky, Rebecca. "Sinclair Chief to Trump in 2016: 'We Are Here to Deliver Your Message.'" Hill, Apr. 10, 2018. https://thehill.com/homenews/media/382441-sinclair-chairman-told-trump-we-are-here-to-deliver-your-message-after-he-won.

Schanzenbach, Diane Whitmore, et al. "Where Does All the Money Go: Shifts in Household Spending over the Past Thirty Years." Hamilton Project, June 2, 2016. https://www.hamiltonproject.org/papers/where_does_all_the_money_go_shifts_in_household_spending_over_the_past_30_y.

Schleiermacher, Friedrich. *The Christian Faith.* Translated by H. R. Mackintosh and James S. Stewart. Edinburgh: T. & T. Clark, 1928.

———. *On Religion: Speeches to Its Cultured Despisers.* Edited by Richard Crouter. Cambridge Texts in the History of Philosophy. Cambridge, UK: Cambridge University Press, 1996.

Schlicke, Jillayne. "The Meaning of Life Is That It Ends." CE Forward, Sept. 6, 2019. https://ceforward.com/2019/09/the-meaning-of-life-is-that-it-ends/.

Schulte, Brigid. "Trump's New Rule to Punish Immigrants Just Shows How Bad American Jobs Are." *Washington Post*, Sept. 5, 2019.

Schürmann, Reiner. "Meister Eckhart." https://www.britannica.com/biography/Meister-Eckhart.

Schuth, Katarina. *Seminary Formation: Recent History, Current Circumstances, New Direction.* Collegeville, MN: Liturgical Press, 2016.

Schwartz, Matthew S. "Global Military Expenditures Are Up, Driven by Top Two Spenders—U.S. And China." NPR, Apr. 29, 2019. https://www.npr.org/2019/04/29/718144787/global-military-expenditures-up-driven-by-top-two-spenders-u-s-and-china.

Schwarz, Jon. "Jimmy Carter: The U.S. Is an 'Oligarchy with Unlimited Political Bribery.'" Intercept, July 30, 2015. https://theintercept.com/2015/07/30/jimmy-carter-u-s-oligarchy-unlimited-political-bribery/.

Schweitzer, Albert. *The Quest of the Historical Jesus.* New York: Macmillan, 1910.

Schelling, Friedrich Wilhelm. *System of Transcendental Idealism.* Translated by Peter Heath. Charlottesville, VA: University Press of Virginia, 1978.

Scott, Eugene. "Comparing Trump to Jesus, and Why Some Evangelicals Believe Trump Is God's Chosen One." *Washington Post,* Dec. 18, 2019.

"SDG7: Data and Projections." International Energy Agency, Oct. 2020. https://www.iea.org/reports/sdg7-data-and-projections.

Secker, Tom. "ClandesTime 157: Two Years inside the CIA's Office of Public Affairs." Spy Culture. https://www.spyculture.com/clandestime-157-two-years-inside-the-cias-office-of-public-affairs/.

Semega, Jessica, et al. "Income and Poverty in the United States: 2019." United States Census Bureau, Sept. 15, 2020. https://www.census.gov/library/publications/2020/demo/p60-270.html.

Sepeda-Miller, Kiannah. "Bernie Sanders Says 49 Percent of 'New' Income Goes to the Top 1 Percent." Politifact, Sept. 29, 2019. https://www.politifact.com/factchecks/2019/sep/29/bernie-sanders/bernie-sanders-says-49-new-income-goes-top-1/.

Setoodeh, Ramin. "'Texas Chainsaw 3D' and Hollywood's Gore Obsession." Daily Beast, Jan. 7, 2013; updated July 12, 2017. https://www.thedailybeast.com/texas-chainsaw-3d-and-hollywoods-gore-obsession.

Seuss, Dr. *How the Grinch Stole Christmas!* New York: Penguin Random House, 1957.

Shalby, Colleen. "The Financial Crisis Hit Ten Years Ago. For Some, It Feels Like Yesterday." *Los Angeles Times,* Sept. 15, 2018.

Shane, Leo, III. "Suicide Rate among Veterans Up Again Slightly, Despite Focus on Prevention Efforts." MilitaryTimes, Nov. 12, 2020. https://www.militarytimes.com/news/pentagon-congress/2020/11/12/suicide-rate-among-veterans-up-again-slightly-despite-focus-on-prevention-efforts/.

Sharlet, Jeff. *The Family: The Secret Fundamentalism at the Heart of American Power.* New York: Harper Perennial, 2009.

Share, Don, and Christian Wiman, eds. *The Open Door: One Hundred Poems, One Hundred Years Poetry Magazine.* Chicago: University of Chicago Press, 2012.

Shaxson, Nick. "Could the Wealth in Tax Havens Help Us Pay for the Coronavirus Response?" Tax Justice Network, Mar. 27, 2020. https://taxjustice.net/2020/03/27/could-the-wealth-in-tax-havens-help-us-pay-for-the-coronavirus-response/.

Shearer, Elisa, and Katerina Matsa. "News Use across Social Media Platforms 2018." Pew Research Center, Sept. 10, 2018. https://www.pewresearch.org/journalism/2018/09/10/news-use-across-social-media-platforms-2018/.

Shellnutt, Kate. "Southern Baptists See Biggest Drop in One Hundred Years." Christianity Today, June 4, 2020. https://www.christianitytoday.com/news/2020/june/southern-baptist-sbc-member-drop-annual-church-profile-2019.html.

Shen, Lucinda. "FBI Director James Comey: 'There Is No Such Thing as Absolute Privacy in America.'" *Time,* Mar. 8, 2017.

Sherman, Erik. "The Incredible Shrinking Corporate Tax Rate Continues to Hit New Lows for These Business Giants." *Fortune,* Dec. 19, 2019.

———. "Median Wealth of Black and Latino Families Could Hit Zero by the Middle of the Century." https://www.forbes.com/sites/eriksherman/2017/09/11/median-wealth-of-black-and-latino-families-could-hit-zero-before-the-centurys-end/?sh=7099e5b950f6.

Sherwood, Harriet. "People of No Religion Outnumber Christians in England and Wales: Study." *Guardian*, May 23, 2016.

Shorrock, Tim. "Who Profits from Our New War? Inside NSA and Private Contractors' Secret Plans." https://www.salon.com/2014/09/24/heres_who_profits_from_our_new_war_inside_nsa_and_an_army_of_private_contractors_plans/.

Shuffelton, Frank, ed. *The Letters of John and Abigail Adams*. London: Penguin Classics, 2003.

Silverman, Ellie. "Facebook's First President, on Facebook: 'God Only Knows What It's Doing to Our Children's Brains.'" *Washington Post*, Nov. 9, 2017.

Silverstein, Jason. "There Were More Mass Shootings than Days in 2019." https://www.cbsnews.com/news/mass-shootings-2019-more-than-days-365/.

Silvestrini, Elaine. "Drug and Device Companies Gave Billions to Doctors in 2016." https://www.drugwatch.com/news/2017/07/03/big-pharma-influence-doctors-2016/.

Singh, Shalini. "Time to Smell the Roses." *Week*, Feb. 21, 2016. https://www.theweek.in/theweek/leisure/time-to-smell-the-roses.html.

Sirota, David. "A Cronkite Moment for the War on Terror." https://inthesetimes.com/article/a-cronkite-moment-for-the-drone-age.

———. "No, Really, You Didn't Build That: How the Rich Became Dependent on Government Subsidies." https://www.salon.com/2014/02/27/no_really_you_didnt_build_that_how_the_rich_became_dependent_on_government_subsidies_partner/.

Smith, Aaron, and Janna Anderson. "AI, Robotics, and the Future of Jobs." https://www.pewresearch.org/internet/2014/08/06/future-of-jobs/.

Smith, Adam. *The Wealth of Nations: Books 1–3*. London: Penguin Classics, 1982.

Smith, Adam B. "Twenty-Twenty U.S. Billion-Dollar Weather and Climate Disasters in Historical Context." https://www.climate.gov/news-features/blogs/beyond-data/2020-us-billion-dollar-weather-and-climate-disasters-historical.

Smith, Christian, and Hilary Davidson. *The Paradox of Generosity: Giving We Receive, Grasping We Lose*. Oxford, UK: Oxford University Press, 2014.

Smith, Christian, with Patricia Snell. *Souls in Transition: The Religious and Spiritual Lives of Emerging Adults*. Oxford, UK: Oxford University Press, 2009.

Smith, James K. A. *Desiring the Kingdom: Worship, Worldview, and Cultural Formation*. Cultural Liturgies 1. Ada, MI: Baker Academic, 2009.

Smith, Peter. "Nativity Story Has Its Share of Skeptics." *Pittsburgh Post-Gazette*, Dec. 23, 2013.

Smith, Richard. "Beyond Growth or Beyond Capitalism?" http://www.paecon.net/PAEReview/issue53/Smith53.pdf.

Smith, Stan. *The Cambridge Companion to W. H. Auden*. Cambridge, UK: Cambridge University Press, 2005.

Smuga-Otta, Kim. "Physician-Monk Leads Stanford Doctors in Meditation." https://scopeblog.stanford.edu/2015/06/30/physician-monk-leads-stanford-doctors-in-meditation/.

Snodgrass, Elizabeth. "Archaeologists Find a Classic Entrance to Hell." https://www.nationalgeographic.com/adventure/article/130414-hell-underworld-archaeology-mount-olympus--greece.

Solomon, Norman. "Why the Washington Post's New Ties to the CIA Are So Ominous." https://truthout.org/articles/why-the-washington-posts-new-ties-to-the-cia-are-so-ominous/.

Sommerfeldt, John R. *Christianity in Culture: A Historical Quest.* Lanham, MD: University Press of America, 2009.

Sorkin, Andrew. "A Tidal Wave of Corporate Migrants Seeking (Tax) Shelter." *New York Times,* Jan. 25, 2016.

Southern Poverty Law Center. "The Year in Hate and Extremism 2020." https://www.splcenter.org/sites/default/files/yih_2020-21_final.pdf.

Spade, Audrey. "New Study Indicates Annual Cost of Incarceration Exceeds $1 Trillion." https://www.prisonlegalnews.org/news/2017/dec/5/new-study-indicates-annual-cost-incarceration-exceeds-1-trillion/.

Spencer, Andrew. "The Complicated Legacy of Max Weber's 'The Protestant Ethic.'" https://tifwe.org/the-complicated-legacy-of-max-webers-the-protestant-ethic/.

Spring, Jake. "Two-Thirds of Tropical Rain Forest Destroyed or Degraded Globally: NGO." https://www.reuters.com/article/us-climate-change-forests/two-thirds-of-tropical-rainforest-destroyed-or-degraded-globally-ngo-says-idUSKBN2B00U2.

Stanford Center on Poverty and Inequality. "State of the Union: The Poverty and Inequality Report 2016." https://inequality.stanford.edu/publications/pathway/state-union-2016.

Stanford School of Medicine. "Where Do Americans Die?" https://palliative.stanford.edu/home-hospice-home-care-of-the-dying-patient/where-do-americans-die/.

"State of Homelessness 2020 Edition." https://endhomelessness.org/homelessness-in-america/homelessness-statistics/state-of-homelessness-2020/. Site discontinued.

Statista Research Department. "Moral Views on Gay or Lesbian Relations in the United States 2001–2021." https://www.statista.com/statistics/226147/americans-moral-views-on gay or lesbian-relations-in-the-united-states/.

Stebbins, Samuel, and Evan Comen. "How Much Do You Need to Make to Be in the Top 1 Percent in Every State?" *USA Today,* July 1, 2020.

Stebbins, Samuel, and Michael Sauter. "These Thirty Companies, including Boeing, Get the Most Money from the Federal Government." *USA Today,* Mar. 29, 2019.

Steele, Anne. "Positive Drug Tests among U.S. Workers Reach Highest Level in Sixteen Years." *Wall Street Journal,* Aug. 25, 2020.

Stein, Ben. "In Class Warfare, Guess Which Class Is Winning." *New York Times,* Nov. 26, 2006.

Stein, Jeff. "The Richest Americans Get a $33,000 Tax Break under the GOP Tax Law. The Poorest Get $40." *Washington Post,* Mar. 30, 2018.

Stephens, Mitchell. "Commentary: The Rise of the Diminished, Ordinary God." *Washington Post,* Feb. 19, 2014.

Sterling, Joshua. "Roae Responds to Philly Paper's Article." *Titusville Herald,* Apr. 5, 2016.

Stern, George. *A Faculty Theory of Knowledge: The Aim and Scope of Hume's First Enquiry.* Lewisburg, PA: Bucknell University Press, 1971.

Stetzer, Ed. "If It Doesn't Stem Its Decline, Mainline Protestantism Has Just Twenty-Three Easters Left." *Washington Post,* Apr. 28, 2017.

Stilwell, Victoria. "What Are Your Odds of Becoming a Millionaire?" https://www.titlemax.com/discovery-center/personal-finance/your-odds-of-becoming-a-millionaire/.

Stockholm International Peace Research Institute. "Global Arms Industry: Sales by the Top Twenty-Five Companies up 8.5 per Cent; Big Players Active in Global South." https://sipri.org/media/press-release/2020/global-arms-industry-sales-top-25-companies-85-cent-big-players-active-global-south.

"The Stockmarket Is Now Run by Computers, Algorithms and Passive Managers." Economist, Oct. 5, 2019. https://www.economist.com/briefing/2019/10/05/the-stockmarket-is-now-run-by-computers-algorithms-and-passive-managers.

Strauss, Daniel. "JPMorgan Chief Jamie Dimon Says Elizabeth Warren 'Vilifies Successful People.'" https://markets.businessinsider.com/news/stocks/jpmorgan-ceo-jamie-dimon-says-warren-vilifies-successful-people-2019-11.

Strauss, Mark. "Powerful New Telescope Finds Whopping 1,300 Galaxies at Once." https://www.nationalgeographic.com/science/article/radio-telescope-new-galaxies-meerkat-south-africa-space-science.

Strauss, Valerie. "New Report Finds High Closure Rates for Charter Schools over Time." Washington Post, Aug. 6, 2020.

———. "Report: Federal Government Wasted Millions of Dollars on Charter Schools That Never Opened." Washington Post, Dec. 6, 2019.

Streeck, Wolfgang. How Will Capitalism End?: Essays on a Failing System. Brooklyn, NY: Verso, 2016.

Strickland, Ashley. "Astronomers Find Galaxy Similar to Milky Way More than Twelve Billion Light-Years Away." https://www.cnn.com/2020/08/12/world/milky-way-galaxy-twin-trnd-scn/index.html.

Suiter, Tad. "After Fifty Years on TV, Has Sesame Street Been Gentrified?" https://current.org/2019/08/after-50-years-on-tv-has-sesame-street-been-gentrified/?wallit_nosession=1.

Sullivan, Andrew. "I Used to Be a Human Being." https://nymag.com/intelligencer/2016/09/andrew-sullivan-my-distraction-sickness-and-yours.html.

Sullivan, Laura. "Prison Economics Help Drive Ariz. Immigration Law." https://www.npr.org/2010/10/28/130833741/prison-economics-help-drive-ariz-immigration-law.

Sullivan, Paul. "All This Anger against the Rich May Be Unhealthy." New York Times, Oct. 16, 2009.

Sullivan, Susan. Living Faith: Everyday Religion and Mothers in Poverty. Chicago: University of Chicago Press, 2012.

"Suicide." https://www.nimh.nih.gov/health/statistics/suicide.

Swaine, Jon, and Ciara McCarthy. "Young Black Men Again Faced Highest Rate of US Police Killings in 2016." Guardian, Jan. 8, 2017.

Swanson, Ana. "Big Pharmaceutical Companies Are Spending Far More on Marketing than Research." Washington Post, Feb. 11, 2015.

Tagliaferri, Lisa. "Lyrical Mysticism: The Writing and Reception of Catherine of Siena." PhD diss., City University of New York, 2017.

Tammeus, Bill. "Central Baptist Theological Seminary on the Rebound." https://www.flatlandkc.org/news-issues/central-baptist-theological-seminary-on-the-rebound/.

Tanzi, Alexandre, and Shelly Hagan. "Public Relations Jobs Boom as Buffett Sees Newspapers Dying." https://www.bloomberg.com/news/articles/2019-04-27/public-relations-jobs-boom-as-buffett-sees-newspapers-dying.

Tate, Nick. "Loneliness Rivals Obesity, Smoking as Health Risk." https://www.webmd.com/balance/news/20180504/loneliness-rivals-obesity-smoking-as-health-risk.

Tavernise, Sabrina. "U.S. Suicide Rate Surges to a Thirty-Year High." *New York Times*, Apr. 22, 2016.

Tax Policy Center. "Briefing Book: Key Elements of the U.S. Tax System." https://www.taxpolicycenter.org/briefing-book/how-do-federal-income-tax-rates-work.

———. "Briefing Book: Some Background." https://www.taxpolicycenter.org/briefing-book/how-does-federal-government-spend-its-money.

Taylor, Adam. "Map: The U.S. Is Bound by Treaties to Defend a Quarter of Humanity." *Washington Post*, May 30, 2015.

Taylor, Jamila, et al. "Eliminating Racial Disparities in Maternal and Infant Mortality." https://www.americanprogress.org/issues/women/reports/2019/05/02/469186/eliminating-racial-disparities-maternal-infant-mortality/.

Taylor, Matthew. "Antarctic 'Doomsday Glacier' May Be Melting Faster than Was Thought." *Guardian*, Apr. 30, 2021.

Teilhard de Chardin, Pierre. *Hymn of the Universe*. New York: Harper and Row, 1961.

Telford, Taylor. "Income Inequality in America Is the Highest It's Been Since Census Bureau Started Tracking It, Data Shows." *Washington Post*, Sept. 26, 2019.

Temin, Peter. *The Vanishing Middle Class: Prejudice and Power in a Dual Economy*. Cambridge, MA: MIT Press, 2017.

Teresa of Avila. *The Interior Castle*. Translated by Mirabai Starr. Reprint, New York: Riverhead, 2004.

Thales. "DHS's Automated Biometric Identification System IDENT: The Heart of Biometric Visitor Identification in the USA." https://www.thalesgroup.com/en/markets/digital-identity-and-security/government/customer-cases/ident-automated-biometric-identification-system.

Thatcher, Margaret. "Margaret Thatcher: A Life in Quotes." *Guardian*, Apr. 8, 2013.

Thérèse of Lisieux. *The Story of a Soul: The Autobiography of St. Thérèse of Lisieux*. Translated by John Clarke. Washington, DC: Institute of Carmelite Publications, 1996.

Thomas, Deja, and Richard Fry. "Prior to COVID-19, Child Poverty Rates Had Reached Record Lows in U.S." https://www.pewresearch.org/fact-tank/2020/11/30/prior-to-covid-19-child-poverty-rates-had-reached-record-lows-in-u-s/.

Thompson, Damian. "Crisis of Faith." https://www.spectator.co.uk/article/crisis-of-faith.

Thompson, Mark. "The U.S. Navy's Titanium 'Tin Can.'" https://www.pogo.org/analysis/2019/01/the-u-s-navys-titanium-tin-can/.

Thornhill, John. "Boldness in Business Person of the Year: Sir Tim Berners-Lee." https://www.ft.com/content/9d3205a8-15af-11e9-a168-d45595ad076d.

Tillich, Paul. *The Shaking of the Foundations*. New York: Scribners, 1948.

Tipton, Steven M. "The Logic of the Holy: Robert Bellah, 1927–2013." https://www.christiancentury.org/article/2013-08/logic-holy.

Tobin, Jonathan S. "Loving Us to Death: How America's Embrace Is Imperiling American Jewry." https://www.commentary.org/articles/jonathan-tobin/loving-us-to-death/.

Toft, Monica Duffy. "U.S. Has Special Forces in 149 Countries and Ambassadors in 144." http://www.allgov.com/news/top-stories/us-has-special-forces-in-149-countries-and-ambassadors-in-144-180327?news=860441.

Tolstoy, Leo. *The Death of Ivan Ilych: And Other Stories*. Translated by Aylmer Maude and J. D. Duff. New York: New American, 1960.

Tomasky, Michael. "At Snopes, a Peek Down the Right-Wing Rabbit Holes." https://www.thedailybeast.com/at-snopes-a-peek-down-the-right-wing-rabbit-holes.

Torrey, R. A. and A. C. Dixon, eds. *The Fundamentals: A Testimony to the Truth*. 2 vols. Grand Rapids: Baker, 2003.

Tracy, Marc. "Gannett, Now Largest U.S. Newspaper Chain, Targets 'Inefficiencies.'" *New York Times*, Nov. 19, 2019.

Trading Economics. "United States Corporate Profits." https://tradingeconomics.com/united-states/corporate-profits.

Trotter, Greg. "End of an Era: Chicago's Last Oreo Line Shut Down Friday." *Chicago Tribune*, July 8, 2016.

Turse, Nick. *Kill Anything That Moves: The Real American War in Vietnam*. London: Picador, 2013.

———. "Target Africa: The U.S. Military's Expanding Footprint in East Africa and the Arabian Peninsula." https://theintercept.com/drone-papers/target-africa/.

———. "The U.S. Military Is Conducting Secret Missions All Over Africa." https://www.vice.com/en/article/ywn5yy/us-military-secret-missions-africa.

Turse, Nick, and wombatman1. "U.S. Special Operations Forces Deployed to 149 Countries in 2017." https://warisboring.com/u-s-special-operations-forces-deployed-to-149-countries-in-2017/.

"Two Hundred Fifty Thousand Mentally Ill Are Homeless. One Hundred Forty Thousand Seriously Mentally Ill Are Homeless." https://mentalillnesspolicy.org/consequences/homeless-mentally-ill.html.

Union of Concerned Scientists. "Underwater: Rising Seas, Chronic Floods, and the Implications for US Coastal Real Estate." https://www.ucsusa.org/resources/underwater.

Union Presbyterian Seminary. "Legacy of BTSR Will Fund New Initiatives in Racial Justice and Theological Education." https://www.upsem.edu/newsroom/legacy-of-btsr-will-fund-new-initiatives-in-racial-justice-and-theological-education/.

Union Theological Seminary. "Episcopal Divinity School to Pursue Affiliation with Union." https://utsnyc.edu/episcopal-divinity-school-to-pursue-affiliation-with-union/.

United States Bureau of Labor Statistics. "Occupational Outlook Handbook." https://www.bls.gov/ooh/.

United States Customs and Border Protection. "Air and Marine Operations: Fact Sheet." https://www.cbp.gov/sites/default/files/assets/documents/2020-Apr/FS_2020_AMO_Fact%20Sheet_FINAL_508__0.pdf.

United States Government Accountability Office. "Face Recognition Technology: FBI Should Better Ensure Privacy and Accuracy." https://www.gao.gov/assets/gao-16-267.pdf.

"The United States Spends More on Defense than the Next Ten Countries Combined." Peter G. Peterson Foundation, July 19, 2021. https://www.pgpf.org/blog/2021/07/the-united-states-spends-more-on-defense-than-the-next-11-countries-combined.

University of Oxford. "Social Media Manipulation by Political Actors an Industrial Scale Problem: Oxford Report." https://www.ox.ac.uk/news/2021-01-13-social-media-manipulation-political-actors-industrial-scale-problem-oxford-report.

Updike, John. *Endpoint and Other Poems*. New York: Alfred A. Knopf, 2009.

———. *The Poorhouse Fair*. New York: Random House, 2012.

Urban Institute. "Lotteries, Casinos, Sports Betting, and Other Types of State-Sanctioned Gambling." https://www.urban.org/policy-centers/cross-center-initiatives/state-and-local-finance-initiative/state-and-local-backgrounders/lotteries-casinos-sports-betting-and-other-types-state-sanctioned-gambling.

"U.S. Census Bureau Releases 2018 Families and Living Arrangements Tables." United States Census Bureau, Nov. 14, 2018. https://www.census.gov/newsroom/press-releases/2018/families.html.

"US Remains Top Arms Exporter and Grows Market Share." BBC News, Mar. 15 (no year). https://www.bbc.com/news/business-56397601.

Vaihinger, Hans. *The Philosophy of the 'As If': A System of the Theoretical, Practical and Religious Fictions of Mankind*. Translated by C. K. Ogden. Oxfordshire, UK: Routledge and Kegan Paul, 1935.

Valverde, Miriam. "Has the Number of Border Patrol Agents Quadrupled Since 2005?" Politifact, Feb. 1, 2019. https://www.politifact.com/factchecks/2019/feb/01/adam-smith/has-number-border-patrol-agents-quadrupled-2005/.

Van Brunt, Alexa. "Adult Interrogation Tactics in Schools Turn Principals into Police Officers." *Guardian*, Mar. 19, 2015.

Van Buren, Peter. "For $178 Million, the US Could Pay for One Fighter Plane—or 3,358 Years of College." Reuters, Sept. 26, 2016. https://www.reuters.com/article/us-college-debt-defense-commentary/commentary-for-178-million-the-u-s-could-pay-for-one-fighter-plane-or-3358-years-of-college-idUSKCN11Q1GE.

Vanden Brook, Tom. "Suicide Rate among Active-Duty Troops Jumps to Six-Year High, COVID-19 Stress Could Make It Even Worse." *USA Today*, Oct. 1, 2020.

Van der Marel, Roland. "How Many Black Holes Are There?" https://www.stsci.edu/~marel/black_holes/encyc_mod3_q7.html#:~:text=In%20the%20region%20of%20the,million%20stellar%2Dmass%20black%20holes.

VanOrman, Alicia, and Linda Jacobsen. "U.S. Household Composition Shifts as the Population Grows Older; More Young Adults Live With Parents." PRB, Feb. 12, 2020. https://www.prb.org/resources/u-s-household-composition-shifts-as-the-population-grows-older-more-young-adults-live-with-parents/.

Varki, Ajit, and Danny Brower. *Self-Deception, False Beliefs, and the Origins of the Human Mind*. New York: Twelve, 2013.

Vibes, John. "Wikileaks Documents Show NSA Spied on World Leaders on Behalf of Big Oil." Free Thought Project, Feb. 23, 2016. https://thefreethoughtproject.com/wikileaks-documents-nsa-spied-world-leaders-behalf-oil-companies/.

Volz, Dustin. "U.S. Spy Court Rejected Zero Surveillance Orders in 2015: Memo." Reuters, Apr. 29, 2016. https://www.reuters.com/article/us-usa-cybersecurity-surveillance/u-s-spy-court-rejected-zero-surveillance-orders-in-2015-memo-idUSKCN0XR009.

Wagner, Peter, and Wanda Bertram. "'What Percent of the U.S. Is Incarcerated?' (And Other Ways to Measure Mass Incarceration." Prison Policy Institute, Jan. 16, 2020. https://www.prisonpolicy.org/blog/2020/01/16/percent-incarcerated/.

Wagstaff, Keith. "Name Recognition Is Apparently Everything in Politics." *Week*, Jan. 8, 2015. https://theweek.com/articles/462156/name-recognition-apparently-everything -politics.

Wall, Mike. "Four Point Five Billion 'Alien Earths' May Populate Milky Way." Space, Feb. 6, 2013. https://www.space.com/19659-alien-earth-exoplanets-red-dwarfs. html.

Walsh, Milton. *Witness of the Saints: Patristic Readings in the Liturgy of the Hours.* San Francisco: Ignatius Press, 2012.

Warrick, Joby. *Black Flags: The Rise of ISIS.* New York: Anchor, 2016.

Washington, George. "Washington's Farewell Address to the People of the United States." Edited by the United States Senate Historical Office. https://www.senate. gov/artandhistory/history/resources/pdf/Washingtons_Farewell_Address.pdf.

Washington Post. "Fatal Force." Washington Post, updated Sept. 6, 2021. https://www. washingtonpost.com/graphics/investigations/police-shootings-database/.

Watson, David Lowe. *Covenant Discipleship: Christian Formation through Mutual Accountability.* Nashville: Discipleship Resources, 1991.

Watson Institute International Public and Affairs, Brown University. "Costs of War." https://watson.brown.edu/costsofwar/.

———. "Costs of War: US Veterans and Military Families." https://watson.brown.edu/ costsofwar/costs/human/veterans.

Watts, Jonathan. "Almost Four Environmental Defenders a Week Killed in 2017." *Guardian,* Feb. 2, 2018. https://www.theguardian.com/environment/2018/feb/02/ almost-four-environmental-defenders-a-week-killed-in-2017.

———. "We Have Twelve Years to Limit Climate Change Catastrophe, Warns UN." *Guardian*, Oct. 8, 2018. https://www.theguardian.com/environment/2018/oct/08/ global-warming-must-not-exceed-15c-warns-landmark-un-report.

Week Staff. "America's Killing Contagion." *Week*, Sept. 7, 2015. https://theweek.com/ articles/575337/americas-killing-contagion.

———. "The Biggest Threats to Humanity." *Week*, Jan. 8, 2015. https://theweek.com/ articles/462317/biggest-threats-humanity.

———. "The Biometrics Boom." *Week*, May 29, 2013. https://theweek.com/ articles/463753/biometrics-boom.

———. "A Brief Guide to 'The Internet of Things.'" *Week*, Aug. 15, 2015. https:// theweek.com/articles/571508/brief-guide-internet-things.

———. "The Cuban Missile Crisis: How Close to Nuclear War Did We Get?" *Week*, Oct. 28, 2015. https://www.theweek.co.uk/66299/the-cuban-missile-crisis-how-close-to-nuclear-war-did-we-get.

———. "Grand Theft Auto V: Harmless Entertainment?" *Week*, Jan. 8, 2015. https:// theweek.com/articles/459626/grand-theft-auto-v-harmless-entertainment.

———. "The Graying of America." *Week*, Aug. 18, 2019. https://theweek.com/ articles/859185/graying-america.

———. "Inside America's Lottery Addiction." *Week*, Feb 7, 2016. https://theweek.com/ articles/603523/inside-americas-lottery-addiction.

———. "Inside Japan's Booming Rent-a-Friend Industry." *Week*, June 26, 2016. https:// theweek.com/articles/631927/inside-japans-booming-rentafriend-industry.

———. "Is Nuclear Armageddon More Likely than Ever?" *Week*, Feb. 27, 2016. https:// theweek.com/articles/608163/nuclear-armageddon-more-likely-than-ever.

———. "Norway: Drowning Our Ideals in Oil." *Week*, Jan. 8, 2015. https://theweek.com/articles/460164/norway-drowning-ideals-oil.

———. "Planning an Artisanal Death." *Week*, Feb. 19, 2018. https://theweek.com/articles/755540/planning-artisanal-death.

———. "Religion: Waning Influence in the U.S." Pressreader, Apr. 16, 2021. https://www.pressreader.com/usa/the-week-us/20210416/281895891052012.

———. "The Rise of Workplace Spying." *Week*, July 5, 2015. https://theweek.com/articles/564263/rise-workplace-spying.

———. "Will You Lose Your Job to a Robot?" *Week*, Sept. 22, 2019. https://theweek.com/articles/866339/lose-job-robot.

———. "The world at a glance. . ." *Week*, Oct. 15, 2021. https://theweek.com/magazine#/reader/readsvg/515470.

Weems, Lovett H. *John Wesley's Message Today*. Nashville: Abingdon Press, 1991.

Weigel, George. *Evangelical Catholicism: Deep Reform in the Twenty-First Century*. New York: Basic, 2014.

Weinberg, Steven. *The First Three Minutes: A Modern View of the Origin of the Universe*. New York: Basic, 1993.

Weinberger, Sharon. "Windfalls of War: Pentagon's Competition for Contracts Abysmal Compared to Other Agencies." Public Integrity, Sept. 2, 2011; updated May 19, 2014. https://publicintegrity.org/national-security/windfalls-of-war-pentagons-competition-for-contracts-abysmal-compared-to-other-agencies/.

Weiner, Rachel. "Almost Half of U.S. Adults Have Seen a Family Member Jailed, Study Shows." *Washington Post*, Dec. 6, 2018.

Welch, Craig. "Melting Arctic Permafrost Could Release Tons of Toxic Mercury." National Geographic, Feb. 6, 2018. https://www.nationalgeographic.com/science/article/melting-arctic-permafrost-toxic-mercury-environment.

Wells, Samuel. "Ministry without God." Christian Century, Nov. 5, 2013. https://www.christiancentury.org/article/2013-10/ministry-without-god.

Wesley, John. *John Wesley*. Edited by Albert Outler. New York: Oxford University Press, 1980.

Westbrook, Robert. Review of *The Age of Acquiescence* by Steve Fraser. Christian Century, Apr. 20, 2015. https://www.christiancentury.org/reviews/2015-04/age-acquiescence-steve-fraser.

White, Tim D., et al. "*Ardipithecus ramidus* and the Paleobiology of Early Hominids." *Science* 326, no. 5949 (Oct. 2009) 64–86.

Whitehead, Alfred North. *Modes of Thought*. New York: Macmillan, 1938.

———. *Process and Reality*. New York: Harper and Row, 1960.

———. "Religion in the Making." In *Alfred North Whitehead: An Anthology*, edited by F. S. C. Northrop and Mason W. Gross, 467–528. New York: Macmillan, 1953.

Whitlock, Craig, and Bob Woodward. "Pentagon Buries Evidence of $125 Billion in Bureaucratic Waste." *Washington Post*, Dec. 5, 2016.

Whitney, Rich. "US Provides Military Assistance to 73 Percent of World's Dictatorships." Truthout, Sept. 23, 2017. https://truthout.org/articles/us-provides-military-assistance-to-73-percent-of-world-s-dictatorships/.

Willimon, William H., and Marcus Borg. "Encountering Jesus: An Exchange between William H. Willimon and Marcus Borg." *Christian Century* 114, no. 31 (Nov. 5, 1997) 1009–11.

Wilson, Edward O. *The Meaning of Human Existence*. New York: Liveright, 2015.

Wilson, Megan. "Analysis: More than 6,000 Lobbyists Have Worked on Taxes in 2017." Hill, Dec. 1, 2017. https://thehill.com/business-a-lobbying/business-a-lobbying/362796-analysis-more-than-6000-lobbyists-have-worked-on.

Wilson, Sarah Hinlicky. "Mission in Spite of Empire: The Story of Bartholomus Ziegenbalg." Christian Century, Sept. 8, 2014. https://www.christiancentury.org/article/2014-08/mission-spite-empire.

WIN-Gallup International. "Global Index of Religiosity and Atheism—2012." https://www.webpages.uidaho.edu/~stevel/251/Global_INDEX_of_Religiosity_and_Atheism_PR__6.pdf.

Witters, Dan. "Millions in U.S. Lost Someone Who Couldn't Afford Treatment." Gallup, Nov. 12, 2019. https://news.gallup.com/poll/268094/millions-lost-someone-couldn-afford-treatment.aspx.

Wittgenstein, Ludwig. Philosophical Investigations. Translated by G. E. M. Anscombe. 3rd ed. New York: Pearson, 1973.

———. Tractatus Logico-Philosophicus. Edited by Mark A. Joseph. Peterborough, Can.: Broadview, 2014.

Wolfson, Andrew. "Ky. Baptists Lure New Worshippers with Gun Giveaway." USA Today, Mar. 3, 2014. https://www.usatoday.com/story/news/nation/2014/03/03/churches-guns-giveaway/5967533/.

"Women in the Workforce: United States (Quick Take)." Catalyst, Oct. 14, 2020. https://www.catalyst.org/research/women-in-the-workforce-united-states/.

Wooden, Cindy. "In Bolivia, Francis Demands Reform of 'Intolerable' Global Economic System." National Catholic Reporter, July 10, 2015. https://www.ncronline.org/news/world/bolivia-francis-demands-reform-intolerable-global-economic-system.

Woodward, Kenneth L. "The Way the World Ends." Newsweek, Oct. 31, 1999. https://www.newsweek.com/way-world-ends-167602.

Woodyard, David O. Living without God, before God. Philadelphia: Westminster, 1968.

"World Press Freedom Index." Reporters without Borders. https://rsf.org/en/ranking#.

World Watch Montor. "Eighty Percent of Religious Discrimination Targets Christians." World Watch Monitor, Dec. 7, 2017. https://www.worldwatchmonitor.org/coe/80-religious-discrimination-aimed-christians/?__cf_chl_jschl_tk__=pmd_ecb1a65d14d8c68b46e6b52e1d0ba9f8a0e39e57-1629142681-0-gqNtZGzNAg2jcnBszQe6.

World Wildlife Fund. "Living Blue Planet Report 2015." https://www.worldwildlife.org/publications/living-blue-planet-report-2015.

Yamada, Frank M. "Message from the Executive Director." https://www.ats.edu/uploads/resources/events/2018-biennial-meeting/2018-biennial-meeting-program-book.pdf.

Yeginsu, Ceylan. "If Workers Slack Off, the Wristband Will Know. (And Amazon Has a Patent for It.)." New York Times, Feb. 1, 2018.

Yen, Hope. "Exclusive: Four in Five in US Face Near-Poverty, No Work." USA Today, July 28, 2013; updated Sept. 17, 2013. https://www.usatoday.com/story/money/business/2013/07/28/americans-poverty-no-work/2594203/.

Yeung, Jessie. "There Are at Least 300 Million Potentially Habitable Planets in Our Galaxy, NASA Finds." CNN, Nov. 5, 2020. https://www.cnn.com/2020/11/05/world/nasa-300-million-habitable-planets-intl-hnk-scli-scn/index.html.

Yoder, John Howard. The Original Revolution: Essays on Christian Pacifism. Scottsdale: Herald, 1971.

———. *The Politics of Jesus*. Grand Rapids: Eerdmans, 1972.

Yokoi, Tomoko. "Female Gamers Are on the Rise. Can the Gaming Industry Catch Up?" Forbes, Mar. 4, 2021. https://www.forbes.com/sites/tomokoyokoi/2021/03/04/female-gamers-are-on-the-rise-can-the-gaming-industry-catch-up/?sh=1c001816f9fe.

Zanona, Melanie, and Brianna Gurciullo. "Boeing's Congressional Base Frays under Pressure." Politico, Mar. 12, 2019. https://www.politico.com/story/2019/03/12/boeing-congress-1264079.

Zeballos-Roig, Joseph. "The Staggering Amount of Wealth Held by the Forbes 400 More than Doubled over the Last Decade. But Their Tax Rates Actually Dropped." Markets Insider, Nov. 26, 2019. https://markets.businessinsider.com/news/stocks/forbes-400-wealth-doubled-last-decade-as-tax-rate-fell-2019-11.

Zengerle, Patricia, and Tabassum Zacaria. "NSA Head, Lawmakers Defend Surveillance Programs." Reuters, June 18, 2013. https://www.reuters.com/article/us-usa-security/nsa-head-lawmakers-defend-surveillance-programs-idUKBRE95H15O20130618.

Zibel, Alan. "Revolving Congress: The Revolving Door Class of 2019 Flocks to K Street." Public Citizen, May 30, 2019. https://www.citizen.org/article/revolving-congress/.

Ziv, Shahar. "Banks Reaped $11 Billion In Overdraft Fees: Here's Why It Matters." Forbes, June 13, 2020. https://www.forbes.com/sites/shaharziv/2020/06/13/banks-reaped-11-billion-in-overdraft-fees-heres-why-it-matters/?sh=5043f80d6ddo.

Zuboff, Shoshana. *The Age of Surveillance Capitalism: The Fight for a Human Future at the New Frontier of Power*. New York: Public Affairs, 2019.

www.ingramcontent.com/pod-product-compliance
Lightning Source LLC
Chambersburg PA
CBHW070909100426
42814CB00003B/111